Atlas of the Languages and Ethnic Communities of South Asia

Atlas of the Languages and Ethnic Communities of South Asia

ROLAND J.-L. BRETON

ALTAMIRA
PRESS

Walnut Creek/ London/ New Delhi

For information address:

AltaMira Press
A Division of Sage Publications, Inc.
1630 North Main Street, Suite 367
Walnut Creek, CA 94596

SAGE Publications Ltd.
6 Bonhill Street
London EC2A 4PU
United Kingdom

SAGE Publications India Pvt. Ltd.
M-32 Market
Greater Kailash I
New Delhi 110 048 India

Printed in New Delhi, India

Library of Congress Cataloging-in-Publication Data

Breton, Roland J.-L.
    Atlas of the languages and ethnic communities of South Asia /
Roland J.-L. Breton.
        p. cm.   (c : alk. paper)
    Includes bibliographical references and index.
    ISBN: 0–8039–9367–6
        1. South Asia—Languages—Atlases. 2. Anthropological
linguistics—South Asia—Atlases. 3. Ethnology—South Asia—
Atlases. 4. Sociolinguistics—South Asia—Atlases.   I. Title.
PK 1541.A1   306.44′6′0954022—dc21   1997   96–51603

97 98 99 00 01 02 10 9 8 7 6 5 4 3 2 1

Interior Design and Production by Print Line, New Delhi
Cover Design by Bharati Mirchandani

To

Nicole
Sophia
Ariadne
Til
Tristan
Nils
Myrtille

CONTENTS

> **PART I:** GENERAL PRESENTATION OF THE LANGUAGES AND ETHNIC COMMUNITIES OF SOUTH ASIA

> **PART II:** THE SIXTY PLATES WITH THEIR COMMENTARIES

Preface to the Second Edition

Language is one of the greatest glories and achievements of humankind. It can win hearts, spread love and solve the most difficult problems. It can express the deepest of human feelings. It is indeed one of the greatest treasures of human civilization. Any linguistic study, therefore, is most welcome.

The multilingual and multiracial nature of the subcontinent is well known. Roland J.-L. Breton's *Atlas of the Languages and Ethnic Communities of South Asia* comprising 60 plates is devoted to graphically analyzing a number of aspects. Cartographic presentation along with commentaries and statistical data give definiteness to the distribution, composition, mother tongue or subsidiary, and other aspects of our languages.

The author shows the Indian languages throughout the subcontinent and the world in the first three plates. The subsequent 33 plates are devoted to the five regions of the area: the Northwest; the Hindi Belt; the Himalayas and the Northeast; Peripheral Indo-Aryan and Central Adivasi Belts; and Dravidian South and Sri Lanka. Three of the plates deal with non-regional languages—Sanskrit, English and non-Indian languages. The next five plates examine languages in the five metropolises, languages by states, while the last six plates deal with the evolution of the political map of India—reorganizations; ethno-linguistic issues; main linguistic minorities; ethno-linguistic structure, flows and foci; and multilingual states in the world.

Apart from the 60 plates and commentaries, this atlas contains (*i*) an introduction dealing in particular with India as an exemplary field for geolinguistics; (*ii*) sections on ethnic subdivisions; linguistic survey and census; the relation between language on the one hand and race, tribe, caste and religion on the other; (*iii*) a conclusion drawing attention to geolinguistic studies, language preservation and territorial management in other countries.

The atlas contains annexures on up-to-date graphs, tables, glossary, index and a summary of the whole text and plates.

Roland J.-L. Breton, Professor of Geography at the University of Paris 8, is an eminent scholar. He has many academic laurels to his credit. He has written nine books on languages, population, civilization and races, and has 140 main contributions to different standard journals. Professor Breton has working knowledge of French, English, German, Russian, Italian, Spanish and Latin. He has held various assignments and participated in numerous missions and conferences, most of which fall in the areas of geography and geolinguistics.

Professor Breton's *Atlas* is an important contribution to the linguistic studies of the world and a significant service to the subcontinent.

Professor Enayat Ahmad
ex-Vice-Chancellor
Magadh University

Preface to the First Edition

A geographer, having a sound comprehension of culture and open to the various horizons of the social sciences, was particularly qualified to carry on the specifically interdisciplinary task of the analysis of the relationship between ethnic groups and space throughout the Indian subcontinent. Roland J.-L. Breton combined the necessary conditions: an extensive stay in the country, a background in both history and geography, a profound fraternity for a population he taught, a knowledge of the language ....

From substantial research drawn from the most reliable sources and from a direct contact in the field, Professor Breton has written a masterpiece which aims at defining and situating the languages in the ethno-cultural structure of India. How far can a language correspond to an ethnic group? An answer to a hypothetical question as this necessitated the exploration of covert relationships between language, race, social groups and religions. Here was an ambitious but indispensable venture to build what should be considered the author's own contribution: the geographical distribution of ethnic groups. That was what the author expected, and he did live up to his expectations.

In all countries with a traditional civilization, each ethnic group has its own specific way of acting over its environment to conveniently fit in space. There are undoubtedly ethnic regions and the criterion for their delimitation is language—a method that is indisputable from our point of view.

We should be grateful to the author as he did not let difficulties detract him from designing and producing an atlas that will be an excellent working instrument for all those interested in knowing about India.

This venture might be too much for one man. Even if his results should be considered as a starting point, we must thank the author for having devoted many years of patient research to it: his work is indeed a step forward towards the better understanding of a world that will weigh ever more with humankind.

Professor Hildebert Isnard
University of Nice
1976

Acknowledgements

The author is grateful to the assistance of the following:

1. Cultural Service of the Embassy of France in India.

2. French Institute of Pondicherry, Department of Social Science, Pondicherry.

3. AtilA (Atelier TIL Architecture) CAD & CAC, Marseilles.

4. CILDA (International Centre of Language Industries and Development) University of Paris 10—Nanterre.

Introduction

The first edition of this atlas was published in French (with bilingual French–English maps) in Quebec in 1976, after 18 years of patient and close scrutiny of the linguistic panorama of the Indian subcontinent, several visits and various publications in this field. Time has elapsed since then, and for the present English edition, I had to revisit the subcontinent to take into account the most recent events and to consider latest available data, including the Censuses of 1981 and 1991.

I had always been fascinated by ethnic diversity, starting from Europe, followed by Asia, America and Africa, wherever my university and research life gave me the opportunity to live, work, and study. In 1947, the Independence of India under sad prophecies struck me; and, then its sound way of resisting all the menaces it faced. In 1958 my first contact with India—and my first appointment as a Faculty member—led me to work under Professor Enayat Ahmad, then Head of the Geography Department of Bihar University in Ranchi. That gave me the opportunity to gain access to in-depth research about the linguistic and ethnic composition of the subcontinent that needed geographical processing, through the steady series of decennial censuses of population; and the huge volumes of the *Linguistic Survey* directed by Sir George Grierson (1902–27) about which O.H.K. Spate, in his monumental work *India and Pakistan* (1957: 143), warned his co-geographers that an attempt to summarize it was a risk of 'the most fatal intellectual apoplexy'.

This arduous attempt at a geographical approach to the languages of India notwithstanding, the success of my earlier books and articles on this issue encouraged me to make it, under Professor Hildebert Isnard, the topic of my Ph.D. thesis presented in Nice in 1973. From this work emerged the first version of this atlas, wherein both the plates and text were based on a complex methodical approach combining seven elements:

- the geographical field surveys conducted throughout the subcontinent where various developments on linguistic questions and on the linguism issue may have occurred;
- the statistical analysis of more than a century of decennial censuses including many detailed answers to various linguistic and ethnic questions, available in Calcutta, Delhi or London;
- after having taken a Sanskrit programme in Aix-en-Provence (1963–65), the study of numerous provisional or definitive conclusions, either convergent or divergent, by Indian or non-Indian linguists, giving the current state-of-the-art teaching in general linguistics about Indian languages; of which, as a geographer, I could not dare correct anything, but to which many discussions, particularly in Mysore at the Central Institute of Indian Languages (CIIL) could bring more light;
- studying social science data in sociology, anthropology and ethnology available with the Anthropological Survey of India in Calcutta and Delhi, collecting information about these highly diverse peoples, comprising one-fifth of the humankind;
- a course on the historical insight of India along subcontinental, national and regional scales that I taught in Aix at the University of Provence (1969–72) which explains various facts ranging from old population patterns to present political options;
- the environmental and biogeographical observation which facilitates the understanding of the importance of environmental factors in the relationships between nature and culture, particularly through maps and other works from the French Institute in Pondicherry;
- the cartographic and general graphic expression, used more as an instrument of scientific research and heuristic investigation rather than a mere means of communication between the author and his readers. The plates do not illustrate the discourse, but, from data storage and processing, and from standardization of figurative tools, constitute the starting point of reflexion and demonstration. It is thus not an addition to the study but an integral step to it.

In this perspective, the atlas comprises two parts. The first part introduces, on a discursive mode, the general relationship between language and ethno-cultural structure of the subcontinent. The second part aims at analyzing the regional distribution of language and ethnic communities through graphic exploration. It is divided into 50 plates (updated and partly redrawn from the first edition) plus ten new ones, six of which were issued through CAD (Computer Assisted Design), as these plates required to take into account the 1991 Census data. Each plate carries a commentary on the facing page.

The whole work follows the rules of contemporary graphic semiology as defined by Bertin (1981 and 1983) and is, thus, a semiographic analysis.

Finally, it is essential to add that geographers mainly work on data of simultaneous signification expressing spatial distribution at a given date, i.e., in synchrony. They may also consider evolutions in time, i.e., in diachrony. Following this double perspective, apart from maps giving instant snapshots of dated situations, many other figures including ethnograms enable the representation of the linguistic reality in its twofold dimensions: either in synchrony or in diachrony.

May everyone who loves diversity enjoy this atlas.

PART I

GENERAL PRESENTATION OF THE LANGUAGES AND ETHNIC COMMUNITIES OF SOUTH ASIA

CHAPTER 1

INDIA AS AN EXEMPLARY LABORATORY FOR THE COEXISTENCE OF LANGUAGES AND ETHNIC COMMUNITIES

The human diversity of the subcontinent has so often been stressed that a brief recapitulation of the main anthropological, linguistic, religious and social characteristics of its ethnic complexity will suffice.

India has been the only part of the world where so many different human races have been living together for thousands of years. These include the Australoids and Veddids from Sri Lanka, Negritoids from the Andaman Islands, dark Melano-Indians, fair North Indians and yellow Mongoloids. There are numerous spoken languages including hundreds of dialectal forms that belong to four distinct families: Indo-European, Dravidian, Austro-Asiatic, Tibeto-Burman. In addition, the subcontinent presents a highly diversified religious panorama with five important native creeds—Hinduism, Jainism, Buddhism and Sikhism—along with numerous tribal religions and four non-Indian faiths: Judaism, Christianity, Mazdaism, and Islam. Through each of these components, a common complex social segmentation is present in changing proportions from one region to another in parallel communities from one geographical end to the other.

After the Partition in 1947, the resultant geopolitical division into seven sovereign states (including some strong provincial units corresponding to some of the biggest old linguistic communities) gave the subcontinent its unique structure expressing its panorama of diversity within a common historical civilization.

The first Census conducted in 1881 and every ten years thereafter, has given a great deal of information about the population of the subcontinent. Besides, the documentation of various mother tongues, religions, tribes, castes, etc., have been so frequently tabulated that it is a definite aid for sociologists, geographers and other social scientists. The complex population of the subcontinent may, thus, be more accurately studied over a span of more than a century.

The comparative growth and spread of communities such as those based on language and religion, before and after the Partition of India, as well as in Nepal and Sri Lanka may easily be delimited and evaluated through census statistics. Since the abolition of untouchability and the secularization and democratization of civil life, there is no distinct registered data on *jatis*. However, Part XVI of the Constitution (Articles 330–42) states that the President should register all 'specific classes' as Scheduled Castes, Scheduled Tribes, Other Backward Classes, or Anglo-Indians (the latter still computed during each census).

In the field of language belonging, the contribution of the Census of India has been highly constant since 1881. In 1886, the World Congress of Orientalists, in Vienna, asked for a systematic and thorough study, which was conducted by the Linguistic Survey under Sir Grierson from 1894 to 1927. This task is now being carried on by the Language Division of the Census of India in Calcutta. Classifying the various languages and dialects of the subcontinent has been a huge task which is still being accomplished though the enumeration of those speaking the various languages has been constantly worked on. This task has been pursued not only throughout the Indian territory but also in most of the other states of the subcontinent, such as Pakistan, Bangladesh, Nepal and Sri Lanka.

In these conditions any observer who wants to scrutinize the composition of the population will find the data either homogeneous or comparable and will encounter four main levels of group identification. The first level is made up of the seven sovereign nations of the subcontinent: India, Bangladesh, Pakistan, Nepal, Sri Lanka, Bhutan and the Maldives that together form SAARC (South Asian Association for Regional Cooperation). Second, the ethno-linguistic communities which correspond to ancient regional sets of population sharing a common language with a particular traditional articulation of social divisions (jatis) and religious affiliation. The best known among these ethno-linguistic communities are named after the broad provincial divisions of the subcontinent—tracing their origin to the ancient *janapadas* up to modern linguistic states—such as Bengalis, Marathis, Andhras, Tamils, etc., and who are considered by the Indian anthropological school as sociocultural or *cultural–linguistic* aggregates. At the other end of the ethnic spectrum, some of these ethnolinguistic communities are conventionally regarded as 'tribes' (termed as Scheduled Tribes in the Constitution of India). The broader regional ethno-linguistic communities can be identified by their language diffusion, while the smaller tribal ones are delimited both by language and Scheduled Tribe statistics in India. Third, the language groups are further subdivided on the basis of religion. These *religious communities* are being commonly enlisted in each census under the heading 'religions'. Finally, social traditional communities called jatis are computed in India alone under Scheduled Castes and Other Backward Classes.

In the context of this fourfold social structure, this atlas will primarily focus on the second level of communities, while the other communities will only be taken into account to explain the proper setting of ethno-linguistic communities within the population.

LANGUAGE IDENTIFICATION AND MEASUREMENT: FROM THE LANGUAGE IDENTIFICATION (THE SURVEY) TO THE MEASUREMENT OF ETHNO-LINGUISTIC GROUPS (THE CENSUS)

The identification of a common speech is not always as obvious as it may appear in daily life. Even inter-intelligibility—i.e., the ability by which speakers of a given language more or less understand those of another language spontaneously without particular training)—which is the basic criterion in the delimitation of language affiliation is inadequate. As one moves from Lahore or Amritsar to Calcutta, as from Amsterdam to Vienna, one may gradually observe only minor dialectal variations in oral expression. Nonetheless, Punjabi is indeed widely different from Bengali, as Dutch is from standard German. A language continuum is a reality, sometimes manifested by a large linguistic area, that ignores sharp inner barriers. However, distinctly differentiated individual languages with low mutual intelligibility may coexist particularly on the periphery.

The second factor of differentiation—besides the geographical distance covering a wide linguistic ex-

panse—is the existence of one or several superordinated common or standardized linguistic form(s): whether it is a spontaneously originated *Koyne*, as in ancient Greek, or a deliberately built national language, a language by *Ausbau* (construction), rather than by *Abstand* (distance), according to the terminology formulated by Kloss (1974). Development, promotion and management of a language reflect the ever-growing conscious and voluntary process that may affect its emergence.

The third element involved in the use and spread of language is the consumption and production of the mass media, which essentially passes through one or the other forms of language.

And, last but not the least, there exists the legal *status* offered to languages of mass consumption which is subject to change in India as anywhere else in the world. It may suffer or benefit according to the disdain or support of the people themselves, followed by the will of the state. Though, linguistic issues in India have often highlighted this situation, the debate has still remained unresolved.

Far from traditional linguistic studies, philological research on these last three modern sociolinguistic aspects of the emergence of language in India, has been conducted by the Census Language Division (see Mahapatra et al. 1989 and McConnell 1992).

To summarize, one may say that, at the turn of the century, most linguistic situations are influenced by three main factors which are on the path to concisely delimit established and emerging languages from simple dialectal forms:
- the existence of a superordinated standard which is already fixed or is in the grammatical, lexical and literary process,
- its actual or potential, widespread use in mass media,
- its eventual legal status or wide consensus to reach it.

A BRIEF UPDATED AND LONG-TERM PANORAMA OF THE LANGUAGES AND ETHNO-LINGUISTIC COMMUNITIES OF THE SUBCONTINENT

To be able to sketch a general map of the languages of the subcontinent from this permanently dynamic situation, it is imperative to refer to the latest available census data of the different states, approximated to the most reliable projections, for instance from the Population Reference Bureau (Washington), i.e., provisionally to those of 1991 when it reached 1,110 million people (cf Plate 59). The following sets should be distinguished from a real language when deliberately omitting dialectal forms and mother tongue variants.

A central *'Hindustani'* group with Hindi (341 million) is the major language in seven Indian states—Haryana, Himachal Pradesh, Rajasthan, Madhya Pradesh, Bihar, Uttar Pradesh, and Delhi. This region is referred to as the Hindi Region or the *Hindi Belt* and comprises 377 million inhabitants. The 36 million difference between the two figures is mainly explained by the existence of two other languages which are very close to Hindi in the spoken use, but strongly individualized and differentiated when written. The first is Urdu (54 million) spoken in India (45 million) by nearly half the Indian Muslims and, in Pakistan (9 million including most of the Partition refugees with their 4 million Muhajir descendants. The second is Punjabi spoken in both the Punjab provinces in Pakistan and in India, with 24 million speakers in India and 70 million in Pakistan, though the written language in Pakistan is institutionally Urdu.

This Hindustani linguistic complex including Hindi, Urdu and Punjabi comprises a total of 489 million people, i.e., 44 per cent of the population of the subcontinent. But within the geographical area of this continuum having three main standard forms of cultural language, it is essential to mention the presence of other local forms which include Rajasthani, spoken by 13 million in 1971 (5 million Marwari), Bhili by 3 million for a provincial population of 26 million, and three 'Bihari' languages (Bhojpuri 14 million, Magadhi 9 million and Maithili 7 million in 1971 of the 56 million speakers in Bihar alone).

Close to this central complex is Nepali with 9.3 million in Nepal and 2.2 million in India, apart from over 5 million Western Pahari dialects now included in the statistics of India.

The peripheral *Indo-Aryan* region includes the eastern group with Bengali (67 million in India, 109 million in Bangladesh), Oriya (27.5 million) and Assamese (13.5 million); the southern group with Marathi (62 million), Konkani (1.8 million) and Sinhalese (12.9 million) and the southwestern group with Gujarati (40 million) and Sindhi (14 million in Pakistan and 2.5 million in India).

Among the *Dardic* languages, half-way between Indo-Aryan and Iranian, are Kashmiri (numerically higher with 4.1 million speakers), Shina, Khowar and the 'Kohistani' language continuum.

The *Iranian* branch of the ancient Indo-Iranian subfamily is represented within the subcontinent by Pushto (15.5 million in Pakistan's North West Frontier Province) and Baluchi (3.6 million).

The 15 major *Indo-European* languages of the subcontinent—12 Indo-Aryan (Hindi, Urdu, Punjabi, Nepali, Bengali, Assamese, Oriya, Marathi, Konkani, Gujarati, Sinhalese and Sindhi), one Dardic (Kashmiri), two Iranian (Pushto and Baluchi) and about six minor ones (Khowar, Kohistani, Shina, Dogri, Bhili and Dhivehi) are spoken by 887 million people, i.e., 79.9 per cent of the population.

The *Dravidian* family gathers the four main southern languages: Telugu (68 million), Tamil (59 million in India and 4.4 million in Sri Lanka), Malayalam (29.5 million), and Kannada (32 million), plus Tulu (1.7 million) and Kodagu or Coorgi (110,000). In addition there are numerous tribal languages: Toda and Kota in the Nilgiri Hills, Gondi (2.4 million), Oraon (1.8 million), Kui (0.6 million), Kuvi (0.2 million), Koya (0.3 million) in central Deccan followed by Malto, Kolami, Parji and Konda (0.4 million altogether), and Brahui (1.4 million) isolated in Baluchistan. Among its 202 million speakers, the Dravidian family had more than 194 million people speaking its four main cultural languages and less than eight speaking 14 local or ethnic languages: 18.2 per cent of the subcontinent's population.

The *Austro-Asiatic* family, from the Austric set of languages, includes 'tribal' languages mainly from the *Munda* branch, i.e., Santali (5.7 million) and its 'Kherwari' sister languages: Mundari (1.4 million), Ho (1 million), Koda, Bhumij, Korwa, Asuri, Birhor and Turi (less than 0.5 million altogether), plus Korku (0.4 million) in the west and Kharia (0.3 million), Savara (0.2 million), Gadaba and Juang (together constituting 1 million) in the south. There are thus about 9 million speakers in 14 languages. *Mon-Khmer*, the other Austro-Asiatic branch, is represented in India by only two outposts: Khasi (0.9 million) in Meghalaya and Nicobarese (32,000) in the Nicobar Islands: i.e., 9.3 million or 0.8 per cent of the population for Austric languages.

The *Tibeto-Burman* family is the most divided. It is represented, in the subcontinent, mainly by ten or more Tibetan or 'Bhotiya' speeches, such as Ladakhi, Sherpa, etc., in Kashmir, Nepal, Sikkim, Bhutan and Arunachal Pradesh with less than 1 million speakers. This family also includes some languages from the Himalayan region of Himachal Pradesh (Kanauri), the Gurung-Tamang group of central to eastern Nepal (Magar, Newari, Rai, Limbu, etc.) covering about 3.7 million speakers; the Mirish languages (Hrusso, Dafla, Miri, Adi, Mishmi) of Arunachal Pradesh, having 0.8 million speakers; and the Assamo-Burman groups of languages including the Bodo group in the northwest (Bodo 0.9 million, Garo 0.8 million, Tripuri or Kokborok 0.7 million, Rabha, Dimasa, Deori, Koch, Lalung together having 0.2 million speakers, Mikir or Karbi 0.3 million, and Meithei or Manipuri 1.3 million) the Naga groups in the northeast (with about 25 speeches numbering 1.2 million speakers) and the Kuki-Chin groups in the south (Mizo 0.5 million, and about 14 Kuki speeches 0.4 million). To sum up, the whole Tibeto-Burman family of 16.6 million people or 1.1 per cent of the population is divided into about 80 ethno-linguistic groups whose mother tongues, except Tibetan and Manipuri, have not yet reached the status of cultural languages and are generally considered 'tribal' languages.

Apart from these three major language families, the subcontinent is the home of two linguistic isolates: *Burushaski* (0.1 million) spoken in the region between Pamir and Kashmir, still without any known external link, and the vanishing *Andamanese* group of languages, spoken in the Andaman Islands by about 100 people. The last isolate has tempted some linguists to tie it to a hypothetic *Indo-Pacific* family including Papuan and former Tasmanian languages.

THE VITALITY AND EMERGENCE OF LANGUAGES IN SOUTH ASIA

Such a picture of the linguistic framework of the population of the subcontinent having about 120 different languages must be considered as provisional and approximate, due to the imperfection of the tools of analysis; it is a mere snapshot. This is because of the constantly changing population figures and also because of the evolution or decline in the definition, use and promotion of a language. Even statistical data are based on a certain amount of 'rationalization', i.e., choices leading to a grouping of dialects under standard language designations. For instance, in post-Independent India, the total number of languages has significantly changed. The 1951 Census numbered 845 mother tongues, including numerous dialects and local, social and non-Indian linguistic forms while the 1961 Census raised the number to 1652. However, several rationalizations and groupings lowered the total in 1971 and 1981 to 105, but these censuses did not include any mother tongue or 'variant' spoken by less than 10,000 speakers.

Perfect, definitive and unquestionable classifications though desirable are not available anywhere. Two national languages—Assamese and Konkani—were once considered dialects. Numerous dialects still remain much discussed with various possible allegiances, and some are eventually considered as 'roofless'. For instance, the ambiguity in rationally classifying Rajasthani speeches such as Mewari, Nimari, Malvi, Harauti, Gojri, etc., under a particular language unit still persists. Their population may eventually choose (though this may take time) between Hindi and any standardized Rajasthani or a Marwari reference speech form. What is the functional audience or the fundamental affinity of the three 'Bihari' languages between Hindi, Maithili and Bengali? Or what about Western Pahari dialects between Hindi and Nepali? Linguistic identifications and administrative decisions regarding rationalization and classification may disagree with the sentiments of the population.

And, in the meantime we must admit that official statistics displaying various linguistic answers from the same population, in the same districts, villages and even families, are indicative of denominational options that may be respected and scrupulously transcribed, but do not in any measure match real different specific uses. Some designations of languages are confusing, as 'Jatapu' or 'Kisan' in Orissa, and there may be a number of people with various mother tongues as well as mixed speeches, such as Nahali in Madhya Pradesh.

In many places the language unit and ethnic group may not appear identical. This can be explained by the process of *language shift* which takes into account the process of acculturation—deculturation, wherein populations shift from one language to another, from one generation to the next, through various degrees of bilingualism. As a direct consequence, this sociocultural process simultaneously leads to a closely related sociogeographical process of the *spread of language* through new communities and in wider areas. And then, beyond the problem of the signification of language use as a conscious, or an unconscious sign of identification to a specific ethnic entity, there remains the bigger problem of the feeling, or the reality, of parenthood between human groups who speak obviously cognate languages, but are geographically and/or historically separated. Does the habit to speak from Munda or Dravidian, etc., populations carry a greater meaning than mentioning people merely sharing languages that sound alike? No anthropological considerations can ascertain it. Nevertheless the linguistic dimension of social, or macrosocial, *societal* units, is a fact of major importance and the modest ambition of this atlas is only to clarify some aspects about distribution of linguistic community through reliable measurements and sensible representations, so as to achieve working relationships between linguistic, ethnological and geographical phenomena.

CHAPTER 2

LANGUAGE COMPARED TO OTHER ETHNIC TRAITS: CONGRUENCES AND DISCREPANCIES

It is usual to extend all the traits of an ethnic group to all its members. But scientific analysis must take into account the specific distribution of traits, particularly those across ethnic limits. This chapter endeavours to do so by comparing the extension of ethno-linguistic communities to the four main referential communities: those based on physical anthropology (race), or ethnic affiliation (tribe), socioprofessional membership (caste) and sociodenominational allegiance (religion).

LANGUAGE AND RACE (ETHNO-LINGUISTIC COMMUNITIES COMPARED WITH ANTHROPOLOGICAL GROUPINGS)

Twenty centuries ago, Strabo, with reference to Megasthenes and other Greek authors, classified the Indian population into two main types: the first type in the north is similar to Egyptians (i.e., Mediterranean type) on account of their features and hair, and the second type in the south is similar to Ethiopians because of the colour of their skin. This broad distinction has for long been accepted by all observers of India. In the same way the Pandits' linguistic classification divided Indian languages into five *Dravidian* and five *Gaurian* languages (the term *Indo-European* was only created later by Westerners). Since then, this simple dichotomy has been widely sophisticated by linguists, historians, anthropologists and other social scientists. Many other languages and linguistic families (Munda, Tibeto-Burman, etc.) as also various other physical types (Veddid, Mongoloid, etc.) have been analyzed and classified, and an attempt has been made to understand their possible relationships, imbrications and interactions. Thus, nowadays, it would be irrelevant to speak of a present Dravidian or Indo-Aryan *race* or population on physical characteristics alone; just as tracing descent from a Jewish, German or Romance *race* in Europe. It

is commonly held that the distribution on the basis of the colour of the skin, features, form and other anthropological attributes is scarcely associated to linguistic areas, particularly with regard to *polymorphic* groups speaking major languages which consist of people presenting different morphologies. Only small isolated tribes may present a certain homogeneity in physical features.

The Indian anthropological school has developed an elaborate taxonomy of physical types from the *primary ethnic strains* (Singh 1992) of India, and the mere enumeration of these big categories shows that their distribution is not based on linguistic criteria.

The Negrito, or the *negritoid* type may only be found among aborigenes from the Andaman Islands. This group is pygmoid, bracycephalic (broad-headed), dark-skinned, having bushy hair, a very low pilosity and a tendency to steatopygy. Traces of this type have been reported among the Dravidian-speaking hill peoples belonging to the Western Ghats, such as the Kadars, Pulayans, Uralis, or those from the Rajmahal Hills, and even among Tibeto-Burman-speaking Nagas: Angamis (Guha 1944) or Konyaks and Kachas (Hutton 1932). According to Elwin (1961), Angamis could be physically akin to Igorots Negritos from the Philippines (who speak an Austronesian language).

The Veddid, or the *veddoid* type, linked with proto-Australoid races from Melanesia and Australia, is represented by the Veddas from Sri Lanka who speak Sinhalese (i.e., Indo-Aryan). This type, characterized by short stature, dolichocephalic (long-headed), brown-skinned, with wavy hair, is also found in the Western Ghats. Examples are the Kannada-speaking Kurumbas from the Nilgiri Hills, the Telugu-speaking Chenchus and Tamil-speaking Yeruvas from the Eastern Ghats. This category is also widely represented among the Adivasis from central India, the Dravidian-speaking Khonds and Oraons, the Munda-speaking Juangs,

Birhors, etc., even the Indo-Aryan Bhils up to Meghalaya, and the Mon-Khmer speakers such as the Khasis.

The dark Indian type, named either *Melano-Indian*, or *South Indian, Paleo-Indian* or *Paleo-Mediterranean*, has often been described as akin to *Mediterranean* and European types, and never to Negro-African *Negroid*, *Melano-Oceanian* or Melanesian ones. This category obviously makes up the majority not only of Dravidian south Indian population but also of numerous Munda-speaking Adivasis, e.g., the Santals, (who would be the darkest among the Indian peoples) and also among many large communities from north India (from Gujarat to the Indo-Gangetic plain and the Himalayan valleys) who speak only Indo-Aryan languages.

The fair Mediterranean type is predominant in northwest India but may be found in smaller proportions all over north India up to the Dravidian-speaking South. Anthropologists recognize among them dolichocephalic types (Indo-Afghan, Iranian, East-Mediterranean and Nordic) as well as brachycephalic (Alpo-Dinaric, Anatolian, Armenoid, and *Pamirian*), but their distribution is crossing all linguistic areas and groupings. In the south, the Dravidian-speaking Todas from the Nilgiri Hills, the Kodagus from Coorg, and the Nayars from Kerala, for instance, belong to one or the other of these types. Biasutti (1953) maintains that the Dravidian Brahuis and the Tibetan-speaking Baltis in the north of the subcontinent are 'pure Europoids'.

The Mongoloid type is also diverse. It is possible to find a tall dolichocephalic and a fair Tibetan (*pre-Mongoloid*?) distributed all over India: from Ladakh to Arunachal Pradesh and among some Nagas or the Adivasis from central India—the Munda-speaking Savaras and the Gadabas, or the Dravidian-speaking Parajas and the Maria Gonds (Hutton 1932)—up to the Pulayans from Wynad in Malabar (Eickstedt 1934). The other smaller brachycephalic and brown *south-Mongoloid* type is found from Limbus in Nepal and Lepchas in Sikkim to most tribal groups in Assam and Burma. But traces of Mongoloid features are present among non-tribal, Indo-Aryan-speaking population in the Bengal area, where they mix with the north- or south-Indian types.

Distribution of racial features can hardly match that of language belonging and use, except for some small closed and isolated communities. But, even among remote tribes, anthropologists may find a juxtaposition of extremely distant types—a strange phenomenon observed among many Southeast Asian hill peoples. The non-coextensiveness between physical–anthropological and linguistic facts is because clear-cut linguistic areas (at both language and language-family levels) are a general historical and functional reality, while homogeneous racial sets of population are exceptional because the larger the ethno-linguistic groups, the more *polymorphic* they become, i.e., various physical types may be present among them.

In this respect, to speak for instance of a *Dravidian* race that includes and is limited to south Indians alone is the expression of a confusion between linguistic vocabulary (Dravidian) and anthropological facts (race). But to believe that the *Melano-Indian* type is a typical feature of the Dravidian-speaking people is an oversimplification which neglects the fact that many Dravidian-speaking communities do not belong to it, e.g., in Baluchistan, while the more numerous Munda- or Aryan-speaking communities do belong to it. Parallel simplifications would confine the extension of the Negritoid type to the Andamanese, the Veddid to the Veddas, or the Mongoloid to Tibeto-Burman tribes. Nowadays, in most cases, there is no direct link between the phenomena of language and race. Though one may trace a long-standing connection between the two phenomena, it has been fundamentally disrupted by centuries and millenniums of migrations, interactions, acculturations, and divergent, or convergent, evolutions.

These disparities in the distribution of the various categories should not lead the reader to neglect detailed anthropological observations that may explain the composition or origin of a certain population. However, it is essential to avoid relating consanguinal descent to linguistic affinities, or to infer one from the other. It is grossly misleading to treat a descent and language group as identical, and further, to assume that the people have a knowledge of these possible kinships. Over the passage of time the connexion between natural and cultural ties may completely be obliterated. Myths are objects of science but not its base.

LANGUAGE AND TRIBE (THE MOTHER TONGUE SETS OF POPULATION COMPARED WITH THE ETHNIC COMMUNITIES)

Language belonging may now be statistically compared with the data of ethnic membership. This is, however, restricted to tribes alone; they being the one ethnic category to be registered in the census (beside Anglo-Indians). This comparison throws light on the acculturation–deculturation process in two ways: first, at the level of an overall confrontation between the number of mother tongue speakers and tribe members, where tribes have languages of their own, and second, the observation of bilingualism within the ethnic groups. The following examples have been taken from the 1961 Census, which includes detailed state-wise data about tribes, mother tongues and bilingualism.

The Khasis, an eastern Meghalaya tribe, numbered 356,000 in Assam (including, at that time, the Meghalaya territory) but their Mon-Khmer language was a mother tongue spoken by 363,000 people. This discrepancy is evidently because of the adoption of Khasi as a mother tongue by non-Khasis. The Khasi Hills are divided into a western part, occupied by 22 former Khasi states, home of the Khasi language; and an eastern part called the Jaintia Hills, where two divergent Khasi dialects are spoken: Pnar, or Synteng, in the northern side, and War in the southern valleys. But, southwest of the Khasi states, the Lyng-ngam, a former Garo clan, is Khasi-speaking; the members do not mix with Garos and consider themselves Khasis (Chatterjee 1968: 237).

The Garos inhabiting the western half of Meghalaya, numbered 258,000, of which 254,000 were Garo (Tibeto-Burman) mother tongue speakers and 2,000 mere Rabha speakers (a close Tibeto-Burman language). But 31,000 among these Garo speakers and half of Rabha speakers spoke Assamese, the regional language, as a second language. At the same time, 47,000 non-Garo people in Assam had Garo as their mother tongue. A rare example, among the tribal peoples, of a linguistic mother tongue group (254,000 + 47,000 = 301,000) that widely exceeded the tribal group (258,000). This strong ethno-cultural situation along with the Khasi situation might have partly helped both the tribes succeed in gaining the creation of their own state, Meghalaya.

In the neighbouring North Cachar Hills Autonomous District in western Assam, the main tribe known as the Dimasas, or the Hairambas, or the Hills Kacharis (as opposed to the Bodos, or the Kacharis from the plains) were 69,000; among them only 20,000 were Dimasa mother tongue speakers and 16,000 'Kachari': together constituting 52 per cent of the tribe. Among other mother tongues were Mikir (spoken in Karbi Anglong district situated towards the east) spoken by 16,000 people, Bengali (the language of the Cachar district towards the south) by 12,000 and Assamese, the regional language, by 4,000. But Dimasa was also the

mother tongue of a second tribe, the Cachar Barmans, numbering 13,000 of which 11,000 (80 per cent) had Dimasa as mother tongue and 2,000 had Bengali. Further, among the Dimasa speakers, 7,000 had Bengali as second language. Again, a third tribe, the Hojais (4,000), in Karbi Anglong, were Dimasa speakers until the beginning of the century. But in 1961, 2,400 of them spoke Assamese as their mother tongue while the rest spoke Mikir or Bodo. Thus, for a total of 86,000 people, split in three traditionally Dimasa-speaking tribes, only 47,000 kept Dimasa as their mother tongue. This was because all the three tribes were being acculturated to Bengali, Mikir or Assamese.

On the contrary, the former Mikirs, now self-designated as Karbis, seemed to be moving towards linguistic and ethnic consolidation. Of a total of 121,000, 119,000 were Mikir mother tongue speakers (of which 68,000 spoke Assamese as second language), but, outside the tribe, 35,000 people were Mikir mother tongue speakers (with 16,000 Dimasas among them). Thus, the linguistic mother tongue group of 154,000 people, widely exceeding the tribe strength, was certainly a positive factor in the affirmation of the Karbi Anglong Autonomous District compared to the weaker position of the North Cachar Autonomous District.

The second tribe of Karbi Anglong is made up of the Lalungs. Of the 61,000 people of this tribe, 5,000 had Lalung as their mother tongue (of which 3,000 spoke Assamese as second language) and 56,000 spoke Assamese as mother tongue (with 8,000 speaking Lalung as second language). However, 6,000 people outside the Lalung tribe retained Lalung as their mother tongue. Nevertheless, a linguistic mother tongue group of 11,000 compared with an ethnic group of 61,000 (even after adding about 8,000 second language speakers) was an indubitable indication of a deep cultural decline.

In the Brahmaputra plains of Assam, the Bodo or Bara people are divided into three tribes: the Mechs in the west across the West Bengal border, the Boros or the Boro-Kacharis in the centre and the Kacharis (or the Plains Kacharis to differentiate them from the Dimasas) in the east. Among 14,000 Mechs of West Bengal, 10,000 were still Bodo mother tongue speakers and the rest were Bengali speakers, while nearly all the 7,000 Mechs of Assam had Assamese as their mother tongue. Among the 346,000 Assam Boro-Kacharis, 245,000 (70 per cent) were Bodo mother tongue speakers (with 160,000 speaking Assamese as a second language) and the remaining 100,000 were Assamese mother tongue speakers (with 25,000 speaking Bodo as a second language). As for the 237,000 Assam Plains Kacharis, less than one-third (31 per cent or 73,000) were Bodo mother tongue speakers (with 57,000 speaking Assamese as a second language) and the remaining 162,000 were Assamese mother tongue speakers (with only 8,000 speaking Bodo as second language). Thus the three tribes seemed differently acculturated: half the Mechs were Assamized, the Boro-Kacharis still had a large ethno-speaking majority (245,000 mother tongue speakers plus 25,000 speaking a second language out of 346,000) with an equivalent number but in an opposite proportion, of Assamized members (100,000 mother tongue speakers plus 160,000 second language ones), and the Plains Kacharis were two-thirds Assamized. Out of a total strength of 590,000 members, the three tribes had only 318,000 native mother tongue speakers plus 35,000 second language ones, while 273,000 had adopted the regional language as their mother tongue, plus at least 217,000 as a second language. The language community was undoubtedly declining as compared to the ethnic community.

Assam, a real conservatory of peoples is rich in such ethnic situations. The east Brahmaputra plain is the home of the Tibeto-Burman Chutiyas, defeated by the Thai Ahoms who held the land from the twelfth to the fifteenth centuries. Most of the Chutiyas, engaged in Hinduization, lost their languages to Assamese, except the small sacerdotal caste of the Deoris. In 1961 the Deoris, registered as a Scheduled Tribe were 13,876, of which 8,457 spoke Deori as their mother tongue (of whom 6,479 were Assamese bilinguals) and 5,337 spoke Assamese as their mother tongue (of whom 1,002 were Deori bilinguals). Such numbers showed, beyond the inevitable acculturation to regional language by a group so small, a strong preservation of linguistic identity: out of 14,000 Deoris, there were 2,000 monolingual Deori speakers, 6,500 bilingual Deori-Assamese, 1,000 bilingual Assamese-Deori and only 4,300 Assamese monolingual ones; plus 500 Deori mother tongue speakers outside the tribe.

Such was not the case of the 163,000 Miris from Assam, of which 134,000 (83 per cent) were Miri (or Mishing) mother tongue speakers, out of which 102,000 were bilingual in Assamese, plus 28,000 Assamese mother tongue speakers (of which 4,000 were bilingual in Miri). No doubt that, in spite of their numerical strength, the Miris from the Assam plains, are not keenly preserving their language as the Deoris are.

The Rabhas, belonging to the former warrior caste of the Bodo people are settled in the Brahmaputra valley,

down the first slopes of the Garo Hills. They numbered 108,000 in Assam, of which only 28,000 kept Rabha as their mother tongue (19,000 were Assamese second language speakers, plus 5,000 Bodo mother tongue ones). But there were 75,000 Assamese mother tongue speakers (1,000 Rabha second language speakers and 4,000 Bodo ones). The 6,000 West Bengal Rabhas had more *ethnic speakers*: 5,000 were still Rabha mother tongue speakers and less than 1,000 were Bengali ones. Out of a tribal community of 114,000, the Rabha linguistic mother tongue group had only 33,000 people, plus, outside the tribe, there were 10,000 mother tongue Rabha speakers in Assam (of which 2,000 were Garos) and 2,000 in West Bengal, totalling the Rabha linguistic group to 45,000.

The case of the Kochs is more peculiar: a former Tibeto-Burman tribe, Hinduized and Bengalized after Rajbangsis, they were enumerated among the Scheduled Castes in West Bengal. A few lived on the fringes of the Hindu society, down the slopes of the Garo Hills or in the Madhupur Jungle in Bangladesh. They are called the Little Kochs or the Pani Kochs, having lower status, and are declining slowly: the 1901 Census enumerated 13,000 in the Madhupur Jungle and 3,000 in the Garo Hills; the statistics of the Linguistic Survey showed 5,000 and 6,000 respectively, and the 1931 Census 10,000. After Independence, though they were no longer registered as a Scheduled Caste or Tribe in Meghalaya, the graph of the mother tongue group has been steadily increasing: 5,000 in 1951, 8,000 in 1961, 14,000 in 1971 and 17,000 in 1981.

The Hajongs, or the Haijongs, also a former Tibeto-Burman tribe, from East Bengal were so completely Hinduized and Bengalized that the Hajong mother tongue was considered a Bengali dialect. After Partition some of them sought refuge in the Garo Hills where they were granted Scheduled Tribe status. In Meghalaya there were 23,000 Hajongs with 8,000 faithful to the Hajong Bengali dialect (of which 3,000 spoke Assamese as second language) and 15,000 were Assamese mother tongue speakers (of which 3,000 spoke Bengali as second language). Here was a striking example of two successive acculturation processes to regional languages: the first gradual while the second progressive.

The language of the Bodo group further towards the south is Tripuri, shared by four geographically close and historically bound, distinct Scheduled Tribes: the Tripuras, Riangs, Jamatias and Noatias, who make up the bulk of the population of Tripura (former Tipperah Hills). The name of the four tribes is also used as dialectal designations within the Tripuri language, which had 300,000 speakers in India: 284,000 in 1961 in Tripura and 16,000 in Assam), plus about 30,000 in Bangladesh Chittagong Hill Tracts. These dialectal designations were commonly used in the old method of naming the speech through the tribe, rather than expressing any clear-cut linguistic divisions of mother tongues. A new standard form, Kokborok, is now proposed as a common link over the possible variants. These four tribes were extremely faithful to their ethnic language. In Tripura, among 190,000 Tripuras, nearly all of them (184,000) were Tripura mother tongue speakers, one-third was Bengalized enough to declare Bengali as their second language, and only 5,000 were of Bengali mother tongue. Among 57,000 Riangs, 24,000 Jamatias and 16,000 Noatias, almost all of them were eth-nophones, with hardly one-fourth speaking Bengali as second language. Thus, among the four tribes which had a total population of 287,000 people, only 5,000 from Tripura were completely Bengalized (Bengali mother tongue) and less than a third (88,000), partly. Outside the four tribes, Tripuri was the mother tongue of some (2,000) Halams, a Kuki tribe in Tripura, and several other small Kuki tribes from Assam and Bangladesh (10,000). The strong linguistic identity of this tribal population was certainly strengthened by the ethnically embedded state of Tripura. However, constant immigration of Bengali settlers, increased by the 1947 Partition and the 1971 Bangladesh War, had reduced Hill peoples to a minority in their own state, while keeping a very narrow congruence between linguistic and ethnic groups: four tribes in one state who exert their influence even outside their territory.

Among the Kuki-Chin people the congruence between linguistic and tribal groups is generally quite perfect. This is evident in Mizoram among the 215,000 Mizos (former Lushais or 'Central Chins') and the neighbouring Maras, speaking Lakher (9,000), and the Pawis, speaking Lai (5,000). Also among 'New Kukis' (former 'Northern Chins') in Manipur comprising the Thadus (48,000 Thado speakers), the Gangtes (5,000) and the Paites (17,000), and again among most of the 'Old Kukis' from Manipur: the Vaiphuis (8,000 Vaiphei speakers). In Assam and Tripura, 'Old Kukis' were subjected to a greater deculturation that was often inter-tribal than Bengalization. Though the 15,000 Manipur Hmars were fully ethnic speakers, 6,000 of the 9,000 Assam Hmars were still Hmar mother tongue speakers. In Assam, other Kukis (19,000) have widely (10,000) adopted Reang (Tripuri) as their mother tongue and in

Tripura, the 16,000 Halams have partly shifted to Tripuri: 2,000 against 14,000 ethnic speakers.

The Nagas too manifest a close congruence between language and tribe. A community with a very strong common ethnic conscience, it is in fact an agglomeration of over 25 groups, each having its own distinct body of speech. It is a rare case presenting a kind of ethnic confederacy with maximum linguistic differentiations through some very rapid divergences. Grierson mentions villages that have split linguistically to the extent of not being able to understand each other anymore within the span of two generations. He explained that the plastic structure of their 'monosyllabic languages, without literature, with a floating pronunciation and numerous prefixes and suffixes vaguely used to meet ordinary needs of grammar' which had led them 'to change very rapidly and independently [of] one from the other' (1902–27). Hutton (1932) gives an example of a village where two languages are spoken on two sides of the main street: one that is common to both while the other kept secret by its speakers.

In March 1969 some southern Nagas had to cross Tuensang District in the northeast of Nagaland. They belonged to the underground organization that signed the 1964 cease-fire agreement with the Indian authorities and were coming home after an illegal training period in China through Burmese mountain tracks. They carried various things including 'Little Red Books', pocket dictionaries, Chinese guns with folding bayonets, grenades, binoculars, compasses, etc. But, while crossing the border by Mount Saramati, they lost their way and found themselves in fellow people's villages. Three Angamis and one Sema reached a village belonging to the Yimchungre tribe. Although the Semas and the Yimchungres are neighbouring tribes, the travellers could not make themselves understood when they asked for food. They were compelled to grab it by force and died in the ensuing fight. As the northeast Nagas were still reluctant to give up the ancestral tradition of head-hunting, the victims' heads were hung with great pomp and ceremony in the Common House gable. A similar incident occurred a while later in a Yimchungre village to five Tangkhuls coming back home and again in a Chang village to two Angamis. The Indian judge, dispatched on the spot, broke off the month long festivities which followed any headhunting. Moreover, some elders had already questioned these celebrations because preparatory headhunting rites had not been respected. This incident, beyond its metaphysical aspect, reflects less the effect of a clash between traditional and modern mentalities and more the result of a common misunderstanding between villagers from the same community speaking different languages.

In Chota Nagpur and central India, more fluidity may be observed between tribal and linguistic identities, with numerous cases of an intertribal acculturation–deculturation process, and the emergence of tribal federations. The biggest Munda tribe, the Santals, had only 3,154,000 members while the language, Santali, had 3,257,000 mother tongue speakers. Santali was also the mother tongue of two minor tribes: the Karmali blacksmiths and the Mahli basket makers. It has also been adopted in the fringes of some related Munda tribes: the Koras (11,000 in West Bengal and 3,000 in Bihar), Bhumijs (7,000 in West Bengal and as many in Orissa), Hos (9,000 in Bihar), 'Mundas' (7,000 in Bengal), and even among the Dravidian Oraons (13,000 in Bihar and 12,000 in Bengal). Simultaneously, some parts of the Santal tribe were linguistically deculturated: less than 2 per cent of 1,514,000 in Bihar had Hindi as their mother tongue, more than 10 per cent of 1,200,000 in West Bengal had shifted to Indo-Aryan, mainly Bengali, and more than 20 per cent of 411,000 in Orissa, to Oriya or to other tribal languages. Everywhere the overlap of the Santal tribe and the Santali-speaking population suffered from strong and increasing discrepancies.

On the Ranchi plateau, of the 629,000 members of the Munda tribe, 78 per cent spoke Mundari, the rest having shifted to Hindi or its local variants like Sadri, or to tribal languages (Oraon 3,000 and Ho 3,000). The greater number of their Oraon neighbours (735,000 : 72 per cent) made it difficult for them to give up their Dravidian mother tongue for some regional or tribal language (Mundari 36,000 or 5 per cent and Santali 13,000 or 2 per cent). In this way we could locate right into their ancestral heartland, 3,000 Dravidian-speaking Mundas and 49,000 Munda-speaking Oraons, i.e., 'Dravidians'. Around the core area their deculturation was higher, not only in favour of regional languages such as Hindi, Bengali and Oriya, but also of intertribal overlaps: 12,000 Santali-speaking Oraons in West Bengal, 7,000 Ho speakers in Orissa, 7,000 Oraon-speaking Mundas in Bengal and 3,000 in Orissa, plus 7,000 Kui (Dravidian) speakers. Ho, the third Munda language, was shared by both the Ho (former Larka Kols or 'Fighting Kols') and the Kol or the Kolha tribes but for long, the linguistic group could not reach the population figures of both ethnic groups because an important proportion had given up their Ho mother tongue, par-

ticularly the long deculturated Kols, e.g., the Orissa Kols (52 per cent).

The Bhumijs were far more deculturated: only 49 per cent were ethnic speakers in Orissa, 38 per cent in Bihar and 1 per cent in West Bengal. The rest of the tribe had adopted Oriya, Hindi, Bengali, Mundari, Santali or Oraon as their mother tongue. Out of the 83,000 Kodas (or Koras) and Khairas—small tank-building tribes/castes in Bengal—a few have kept their Munda Koda (12,000) or Khaira (18,000) languages.

The Kharias, often mistaken even in official statistics for the Khairas in spite of their different home area (in west Chota Nagpur), their language (from another Munda branch) and their traditions (ancient Hinduization), were also involved in a deep acculturation process which strengthened after their displacement from their home area: the mother tongue group represented 84 per cent of the tribe in Bihar, 74 per cent in Madhya Pradesh, 53 per cent in Orissa, and 44 per cent in West Bengal, while the rest spoke some regional language: Hindi, Oriya or Bengali.

The 138,000 Kisan (peasants) tribe members presented even more amazing data. In Bihar all of them (12,000) have adopted Hindi or its local variants. But in Orissa, of the 126,000, only 74,000 (59 per cent) have adopted Oriya while others have stated a 'Kisan' mother tongue, leaving experts with no clue to decide what it is, or in which proportion to put it under the Munda (Koda) or Dravidian (Oraon) grouping; until the Linguistic Survey experts advised the census to include it in the Dravidian language list.

The Korwas experienced a parallel process when giving up their Munda language (Korwa, including Koraku) in Madhya Pradesh, their main area, 74 per cent (of the total 42,000), 80 per cent in Bihar (out of 21,000) and 100 per cent in West Bengal (out of 3,000).

The case of the Asuri Munda language shared by three small forest-dwelling tribes is somewhat puzzling: the Birs (the Asurs proper), the Birjias (different from the Binjhias) and the Agarias whose mother tongues were considered as three dialects from the Asuri language numbered 3,126, 1,423 and 323 speakers respectively in 1901 and 4,540, 2,395 and 98 in 1961. This steadfast preservation of the Asuri and Birjia languages is surprising as only a part of each tribe has kept its linguistic identity—in Bihar (in 1961) less than half of the 6,000 Asurs, and 1,500 out of the 4,000 Birjias; the others have adopted Hindi.

Language preservation among Birhors, the 'jungle people', the least in number (3,300) among the Munda tribes from Chota Nagpur, with one out of six still speaking the Birhor language is even more surprising. In Bihar only 250 out of 2,400 were ethnic speakers, about half the population had shifted to Hindi or its variants and quite as many to Santali (700) or Mundari (300). Among the 513 Birhors of Madhya Pradesh, there were 289 Hindi mother tongue speakers against 174 Birhor speakers, but there were also 133 Birhor mother tongue speakers outside the tribe. A curious retention of a microscopic language whose 590 mother tongue speakers were, in 1961, extremely close in number to the 562 in 1901 when Grierson (1902–27) concluded his chapter about Birhors as follows: 'The tribe may probably have been more numerous in the past than now, and it is likely only a question of time to see Birhor dialect cease to exist.' That time has yet to come.

In the heart of the Santal Parganas, the far northeastern Dravidian language, Malto, has survived and is spoken by two Paharia ('hill people') tribes, with no geographical or affinal ties, still practising slash-and-burn shifting cultivation. In the north, in the Rajmahal Hills surrounding the Ganges, there are the 56,000 Sauria Paharias, or the Malers ('hill people' in Dravidian); 91 per cent (51,000) of them are ethnic speakers of which only 6,000 speak Hindi and 5,000 speak Santali as second language, and 5,000 speak Hindi as their mother tongue. The Mal Paharias present further south in the Ramgarh Hills are more acculturated to Hinduism and Hindi. Numbering 45,000 in Bihar, 69 per cent (31,000) of them were ethnic speakers of which 3,000 spoke Santali, 2,000 spoke Bengali and 1,000 spoke Hindi as their second language, and the others (14,000) have adopted either Bengali or Hindi as their mother tongue. But, most of the 16,000 Mal Paharias in West Bengal were Bengali mother tongue speakers, including those speaking 'Mal Paharia', currently considered as a Bengali dialect.

Besides all these Chota Nagpur tribes faithful to their Munda or Dravidian linguistic expression and identity, there exist other tribes that lack a specific language though many may claim either a Munda historical tradition, descent or kinship. They include the Kharwars regarded as the oldest inhabitants of Palamau, apparently the same as the Kherwars, a name used for the main linguistic Munda subset—the Cheros, Binjhias, Baigas, Bedias, Chik-Baraiks, etc. These tribes are nearly Aryanized with the exception of the Lohars (blacksmiths) who have partly adopted the Mundari or Santali speech of the tribe to which they are associated.

Southwards, the same linguistic Aryanization is ob-

served among the tribes of Chhattisgarh. The 334,000 Kawars have fully shifted to Hindi or its variant which is called Chhattisgarhi here. In the west, the 130,000 Halbas are divided into Hindi-speaking (3,000), Chhattisgarhi-speaking (98,000) and those speaking their own Halabi dialect, a transition between Hindi and Marathi. In the east, the Hindi-speaking Binjhwars of Chhattisgarh are closely related to the Oriya-speaking Binjhals, as also to the Hindi-speaking Binjhias from Bihar.

Among the Orissa tribes, more than half (12,000) of the 22,000 Juangs were ethnic speakers, others had shifted to Oriya (8,000) or Dravidian Kui (1,000); but as Juang was at the same time a mother tongue for 4,000 non-Juang people, the Juang-speaking group numbered 16,000—a relatively stable small linguistic community (11,000 in 1901, 13,000 in 1951, 16,000 in 1961, 12,000 in 1971, 19,000 in 1981).

The case of the Khonds (alternatively written as Kondhs or Kandhas) is more complex due to their fundamental linguistic plurality and numerous inter-ethnic overlaps. This unique tribe has three Dravidian languages of its own: Kuvi (ex-Khondi), Kui and Konda (or Kubi). Out of the 819,000 Orissa Khonds, 45 per cent (365,000) speak Kui as their mother tongue (of which 100,000 speak Oriya as their second language), 16 per cent (165,000) speak Kuvi (of which 51,000 speak Oriya as their second language) and 1 per cent (11,000) speak Konda, i.e., 62 per cent ethnic-speaking members altogether. Further 15 per cent (119,000) had stated Oriya as their mother tongue but some had shifted to other regional languages such as Telugu (5,000) and Hindi (16,000) from the Laria dialect. Some spoke neighbouring ethnic-mother tongues: 5 per cent (41,000) spoke Savara (Munda) and 3 per cent (22,000) spoke Koya (Dravidian). The 22,000 Khonds of Andhra Pradesh were still in a majority (59 per cent) with Kuvi as their mother tongue (13,000), while the others had adopted the regional language, Telugu. As for the Khonds from Madhya Pradesh, they had all shifted to Oriya or Hindi (Chhattisgarhi) in nearly matching proportions.

The next Dravidian-speaking tribe, the Koyas, are divided between the states of Orissa and Andhra Pradesh. Out of the 55,000 Orissa Koyas, 96 per cent (53,000) speak Kui (the main Kondh language) as their mother tongue and 2,000 speak Oriya. Thus we notice that this state oscillates linguistically, for 22,000 Khonds spoke Koya as their mother tongue while 53,000 Koyas spoke Kui. As for the 220,000 Koyas from Andhra Pradesh, they were more deculturated in favour of a regional language, since 54 per cent

(118,000) were Telugu mother tongue speakers and only 46 per cent (102,000) spoke Koya as their mother tongue, among whom 69,000 spoke Telugu as their second language. It is thus seen that the Koya language has become the mother tongue for less than half (102,000) the Koyas from Andhra Pradesh, and for a smaller part (22,000) of the Kondhs from Orissa, plus for some other (17,000) people. The last category includes more than half the 11,000 Oriya Jatapus, the sister tribe of the Koyas, while the rest have moved to Oriya (3,000) or Telugu. The acculturation of the Jatapus is higher in Andhra Pradesh, as also their social status, and they have given up Kondh or Koya ethnic mother tongue: many of them now state a 'Jatapu' mother tongue, which may be a Telugu dialect, and has been listed with yet-to-be classified speeches (19,000), such as 'Kisan' in the Dravidian list. As for Konda-Doras (17,000) from Orissa and Konda-Dhoras (87,000), Konda-Kapus (30,000) and Konda-Reddis (35,000), from Andhra Pradesh, they are almost completely acculturated to the Telugu linguistic group with only 1000 Konda-Doras and as many Konda-Dhoras speaking Kui or Kuvi as their mother tongue.

The Paraja, or Paroja, tribe of southern Orissa and its Parji language was described by Grierson (1907–27) as a Gondi dialect but is now classified as a distinct Dravidian language. Among the 160,000 Parajas of Orissa, only 53 per cent (84,000) speak their Parji mother tongue while, nearly half have shifted to Oriya (41 per cent or 66,000), or to Kui (4 per cent or 7,000). The Parajas of the neighbouring Bastar District of Madhya Pradesh have Dhurwa (25,000) as their mother tongue, a Parji dialect, also spoken by Gonds while most of the Parajas (85,000) speak the Oriya Bhatri dialect.

In Savaras (Sauras or Saoras), a Munda tribe concentrated in the Mahendragiri massif, in the *Thermopylae* of India, that shows the coastal limit between the Indo-Aryan north and the Dravidian south, we find a far less obscure people, which most probably matches Pliny's *Suari* (in his first century, *Natural History*), Ptolemy's *Sabarae* (in his second century, *Geography*) and the *Shabaras* from the Sanskrit literature. They may have migrated from southwest Bihar by the fifth century across Chota Nagpur and Orissa, and may have been involved in a deep Hinduization and acculturation process. Among the 312,000 Savars from Orissa, distributed from the Mahanadi basin down to the South, hardly more than one out of three (116,000 or 37 per cent) still spoke Savara as a mother tongue while more than half (180,000 or 58 per cent) have shifted to Oriya and to

various other speeches including those from other tribes, such as the Bhumijs (9,000 or 3 per cent). In Andhra Pradesh the 68,000 Savaras were mostly ethnic speakers (48,000 or 70 per cent) and the rest (19,000 or 30 per cent) had shifted to Telugu. But though the speech had lost ground within the Savara tribe itself, it was adopted by other tribes, i.e., by 41,000 of the earlier mentioned Khonds from Orissa.

The Gadabas, a Munda tribe, southwards from the Savaras, live on the Orissa–Andhra border. Out of the 44,000 Gadabas from Orissa and 22,000 from Andhra Pradesh, 73 per cent (32,000) and 36 per cent (8,000) respectively still spoke Gadaba as mother tongue, while 24,000 from Orissa spoke Oriya and 7,000 from Andhra Pradesh spoke Telugu as their second language. The rest of the tribe were already Oriya or Telugu mother tongue speakers. This divergent acculturation now seems to be overlapped by an older and inner sociolinguistic break-up between the four main subtribal clans or gotras: three of them faithful to the Munda dialects—Gutob (or Guta, or Gata), Remo and Didey—and the fourth one to Ollari, a Telugu dialect or perhaps a distinct Dravidian language.

The Gonds though numerous are geographically distributed over a wide region. They are the first tribe in India with a numerical strength of 3,992,000, but their language ranks the third in tribal languages, with 1,501,000 mother tongue speakers, equivalent to 38 per cent of the tribe, far behind Santali and Bhili (3.2 and 2.4 million). As among the Gondi mother tongue population there were 325,000 non-Gonds and only 1,176,000 Gonds; the ethnic-speaking Gond proportion was lowered to 29 per cent of the whole tribe with high variations from one state to another.

Out of the 3,094,000 Gonds from Madhya Pradesh, (Gond-Darois, Gond-Patharis, etc.) 895,000 (29 per cent) still spoke Gondi (or Dorli and Maria dialects) as their mother tongue; most (69 per cent) of the others have shifted to Hindi or its variants (Chhattisgarhi, Halabi, Bagheli, etc.), and a small number to Oriya (28,000 or 0.9 per cent) or to another tribal language, i.e., Dhurwa, a dialect from Parji, from the Parajas (23,000 or 0.7 per cent). But outside Madhya Pradesh and even in the two strongholds of Bastar District and Gondwana, in Mahadeo and the Maikal massifs, the use of Gondi is rapidly declining. It is spoken by only 1 per cent of the 34,000 Gonds in Bihar, and by 4.5 per cent of the 446,000 Gonds in Orissa. As a result of higher concentration in hilly and forest border sectors there were still 144,000 (52 per cent) Gonds in Andhra Pradesh and

278,000 (68 per cent) Gonds in Maharashtra as genuine ethnic speakers.

The Kolams, geographically close to the Gonds, and living mainly in the Kandi–Konda Hills on the Andhra-Maharashtra border speak Kolami, differentiated from Gondi by Grierson who supposed it to have belonged to a former non-Dravidian population such as Toda in the Nilgiri Hills. Kolami has been enjoying a steady increase in its stated mother tongue speakers from 23,000 in the Survey to 43,000 in 1951, 51,000 in 1961, 67,000 in 1971 and 79,000 in 1981.

The Korkus living in the Gawilgarh Hills on the Maharashtra–Madhya Pradesh border are the only western offshoot of Munda peoples barring some old communities such as the Kolis which may also have been Kolarian speakers. Part of them, like the Nahalis in the west, and the Muwasis in the east, have mainly left the Hills and dacoity, and have settled as herdsmen. Of the 204,000 Korkus (154,000 in Madhya Pradesh and 50,000 in Maharashtra), a large majority (149,000 or 73 per cent) spoke Korku as their mother tongue, of which half (73,000) spoke Hindi as their second language while the remaining part spoke either Hindi (41,000 or 20 per cent) or Gondi (12,000 or 6 per cent) as their mother tongue. And, in both the states, the number of Korku mother tongue speakers exceeded the ethnic-speaking Korkus: 159,000 against 99,000 in Madhya Pradesh and 61,000 against 50,000 in Maharashtra. This implies that 60,000 and 11,000 non-Korku people in Madhya Pradesh and Maharashtra respectively spoke Korku as their mother tongue. The detribalized group of Korku descent is thus another example of these important ethno-linguistic discrepancies.

The Bhils habitating a vast area from the Western Ghats to the Aravalli range in the hilly and forest bounds of four states—Maharashtra, Gujarat, Madhya Pradesh and Rajasthan—have a lower rate of linguistic deculturation than the Gonds. There were 2,439,000 (72 per cent) Bhili mother tongue speakers against 3,838,000 tribe members. This is perhaps because the Hindi and Bhili Indo-Aryan languages could sometimes be confused with Bhilali, a Bhili dialect from the Bhilala community, half-way between Bhils and Rajputs, which may be considered as belonging to Rajasthani. But here too one may note large fluctuations between linguistic and ethnic delimitations.

Of the total 575,000 Bhils in Maharashtra, half the number had Marathi as their mother tongue, the rest spoke either Bhili (217,000 or 37 per cent) or some form of speech akin to Khandeshi, Ahirani, etc., at the border of Madhya Pradesh and Maharashtra. The affiliation of these forms of speech could be reported to either Hindustani or Marathi, and have been lately raised in the Census of India as a separate language under the designation of Khandeshi. The 1,123,000 Bhils of Gujarat were quite exclusively (1,051,000 or 94 per cent) Gujarati mother tongue speakers, while Bhili and its dialect Bhilodi stood far behind (4 per cent), followed by the Dangi dialect of Khandeshi in Dangs District hills. Two-thirds (820,000 or 67 per cent) of the 1,222,000 Bhils in Madhya Pradesh spoke Bhili as mother tongue, some spoke one of its variants (Bhilali or Barel) and less than a quarter (293,000 or 23 per cent) spoke Hindi. The majority (360,000 or 40 per cent) of the 907,000 Bhils of Rajasthan, stated Wagdi, a Bhili dialect spoken in the Vagad country, as their mother tongue, followed by two main Rajasthani dialects, Mewari and Marwari (309,000 or 34 per cent), and numerous other dialectal designations.

Thus the linguistic acculturation of the Bhils to regional languages was to a large extent achieved in Gujarat, much advanced in Maharashtra, less in Rajasthan and low in Madhya Pradesh where they enjoy a more isolated geographical position. Of a total of 3,727,000 Bhils in these four states, only about one-third (1,659,000 or 39 per cent) stated Bhili or a Bhili dialect as their mother tongue. Except in Madhya Pradesh where almost all Bhili speakers were from the Bhil tribe, in the three other states Bhili was spoken by nearly 1 million members of other Scheduled Tribes or Castes. A similar case was noted in Rajasthan, for instance, among a part of the Mina tribe, the fourth in India by its number (1,156,000), which no longer has any specific speech. A majority of its members (47 per cent) stated one or another Rajasthani dialect as their mother tongue and 45 per cent Khari Boli, the purest form of Hindi. However, a small proportion (7 per cent) still spoke Wagdi, the Bhili dialect, as their mother tongue.

Other tribes—the Dublas, Dhodias, Gamits, and Dhankas in Gujarat; and the Chodharis and the Mavchis in Maharashtra—state the Bhili dialect as their mother tongue along with Dubli, Dhodia, Gamti, Dhanki, Cohdari, Mawchi, etc., (usually spoken by only a small number of them). This was observed among the Varlis or Warlis (244,000 in Maharashtra and 98,000 in Gujarat), nearly all of whom had shifted to either Marathi or Gujarati. The Varli dialect, once classified under Marathi, and now under Bhili, was widely spoken in the tiny Union Territory of Dadra and Nagar Haveli (58,000 inhabitants), situated at the border of Gujarat and Maharashtra, where the Varlis are in a majority (of a total of 33,000, there were 30,000 Varli, 2,000 Marathi and 1,000 Gujarati mother tongue speakers), the other inhabitants stated Bhili dialects (Dhodia and Kokna 11,000), Gujarati (10,000) and Marathi (2,000).

Close to them in the Western Ghats, the Koli tribe, an eponym of the *Coolies* (porters), have long lost any specific language. One may be inclined to assume that it was Munda, i.e., *Kolarian*; but their anthropological features make them akin to the oldest inhabitants of the peninsula. With 432,000 members altogether (of which 419,000 are in Maharashtra alone), they are the thirteenth largest tribe in India, but second to the Minas, to be without a language of their own.

In the Dravidian region the Scheduled Tribes distinguish themselves by their own dialect and seldom identify with the regional language or a specific language. The main tribe in Andhra Pradesh, the Chenchus (18,000), living in the Nalamalai Hills between the Krishna valley and the Andhra Littoral, speak only Telugu, like the Pardhis from Telangana. In the south, the nomadic tribe of the Yerukala basket makers is losing its Tamil dialect in favour of the Telugu regional language. Of a total of 128,000 living in Andhra Pradesh, 77,000 were Telugu mother tongue speakers (of which only 2,000 knew Yerukala), and out of the 50,000 faithful to the Yerukala Tamil dialect, 34,000 were Telugu second language speakers. This is a significant example of a language adapting to the regional cultural environment. In the Western Ghats, nearly all the 64,000 Koragas stated Tulu, (the language of Mangalore District), as their mother tongue. In Coorg District away from the non-tribal, Kodagu speaking Coorgs in the hills, the 14,000 Yeravas, somehow akin to the Yerukalas, have their own Malayalam dialect, the only one that's so differentiated.

In the Nilgiri Hills of Tamil Nadu, the Kurumba shepherd tribe is distinct from the neighbouring Toda herdsmen and Kota craftsmen, whose Toda-Kota language is strongly individualized between Kannada and old Tamil. Kurumbas speak a Kannada dialect, as do the Badaga peasants who are not a tribe but a non-scheduled caste, evenly divided between Coorg and the Nilgiris. Their number has been constant (i.e., 9000) in 1961 as in 1901.

As for the two famous Nilgiri Hills tribes (the Todas and Kotas), their linguistic preservation is as noticeable as their physical and cultural origins, and this despite their numerical weakness. However in 1961, out of the 714 Todas, only eight stated Tamil as their mother tongue against 706 who stated Toda (of which only 171 speak Tamil as their second language). Further, out of the 833 Kotas, only four spoke Tamil as their mother tongue against 829 who stated Kota (of which 226 spoke Tamil as their second language).

Several small tribes live in the Western Ghats near Kerala where Negritoid or Vedda-Australoid traits may be clearly noticed. The Veddas from Sri Lanka have neither preserved any language of their own nor any linguistic feature. As a result, it is difficult to assess what they might have spoken before adopting one of the regional Dravidian languages. The Pulayan tribe, or Hill Pulayans (Mala Pulaya) comes from northern Malabar, and is not to be confused with the more numerous homonymic Pulayan caste from the south. These 61,000 Pulayan tribesmen from Kerala all speak Malayalam, while their 3,000 kinsmen from Tamil Nadu speak Tamil. The same phenomenon is observed among most tribes from this region, e.g., the 9,000 Kanikkars, hill dwellers of former Travancore state who still practise slash-and-burn cultivation speak Malayalam; but out of their 1,800 kinsmen who have crossed the hills to settle in Tamil Nadu, only 600 retained Malayalam while 1,200 adopted Tamil. Other tribes from Kerala, such as the 37,000 Paniyans, 14,000 Malayarayars, 3,000 Uralis, 3,000 Ulladans, etc., speak only Malayalam. The main exceptions are the 5,000 Muthuvans, Negritoid blowpipe hunters, where the majority (4,000) speak Tamil while the rest speak Malayalam; and the Irulars who are all Tamil speakers, numbering 11,000 in Kerala and 80,000 in Tamil Nadu.

In the heart of Tamil Nadu, the small Shevaroy massif is the home of the Malayali tribe (not to be confused with the homonymic Malayalam speakers of Kerala), numbering 130,000 members. They speak pure Tamil, though they differ by their physical traits and material culture from other inhabitants of Tamil Nadu.

As regards the linguistic situation of tribal populations, one may conclude that the basic formula 'one tribe one language' suffers from various exceptions. First, most tribes are involved in a general process of linguistic acculturation in favour of the regional language of the surrounding dominant population. The proportion of bilingual tribesmen is increasing with a fringe of fully acculturated tribesmen everywhere, i.e., those who have kept the tribal language as a second language and have adopted the regional language as their mother tongue, while those who have not done so, have become monolingual in the regional language. This fringe of people within the tribe includes, beyond monolingual tribesmen, three categories of people showing three successive stages of acculturation: bilingual with a tribal mother tongue and a regional language as their second language, bilingual with a regional mother tongue and a tribal language as their second language, and, finally, monolingual in a regional language. In this respect we can characterize this situation as 'one tribe with two languages: a declining tribal language and an increasing regional one'.

The ultimate point is reached when a tribe has completely lost its own language, and there is no surviving trace of it. This is the case of many tribes in the Bengal area, central India, and the Dravidian South, where we may observe: 'one tribe and no tribal language'.

But we may also notice an intertribal acculturating process, i.e., some part of a tribe which, for proximity or historical or social reasons, has adopted the mother tongue of another tribe. This kind of an overlap between the tribe membership and the tribal language use is common, and is somehow more puzzling than the acculturation to the regional language. This situation could be summarized as: 'one tribe with two languages: its own plus the one belonging to the next tribe'.

Further, there are various cases of: 'one tribe with several languages of its own'. In most examples, 'several' ranges from few to many. This is illustrated by the Khonds who have three languages and the Nagas, 25 or more languages, whatever the official number of listed Naga tribes may be.

The last case is that of 'several tribes with a single shared tribal language', such as Malto which is spoken by two tribes, Bodo and Dimasa, or Asuri which is spoken, by three tribes, Tripuri by four, etc.

One can find more situations where the various aforesaid cases mix and have mutual effects such as deculturation towards many regional languages with intertribal overlaps. This highlights the dynamics of the Indian society and its constantly changing cultural panorama even though, in the linguistic field, basic changes need a minimum of one generation to manifest themselves. And, within this approach to the increase in diverse situations, language is only one clue among others. However, among all cases of *language shift*, the prevailing phenomenon of *language spread* in favour of regional languages remains.

LANGUAGE AND CASTE (THE ETHNO-LINGUISTIC COMMUNITIES COMPARED WITH THE SOCIAL COMMUNITIES)

Tribes may enjoy a large variety of linguistic situations: some have an *ethnic-speaking* population (speaking, as

a rule, a language of their own), others have a multilingual one (divided between *ethnophones*, i.e., *ethnic speakers* and *allophones*, i.e., speakers of mother tongues that do not belong to the ethnic group) while still others may be fully acculturated (who do not speak any language of their own). Tribes belonging to this last category are likely to be considered as simple subgroups of the regional ethnic group, for instance, the Minas, Chenchus or Irulas are linked to the Rajasthanis, Andhras or Tamils by a shared linguistic culture. As a result of the shared feelings, they tend to be assimilated as castes rather than as tribes. On the other hand, the Khasis, Nagas, Santals, Khonds or Todas are clearly seen as strong ethno-linguistic groups. But the Cheros, Kolis or Yerukalas seem to be more akin to Hindi-Marathi- or Tamil-speaking castes because they are deprived of the main ethnic characteristic: a specific language. In this way the same community may be officially registered as a Scheduled Tribe in one state and as a Scheduled Caste in another.

India's social history is full of such evolutions through the multimillenary, complex process of acculturation, including *Brahmanization, Sanskritization* and *Aryanization*. Many marginal communities then enjoyed the opportunity to cross the Hindu Pale and become, within it, simple castes, and others earlier excluded because of their impure status, became clean castes. If few had then been integrated as a whole, fewer could keep their own language, as it occurred for the Manipuris with Meithei, who are not a tribe but a Hindu people—a *jana*. This warranted a split in the tribe, as seen among the Raj-Gonds who seceded from the Marias, the Gondi-speaking Forest Gonds, to join the Hindu and Hindi-speaking society. Though they seem to be a high status jati, they are nevertheless still listed as a Scheduled Tribe (at least in Maharashtra). In northern Bengal, the Rajbangsis and the Kochs have since long lost any Tibeto-Burman speech and have become Scheduled Castes; as in the neighbouring central delta, the Namasudras or the Chandals may have done with their lost and forgotten Munda languages and, westwards, possibly the Bagdis, with a former Dravidian one. But the alleged ancestry may not directly reflect the anthropological origin, since the Bagdis present themselves as descending from the Radha warriors, as do the Pods, another Scheduled Caste claiming ancestry from the Pundras—the other legendary founders of the western Bengali settlement. A similar case is noticed among the Marathi-speaking Kolis, probably, a former Munda (Kolarian) tribe, now listed among Scheduled Tribes; or the autochthonous

Mahars listed among Scheduled Castes. They have been speaking the Marathi language for centuries as do the peasant caste of the Kunbis. Many mother tongue designations such as 'Mahari' in Maharashtra, 'Rajbangsi' in Bengal or 'Badaga' in the Nilgiri Hills may be a mere social designation with no significant linguistic basis or originality.

Some wandering castes have kept their Rajasthani dialect, for instance, the Gujjars in Kashmir speak Gojri, and the Banjaras-Lambadas in Deccan speak Banjari-Lambadi; these are examples of faithfulness to the language even when far away from home. So also the Tamil-speaking, Kaikadi basket makers in Marathi Vidarbha, who numbered 8,000 and 15,000 in 1891 and 1901 respectively, and 4,000, 8,000 and 12,000 in 1951, 1961 and 1971 respectively. In Maharashtra, the Vadari quarrymen, who speak Telugu, numbered 27,000, 4,000, 2,000, 21,000 and 36,000 in the same years. The Golar herdsmen and the Holija saddlers and musicians of Madhya Pradesh may exemplify the same spirit of preservation with nearly the same small number of 3,500 Kannada speakers in 1901 and 1961. The Saurashtra Gujarati silk weavers around Madurai in Tamil Nadu are a far more numerous case with 124,000 Saurashtra Gujarati dialect speakers in 1951 and 217,000 people speaking Gujarati mainly in their households in Tamil Nadu in 1981 (94,000 in the Madurai District itself).

In the same state the three-century-old political influence of the Marathas is still partly responsible for the presence, in 1981, of a Marathi-speaking home population of 65,000; of which there are 20,000 in Madras and 12,000 in North Arcot district, the two strongholds of Maratha power in Tamil Nadu. Some social strata of the Vijayanagar empire that was left in Tamil Nadu may still contribute to the fact that nearly 4 million people speak Telugu in this state. Language maintenance with social cohesion may not only survive thousands of kilometres but also centuries of separation from the original homeland. Within the social framework of the traditional caste system, made cohesive by the economic *jajmani* system, additional communities speaking different mother tongues could coexist. Nowadays numerous social associations and interminglings reduce this linguistic conservation as it is more pragmatic to speak in a mutually comprehensible medium.

The Turis (or Turias), basket makers and farmers of Chota Nagpur, is the only Scheduled Caste having its own Munda language which is close to Birhor. The Birhors are also basket makers but registered as Scheduled Tribe. They are divided into four subcastes,

two of which are Hindi-speaking, the other two faithful to the Munda language; while the Birhors are considered to be a fifth subcaste which is still partly tied to its own Munda language. The Turi language, more used than Birhor, had 4,000 speakers at the beginning of the century; the number fell to 2,300 in 1951 and 1,600 in 1961.

The demarcation between tribe and caste is far from being always neat. The Gonds, the first Indian tribe by its registered number, though partly losing their Gondi language particularly in the northern periphery of their area of dispersion, are registered in Bundelkhand and Uttar Pradesh as Scheduled Caste instead of Scheduled Tribe. The Kharwars and Cheros, Hindi-speaking tribes of Chota Nagpur, have for long been registered as castes in Uttar Pradesh, because of being geographically distanced from their homeland which is also the heartland of Kherwari (Munda) languages. The Bhumijs, a Munda tribe from Chota Nagpur are registered as a caste in the plains of north Bihar and were provisionally so (1950–56) in West Bengal and Orissa under presidential orders. This was also the case among the Koras, another Munda tribe, and the Khairas who adopted the caste status after 1956. Another example of transition was observed in West Bengal among the Mundari-speaking Loharas (iron-casters) and the Santali-speaking Mahli basket makers: a brief passage to the caste status outside their homeland. Around the Rajmahal Hills, Malto, the northern Dravidian language is the main cultural trait of the hill tribe with the same name. Malpaharya, a Bengali dialect of Malto, is increasingly gaining in audience as the caste status gains over the tribal one.

In principle, it may be stated that social communities such as castes, surviving through their native language or striving to keep it, are now exceptions in the Indian panorama. Tribes need to maintain their identity through the survival and maintenance of language—the key shared link. Occupational groups known as jatis are usually cohesive enough to not require an original speech that may give them the semblance of a tribe.

LANGUAGE AND RELIGION (ETHNO-LINGUISTIC COMMUNITIES AS COMPARED TO RELIGIOUS COMMUNITIES)

Despite abundant literature on religious communities in India, these communities are yet to be viewed from a linguistic point of view. This section attempts to analyze them in this regard by dividing them into three categories: the *monoethnic* community, where members mainly belong to a single ethnic group, such as specific tribal cults, Parsi and Sikh communities; the *oligoethnic* group comprising a small set of ethnic groups like modern Buddhism in India, and Jainism, and the *trans-ethnic* community including those religions which are well-represented on the whole subcontinent—Hinduism, Islam and Christianity.

Language has established a close link with religion in liturgical and sacred texts. Sanskrit, Pali, Hebrew, Latin or Aramaic, old Persian and Arabic are languages which have been used in priestly societies by believers of specific faiths. But the use of classical or dead languages is far from being a mass phenomenon, and may only be approached through small numbers in statistics on bilingualism.

The correspondence between religious and ethnic communities may be more obvious provided the latter are numbered, just as tribes and religions have always been computed in each census. No wonder that ethnic cults are found in tribes; besides an increasing proportion of their population belongs to worldwide denominations such as Hinduism, Islam or Christianity. The comparison between the strength of tribe and its religion, will be discussed subsequently from the exhaustive 1961 Census data.

At that time the Garo religion was stated by 57 per cent of the Garos along with a few other similar tribes; and the Khasi religion by 49 per cent of the Khasis. Among the Nagas the attachment to ethnic cults varies according to communities: it is high among the Konyaks (60 per cent) but very low among their neighbours from the oriental group—the Yimchungres, Changs, and Wanchos—though they have recently given up head-hunting rituals. Among other northeastern people, a significant section (14 per cent) of the Karbis (Mikirs), famous for their royal cobra cult, stated their exclusive attachment to the ethnic religion. Ethnic religions of the Boros, Rabhas, Miris, and Hajongs, each have about 1,000 followers; while the Manipuris and Mizos have even less. But religious preservation seems higher in Arunachal Pradesh, at least for 'Doni Polo' tribal cults among the Dafla and Adi, and subtribes in Apatani, Tagin, Gallong, Minyong, Padam, etc.

In Chota Nagpur the main ethnic religious survival was that of the Ho cult, the first in India, stated by 41 per cent of the Hos in Bihar. The Santal religion, the second ethnic one in India, was practised by 6 per cent of the Santals in Bihar alone and by nearly no one in Bengal and Orissa. The Munda, Bhumij and Mahli cults have only between 1,000 and 100 followers. But this relative decline of tribal monoethnic cults is widely made up by the tribal 'Sarna' (from the Sacred Grove) religion which still had 429,000 believers in many Bihar tribes: 32 per cent of the Hos, 17 per cent of the Oraons, 16 per cent of the Mundas, 11 per cent of the Kharias, etc. Others should be added to this cult which, though they may not be exclusive from the former on a metaphysical basis, were definitely so on the census registers: Sansari (mainly among the Mundas: 3 per cent), Bonga or Sing Bonga (Sun God), Adivasi (from Autochthonous), Marang Buru (Mountain God), Adid-harma (Old Faith), etc. Though some of them had few registered believers, their total allegiance could be rather high among certain tribes, for instance, 73 per cent of the Hos, and 20 per cent of the Mundas. Revivalist cults, aiming at restoring the ethnic feeling of the Munda or Kherwari peoples had less believers: the 'Kharwari' and Birsa (the 1895 Munda uprising hero) cults.

It is difficult to ascertain the future of these ethnic or interethnic cults established on tribal bases because their audience is being steadily eroded by the expansion of more universal religions such as Hinduism, and, over the past few centuries, Christianity. The admission of a people as a whole within the Hindu Pale since the fifteenth century as seen in the Manipuri case is exceptional among mountain dwellers, and more frequent in the Brahmaputra plains, among the Mechs, Bodos, Kacharis, or in the neighbouring hills among the Rabhas, Lalungs, Hajongs, Dimasas, Cachar Barmans or Miris. For instance, nearly all the 13,876 Deoris were Hindus (13,780 or 99 per cent), not a surprising fact for the former Chutiya sacerdotal caste, but which nevertheless reflected choice to a certain extent. The main mountain peoples, however, were still far from Hinduization: scarcely 4 per cent of the Garos, Khasis or Nagas were Hindus and there were fewer still (1 per cent) among the Mizos. Only the Karbis (Mikirs) have substantially (75 per cent) shifted to Hinduism, which may be explained because of their strong ties with the Congress party and their decision, taken with the Hinduized Dimasas, Hojais and Lalungs, not to join their two districts (Karbi Anglong and North Cachar Hills) to the new Meghalaya state seceding from Assam (set up to meet the requirements of the Garos and Khasis).

These three tribes (Garos, Khasis and Karbis) stand at various stages of the same denominational tripartition in three basic sets:
* an old stock of the population faithful to tribal cults in a relatively constant diminution: still in majority

among the Garos and Khasis but in residual numbers among the Karbis,

- a very small early Hinduized fringe seen among the Garos and Khasis but which now includes three out of four Karbis,
- a recently Christianized fringe, big among the Garos (43 per cent) and Khasis (48 per cent), and small among the Karbis.

These situations are evolving quickly, some tribes tend to become nearly unidenominational, for instance, 97 per cent of the Mizos are Christians, and the Nagas too are increasingly adopting the Baptist faith. The progress of Christianity in Nagaland is steady (46 per cent in 1951, 53 per cent in 1961, 67 per cent in 1971 and 80 per cent in 1981), while that of Hinduism has been 4, 9, 11, 14 per cent; both at the expense of ethnic cults (50, 37, 21, 4 per cent). The trend has been adopted by the small tribes as well, such as the Southern Chins in Mizoram and the Pawis who have all been Christianized, and three-fourths of the Lakhers in Manipur, the 'Old Kukis' (Vaiphuis, Koms) and the 'New Kukis' (Thadus, Chirus, Gangtes, Simtes, Zous and Paites) are already Christians in majority. But the Kukis living in the far west towards the Cachar District plains and the Tripura hills are under the cultural influence of Bengalis, Tripuras and Riangs. The process of Hinduization here widely counterbalances with that of Christianization and is accompanied by a simultaneous significant shift to other mother tongues. For instance, the 15,000 Manipur Hmar were Christians with Hmar as their mother tongue, while among the 9,000 Assamese Hmar, divided into 5,000 Hindus and 4,000 Christians, only 6,000 had kept their Hmar mother tongue. At the same time the 19,000 Hinduized Assamese Kukis had overwhelmingly shifted to the Reang Tripuri dialect and a part of the Hinduized Halams from Tripura had shifted to the Tripuri mother tongue. Generally speaking, we may notice, in the northeastern states, that Hinduization accompanies acculturation to the regional language—Assamese or Bengali in Cachar—or to a locally prevailing tribal language such as Tripuri. While Christianization seems to be linked to a conservative linguistic behaviour that tends to better preserve and develop the ethnic tribal languages.

In Chota Nagpur the same kind of tight linkage between language and religious shifts is not found because tribes are involved in a wider geographical diffusion out of their homelands across three or four states: Bihar, West Bengal, Orissa and Madhya Pradesh. That leads them to an even deeper process of religious and linguistic acculturations. For instance, the overall religious tripartition of Oraons between native Sarna cult (9 per cent), Hinduism (69 per cent) and Christianity (22 per cent) suffers from many disparities: Sarna was higher in Bihar (18 per cent), Hinduism in Bengal (91 per cent) and Orissa (76 per cent), and Christianity in the remote hilly tracts of Madhya Pradesh (37 per cent). Among the Mundas (Mundari-speaking tribe), the matching tripartition (13 per cent, 67 per cent, 20 per cent) was more favourable to Sarna in Bihar (20 per cent), to Hinduism in Bengal (95 per cent) and Orissa (85 per cent), and to Christianity in Bihar (20 per cent). The Hos were similarly more largely Sarna believers (32 per cent) than Hindus (24 per cent) in Bihar, but thoroughly Hinduized in Orissa. The best example of a Christianized tribe was that of the Bihar Kharias (13 per cent Sarna believers, 27 per cent Hindus, 60 per cent Christians), but they were better Hinduized outside: widely (77 per cent) in Orissa and almost completely in Bengal and Madhya Pradesh which decreased their overall tribal Christian proportion to 29 per cent.

This polymorphic acculturation of tribes, overwhelmingly favouring Hinduism and regional languages, may be found in the tribal belt in central India and in the southern Dravidian zone. The main exceptions are two small Kerala tribes: the 14,000 Malayarayars who are divided into Christians and Hindus, and the 3,000 fully Christianized Hill Pulayas. The Nicobarese too, the second Mon-Khmer tribe after the Khasis, were evangelized by Danish Lutheran missionaries long ago. This, however, is in no way indicative of Christianity becoming a tribal religion in India, for there are millions of Malayali, Tamil, Andhra and Konkani Christians who outnumber thousands of Christianized Khasis, Garos, Nagas, Mizos, Kukis, Kharias, Oraons and Mundas. However, one may note that among the Mizos, for instance, Christianity is on its way to becoming, along with the specific mother tongue, a shared ethnic feature of the group.

Another religion confined throughout the subcontinent to some ethnic groups is Buddhism. The most famous ethnic example of a strong affinity to Buddhist faith and to the ethnic language is the case of Sri Lanka Sinhala-speaking people, who comprise the bulk of the island's population. They have not only kept intact their faith in Buddhism but also initiated and propagated, from the thirteenth century onwards, a deep reformation of its old Hinayana or Theravada way, to most Southeast Asian countries: Burma, Thailand and Laos, and Cambodia.

The second traditionally Hinayana Buddhist group

are the Arakanese, speaking a Burmese dialect, whose members are called Moghs, Maghs or Marmas in Bangladesh and in the state of Tripura in India. Their language is locally called 'Buddha Bhasa' (Buddha's language) by opposition to the prevailing 'Banga Bhasa' (Bengali). The Chakmas, the main hill tribe from the Chittagong Hill Tracts have acquired the Buddhist faith under the Arakanese influence, and speak a Bengali dialect Chakma as their mother tongue and even claim Indo-Aryan Kshatriya descent. Buddhism has penetrated other tribes marginally: only 1 per cent (3,000) of the Mizos are Buddhists while 3,000 Chakmas have been Christianized and have adopted as their mother tongue the Pawi language of the southern Chins who received the same evangelization as the Mizos. Two other small ethnic groups have got connected to Buddhism: the Chaks and the Khyangs. The Chaks are the survivors of the former Loi people who set up the Pyu kingdom at Prome in the sixth century before the Burmese invasion and the foundation of Pagan in the ninth century. The Khyangs are part of the Chin Hills people who have adopted the Arakanese way of life while keeping their Chin mother tongue.

Close to them in the Chittagong Hill Tracts, three fully Hinduized groups are to be found, all of whom are Tripuri-speaking: 'Tipperas' or Tripuras, infiltrated from Northeast; Mrungs, descendants of the Arakan kings' prisoners of war; and the Chins who have adopted the Reang dialect. These groups form three cases of convergent religious (Hinduization) and linguistic (towards Tripuri) acculturations.

The last category of hill dwellers in the Chittagong area is that of the Chin or Kuki (true mountain peoples) groups, settled on the crests and attached to slash-and-burn shifting cultivation. The language of the Mrus, towards the south, was classified in the Linguistic Survey more as Burmese than as Chin, and the Kumis (or Khamis) from the southern Chin group have both remained faithful to the tribal animist cults of their ancestors. Towards the northeast, some central Chins including the Pankhuas, Bonzogis and Boms are on their way to becoming Christianized like their Mizo brothers.

Thus, the Chittagong Hills are increasingly tending towards a typical cultural tripolarization: (*a*) tribes still speaking Kuki-Chin, who are animists or are in the process of being Christianized, (*b*) Buddhist tribes, traditionally Burmese-Arakanese speakers (the Marmas), or those who have shifted to Bengali (the Chakmas) looking towards the Hindu social organization, and (*c*) the Hindus who in turn have shifted to the Tripuri

dialects or language. At the same time, the Marma dialect, a former Arakanese lingua franca in the hills, has gradually given place to Bengali which bore Hindu values instead of Buddhist ones, before the advent of the Muslim influence in the hills, later supported by the states of Pakistan and Bangladesh.

The third refuge of Buddhism in the subcontinent is the Tibetan area where the Tibetan-speaking population, or Bhotiyas, of remote Himalayan valleys, appear to follow the Mahayana Lamaist Buddhist faith which is radically different from the reformed Hinayana or Theravada way propagated from Sri Lanka to Burma.

The Mon-Pas (or Monbas) speaking a Tibetan dialect or a Himalayan language, located mainly in Tawang District (or Mon-yul, the Mon country) in Arunachal Pradesh, are followers of Buddhism; the lamas here belong to the 'yellow caps' sect originated from the sixteenth century reform of Tsong Kha-pa. The rest of the population of the valley comprising the Hrussos, Daflas, Adis, Mishmis (all speaking Mirish non-Tibetan languages) owe allegiance to their tribal cults and are now under closer Hindu influences.

In Bhutan, the prevailing autochthonous Tibetan people from the upper valleys follow Buddhism with lamas of the 'red caps' belonging to the non-reformed Kargyupa sect. They are called 'Druk-pa' from the Tibetan name of Bhutan, Druk-yul, the Land of the Dragon. However, the Nepalese immigrant population that settled in the southern hills is Hindu.

In Sikkim, the traditionally prevalent religion is Buddhism with lamas from the 'red caps' Nyingma sect, founded in the seventeenth century. They converted the still animist, ruling Lepcha autochthonous tribe to the Buddhist faith and since then, the ethnic groups of the Tibeto-Burman-speaking Lepchas and the Tibetan-speaking Bhotiyas, form most of the Sikkim state. But the influx of Nepalese migrants has introduced a Hindu majority which is increasing in numbers and spreading from the south. Among some of the migrant descendants acculturated to the Bhotiya language and to a socially prevalent group, but have retained their ancestors' faith, we may notice the appearance of a fringe of neo-Tibetan Hindu Bhotiya speakers. This discrepancy confirms the importance of religion as a capital sign of ethnicity and ethnic origin, second only to language, and most often, of longer persistence among groups of composite societies.

In Nepal, most of the population (88 per cent in 1961 and 86.5 per cent in 1991) was Hindu as stated explicitly in the 1967 Constitution. Article 3-1 of the Constitution lays down that the state of 'Nepal is a monarchic, Hindu, independent, indivisible and sovereign state' and that the king 'belongs to the Aryan civilization and Hindu religion' (Article 30-1). Nearly all ethnic groups from the country have become Hindus, with two firmly proclaimed Buddhist exceptions: the Tibetan-speaking Bhotiyas, or Sherpas (people of the East) from the eastern upper valleys, and part of the Newars, autochthonous inhabitants of the Kathmandu valley who since long are divided into two kinds of social communities or castes: the Hindu Shivmargis and the Buddhamargis who share the same life and settlement pattern and their common Tibeto-Burman Newari language. Both Sherpas and Buddhamargis constitute the basic part of the Buddhist population of Nepal (9 per cent in 1961, but 2.4 per cent in 1991). Furthermore, some craftsmen communities, such as the Ansari (weavers) or the Dhobi (washermen) speaking Urdu in the Terai Gangetic plain make up the small (3.5 per cent in 1991) Muslim minority. Here Buddhism is obviously a collective feature of one ethnic group and of social subgroups of another.

In India, the upper valleys of central and western Himalayas are inhabited by the Tibetan-speaking Bhotiyas who are Buddhists. The mountain areas of Uttar Pradesh—Upper Kumaun—facing the Nepal border along the Mahakali valley is called 'Bhot country'. Its inhabitants display Mongoloid traits and a Tibetan-like way of life, associated with pastoral and commercial displacements. But they are culturally Hinduized and their Himalayan languages—Byangsi, Chaudangsi, Darmiya and Rangkas—though still listed in the Linguistic Survey, have disappeared and are not listed in the census any more. Srivastava (1960) hardly came across any old man remembering his father speaking Rangkas and states that the three other languages may be used in daily or ceremonial life. Anyway, these languages were under a process of an internal grammatical and lexical transformation, already noted by Grierson (1902–27), and were replaced in social life by the Kumauni Pahari dialect and Hindi. In Upper Garhwal, a similar thing occurred to the Tibetan Jad dialect speakers from the Baghirati valley, while the Garhwal Bhotiyas from the two Alaknanda valleys seem to have better preserved their Tibetan dialect (8,000 Bhotiya mother tongue speakers in 1961) despite being strongly influenced by Hinduism in its famous high places of pilgrimage.

In Himachal Pradesh Kinnawar, or the Sutlej upper valley, there were 2,000 Buddhist Bhotiya-speaking Jads and 27,000 Kanauras down the river, of which 3,000 were Buddhist Bhotiya speakers and 24,000 Hindu Himalayan Kanauri speakers. In Lahul and Spiti District, the 12,000 Bhots have preserved their two Tibetan dialects, Lahuli and Spiti, but are divided into 4,000 Hindus and 8,000 Buddhists, from the 'red caps' sect. In Chamba District, the 3,000 Lahaulas, faithful to their Himalayan Chamba Lahuli language are Hindus. Among the Jad, Bhot, Kanaura and Lahula ethnic groups that enjoy a Scheduled Tribe status, only Jads and Bhots are Tibetan-speaking Buddhists while the latter two groups are Himalayan-speaking Hindus except the Tibetan-speaking part of the Kanauras. Again, Tibetan is considered Buddha Bhasa in opposition to Pahari dialects or even to the Himalayan languages from the Hindu populations.

In Jammu & Kashmir the same opposition is not stated any more because the far west portion of Tibetan-speaking population has been converted to Islam: the Baltis from Baltistan and the Puriks from Purig-Yul, i.e., the Kargil area, while the population of Leh typically remained within the Buddhist culture. All the 89,000 inhabitants from Ladakh (including Kargil and Leh in 1961) were divided into 40,000 Muslims, mainly Balti Tibetan dialect speakers (34,000) and 48,000 Buddhists, less than both the speakers of both the Ladakhi Tibetan dialect (53,000) and Bhotiya Tibetan language (2,000) mother tongue speakers; this slight discrepancy shows that some Ladakhi speakers have also been Islamized.

Until the middle of the twentieth century, Buddhism remained confined to a small number of ethno-linguistic communities spread at the three ends of the subcontinent: the Sinhala in Sri Lanka, the Arakanese and Chakmas in the Chittagong Hills; and the Bhotiyas all along the Himalayas, the Lepchas in Sikkim and part of the Newars in Nepal. It was a typical *oligoethnic* situation, complicated by the opposition between the Hinayana or Theravada way of Sri Lankan and Burmese Buddhism, and the Tibetan tantric lamaistic, a more syncretic way reigning over the Himalayas.

As opposed to this, the tantric Bengali way in the Chittagong Hills seems to have yielded to the Sinhala–Burmese way in the nineteenth century. A third Buddhist form appeared, after the Independence of India, in the heart of the country: the 'neo-Buddhist' form adopted under Dr Ambedkar's leadership by Marathi-speaking former Scheduled Castes, the Mahars. Buddhism as a result found a sudden resurgence with 3 million followers, when earlier they were only 200,000 in India, 50,000 in Sikkim, less than 400,000 in

Bangladesh and a million in Nepal, but definitely more than 6 million in Sri Lanka. This mass actually added one more ethno-linguistic component to Buddhism as the neo-Buddhist community is closely confined to Maharashtra and its eastern part, Vidarbha, with approximately 4 million people in 1991.

Compared with the tight ethnic partition of Buddhists, the distribution of Jains is notably more diffuse through linguistic limits and thus are *transethnic*. Though the spread of Jainism and Buddhism over the subcontinent dates back to more than two thousand years, Jainism declined in western India. Over the past few centuries Jains are mainly found in Gujarat and southern Rajasthan, where the main Jain temples are located in Mount Abu, Girnar, Shetrunji, and Ranakpur. Never heavily concentrated, they seldom reached more than 3 per cent of a district population; they spread through Rajasthan, Madhya Pradesh and Maharashtra, carrying with them their Marwari, Gujarati or Marathi speeches, though increasingly it is Hindi which they have promoted as a lingua franca. Their second core area lies in the bordering Marathi districts—Belgaum, Kolhapur, Sangli—along the Kannada country where before the Lingayat emergence in the twelfth century they were culturally pre-eminent. Nowadays, they are widely scattered all over India, and are known as 'Marwaris', contributing better to the expansion of Hindi, the language of the Union, than their own western speeches.

The Parsis, since their settlement in the eighth century on the southeastern coast of Cambay, stuck to Gujarati, and in the nineteenth century brought it to Bombay where three quarters of them live. Persian has been forgotten by their ancestors. It is only retained under its older Avestic form as a liturgical language. Nowadays, however, a predominant western influence supports the use of English and this cultural impact is basically overtaking their small number—100,000 people or less.

The same phenomenon occurred among the smaller Jewish community, which, since the departure of most Malayalam speakers of Cochin to Israel, is limited to 20,000 highly Anglicized Jews in Bombay.

Sikhism, born in the Hindustani plains (Guru Govind Singh was from Patna), found its main area of diffusion in Punjab in the eighteenth century. The community dominated the entire province until 1846, in political terms and not in terms of number of followers. As a direct consequence of the 1947 Partition, the refugees following mass movements were concentrated in the area east of the Sutlej and became a majority in some districts. But their attachment to the Punjabi language in which most of their sacred texts are written, and to their Gurumukhi script makes the Sikhs indefectible supporters of this particular form of Hindustani. Many aspects of community oppositions manifested in social, cultural, linguistic, religious and political grounds have strongly tied Sikhism to Punjabi, the issue regarding the Punjabi Suba (Punjabi Province), and all other issues relating to Punjab. At the same time the wide diaspora of the Sikh community all over India makes its members active agents to spread the Hindustani language (though through the Gurumukhi script) in provinces far beyond the Hindi Belt, just as Muslims do with Urdu.

The strong tendency to consider Punjabi as the expression of a religious community is new. The division of Hindi has been geographical until the beginning of the twentieth century: Punjabi in the west and Hindi in the east. Punjabi is still considered as a western colloquial form of Hindustani in Pakistani Punjab where the cultural form is Urdu. Even in India, all through the 1961 Census the parallelism between the distribution of Sikhism and Punjabi as a mother tongue shows some discrepancies (see Plate 9). In Delhi, Uttar Pradesh and many other provinces there were three Punjabi speakers for every two Sikhs: Delhi had 317,000 against 204,000, Uttar Pradesh 419,000 against 284,000, Madhya Pradesh 110,000 against 66,000, Bihar 58,000 against 34,000, Maharashtra 104,000 against 58,000, Gujarat 15,000 against 10,000, Assam 12,000 against 10,000, Orissa 7,000 against 5,000, Andhra Pradesh 11,000 against 9,000, Karnataka 5,000 against 3,000 Tamil Nadu 4,000 against 3,000—the parallelism remained fixed from the state to the district level. The number of Sikhs is decreasing to half of the Punjabi speakers in big cities such as Bombay (25,000 against 55,000) or Madras (710 against 1,429). Sikhs rarely exceed Punjabi speakers: in four Ganga–Yamuna Doab Districts (Bulandshahr, Aligarh, Etah, Etawah) and in five scattered districts which may be explained as either due to local conversions to Sikhism or due to Sikhs who have given up Punjabi. Only in Himachal Pradesh and Jammu & Kashmir one may find some Hindu Punjabi-speaking populations, in fact mother tongue speakers of dialects such as Kangri which is now classified under Pahari or Hindi, and Dogri, now considered as a distinct language.

Beyond these local situations, the large number of Punjabi speakers is in fact split between more than 70 million Pakistani Punjab Muslims (in 1991), oral users of western Punjabi dialects, though they use Urdu for written expression, plus 24 million Indians mostly Sikhs attracted by Punjabi written in Gurumukhi, and 2 million Dogri speakers mostly Hindus, who can write it in Nastaleeq Arabo-Persian script, but who in fact increasingly use Urdu, the official language of Jammu & Kashmir. Punjabi-speaking populations are widely tridenominational: Muslims, Sikhs and Hindus. But the Sikh community, despite a diaspora spread all over India, is still basically *monoethnic* because most of them are Punjabi speakers, whereas the Muslim and Hindu communities are *transethnic*, i.e., spread in nearly all language communities of the subcontinent.

The only ethnic groups which seem to be unidenominationally Muslim live on the Iran-Afghanistan border: the Baluchis, Brahuis, Pashtuns, Western Dards, Burushos and Tajiks. The most uneven division may be found among the Kashmiris, where more than 95 per cent have been converted to Islam with the only exception of the Brahmanical community of the Pandits. Among the Sindhis, only one-fourth stuck to Hinduism while others left Sind for India in 1947. The Partition left the Bengalis divided into two bidenominational states: West Bengal (with four-fifth Hindus and one-fifth Muslims) and Bangladesh (with five-sixth Muslims and one-sixth Hindus). In Kerala, three-fifth of the Malayalis are Hindus, one-fifth Christians and another fifth Muslims. Among the Hindustani-speaking population of the Hindi Belt, the stated attachment to Hindi, Urdu or Punjabi roughly displays the division between the Hindu, Muslim and Sikh communities, though not always precisely. Outside the Hindi Belt, many Muslim communities living in Dravidian South, for instance, have not given up their Urdu language, just as the Partition refugees (Muhajirs) in Sind or in Bangladesh. All these diasporas, such as the Sikh one, are spreading one or another form of Hindustani.

But, different from the very close association between the Punjabi language and Sikhism, there is no such congruence between Urdu and Islam (see Plate 13). Within the Hindi Belt, or within the linguistic Hindustan, an excess of up to 50 per cent of Muslims compared to Urdu speakers can usually be found, which means that one Muslim out of three states Hindi or one of its local dialects as his mother tongue. In the heart of Hindustan the margin is slighter: 7.9 million Urdu speakers against 10.8 Muslims in Uttar Pradesh, 4.1 against 5.8 in Bihar, and in Delhi, where the linguistic division merges with the religious one, there are 153,000 against 156,000. In the outer provinces the margin widens: 6,000 Urdu speakers for 26,000 Muslims in Himachal Pradesh and 740,000 against 1,318,000 in Rajasthan. Within the Hindi Belt, there are 13.7 million Urdu speakers for 19.8

Muslims, i.e., 69 per cent Urdu speakers among Muslims or 100 Urdu speakers out of 145 Muslims.

In the eastern peripheral Indo-Aryan states of India (West Bengal and Assam), in Bangladesh, or in the western provinces in Pakistan (Sind and Punjab), Urdu mother tongue speakers form small minorities among Muslims. In Jammu & Kashmir, where Urdu is the official language, out of 2.4 million Muslims, mostly Kashmiris, only 13,000 Urdu mother tongue speakers could be found; among 1.9 million Kashmiri speakers, out of 199,000 second language speakers, 157,000 stated Urdu (including the Pandits) and 13,000 Hindi. But the ratio is changing in the southern Indo-Aryan states: 595,000 Urdu speakers for 1,745,000 Muslims (34 per cent) in Gujarat, 2.7 million against 3 million in Maharashtra (90 per cent) and 213,000 against 215,000 in Orissa. In the Dravidian states of central Deccan the difference is minimal: 2.5 million Urdu speakers against 2.7 Muslims in Andhra Pradesh, 2 million against 2.3 in Karnataka, leaving a small fringe of 6 per cent and 14 per cent non-Urdu speakers among Muslims. In Tamil Nadu, where the shift made by Muslims from Tamil to Urdu is recent and incomplete, there are 616,000 Urdu speakers among 1,560,000 Muslims (39 per cent). In Kerala this shift has not occurred among the 3 million Muslims, which has 9,000 Urdu mother tongue speakers and 1,500 speaking Urdu as a second language.

Finally, Urdu is the language of two-thirds of the Muslims of the Hindi Belt, of the Muhajirs in Pakistan, and of nine-tenths of the central Deccan Muslims. But, outside the historical area of its birth between the twelfth and the eighteenth centuries, Urdu has reached the bulk of Muslims only recently. In 1971 the *polyethnic* make-up of the Muslim world within the subcontinent had more than 60 million Bengalis (including 10 million in India), 35 million Pakistani Punjabis, nearly as many Urdu native speakers (30 million in India and 5 million in Pakistan), 9 million Pathans (not to mention Afghanistan refugees), 6 million Sindhis, 4 million Malayalis and 2 million Kashmiris. Plus 2 million Tamils in India and 600,000 Moors in Sri Lanka, 1.5 million Pakistan Baluchis, several Gujaratis and half a million Brahuis.

Hinduism, a genuine *transethnic* religion spread all over the subcontinent, declined substantially faced with the introduction of Islam among the Kashmiris, Punjabis, Sindhis and Bengalis, but is still spreading among the tribal (Adivasi) populations of central India and among the Tripuris, Bodos, Karbis, etc., in the northeast, and even among the Bhotiyas from Himalayas.

Historically, Christianity reached the Malayalis,

Konkanis, Tamils and Andhras successively, all of whom were originally Hindus; the Sinhalese who were Buddhists; and, then the Adivasis from central India and the Mizos, Kukis, Nagas, Khasis and Garos, on the eastern border, at the expense of their tribal cults.

Islam was spreading to a lesser extent over the entire Hindu world at the same time within the Buddhist area (Baltistan and probably Bengal), but not among animistic tribal ethnic groups.

Jainism, another *transethnic* religion, after having spread all over the Hindu world, slowly withdrew into small minorities, in the west and southwest.

Buddhism declined from India at the same time as a distinct religion and only remained in areas such as Sri Lanka, Burma and Tibet until the twentieth century, till it was revived by some Marathi speakers as neo-Buddhism. In this way its limited grip on specific ethnic communities has transformed it to a strictly *oligoethnic* religion in the subcontinent, rather than the *transethnic* one it used to be. Similarly, the intertribal Sarna religion in Chota Nagpur is typically *oligoethnic*. Sikhism, mainly confined to Punjabi-speaking populations is a *monoethnic* religion, as is Parsism (Mazdaism) which exclusively reached a small part of Gujarati speakers.

The ethnic religions such as the Ho, Garo, Khasi, etc., are *monoethnic* religions.

Nowadays few ethnic groups are monodenominational. Most of them are heterogeneous in the religious field, e.g., the Kashmiris, Sindhis, Bengalis or Hindustani-speaking populations are mostly Hindus or Muslims in various well-known proportions; the Newars are Hindus or Buddhists; the Punjabis are Hindus, Muslims or Sikhs; as also Keralites, Konkanis and Tamils who could be Hindus, Christians, or Muslims; or the Adivasis who could be animists, Hindus and Christians. Among Telugu, Kannada, Marathi and Gujarati speakers, and more recently among the Tamils, the tripartition between Hindus, Christians and Muslims, (by the way the latter stick to Urdu), has experienced both an ethnolinguistic and a religious secession since a long time.

But few religious situations have had a direct impact on the linguistic use, such as Islam for Urdu, Sikhism for Punjabi and Christianity for some tribal languages. Anyway, beyond all the various historical and environmental situations, religious identity is second to none, except sometimes to language, as a conscious and definite symbol of collective identification and behaviour, and both remain basic and interrelated clues about ethnic groups and subgroups.

CHAPTER 3

FROM LANGUAGE DYNAMICS TO LINGUISM

The population of the Indian subcontinent holds plenty of work in store for human science researchers studying the intermingling of its more than hundred languages, ten religions (six Indian-originated and four non-Indian), at least four main racial types, and countless jatis, janas and tribes, widespread within its seven sovereign nations. The present huge series of the Anthropological Survey of India, in publication since 1993, is an impressive illustration of the wide scope of the needed task, and its selected title, *The People of India*, written in the singular, is highly significant.

The modest ambition of this atlas is to emphasize the importance of the linguistic component, and to clearly present its development to non-specialists, as far as data available on language can make a geographical and historical analysis possible. The issue is not to give more importance to linguistic identities over national, social, tribal or religious ones but to stress its role and manifestation among the universal and permanent process of acculturation and deculturation. This atlas also seeks to explain and illustrate how this cultural factor has been strong enough to deeply change the political framework and map of India.

These acculturation–deculturation processes have been constantly at work for thousands of years all over the subcontinent. Among other examples, a case in point is that of Nepal where national unity is based on the settlement of Hindu castes from the noted Aryan descent, the Brahmins or the Kshatriyas (Thakurs, Khas or Chetris), whose members were basically the Himalayan Mongoloids but linguistically Aryanized, religiously Hinduized and socially promoted as ruling classes over their Gurkha brothers. Fuerer-Haimendorf (1960) comments on the rapid spread of Nepali as a lingua franca among local dominant populations coinciding with the expansion of the Gurkha empire while the Brahmins and the Chetris infiltrated all along the Himalayas. The Newars, on the other hand, had been unable to make Newari adopted as a second language by any other ethnic group, and were even losing their own language after two or three generations of settlement outside the Newar towns; though the Gurkha power gained its hold only in the eighteenth century, i.e., after eight centuries of Newar influence. A similar cultural influence, linked more to sociopolitical supremacy than to mass migration, may also explain for instance the linguistic *Urduization*, or Islamization, of large sectors of the Deccan population.

In many historical circumstances, the spread of language is due more to social prestige than to invasions and population changes. However, within large linguistic areas, a divergent particularism may counterbalance the main antagonistic tendency to a convergent standardization. This is what seems to be happening in the heart of India within the Hindi Region or the Hindi Belt or 'Hindi Sansar' over seven provinces with nearly 500 million inhabitants. Among them, most consider themselves Marwaris, Avadhis, Maithils, etc., or are considered by others as Rajasthanis, U. P. ites, Biharis, rather than as *Hindustanis*, which is hardly an ethnic designation and not even a proper linguistic one. This, in spite of the ancient Maurya, Gupta, Harsha or Mughal unity, and notwithstanding former Marxist debates on the so-called *developing* Hindustani nation. Divergences in the designation of mother tongues are actually pointed out from one census to another, e.g., hesitations among populations in deciding whether to state standard languages (Hindi or Urdu) or regional speech forms (Bhojpuri, Maithili, etc.) as their mother tongues though everyone locally speaks the same language as their neighbours. Mother tongue designations are, therefore, a mere symbolic manifestation of allegiance and not of any real cultural practices.

Historical evolution may efface clerical or cultural languages that may exist only as a vestige in present-day life. Sanskrit, Pali, Hebrew, Syriac, Avestic Iranian, Quranic Arabic present examples of their survival in varying degrees among the various religious communities. Persian—officially used by Turko-Afghan Sultans, Mughals, Marathas and the East India Company (until the Macaulay Report in 1829) and, up to the twentieth century, as a literary language by Iqbal and Tagore—is still a cultural language in Pakistan and in Bangladesh, besides Urdu, Arabic and English. In 1961, there were 26,000 Iranian mother tongue speakers in west Pakistan, but 288,000 people spoke Persian as an 'additional' language; 303,000 knew how to read and write it; while 22,000 could only read it. In Bangladesh, along with 64 Iranian mother tongue speakers, there were 61,000 speakers with an 'additional' language; 301,000 who could read and write it, while 38,000 could only read it. After seven centuries of prominence, Persian is slowly on the wane.

Languages that are disappearing among their native speaking population since the Linguistic Survey and the census mentioned them are rare. Such a fate seems destined for some Himalayish pronominalized languages, such as Rangkas or Byangsi; and for some speeches from eastern Iran, such as Wanetsi, Ormuri or Parachi, in the North West Frontier Province, submerged by Pushto, along with some other southwestern Dardic relics, such as Tirahi. In Assam, the Moran language of the first Tibeto-Burman tribe subjugated by the Thai Ahoms in the thirteenth century, had, according to Grierson (1902–27), 78 speakers in 1901 and none in 1921. Ahom, the language of their conquerors, in spite of its unique historical chronicles (the *Buranjis*) apparently disappeared from the population in the eighteenth century, and from among the priesthood (the Deodhais) by 1850. Grierson only found a dozen priests with a 'decent knowledge' of it. Present Ahoms numbering several hundred thousands are a fully Assamized jati, too proud of its past to accept any Scheduled Caste or Tribe status.

Besides the disappearance of some specific languages, and the additional spread of others, Indian history shows many examples of persistence in territorial occupation. Some ancient ethnic groups born in delimited areas seem to have survived through centuries: Magadh and Mithila, for instance, are examples of ancient *janapadas* (ethnic territories) that have survived through centuries while keeping their linguistic identity intact, in spite of inevitable speech evolutions. The whole complex history of India through its multiple dynasties, empires and capitals, can not be understood by anyone who is not acquainted with its constant formation into big ethno-linguistic sets of people linked with the emergence of present major languages. The

long series of events of the Deccan can not be unravelled without the clue of the Tamil–Telugu–Kannada–Malayalam divergence, or of central India without the Marathi–Gujarati history, or of eastern India without the Bengali–Oriya–Assamese–Maithili relation, and so on despite the basic shared cultural link provided by languages such as Sanskrit, Pali, Persian or Hindustani.

Many troubles from the late British Raj period, as from the early Independence times, occurred due to wrong appreciation of the basic components of the subcontinent's population and its cultural setting: the basic search for unity with regard to regional conscience. The difficult redrawing of the political map of India, final *reorganizations* and birth of *linguistic states* as an outcome of decades of controversies, illustrates the misconception the former paramount power had about India, and the sudden excessive cautiousness on the part of the *founding fathers* facing the implementation of the motto—the redrawing of administrative units according to main language areas—they had long supported and their reluctant surrender to linguism. In fact, modern history will tell if the achievement of most of the claims to linguistic divisions, through successive reorganizations, was one of the secrets of Indian democracy that preserved it from the explosion seen in other regimes and states, such as the USSR, Yugoslavia or Czechoslovakia, which failed to cope in time with the aspirations of their regional populations. Not to mention Belgium or Canada, where long-standing linguistic issues take decades to reach a solution acceptable to every component of the population.

Admitting the fact that any population should be entitled to fully use and promote its own language at any level of education, administration and mass media, and extending this right to its whole territory under a shared self-nominated power is evidence of wisdom that few states, except India, have given. Many tensions did not reach such a high stage of conflict and were resolved thanks to central arbitration from 1953 to 1972 as well as through local agreements like the Bihar–Bengal (1956) or the Tamil–Andhra (1960) ones. Some, however, have lasted over time such as the Marathi–Kannada border issue over Belgaum in spite of the arbitrary Mahajan Report (in 1967). Others appear and disappear periodically like the Loch Ness monster, in eastern India such as the Jharkhand, Gorkhaland, Udayachal (Bodoland) movements, waiting for a future that Nagaland, Meghalaya, Mizoram or Arunachal Pradesh have already won in various ways.

These lasting incertitudes notwithstanding, and partly

due to them, the Indian geopolitical landscape seems as if it were potentially evolving. Among all significant factors, the ethno-political and -linguistic factors are constantly taken into account in the democratic process. The experience of the last four decades shows that, after the inclusion of major 'constitutional' languages, populations got all they wanted, and that the limit of compromises to middle-sized groups may have been reached. Nowadays, however, minor ethnic communities are gradually seeing their initial goals of the promotion of their ethnic language rather out of prospect, even at the local level where it has been proved that sections of ethnic mother tongue speakers are prone to give preference to regional languages as a vehicle for education and culture.

This lesson of multilingualism and ethno-political framework of a federal India, though not adopted as such by the neighbouring states of the subcontinent, may have a specific influence abroad and help to avoid internal troubles. No nation can pretend to teach others what they ought to do, each one may find some solutions to its own problems which could be a remedy for other crises. India may still face fresh developments to the principle of autonomy it has been instilling in its decentralized structure, while the other states from the subcontinent, such as Sri Lanka or Pakistan, may take further steps in the paths of multilingualism or federalism. While sharing a population within a single environmental and historical framework, with common languages, traditions and customs, all the nations now grouped together in the South Asian Association for Regional Cooperation (SAARC) may jointly agree on a similar treatment of many cultural issues as well.

Among them, the tradition of the census of population computed for more than a century may be extended, standardized and synchronized throughout the subcontinent: here is expressed a researcher's earnest wish. The success of self-determination, self-expression and home rule for so many communities may tend to extend them to all sections of society where unity in diversity and tolerance of all forms of life are well-known watchwords: here rests the hope of the citizens.

PART II

THE SIXTY PLATES WITH THEIR COMMENTARIES

CHAPTER 4

INTRODUCTION: THE REGIONAL SEMIOGRAPHIC ANALYSIS

When studying the regional distribution of languages and language families, and complex local situations, the chosen method was basically that of graphic treatment of statistical data. The discursive analysis beginning from graphic evidence reached through a unified process of representation is as such the opposite of the usual process followed for the representation of research through graphic illustrations. The importance of the graphic method along with the semiologic options it implies is the basis for describing this method as semiographic.

The second part of this atlas is made up of 60 plates including maps and graphs along with descriptions and commentaries. The numerical data is also accommodated in the text and in cases where it cannot be, it appears at the end of the plate series.

The 60 plates follow in a geographical order, beginning from the northwest to the south of the subcontinent. This order, along with mention of the main places of settlement of big linguistic groups (Indo-Aryan, Tibeto-Burman, Dravidian, etc.) enables their study. According to their importance, the distribution of main languages is covered on several plates while that of minor ones is shown on a single plate. The first three plates cover the subcontinent; the following 33 plates display regional situations; 14 others deal with non-regional phenomena extending all over the subcontinent—all these 50 plates are updated from the first edition. The last set of ten plates is based on the 1991 Census data, treated by CAD/CAC (Computer Assisted Design and Cartography) at the ATILA (Atelier TIL Architecture) workshop in Marseilles. Unless otherwise specified, numerical data is taken from either the 1961 (the first 53 plates) or the 1991 (the last seven plates) Census; the plates also display the 1941, 1951, 1971, 1981 Census data, or those from 1881 to 1931 with required specifications.

Most data refer to the mother tongue use (after gathering local variants and designations under the shared relevant identifiable or standard language name). Regional and subcontinental maps mention the distribution of mother tongues by districts within provinces (state or territory). The regional maps show the language within its physical environment. The methods of representation used are shaded areas and proportional symbols. Dotted maps are used (having circles, squares, triangles, etc.) where surface area is directly proportional to the amount of people considered. However, from Plate 54 onwards, proportional spheres have been preferred to circles as the apparent use of the third dimension enables a better representation of population volume with higher differences. In Plate 59 the same sphere scale has been retained but without the illusion of the third dimension when changing the circumference of the sphere to that of a circle so as to divide it into parts proportional to the percentages of each circle/sphere.

As regards graphs, different systems are chosen in accordance with various requirements. Anamorphosis makes uneven volumes perceptible when kept in their relative geographical position (Plates 1, 2, 3). Histograms are convenient either to represent variations (Plate 19) in the same spatial framework or to compare the sizes of different contemporaneous linguistic situations (Plates 43, 44). Simple Cartesian graphs are chosen for parallel historical evolutions (Plates 12, 19, 28, 40, 44).

The ethnogram has been elaborated to mention the percentage of ethno-linguistic communities sharing a common territory. The vertical axis shows graduation in per cent while the horizontal one may (or not) be used to denote the absolute value of the whole set of population: in this case the proportionality of absolute values may be visually appreciated through surface areas, sizes as well as per cent relative values. The ethnogram may be synchronic when allowing the comparison of neighbouring regional situations at the same time or diachronic when used for the same region at successive times.

The cumulative use of these various ways of representation was dictated by the will to quantify the linguistic phenomenon in space as in time in its whole complexity; particularly with regard to ethnograms which give a visually perceptible idea about language dynamics.

This research, at the crossroads of linguistics, ethnology, history and ecology, has been deliberately carried out through graphic and cartographic methods of geography. The scale may be regarded as too small for one-fifth of humanity, however, this one-fifth is unduly considered as little known because it is precisely the only one for which we have exhaustive decennial data for more than a century about language use compared to other sociological and anthropological characteristics. And, from this rich scientific database, not only is it possible to form monographs but also a macroanalysis based on precision, though at another scale.

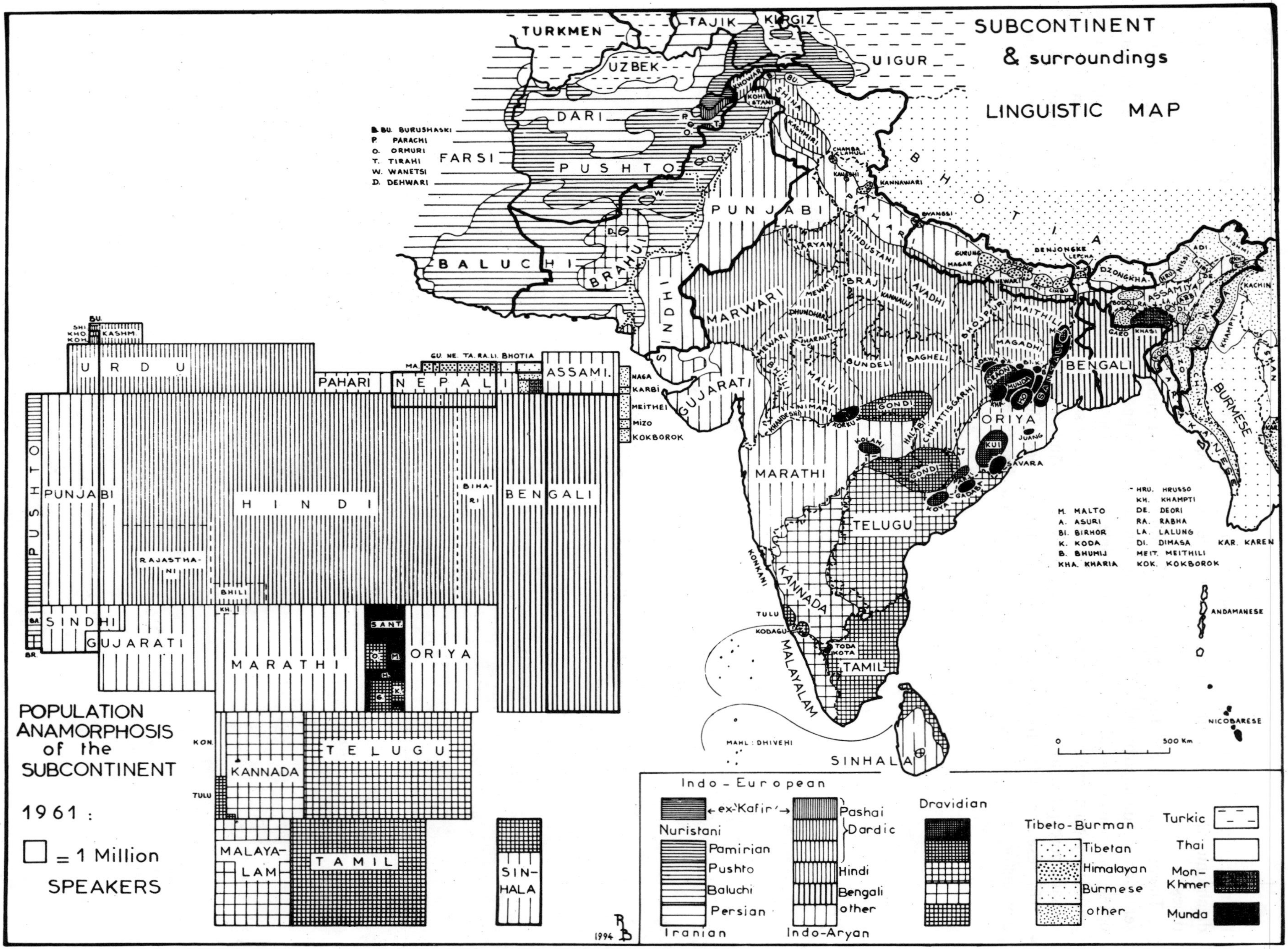

Plate 1: The Languages of India

CHAPTER 5

INDIAN LANGUAGES THROUGHOUT THE SUBCONTINENT AND THE WORLD

PLATE 1: THE LANGUAGES OF INDIA

The distribution of Indian languages among the population and in the territories is jointly shown through two different graphic methods:

- a map of the linguistic areas of the subcontinent (upper right),
- and an anamorphosis, i.e., a schematic, multirectangular representation of the population proportional to its volume (in 1961) by state and within them, by language community (down left). Both the map and the anamorphosis have same shadings and a common key.

The map extends the representation of the area beyond the seven constituent states of the subcontinent bound together by SAARC[*] to neighbouring regions belonging to Iran, Afghanistan, Turkmenistan, Uzbekistan, Tajikistan, China and Myanmar. It shows territorial linguistic continuities across the borders. The anamorphosis is, however, strictly limited to the states of the subcontinent (delineated by thick lines), main linguistic communities within them (by thin lines) and main dialect sets (by hyphenated lines).

Comparison between both representations—area map and population anamorphosis—leads to some reassessment of the relative importance of various groups. For instance, in the anamorphosis, the less densely populated regions such as Bhutan, Nepal, or Pakistan seem to decrease compared with their more widespread image conveyed by maps while communities enjoying a denser settlement seem to extend e.g., those speaking Bengali, Malayalam or Tamil.

Both the images—the territorial map and the population anamorphosis—equally represent and show the settlement and strength of the language and linguistic communities. They only differ in emphasizing one language asset over the other, i.e., either the spatial or the communal. The human community is basically the direct real asset of any language while territory is only man's asset.

---

[*] SAARC: South Asian Association for Regional Cooperation. The seven nations forming SAARC are India, Pakistan, Bangladesh, Sri Lanka, Bhutan, Maldives and Nepal.

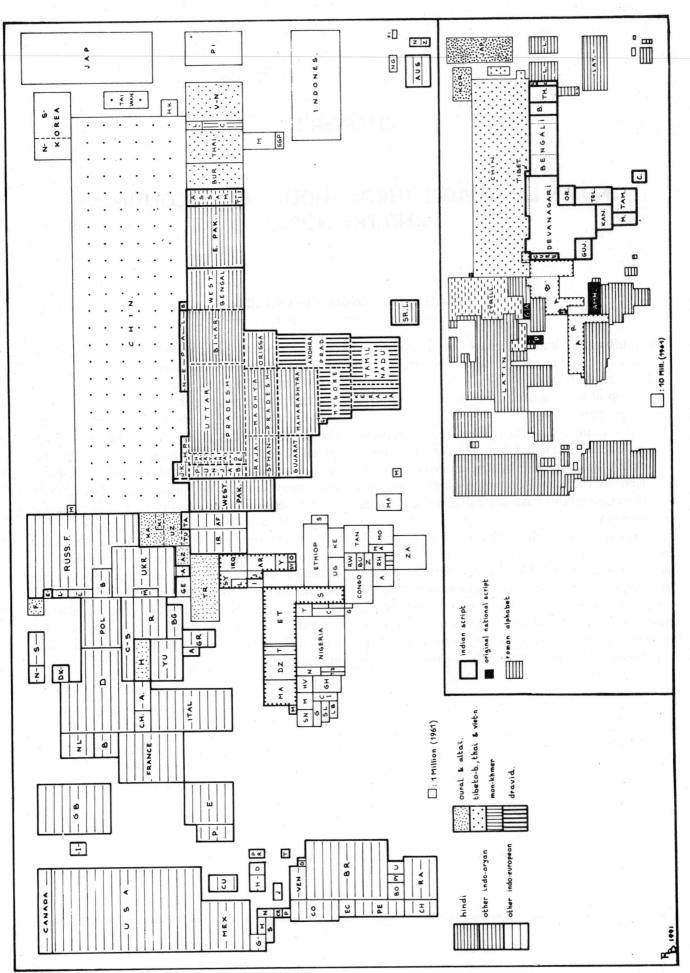

Plate 2: Indian Languages and Scripts in the World

PLATE 2: INDIAN LANGUAGES AND SCRIPTS IN THE WORLD

Two anamorphosis of the (1961) world population distributed by state are used to show the diffusion of:

Indian languages (main, upper part),
and Indian scripts (minor, lower right).

- The language anamorphosis displays the population of the world according to its national distribution and that of India by its provincial one. Each state is covered by a shade related to the official language in use or, precisely, to the linguistic family of the particular language: Indo-Aryan (with a particular representation for Hindi), other Indo-European, Dravidian, Mon-Khmer, Tibeto-Burman, Uralic-Altaic language families, or any other language family (blank areas with a particular representation for Arabic: a dotted line).

- It also shows the importance of Indian language families in the administrative setting of the world population in terms of both its mass (one-fifth of the world population) and the size of the political units that each one covers: in this way the Indian states may be compared with European nations.

- The anamorphosis by script deals with the alphabetic or ideographic systems used by official languages. It shows the global population distribution between Indian, Latin, Arabic, Cyrillic (Russian), Chinese, and other original national systems (Hebrew, Greek, Amharic-Ethiopic, Armenian, Georgian, Mongolian, Korean and Japanese). It illustrates the vast spread of Indian scripts in the subcontinent and most of Southeast Asia, second only to Latin script areas. It also shows the exceptional division of this contiguous sphere with about 15 different areas where there is prevalence of one form of script derived from the original Brahmi (Devanagari, Bengali–Assamese, Tibetan, Oriya, Gurumukhi [Punjabi], Gujarati, Telugu and Kannada, Tamil, Malayalam, Sinhala, Burmese, Thai and Lao, Khmer). This huge sphere thus appears as the most diversified of scripts in the world, i.e., excluding the link set up by English and its Latin script.

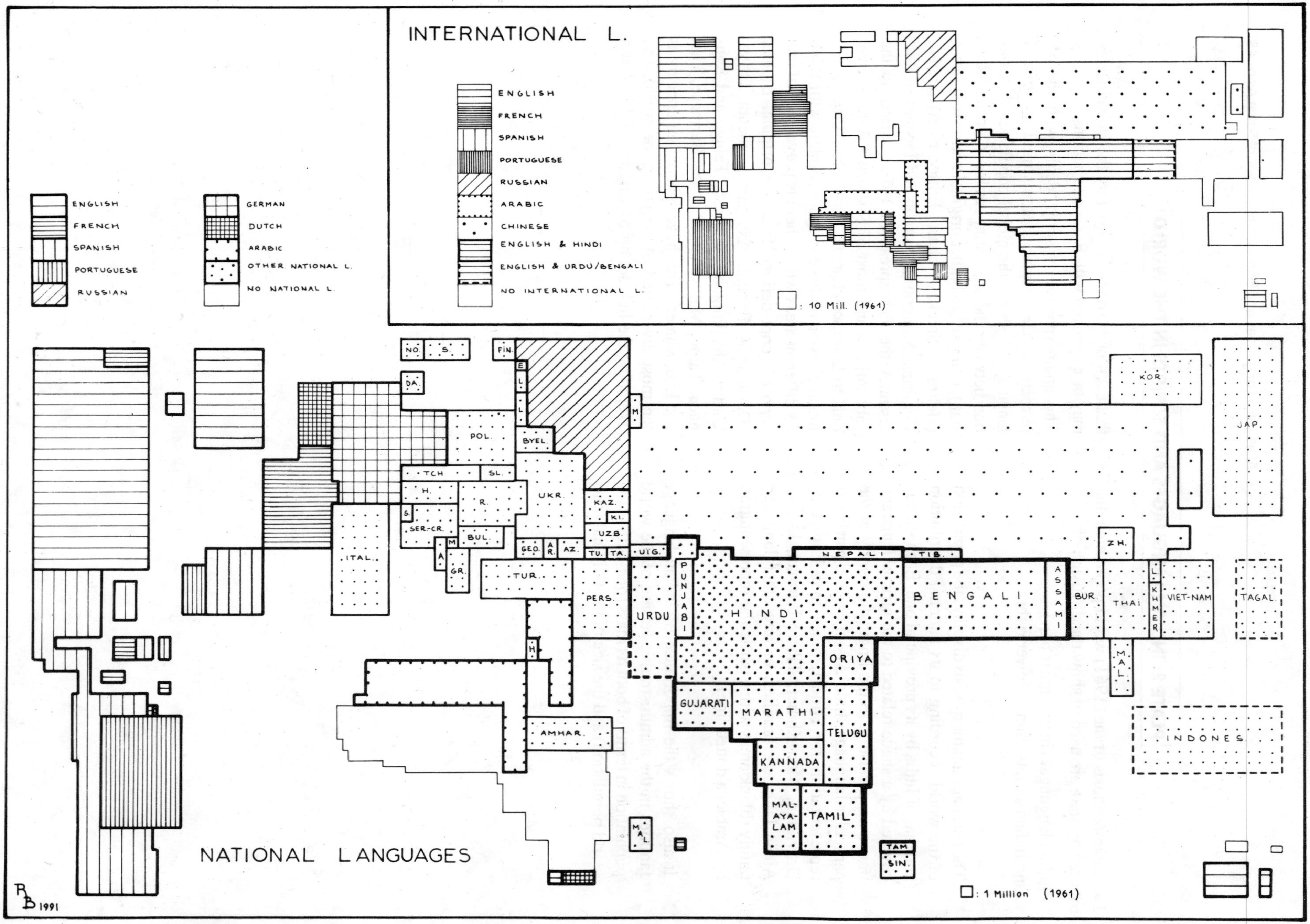

INTERNATIONAL L.

: 10 Mill. (1961)

ENGLISH
FRENCH
SPANISH
PORTUGUESE
RUSSIAN
ARABIC
CHINESE
ENGLISH & HINDI
ENGLISH & URDU/BENGALI
NO INTERNATIONAL L.

GERMAN
DUTCH
ARABIC
OTHER NATIONAL L.
NO NATIONAL L.

ENGLISH
FRENCH
SPANISH
PORTUGUESE
RUSSIAN

NATIONAL LANGUAGES

: 1 Million (1961)

JAP.
KOR.
ZH.
VIET-NAM
TAGAL.
INDONES.
THAI
BUR.
MAL.
ASSAM
BENGALI
TIB.
NEPALI
ORIYA
HINDI
TELUGU
GUJARATI
MARATHI
KANNADA
PUNJABI
MAL-AYA-LAM
TAMIL
URDU
PERS.
UIG.
TU. TA.
AZ.
GEO.
TUR.
GR.
M.
BUL.
SER-CR.
A.
S.
H.
R.
SL.
POL.
TCH.
UKR.
BYEL.
KI.
UZB.
KAZ.
Σ
FIN.
E.
L.
L.
NO.
S.
DA.
ITAL.
H.
AMHAR.
MAL.
TAM
SIN.

R B 1991

Plate 3: Official Languages

PLATE 3: OFFICIAL LANGUAGES

The two world population anamorphoses represent the distribution of official languages considered as:

i) national languages (shown below), i.e., about 70 state home languages,

ii) or international languages (shown above), i.e., the first seven international languages.

- In the main anamorphosis, the spread of national languages in their state (sovereign or federal) population shows the relative weight of each main language of India compared, for instance, with those of Europe. Particularly if we take into account the fact that there are altogether less than 15 national languages in India while there are about 30 national languages in Europe and that too for a smaller population.

- In the minor anamorphosis, the spread of the seven major international languages—either as the national home language or as an official additional one—covers a wide majority of the population in the world, including the Indian subcontinent where English is used in addition to Hindi, Urdu or Bengali. But it leaves big compact regions rather untouched (denoted by blank areas), mainly in eastern Europe and eastern Asia, where only national languages are in use, at least in everyday life (including administrative and teaching fields). At the same time we may see that the subcontinent is the widest compact human set with only one link language in the world.

CHAPTER 6

THE NORTHWEST

PLATE 4: PUSHTO, BALUCHI AND BRAHUI

Plate 4 deals with the three languages spoken along the western border of Pakistan: Pushto (or Pashtu, or Pushtu), Baluchi and Brahui. It is divided into two parts:

- On the left, a general map of Pakistan and Afghanistan shows the extension of the linguistic majority areas of the three languages.
- The map on the right presents, through different administrative inset maps on a smaller scale, the detailed distribution of each of these three languages.
- The general map is political (with international boundaries and the provincial borders of Pakistan along with district limits and names) and physical (main rivers, mountain foot lines, main mountain passes and desert areas). Upon this background, the extension of the majority areas of the three languages are displayed according to key shadings.

Pushto, an east Iranian language, prevailing along most of the border between Afghanistan and Pakistan extends from the hills to the piedmont basins in Pakistan, and all around the central mountains of Afghanistan.

Brahui, the only Dravidian language isolated in the northwestern part of the subcontinent (probably since the Harappan civilization), prevails throughout most of the Kalat massif in the middle of Pakistani Baluchistan, and may slightly exceed the border to cover a small end of Afghanistan.

Baluchi, another Iranian language but from the western group, is divided into two main areas: (*a*) the widest in the west covers southeastern Iran where a province also bears the name of Baluchistan, the southwestern end of Afghanistan, the three westernmost districts of Pakistani Baluchistan: Chagai, Kharran and Makran; and (*b*) the smallest area, eastwards of Kalat

and Quetta, around Sibi, extends both in the southern Sulaiman Range and the Kachhi plain from the eastern–central part of Pakistani Baluchistan.

The geographical extension of these three languages in Pakistan is mainly but not exclusively seen in the hilly region and some piedmont foothills in the western part, i.e., the Indus plains. The extension continues westwards of the international frontier over hundreds of kilometres, across other hills, basins and piedmonts. Linguistic Pashtunistan and Baluchistan widely exceed the geopolitical limits of the subcontinent, in other words these Iranian language areas are the eastern fringes of the Iranian world within the subcontinent area.

- The map on the right gives further details about the concentration of the three languages, from the Pakistan frontier to the Indus plains across each district of the four provinces (North West Frontier Province, Baluchistan, Sind and Punjab) and Karachi. Any district concentration of 2,000 speakers or more is shown by a proportional circle and the percentage (over 10 per cent) of the district population that it represents is given by a shading.

Pushto prevails, among more than 50 per cent of the population, in most parts of NWFP and northern Baluchistan except in the NWFP northern Dardic tip (less than 10 per cent in Chitral and Kalam) and between 10 and 50 per cent in Hazara, Dera Ismail Khan and Sibi districts. Of these, Hazara and Dera Ismail Khan are predominantly Punjabi-speaking while Sibi is Baluchi-speaking. The heavy concentration of Pathans in Pakistan speaking Pushto (in Afghanistan they are called Afghans) in the Frontier hills and basins comes with a sprinkling in the Punjab and Sind plains up to Karachi.

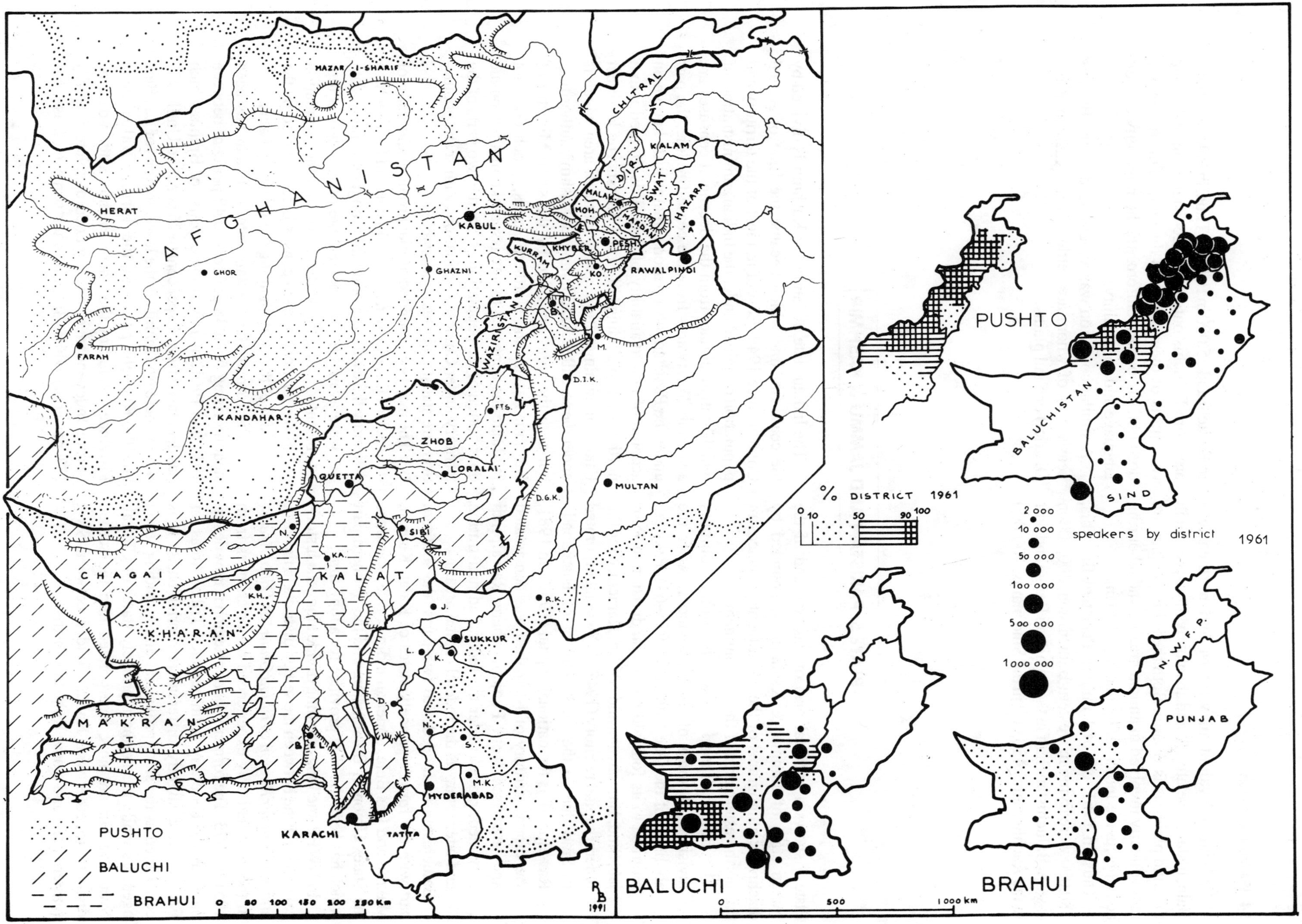

Plate 4: Pushto, Baluchi and Brahui

Baluchi, prevalent in western and northeastern Baluchistan, is relatively and absolutely more present in the Sind plains as is Brahui. Both these hill peoples are more directly involved in animal grazing and labouring activities in the Indus valley than the Pathans.

Thus, in 1961, out of 1 million Pakistani Baluchis, 280,000 were living in western Baluchistan, 200,000 in eastern Baluchistan (half in the Sulaiman Range and half in the Kachhi Plain) 430,000 in the Sind plains, 100,000 in Karachi and 25,000 in Punjab. Thus, in Pakistan, there are more Baluchis outside Baluchistan than inside and two-thirds of them are plain dwellers. This dispersion does not, of course, reinforce the homogeneity of their language and community.

A similar condition was experienced by the Brahuis nearly half of whom are settled in the Kachchi (Kalat District) or Sind plains.

PLATE 5: PAKISTAN AND JAMMU & KASHMIR

Plate 5 shows a political map of Pakistan and of the Indian state of Jammu & Kashmir, surrounded by diachronic ethnograms of the constituent provinces of this northwestern area of the subcontinent.

- The political map shows the inner complex divisions of some of these provinces. After the abolition of the One Unit Act (1955–69), Pakistan returned to its fourfold provincial division in Punjab, Sind, Baluchistan and NWFP. Karachi, once the federal capital territory (1948–61) was incorporated in Sind due to the establishment of Islamabad–Rawalpindi as the national capital (1959). In 1981, the capital territory of Islamabad was demarcated and separated from Punjab, where Rawalpindi remained, placed under the federal administration and later set up as the federal capital area.

Baluchistan is divided into two parts: the southern part with the former princely states of Kalat, Kharan, Makran and Las Bela, under an indirect rule, was once the States Union of Baluchistan, and the northern part which has been the only province for a long time.

In NWFP, the long-standing divide along the historical Durand Line between the settled districts in the east, and the *Frontier Region* or *Illaqa Ghair*, or *Tribal Areas*, in the west had only experienced minor changes from 1951 to 1973. The former Frontier Region is now designated as the Federally Administrated Tribal Areas, or FATA, on a slightly different territorial basis. It is considered as the sixth provincial unit including seven agencies while the northern princely states of Chitral, Swat and Dir are now incorporated into the settled districts, together with Kalam divided between Swat (eastern part) and a new Kohistan District.

The Indian state of Jammu & Kashmir is divided by the cease-fire line which became the Line of Actual Control since 1949. East of it, most of the territory and population remained under the Indian administration, of which statistical data from the decennial censuses are available. Westwards from the cease-fire line, the part under the Pakistani occupation remains little known on account of non-availablity of data. It is divided into a northern area including Gilgit and Baltistan under direct Pakistani administration, and a southern area which is under the so-called Azad Jammu & Kashmir authorities; but both the areas are ruled by the same Ministry of Kashmir Affairs and Northern Areas, which does not facilitate the approach to any issue like mother tongue distribution of the population. Also, the two parts of the territory under Chinese occupation, with scant population, are statistically less accessible.

- The map is surrounded by diachronic ethnograms of each of these provinces of Pakistan and India, which show the evolution of mother tongues as far as data were available. The percentage of speakers is represented along the vertical axis and the population of the territory at each census is represented by the width of the column along the horizontal axis.

In the former Baluchistan states, Baluchi has been steadily rising from 38 per cent to 48 per cent between 1911 and 1961, mainly at the expense of Brahui which has decreased from 46 per cent to 26 per cent. Until 1931 Sindhi increased mainly in the lower regions of Las Bela and the Kachchi plain. In the former Baluchistan Province, excluding the states, Pushto, after a decline before Independence, has regained absolute majority (53 per cent) while Baluchi, after some increase, has

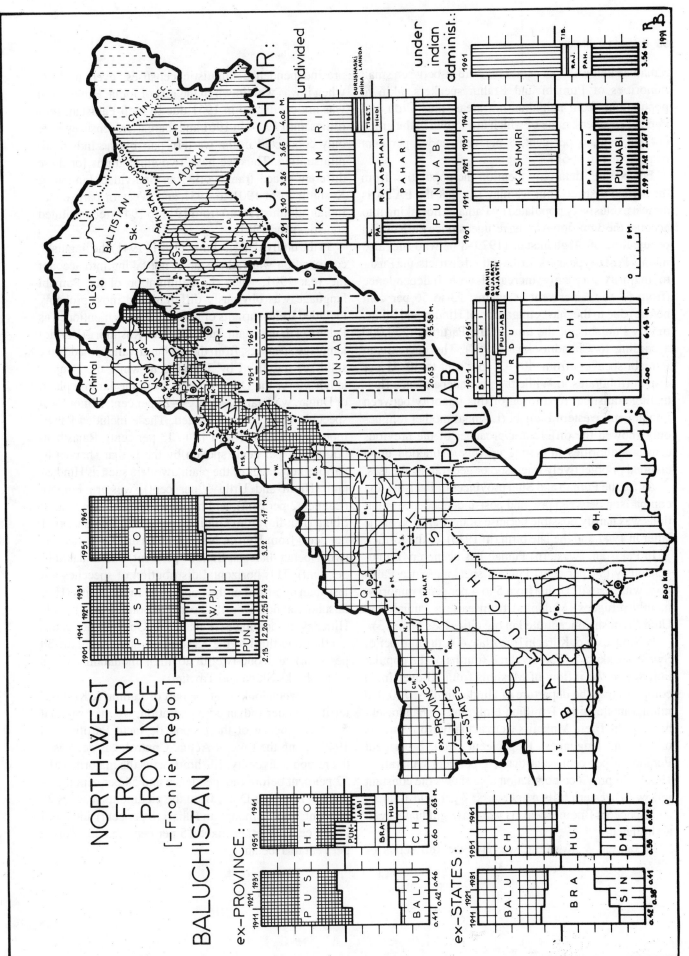

Plate 5: Pakistan and Jammu & Kashmir

remained below 20 per cent. There are in-between small minorities of Punjabi and Brahui speakers, akin to populations from neighbouring areas, plus Urdu and Persian speakers, none of which are shown in the graph (14 per cent, 6 per cent, 3 per cent and 2 per cent respectively in 1961).

For NWFP, data only mention the population from the settled districts, but we may say that the FATA is almost exclusively populated by Pathans, not taking into account the 3 million Afghan refugees since the Russian occupation of Afghanistan (1979–89), who are also mainly Pushto speakers. In the settled districts, the Pushto majority suddenly increased with Independence (from 67 to 64 per cent as against 53 to 56 per cent before) due to the mass emigration of Hindus and Sikhs, mostly Punjabis, at the time of the Partition (250,000 according to Chandrasekhar, 1950). The decrease in Punjabi speakers from 40–45 per cent to 30–31 per cent corroborates it. While the pre-Independence fluctuating statistical repartition of this minority between Punjabi and western Punjabi (Lahnda) mother tongues only showed the different approaches of the previous census authorities in setting up this distinction upon claimed or objectively linguistic or geographical bases.

As for the Punjab and Sind provinces of Pakistan, the comparison between pre- and post-Independence situations was hardly possible because of the Partition of the latter in 1947 and the late birth (in 1936) of the former.

In Pakistan, (western) Punjab has been very homogeneously (94 per cent) Punjabi-speaking since Partition, with a small Urdu (from 5 to 4 per cent) minority, mainly refugees (Muhajirs) from eastern Punjab and Uttar Pradesh concentrated in big cities (see Plate 13).

In Sind, except Karachi (see Plate 40), the number of Sindhi speakers fell below three-fourths of the population due to the inflow of Muslims from all over India compensating the departure of Hindu Sindhis: 700,000 immigrants against 1 million emigrants (Chandrasekhar, 1950). These Muhajirs were actually from various origins and languages: 10 per cent Urdu, 5 per cent Punjabi, 2 per cent Rajasthani, 1 per cent Gujarati in 1961. The province population also shows the constant inflow of western hills neighbours: 7 per cent Baluchi and 2 per cent Brahui speakers who have gradually been assimilated.

In Jammu & Kashmir, we have the full series of pre-Independence linguistic censuses, even in 1941 when it was withdrawn in the rest of India. However, it was not conducted in 1951 due to Indo-Pakistani hostilities until 1949. In 1961 and thereafter, censuses were only conducted in the western part by the Indian administration. Thus we have two ethnograms for these different space frameworks: an undivided Jammu & Kashmir from 1901 to 1931 and Western part (under Indian administration) from 1911 to 1941 (reconstituted statistics) and 1961.

In the undivided Kashmir, (1901–1941) the linguistic composition was rather stable, not taking into account the year 1901, when the delimitation of the Punjabi language was obviously different and most probably included some variants of mother tongues mentioned as Pahari or Hindustani later on. The Kashmiri (Dardic) language speakers, from the Kashmir valley, made up a solid set stabilized by 38 per cent while the Punjabi language (or the Dogri dialect) from the Jammu plain, or Dugar, was stabilized by 24–25 per cent. Minor local speeches appeared annihilated. These included Pahari mountain dialects (from 18 to 13 per cent), Rajasthani (Gojri 9–7 per cent) spoken by the Gujjar shepherds, various languages of the plain dwellers such as Hindustani (Hindi and Urdu 5 per cent), western Punjabi (Lahnda 2 per cent), and highland people's languages: Shina (Dardic) from Gilgit (2 per cent), Burushaski (1 per cent) from Hunza, Nagir and Yasin, Tajik, and the two Tibetan dialects. Balti (4 per cent) and Ladakhi (1 per cent). This horizontal distribution of speeches left less than one-third of the population in the plains (Hindustani, Lahnda, Dogri: 32 per cent), one-fifth in middle Himalayan mountains (Pahari and Gojri 20 per cent), another one-third to the Kashmir valley (Kashmiri 38 per cent) and one-twelfth to high mountain valleys (Burushaski, Shina and Tibetan).

Now, when looking at the part of Jammu & Kashmir territory under Indian administration, we may say that the consequence of the second de facto Partition (in 1949) along the Line of Actual Control, has decreased the region's diversity: Kashmiri wins the majority (51–52 per cent before Independence and 54 per cent thereafter), Punjabi or Dogri from the piedmonts reaches 28 per cent, middle mountain Pahari (8 per cent) and Gojri (7 per cent) together make 15 per cent, leaving only 2 per cent to Tibetan.

PLATE 6: KASHMIRI AND DARDIC

Plate 6 presents a territorial overview of the northernmost section of the subcontinent. This physically, politically and linguistically complex area, due to the lack of homogeneous numerical data, is treated qualitatively and not quantitatively, with a small inset political map and a general linguistic one.

- The political inset map shows, with bold lines, the international boundaries between sovereign states: India, Pakistan, Nepal, China, Afghanistan, Tajikistan, Uzbekistan and Kirgizstan. Thin lines draw the states of India and dotted lines outline the autonomous (*Zi Zhi*) provinces (*Qu*), prefectures (*Zhou*) or districts (*Xiang*) of China and the former autonomous district of High Badakhshan in Tajikistan.

- The general linguistic map shows all these political limits and adds the Kashmiri Line of Actual Control and the unrecognized limits of Chinese occupied territories (shown with broken lines). It displays the main hydrographic network and the foothills line between Himalayas and the Indo-Gangetic plain, between the Karakoram-Tibet and Xinjiang plain, and between the Pamir uplands and the Amu-Darya middle basin. It also shows the main mountain passes and summits.

Within this general physical and political framework, the map locates the space extension of each language in its core majority area. The key on the right shows the different shades that are used for language families and separate languages.

From north and west to south and east, we can see different linguistic areas. At the westward end the Iranian languages mainly include Tajik, covering most of Tajikistan and northeast Afghanistan, and Pushto, spread across all southeastern Afghanistan and Pakistan NWFP and FATA.

Belonging to the same linguistic area, eastern Tajik, or Galcha, includes a chain of more than ten Pamirian dialects or languages, each isolated in its own valley in Tajikistan Upper Badakhshan (Wanchi, nearly extinct, Yazgulami, Rushani, Bartangi, Oroshori, Shugnani), in Afghan Badakhshan (Wakhi, Ishkashimi, Sanglishi, Munjani), plus Yidgha in one Chitral valley from Pakistan. South of Tajikistan and the Afghanistan Wakhan

territorial peninsula, the Wakhi dialect overlaps with the upper Chitral reaches in Pakistan, south of the Baroghil Pass, and with Jammu & Kashmir in the upper Karambar (Ishkoman) and Hunza valleys of Gilgit, where it is known as Gojali from the Gojal ethnic group. East of the Karakoram and the Khunjerab pass in China, the Pamir Tajik dialect, called Sarykoli, is spoken in three other upper valleys of the Yarkand basin which have been set up in a Tajik Autonomous District (Taxkorgan Tajik Zizhixian) where the main town is Taxkorgan (Tashikuergan). The High Badakhshan has been set up in an Autonomous Region within USSR's Tajikistan, as an acknowledgement of the Pamir Tajik identity from the government of Moscow, a concern that the succeeding government of Duchambe does not seem to share. In this way the small ethnic community speaking the Pamir Tajik dialect/language chain—all Ismaili Shiah Muslims as the Burushos—is scattered all over isolated remote valleys and enjoys the rare privilege to live in the five countries which exert their sovereignty over the slopes of the roof of the world: Tajikistan, Afghanistan, Pakistan, India and China.

Similar to the official language of Iran which is Iranian (i.e., Farsi), the language of Kabul, called Farsi-Kabuli, or Kabuli, and officially Dari (i.e., the court language), the latter being the standard language in Afghanistan besides Pushto, could not be distinguished here from the other Tajik standard, imposed in Tajikistan by Russians. This was deliberately meant to be different, with a lexical inflow of Russian words instead of Persian and Arabic, and with the imposition of the Russian (Cyrillic) script, now officially given up. But residual linguistic isolates of Parachi and Ormuri have been shown on the map, both belonging, like Baluchi and Persian, to the western group of Iranian languages and not to the eastern group, like Pushto and Pamir Tajik.

In the province of Nuristan (ex-Kafiristan) of Afghanistan, between the Iranian and Indo-Aryan families of languages, the small group of the so-called Kafir, or Nuristani languages may have been considered as the third in-between branch of the old Indo-Iranian family (see Fussman 1972). It mainly includes four surviving languages (Kati, including Bashgali, Prasun, or Wasi, or Veron, Ashkun and Waigali), plus Tregami, restricted to three villages, all clustered in the four valleys north

LANGUAGE LANGUAGES:
FAMILIES:

TURKIC
UIGUR
KIRGIZ

IRANIAN
TAJIK
PAMIR TAJIK
NURISTANI ("KAFIR")
PARACHI & ORMURI

PUSHTO

DARDIC
PASHAI & TIRAHI
KHOWAR
"KOHISTANI" & SHINA
KASHMIRI

INDO-ARYAN
PUNJABI
PAHARI & GOJRI
PAHARI

TIBETO-
BURMAN
TIBETAN
BURUSHASKI

LINE OF CONTROL
& CHINESE OCCUPATION

CHINESE CLAIMS

CHINA

XINJIANG WEIWUER Z.Z.Q.
(SIN-KIANG UIGUR Z.Z.Q.)

XIZANG ZZQ.
(TIBET Z.Z.Q.)

KIRGIZSTAN

TAJIKISTAN

HIGH
BADAKHSHAN

UZBEKIST.

AFG.

INDIA

JAMMU & KASHMIR

HIMACHAL PRADESH

PUNJAB

UTTAR P.

PAK.

Plate 6:   Kashmiri and Dardic

of Jalalabad and Kabul river.

The Dardic group of languages is the first to definitely belong to the Indo-Aryan family, with some archaic forms resembling those of the Prakrit stage. From west to east in Afghanistan, we first encounter Pashai spoken down the valleys of the Kafir languages, with six smaller language units which are not shown on the map because they only extend to a few villages: Shumashti, Grangali, Ningalami, Savi spoken in one village; Wotapuri in two villages; Gawarbati in three villages; and the residual isolate of Tirahi spoken in the region south of Kabul river.

In Pakistan, the upper valley of Chitral is mainly the home of Khowar with some minor language units such as Kalasha, Phalura and Dameli, the latter possibly affiliated to Kafir. These languages are found close to the Afghan border. Further east in NWFP, Dir is the home of Bashkarik or Garwi, or Diri, and Swat is the home of Torwali, or Swati, which are both disappearing in the upper reaches of these valleys. In the Indus valley Maiya is hardly surviving, some other minor dialectal units such as Palasi, Chillisso and Bateri, usually confused under the common designation of Kohistani. This is because Kohistan (mountain land) is the name of this region, recently set up as a new district on both sides of the Indus after the abolition of the Kalam District and the transfer of the eastern part of its territory to Swat. But the Kohistani designation has also been used to name the whole language (or dialect) chain of the three valleys of Dir, Swat and the Indus.

In Jammu & Kashmir, beyond the region of the eastern Khowar speakers in the upper Ghizar valley (western Gilgit), there are eastern, and widely spoken, Dardic languages: Shina from the middle Gilgit valley to Kargil, where it is named Brokskat, the language of the Buddhist Brokpa (hamlet people) or Minaro, and Kashmiri, in the Srinagar valley (upper Jhelum, or Kashmir proper) and in the northern Chenab part of Doda District in Jammu.

North of the Dardic lands, still higher through the Karakoram range, the Burushaski language is present in the Yasin valley and the middle Hunza valley (states of Hunza and Nagir). It is an isolate, not affiliated to any language family and spoken by the Burushos only.

Further north, just beyond the Wakhi-Gojali-Sarykoli Pamir Tajik language chain with the Tajik Autonomous District (Zizhixian), the Turkic area of Altaic languages begins with Kirgiz in upper Wakhan, eastern Pamirs and the Kirgiz Autonomous Prefecture (Zizhizhou) of Kizilsu, within the Chinese Xinjiang Autonomous Province (Zizhiqu) whose main language, Uygur, is spoken all over the line of oases down the Karakoram and the Tibetan plateau.

South and east of Karakoram, the upper valley of the Indus is the area of the Tibetan population, with three dialects: Balti from Baltistan where Skardu is the main town, Purik from Purik Yul where Kargil is the main town, and Ladakhi from Ladakh where Leh is the main town. This extreme western vanguard of the Tibetan settlement has been culturally influenced by the West because if Ladakhis are still Buddhists, Baltis and Purikpas are Muslims.

South of the Dardic lands, hills and plains belong either to Pushto in NWFP, east of the Indus, or to the huge Indo-Aryan area with all forms of Hindustani, mainly Punjabi in plains and lowlands. Eastwards, in middle mountains, various Pahari dialects are spoken along with a migrant Rajasthani dialect, Gojri, brought by groups of Gujjar shepherds.

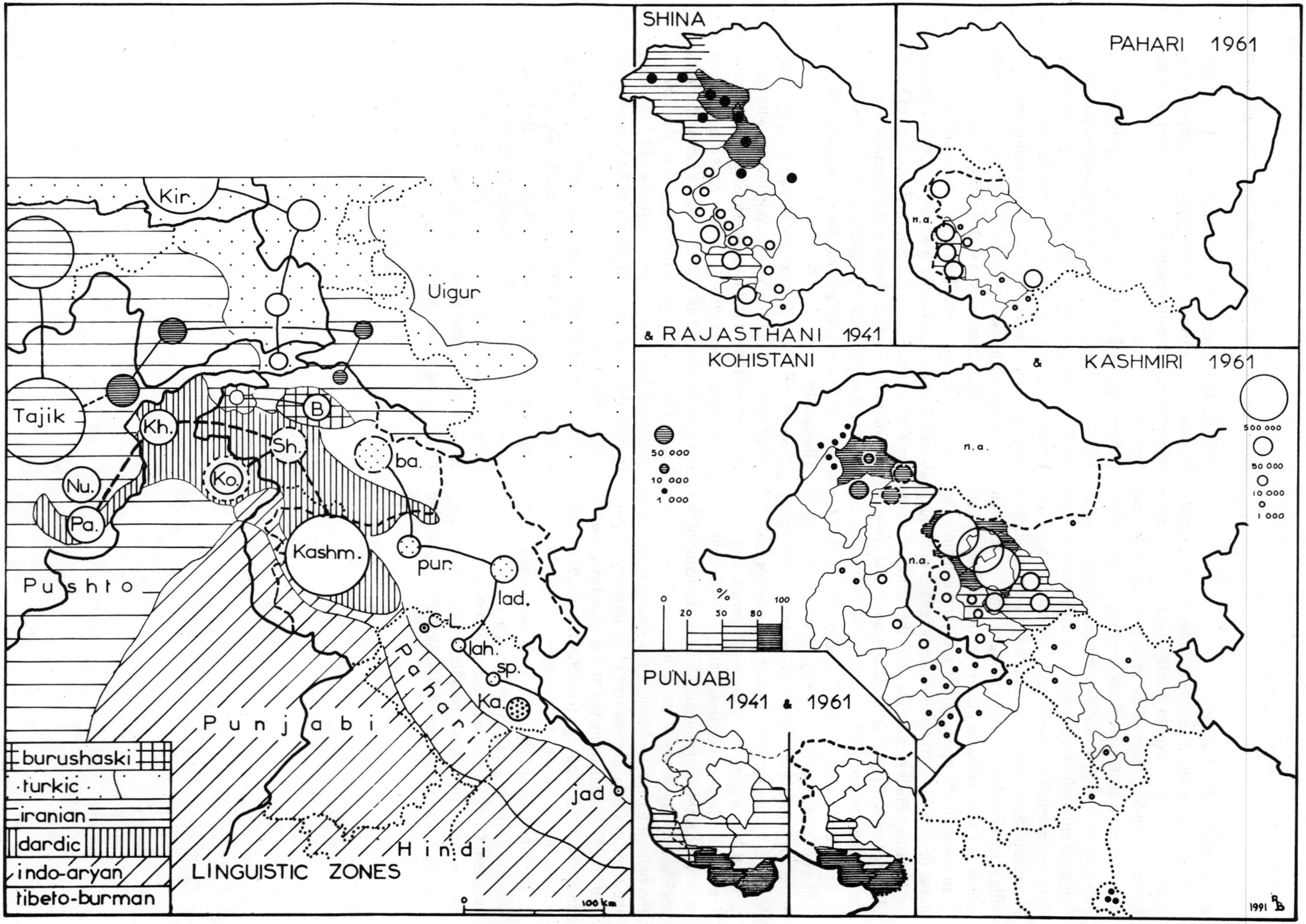

Plate 7: Jammu & Kashmir and 'Frontier Illaqas'

PLATE 7: JAMMU & KASHMIR AND 'FRONTIER ILLAQAS'

Plate 7 tries to give both a spatial and quantitative image of the language distribution of Jammu & Kashmir, including former Gilgit *Illaqas*, in connection with neighbouring regions, with an overall map of the linguistic areas, and separate inset maps of the six main languages.

• The overall map of linguistic areas, on the left, introduces a simplified area map of the whole northern end of the subcontinent in which proportional circles, giving an idea of the volume of speakers of main regional languages by state, are linked to show their grouping:

Tajik in the Iranian area plus Pamir Tajik dialects, and Nuristani or Kafir,

Kirgiz in the Turkic area, the Burushaski language isolate in two territorial spots,

Pashai, Khowar, Kohistani, Shina and Kashmiri in the Dardic area,

Balti, Purik, Ladakhi, Lahuli, Spiti and Jad, all Tibetan languages/dialects, plus Chamba Lahuli and Kanauri which are distinct Himalayan languages in the Tibetan area.

South (and northeast) of the core of the Himalayan area, Pushto, Punjabi, Hindi, Pahari, (and Uygur) are not shown with quantifying circles here.

• The separate inset maps on the right represent one or both languages for which numerical data have been found at the district level in the census of undivided India (1941), or Independent India and Pakistan (1961). A shared scale of proportional circles for absolute values and shadings related to the percentage of population, both by district, allows some comparisons.

Shina predominated in northern *Illaqas* of Gilgit and Astore (Gilgit Wazarat) but was superseded in the western part by other Dardic speeches such as Khowar.

Rajasthani (i.e., Gojri), spoken by the semi-nomadic Gujjar shepherds who are localized in the low Himalayan Pir Panjal range, was everywhere a minority.

Pahari was a similar minority particularly in Poonch and southeastern Jammu.

Kohistani, used in 1961 in Pakistan as a generic designation for all the Dardic chain of languages from the Hills (Kohistan), east of Khowar; thus Bashkarik, Torwali and Maiya, and some minor designations, predominated in the former Kalam District and were significantly present in the northern Hazara and Swat District, and less so in Dir and Chitral.

Kashmiri, at the same time, was widely predominant in the valley of Srinagar, less in Doda and Udhampur districts where it was confined to the northern part of the Chenab river. There were also some scattered Kashmiri speakers in the surrounding hills and plains except west of the Line of Actual Control for which data are not available.

Punjabi, as it was named in 1941 and 1961 but now designated in Jammu & Kashmir as Dogri, is widely predominant—more than 80 per cent—in the core area of the Jammu plains (Jammu and Kathua districts) but had still the majority in the Jhelum–Chenab doab plains (Mirpur district) and a significant minority (20–49 per cent) in the Rias–Udhampur lower hills. In the northern hill districts (Poonch and Muzzafarpur) it fell under the 20 per cent mark where it yielded to Pahari, Rajasthani and Kashmiri.

CHAPTER 7

THE HINDI BELT

PLATE 8: PUNJABI

Plate 8 deals with the Punjabi language distribution comprising two maps: on the left, the physiographic–political map of the larger Punjabi region with shadings that shows the relative percentage of Punjabi speakers in each district population; and, on the right, a subcontinental map with proportional circles that shows the absolute number of Punjabi speakers in each district from all provinces.

- The Punjab map, with a sketch map above it, represents the political division of this natural and linguistic region between the states of Pakistan and India and their provinces.

Punjab is made up of the plain area interspersed with five rivers (Indus, Jhelum, Chenab, Ravi, Satluj) with the Potwar plateau at its northern corner and is unevenly Punjabi-speaking. All the districts of Pakistani Punjab (former western Punjab) are quite evenly peopled and have more than 90 per cent Punjabi speakers while the plain districts of Jammu & Kashmir have Dogri mother tongue speakers. In the Indian province of Punjab most districts only exceed 50 per cent of Punjabi speakers, such as the districts of Dera Ismail Khan and Hazara in NWFP. Eastern Indian Punjab, western Haryana, Delhi, northern Rajasthan, central Sind, western Baluchistan, the Peshawar basin (NWFP) and the middle Himalayan Jammu & Kashmir, the outposts of the Punjabi-speaking area form minorities of 10 per cent or more.

- The map of the subcontinent confirms this concentration and diffusion of Punjabi. It also adds another fact: the wider presence of Punjabi speakers in inner and eastern parts of the peninsula on account of the Sikh diaspora, accelerated and extended by the Partition.

When looking at both maps depicting the distribution of Punjabi speakers—a big majority in the Punjabi region with widespread minorities around it and much further on—we must always keep in mind that (a) Punjabi is part of the huge set of languages, mother tongues, dialects and local variants, gathered together under the shared designation of Hindustani, and (b) that reciprocal intelligibility enables speakers of one oral form of speech to easily use one or another of the three standardized languages, whatever they may state, or claim as their mother tongue. Among standard and official languages, Punjabi has a lesser political stand than both its main rivals, Hindi and Urdu. The former is the language of the Union and of eight states in India, and the latter is the national language of Pakistan and the only official one in its provinces, plus the official language in the state of Jammu & Kashmir in India. At the same time Punjabi was the official language in the state of Punjab in India where the joint use of Hindi largely superseded its theoretical stand until recently.

Therefore, if Punjabi mother tongue speakers make up nearly one-fifth out of about 500 million Hindustani mother tongue speakers, it is indeed considered as the potential official language of only less than a quarter or a fifth of the inhabitants of the Punjab state in India (20 million in 1991), and more precisely of its Sikh community which is its main if not only support within Punjab, and which makes up 60 per cent of its population (i.e., 12 million in 1991). Everywhere else Punjabis may be or are compelled to use other Hindustani written standards. Thus, within the potential bulk of 100 million people using Punjabi as their oral mother tongue, only a small eighth of them is willing, and can keep Punjabi as their cultural language in its original Gurumukhi script.

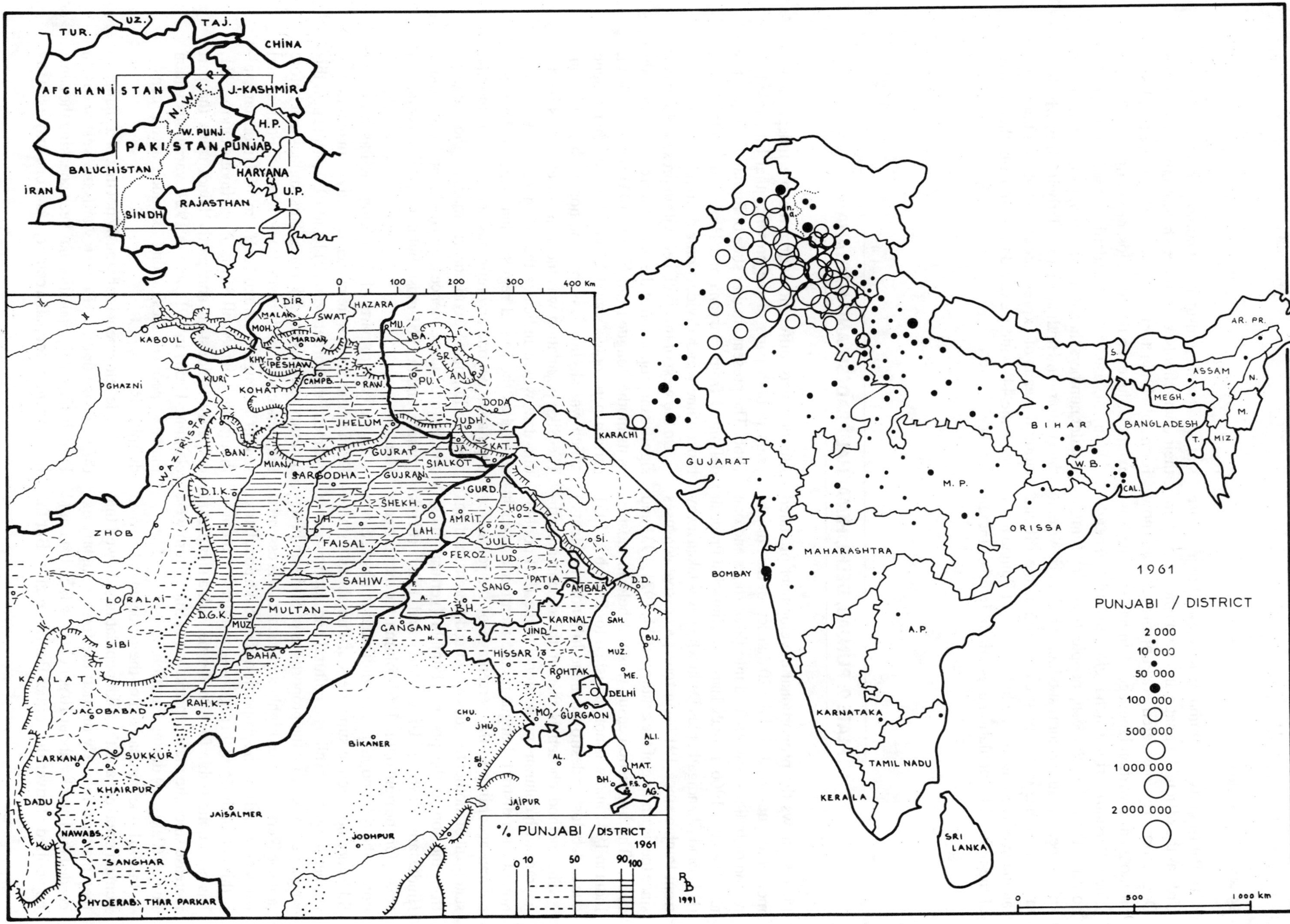

Plate 8: Punjabi

In Pakistan as in Jammu & Kashmir, Punjabis use Urdu as the official language. In Jammu they may claim Dogri, formerly considered as a Punjabi dialect and now promoted as a written language of India using the Nastaleeq (Persian) script which is close to Urdu. In neighbouring Himachal Pradesh, people from the Kangra valley speaking the Kangri subdialect of Dogri, write it in the Devanagari script used in Hindi, the official language of the state. In the Indian state of Punjab most of the non-Sikh population uses Hindi. In other Indian states where their insufficient numbers deprives them of their own schools, even the Sikh community uses other forms of Hindustani, i.e., mainly Hindi and to a lesser extent Urdu, even if orally closer to Punjabi.

Punjabi, used in its standard written form, has far smaller numbers than its mother tongue population; it is the contrary in Hindi and particularly in Urdu which as cultural means of expression and as second languages (see Plate 44) widely exceed the number of their native speakers.

PLATE 9: PUNJAB, DELHI, HIMACHAL PRADESH AND HARYANA

Plate 9 shows the proportional development of stated mother tongues in each of the 20 districts of the Punjabi region of India—now divided into three states and one territory since 1966: Punjab, Haryana, Himachal Pradesh (H.P.) and Chandigarh, plus Delhi which was taken away from Punjab since 1912—in four successive censuses since the beginning of the century: 1911, 1921, 1931 and 1961. (The linguistic census was not held in most of India in 1941 and was not published for Punjab in 1951 due to data lost or destroyed in the Jullundur incidents.)

The method chosen is that of the diachronic ethnogram with columns proportional to the 1961 population of each district. Languages are mentioned in each column according to the percentage of the registered statement of mother tongues by using different shadings from the top to the bottom: Punjabi (vertical lines), Hindustani (dashes), Urdu (dots) and Hindi (blank areas). On the right of the 1961 column, the then proportion of the Sikh population is indicated in black. Since Sikhs are now active supporters of Punjabi as a stated mother tongue as well as a cultural and administrative language, comparing the proportions of Sikhs and Punjabi speakers becomes highly significant. It is essential to bear in mind that the proportion of the Sikh population in this part of the Punjabi region—the highest in India—has been quite stable for a long time with a significant increase since the mass repatriation of Sikhs from west Punjab (Pakistan) during Partition.

In 1961, the comparison of the percentage between Punjabi speakers and the Sikh populations showed that they matched in every district: the former slightly exceeded the latter by about 10 per cent—a fact that could be verified all over the former Punjabi region. But the situation was different during the pre-Independence years in both parts of the province that bifurcated in 1966. The present smaller state of Punjab in the west is delimited from Haryana and Himachal Pradesh by a broken line which divides some districts.

On the west of this line, i.e., within present Punjab, a significant proportion of the population claimed Punjabi as its mother tongue from 1911 to 1931 while in 1961 a certain percentage stated Hindi as its mother tongue which was slightly less than the non-Sikh population. The Sikh population was the same or even less before this date which indicates that Punjabi was then considered as the shared regional language of the whole population beyond any religious demarcation, and that now the linguistic divide nearly matches the religious one. Before Independence both Hindus and Sikhs spoke Punjabi, and in 1961 most (but not all) Hindus claimed Hindi.

In the eastern parts of the region such as Karnal or Delhi where Sikhs were numerous, only a small minority claimed Punjabi between 1911 and 1931, while now this minority exceeds the Sikh one. This implies that before Independence nearly everybody ignored Punjabi and sought belonging to another form of Hindustani, although they named all forms of it: Hindustani in 1931, or partly Hindustani and partly Hindi (plus the part claiming Urdu) in 1911 and in 1921, variations which matched people's hesitations as much as the census definitions.

This development is obviously not that of a change in the language oral use. Either towards the west or east in Punjab, the local population has been speaking the same mother tongue for half a century. And one may even say

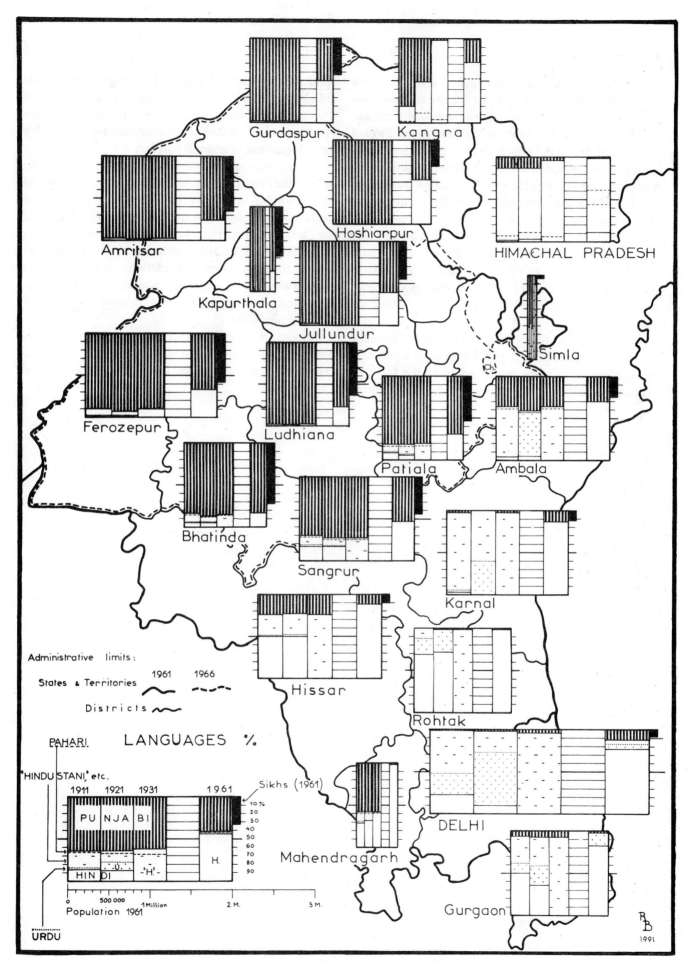

Gurdaspur

Kangra

Amritsar

Hoshiarpur

HIMACHAL PRADESH

Kapurthala

Jullundur

Simla

Ferozepur

Ludhiana

Patiala

Ambala

Bhatinda

Sangrur

Karnal

Administrative limits:

States & Territories   1961   1966

Districts

LANGUAGES %

Hissar

Rohtak

PAHARI.

"HINDUSTANI," etc.

1911 1921 1931   1961   Sikhs (1961)

PUNJABI

10 %
20
30
40
50
60
70
80
90

H.

HINDI   "H."

Mahendragarh

DELHI

URDU

0   500 000   1Million   2 M.   3 M.

Population 1961

Gurgaon

R
B
1991

Plate 9: Punjab, Delhi, Himachal Pradesh and Haryana

that, within this whole area which is a few hundred kilometres wide, variations in speech are so minor that it is basically the same language or dialectal form and not the typical westernmost nor the easternmost form of Hindustani. But in the west it was designated as Punjabi (from the Satluj banks to the Indus banks) while in the east (from the Yamuna banks to Varanasi) it was named Hindi or Hindustani, according to various accidents. No clear-cut line could be drawn in the geographical divide, (or Sirhind) between the Indus and Ganga basins. And now the linguistic division is shared: Sikhs everywhere register themselves as Punjabi speakers, Muslims as Urdu speakers, and most Hindus as Hindi speakers with a small fringe claiming Punjabi and an even smaller one Hindustani.

If anything has changed it has certainly not been the oral form of speech of the population or of a part of it but the way they name it, according to the fact that claiming a mother tongue now sounds like claiming some religious, shared or ethnical belonging, or a political choice. This mother tongue option may not really match practical behaviour, as its shows the use of the Hindustani form of language rather than another one for any educational or cultural purpose.

The last ethnogram at the bottom left shows the whole area of the Punjab before bifurcation, now in India and the historical results of long hesitations and final decisions: a strong claim for the Punjabi language and the Punjabi region (Punjabi Suba) by Sikhs, a decrease in the Punjabi-speaking population almost entirely related to the Sikh community, and a development where most Hindus claim Hindi, not Hindustani, while Muslims (now very few except in Gurgaon, southwest of Delhi) claim Urdu.

Nowadays, wherever there are no Sikhs, there is actually no Punjabi written language, except in Kangra (Himachal Pradesh) where the Kangri subdialect of Dogri is spoken.

PLATE 10: PUNJAB AND RAJASTHAN

Plate 10 seeks to test the development of language identity of Punjabi and Hindi in both the neighbouring regions of Punjab and Rajasthan within the big Hindustani linguistic area in undivided India and since the Partition through the longest series of censuses.

- The political map in the centre of the plate shows how the Partition line cuts both former British provinces (horizontal lines) of Punjab and Ajmer-Merwara and both sets of princely states (dotted areas) named Punjab states and Rajputana states.

The Punjabi province was divided into two parts: the western part with the western Punjab state of Bahawalpur which became the Pakistani province of Punjab; and the eastern part which became the Indian state of Punjab while the eastern Punjab states were united in two states: those of the plains called the PEPSU (Patiala and East Punjab States Union) and those of the mountains (Himachal Pradesh). However, under the 1956 states' reorganization, PEPSU has been incorporated in the Punjab state. Finally, during the Punjab bifurcation in 1966, the two states were reorganized into the three present states of (smaller) Punjab, (newly set up) Haryana and (extended) Himachal Pradesh, plus the union territory of Chandigarh which is the capital of Punjab and Haryana.

Southwards, the Rajputana states became Rajasthan state, while the Ajmer-Merwara province became the Ajmer state. These two states were subsequently united to form the (present) state of Rajasthan during the states' reorganization in 1956.

- Ethnograms show the linguistic development of each main political unit: on the left within the pre-Partition limits and dates until 1931 and on the right within the 1961 delimitation, between 1911 and 1961. In all these diachronic ethnograms, each column changes in width according to the size of population at the census time on a scale specific to each province drawn at the bottom of the ethnogram. The percentage of language claimed by the population is mentioned with a shared shading displayed in the key below based on various designations used by different censuses for the Hindustani set of languages—western Punjabi (or Lahnda), Punjabi, Hindustani, Urdu, Hindi, Rajasthani—and other main languages—Pahari, Pushto and Bhili. Other language designations are left blank. The main purpose of these ethnograms (as in Plate 9) is

to highlight the utmost importance of the choice in the linguistic designation compared with the genuine actual development in using these languages.

In the Punjabi province within the pre-Partition limits, it is interesting to notice the confusion of other names in 1881 as for the Hindustani designation, which were subsequently used as Hindi, Pahari, and Rajasthani and would experience some unpredictable changes. Pushto is dying only due to the secession of the North West Frontier Province in 1901 and because of a newly formed Punjab with new and more homogeneous assets. Simultaneously, the rather even increase in western Punjabi over Punjabi may show as much the intentions of the authorities as those of the population itself to differentiate two kinds of languages in the Punjabi area itself. The stable minority-stand of Hindi, located in the southeastern corner of the province on the other side of the Indo-Gangetic divide, is noteworthy and is already shown in the previous plate. Finally, minor fluctuations in Pahari and Rajasthani show uncertainties in the linguistic designations of geographically marginal populations.

Similar stabilities and fluctuations existed within the Punjab states from 1891 to 1931. Pahari was stable in the Himalayan states, Hindi in the southeastern states, while there were some fluctuations in the use of designations like western Punjabi (rather peculiar in eastern Punjab) or Rajasthani (more prevalent in Bahawalpur).

In Rajputana, between 1901 and 1931, there was a relative decline of Hindi (divided into western Hindi and Hindi in 1911) as compared to Rajasthani and even minor Bhili. The same thing occurred even more obviously between 1891 and 1931 in Ajmer-Merwara: Hindi suffered a decline against Rajasthani (Ajmeri dialect). Now, looking back at these developments within the geographical limits of post-Partition provinces suggest other motivations and interpretations.

Within the 1961 delimitation of Punjab including present Haryana, the opposition between pre-Independence times (from 1911 to 1931) and now is impressive because of (a) the drastic decrease in the Punjabi designation and the opposite development of Hindi, and (b) the dying designation of Hindustani and Urdu due to Partition consequences. The significant decline of Pahari compared to its previous development may also

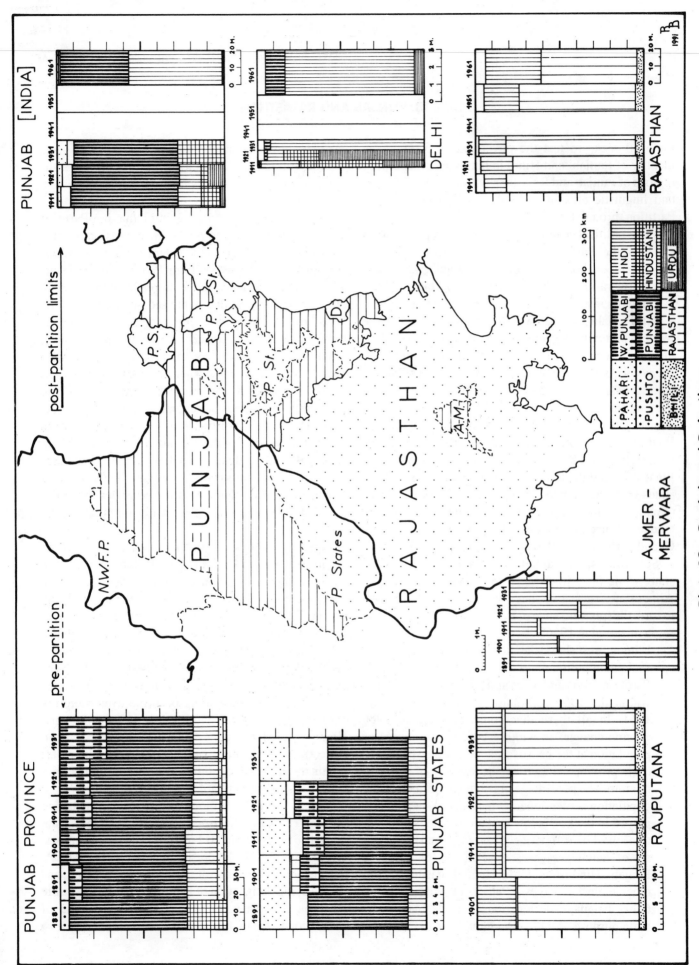

Plate 10: Punjab and Rajasthan

be explained by the preference for the Hindi designation.

The Delhi ethnogram with columns whose width is proportional to the population size is more expressive than the one in Plate 9 with identical columns. It displays the significant increase in Punjabi because of the inflow of the Sikh population, the decrease in Urdu due to the migration of Muslims, and the relative moderate decline of Hindi in spite of the significant inflow of the Hindu population. It also shows, for the period from 1911 to 1931, how changes in the linguistic designation could be significant of anything other than language use. The Muslim city of 1 million in 1941 was, in 1961, a metropolis with 2.5 million inhabitants due to the departure of most of the Muslims and the arrival of half-a-million Sikh and Hindu refugees. There was also a rather sharp correlation between linguistic and religious communities: Muslims and Urdu were both 6 per cent, Hindus 84 per cent and Hindi 77 per cent, Sikhs 8 per cent and Punjabi 12 per cent.

As far as Rajasthan is concerned (1911–61) the post-Partition developments are quite opposite to the pre-Partition ones: there was a development of standard Hindi from 14 per cent to 33 per cent over Rajasthani (dialectal forms) which declined from 79 per cent to 56 per cent and Bhili (a tribal language) from 3 per cent to 5 per cent and 4 per cent in an absolute increase: 334,000 in 1911, 832,000 in 1961 (see also graph in Plate 12).

To summarize the lessons of the development of this western part of the large Hindustani area, it can be said that two main trends prevail: the growing preference for major designations of standard languages (Hindi, Punjabi and Urdu) over local dialectal ones such as western Punjabi or Rajasthani, and the decrease in minor marginal language units such as Pahari and Bhili. However, this simplification of linguistic identity on the basis of mother tongues is outnumbered by the growing concentration of cultural uses of the three standard languages in their respective territorial (Pakistan, Indian Punjab, India) and shared (Muslim, Sikh and Hindu) assets.

speakers outside HINDI REGION.

1961

2 000 10 000 50 000 100 000 500 000

In Hindi Region:
% HINDI 1961

0 10 50 90 100

1 000 km.
500
0

HINDI REGION
> 50%

RAJASTHANI
/BIHARI

URDU > HINDI

PUNJABI > HINDI

ASS.
BANGLA.
W.B.
ORISSA
BIHARI
RAJASTHANI
JAMMU-KASHMIR
PUNJAB
PAK.
GUJARAT
MAHARASHTRA
NAGPUR
A.P.

RAJASTHANI
/BIHARI

1961:
2 000
10 000
50 000
100 000

500 000
1 000 000

HINDI

HINDI &
RAJASTHANI
/BIHARI

Bihari
BHOJPURI
MAITHILI
SADRI

minorities:

RAJASTHANI

PAKISTAN
NEPAL
J.K.
H.P.
PUNJ.
HA.
RAJ-ASTHAN
GUJARAT
UTTAR PRADESH
Dhundhari
Marwari
Malvi
MADHYA PRADESH
Maithili
Bhojpuri
Magahi
Sadri
BIHAR
ASSAM
AR. P.
ME.
MA.
TRI.
E. PAK.
W.B.
ORISSA
MAHARASHTRA
GOA
KARNATAKA
ANDHRA PRADESH
TAMIL NADU
KERALA
Gojri

1000 km
1961

1961:
50 000
100 000
500 000

1 000 000

PLATE 11: HINDI, RAJASTHANI AND BIHARI

Plate 11 shows, for the whole subcontinent, the distribution of Hindi and two other languages or language groups which are directly akin to Hindi: Rajasthani and Bihari. As both are increasingly considered as simple groups of Hindi dialects but been listed separately for a long time, it is interesting to begin the study with these marginal components before the main central language, i.e., starting with the two small maps on the left devoted to Rajasthani and Bihari and ending with the Hindi subcontinental language.

• The first Rajasthani and Bihari map shows the settlement of Rajasthani and Bihari in 1961, with proportional circles in each district of the Hindi Region or the Hindi Belt including the eight states or territories where Hindi is the provincial language (circled by a bold line). Within it, every district where these dialects reach 50 per cent of the population is dotted. Outside the Hindi Belt, areas where the Punjabi mother tongue outnumbers Hindi are mentioned with vertical hatching: Punjab and Jammu & Kashmir. Areas where Urdu outnumbers Hindi are shown with horizontal hatching, i.e., most of the remaining part of the subcontinent: the west, south and partly east (Orissa Littoral and Bangladesh). The only regions outside the Hindi Belt where Hindi mother tongue outnumbers Urdu are found along the outer limits of the Hindi Region: Marathi Vidarbha and inner Orissa in the south, and West Bengal and the whole northeastern India plus the Himalayan states in the east.

Within the Hindi Belt, the main variants, Rajasthani and Bihari, do not exactly match their corresponding provinces. In the southwestern corner, Rajasthani reached a majority stand in most Rajasthan and was significantly claimed in the southwest part of Madhya Pradesh (Malwa and Nimar plateaus). At the eastern end of the Hindi Belt, Bihari got the majority as a stated mother tongue in western and central northern Bihar, and a significant minority in southern Bihar, but could garner no support in eastern Uttar Pradesh where the Bhojpur country is the core of one form of Bihari.

Again, the census data based on mother tongues stated by people does not allow to draw maps of actual linguistic uses or the limits of dialectal areas but only of the preference for some linguistic designations (as sectarian denominations) within some populations, showing psychological or political feelings and behaviour. Moreover, among the same population, some state the name of one standard language as their mother tongue, while others state some dialects or even some uncommon, dead languages.

• The second Rajasthani and Bihari map shows the extension of Rajasthani and Bihari outside the Hindi Belt in 1961. Rajasthani has two main areas of long-range diffusion brought about by semi-nomadic Scheduled Castes: the Jammu hills where the Gojri dialect is spoken by the Gujjars, and central Deccan where Banjari-Lambadi is spoken by the Banjaras and Lambadas from Maharashtra, Karnataka and Andhra Pradesh. Bihari has a traditional settlement beyond the administrative limits of Bihar in Madhya Pradesh, West Bengal and, above all, in eastern Terai in southern Nepal.

Main dialectal designations are only memories in their areas of origin. Marwari, Mewari, Dhundari, Malvi and Nimari only represent the selection of the preferred forms from among the wide range of multiple Rajasthani dialectal and subdialectal names. On the other hand, Maithili, Magadhi and Bhojpuri (plus Sadri, the latest southern variant) are the only significant subdivisions of the Bihari threefold linguistic group.

• The Hindi subcontinental map separately uses two means of representation. Within the Hindi Belt, the shading is according to the percentage of stated Hindi mother tongue speakers. This allows the specification of the actual geographical core of Hindi which comprises southern and eastern Uttar Pradesh and northern Madhya Pradesh (denoted in black). The preference in this region of more than 90 per cent of the population is to state Hindi as their mother tongue. The map also shows the marginal regions where Hindi competes with Rajasthani, Bihari or Pahari designations, or coexists with other language settlements (Punjabi or tribal languages in southern Bihar and Madhya Pradesh; denoted by a shading that moves from a lighter shade to a full blank).

Outside the Hindi Belt where Hindi has always had a rather small minority stand, the method of proportional circles bring out all types of concentration (as in Calcutta) or dispersion (as in Deccan) of Hindi mother tongue speakers.

PLATE 12: THE HINDI REGION

Plate 12 is dedicated to the Hindi Belt, the region made up of provinces where Hindi prevails in administrative as well as in everyday use. Two maps, one linguistic and the other historico-political at the top right, and a historico-demographic graph in the middle with six provincial diachronic ethnograms around it are designed to show the increase over space and time in the main language of India in its core area, the Hindi Region or the Hindi Belt. A shared key of shadings used in the linguistic map as also in the ethnograms in given on the top left corner.

- The first map entitled 'Provinces and linguistic zones' at the top in the centre shows the respective areas for each of the main broad dialectal groups within Hindi: Rajasthani is spoken in most of Rajasthan and western Madhya Pradesh (Malwa); western Hindi covers Haryana, Delhi, western Uttar Pradesh and central Madhya Pradesh; eastern Hindi is prevalent in central Uttar Pradesh and eastern Madhya Pradesh; and Bihari in eastern Uttar Pradesh and the whole of Bihar. Other very close language areas include those of Pahari also belonging to the central Hindustani language set; Bhili and Gujarati which can be linked to the central zone; and Marathi which definitely belongs to the southern Indo-Aryan zone.

- The geopolitical map entitled 'Ex-Provinces' presents, within the framework of present provinces (which is also that of the linguistic map), the situation before the reorganization of former princely states and provinces whose names are also mentioned in some ethnograms.

- The central graph allows one to compare through a century of censuses (from 1881 to 1971), the demographic growth of the main provincial units in the Hindi Belt along with the growth of two main regional language forms grouped together within Hindi: Bihari and Rajasthani. Though regular data are available for the provincial population, it is not always so for dialectal forms of speech, as a result of which some discrepancies may be brought into evidence.

Bihari speakers declined from 1901 to 1931 and even until 1961 from 37 to 17 million. However, there was a significant increase in 1971 up to 30 million, though, at the same time, the inhabitants of Bihar province in-creased from 37 to 60 million; i.e., Bihari speakers decreased to half the population of the province.

As regards Rajasthani, figures stand quite steady from 1901 to 1971 as far as speakers are concerned—between 10 and 15 million—while the population of the province increased from 10 to 25 million. The comparison of data within each province helps to balance this decline which was relative in Rajasthan and absolute in Madhya Pradesh.

Both Bihari and Rajasthani speakers outnumbered their respective province's population at the beginning of the century but are now far behind. This decrease in the proportion of provincial populations claiming faithfulness to their regional languages is a significant stand highlighting the strengthening of the national language. This, as a preference for at least some designation and maybe beyond that as a potential choice facing various written and oral forms of expression.

- Ethnograms may clarify the extent of these shifts. In Central India Agency and Gwalior (western and northern parts of Madhya Pradesh), no substantial change was noticed from 1901 to 1931, in the tripartition between Rajasthani, western and eastern Hindi. There was an indication of increase in Rajasthani at the expense of western Hindi before the First World War, which was reversed afterwards. In the whole Madhya Pradesh area, from 1911 to 1961 the main noticeable fact is the gradual prevalence of the Hindi designation compared with the decrease in Rajasthani and other local forms, and the steady marginal stand of Marathi.

At the turn of the nineteenth century, the change in designations of Agra and Oudh (Uttar Pradesh), the nucleus of the core area is obviously an administrative one: the same 98 per cent majority stated that they spoke Hindustani in 1881, Hindi in 1891, and, in 1901, split between western and eastern Hindi and Bihari. Then, in 1911, 1921 and 1931, the whole population once again stated Hindi, with the exception, in 1911, of 8 per cent who stated Urdu. In Independent India the situation came to a more rational balance. In 1951, besides 80 per cent Hindi speakers there were 7 per cent Urdu speakers and 11 per cent Hindustani speakers; subsequently in 1961, besides 80 per cent Hindi speakers, there were 11 per cent Urdu speakers and no Hindustani speakers. These Urdu and Hindustani percentages compared to

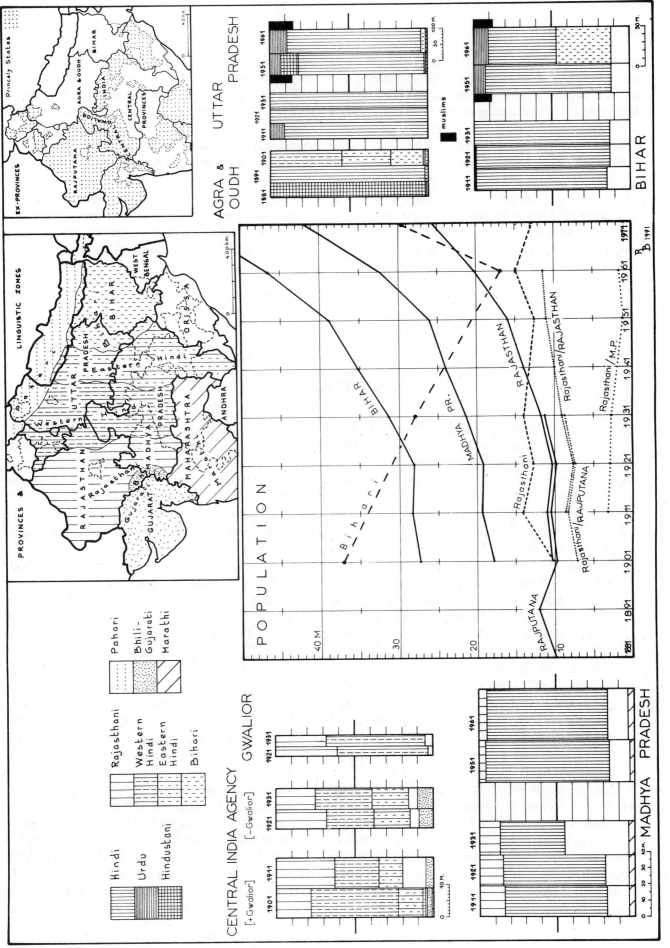

Plate 12: The Hindi Region

those of Muslim/Hindu populations (15/85 per cent) show that most of the Muslim population was attached to Urdu, and that a fringe of Muslims and Hindus, after having stated some neutral speech form like Hindustani are now grouped (and maybe more than statistically mentioned) with Hindi speakers.

Nearly the same situation is found in Bihar where the number of Urdu speakers (7 per cent and 9 per cent in 1951 and 1961 respectively) tends to come closer to but still under the Muslim population (11 per cent and 12 per cent). The stand of Bihari was extremely uncertain with 112,000 speakers in 1951 and 6 million ten years later while the proportion of minor tribal languages from Chota Nagpur was steady.

It is finally worth mentioning that all the fluctuations noticed in the enumeration of languages indeed show changes in speakers' own statements regarding their mother tongue, drawn from their specific cultural feelings about their identity. They also increasingly reflect the will to rationalize the census after thorough registration, particularly when referring to regional (Rajasthani, Bihari, Pahari, etc.) or general (Hindustani) designations now officially considered as simple *mother tongue variants* and bracketed together as constitutional languages.

PLATE 13: URDU

Plate 13 displays the geographic distribution of Urdu as a mother tongue throughout the subcontinent in 1961 with the help of two maps: on the right a large dotted map for absolute figures, and on the left, a small shaded map for the percentage of population, plus, at the bottom left another shaded one showing the main agents of diffusion of Urdu: the Muslims.

- The dotted map called 'Urdu speakers by district' is drawn on the same scale as that of Hindi speakers in Plate 11. It enables the identification of various regional amorphous groupings of Urdu speakers. The main cluster is found in the Gangetic plains of Uttar Pradesh and northern Bihar, i.e., in the core of the Hindi Belt; the second in central Deccan, i.e., Maharashtra, Andhra Pradesh, Karnataka and northern Tamil Nadu; followed by some minor groupings around Calcutta, in western Madhya Pradesh and central Gujarat, Pakistani Punjab and the Sind provinces, and parts of Bangladesh and Orissa; and finally some traces in Himalayas, Assam and the Northeast, Kerala, Sri Lanka.

This distribution shows the origin of this language which first appeared in northern Deccan as 'Dakshni', the *southern* language of the Muslim conquerors there, and then as Urdu, the language of the court, the *Horde*, in the main stronghold of northern Hindustan. It was eventually adopted as the distinctive cultural form of Hindustani by most of the Muslim communities, particularly by those from Northern Deccan, the Gangetic valley and in various centres of activity, some traditional such as Bhopal, Gujarat, and others modern like Calcutta or Madras. Subsequently, an influx of Partition migrant refugees (Muhajirs) carried it to Pakistan and Bangladesh. There was however a marked absence of Urdu speakers in regions such as Kashmir, Assam, Kerala, southern Tamil Nadu and Sri Lanka where the Muslim communities stuck to local languages.

- The two small shaded maps drawn on a same scale and with the same key, compare the percentage of population in the subcontinent in 1961 that spoke Urdu (the top map) or was Muslim (the bottom map). The similarity in repartition is complete in central Deccan and very high in the Gangetic plains. But, everywhere else, the percentage of Muslims is higher than that of Urdu speakers which indicates that most of the Muslims, outside northern Deccan, Uttar Pradesh and Bihar speak a mother tongue other than Urdu. The opposition is strikingly obvious all over the predominantly Muslim states of Pakistan and Bangladesh where Urdu is not a native language; even in Jammu & Kashmir where Urdu is the official language as in Pakistan; and in three other areas of India where Muslims are numerous: West Bengal, Assam (and Tripura) and Kerala.

From this overview it is clear that if Urdu is undoubtedly the distinctive language of most Muslims from the Hindi Belt and Deccan, the numerous Muslim populations of Pakistan, Jammu & Kashmir, West Bengal,

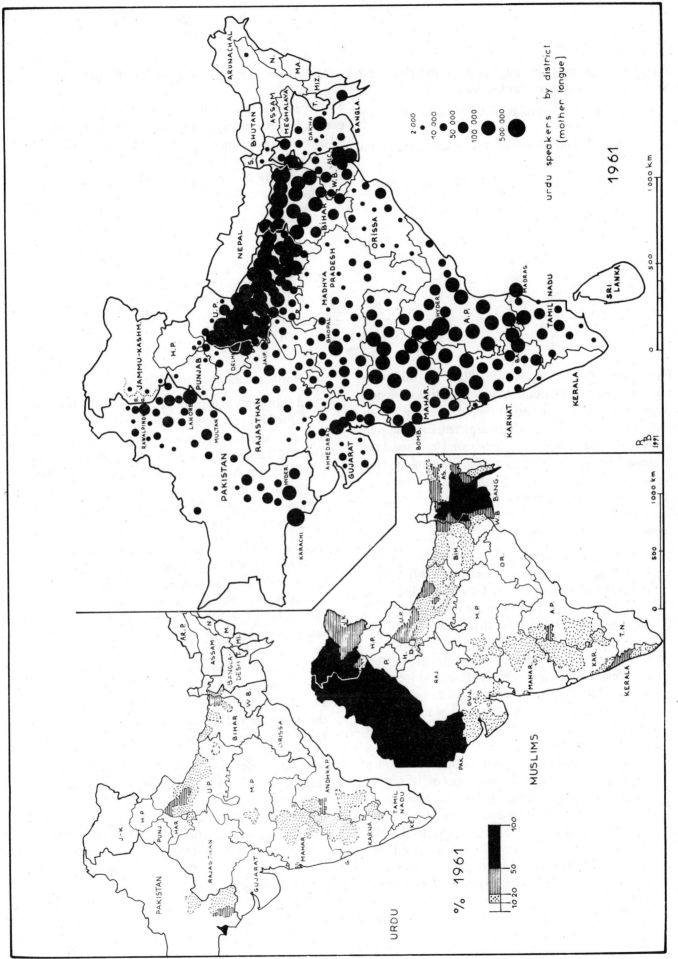

urdu speakers by district
(mother tongue)

2 000 ·
10 000 ·
50 000 ●
100 000 ●
500 000 ●

1961

1000 km

500

0

R
B
1971

MUSLIMS

% 1961

100

50

10 20

URDU

Plate 13: Urdu

Bangladesh, Assam, Tripura, Kerala, Tamil Nadu and Sri Lanka have other mother tongues:

Punjabi, Sindhi, Pushto, Baluchi, Brahui, and various Dardic languages in Pakistan,

Kashmiri, Punjabi, Shina, Burushaski, etc., in Jammu & Kashmir,

Bengali in West Bengal, Bangladesh, Assam and Tripura,

Malayalam in Kerala, and Tamil in Tamil Nadu and Sri Lanka.

However, in spite of these significant regional divergences, Urdu (besides Hindi) enjoys the widest diffusion all over the subcontinent as a mother tongue (and in fact in many areas ranks before Hindi), without taking into account its official stand as a second language in Pakistan and Jammu & Kashmir.

PLATE 14: URDU–HINDI

Following the conclusions from Plate 13, this plate highlights more precisions about the relative diffusion of the major twin languages of the subcontinent, Hindi and Urdu, in 1961. This has been depicted, first, through a mathematical ratio—the number of Urdu speakers against Hindi speakers, both as a mother tongue (the bigger map on the right) and as an additional language (the smaller map at the bottom left). A third map (at the top left) shows another ratio—the number of Urdu speakers against Muslims.

• The bigger map shows, at the district level, the ratio U/H (Urdu mother tongue speakers/Hindi mother tongue speakers) with a visual scale extending from U/H = 0.5 to U/H>10. The lower limit (U/H = 1) is indicated in central and eastern India by a dotted line and shows that Urdu speakers are less numerous than Hindi speakers all over the Hindi Belt, in most of West Bengal and the Northeast, and eastern Maharashtra. But everywhere else they outnumber Hindi speakers particularly in most of the Deccan, where the ratio is more than ten Urdu speakers for one Hindi speaker.

• At the provincial level, we can see (in the small map on the bottom right) that this ratio of 10:1 is as applicable in Andhra Pradesh, Karnataka and Tamil Nadu as it is in Pakistan and a ratio of 5:1 is applicable in Kerala, Maharashtra, Gujarat and Bangladesh. This leaves few provinces outside the Hindi Belt where Hindi mother tongue speakers outnumber Urdu speakers, i.e., in Orissa, West Bengal, the Northeast and Jammu & Kashmir.

• As a subsidiary language (the map on the bottom left), the U/H ratio seems to bring a different repartition at the provincial scale: Urdu outnumbers Hindi in Pakistan, Jammu & Kashmir, Bangladesh, Andhra Pradesh and Tamil Nadu. The rectangular surface areas make the proportion more accurate in each province where there are additional language speakers of Urdu and Hindi.

• The map on the top left of the plate dedicated to the U/M ratio (Urdu mother tongue speakers to Muslims) clearly shows that only in four southern states (Andhra Pradesh, Karnataka, Maharashtra and Orissa) Urdu speakers outnumber 80 per cent (ratio = 0.8) of the Muslims. In most of the Hindi Belt the ratio is between 0.5 and 0.8; in West Bengal, Rajasthan, Gujarat, Himachal Pradesh and Tamil Nadu, it is between 0.1 and 0.5; while elsewhere, i.e., in Pakistan, Jammu & Kashmir, Nepal, Bangladesh, the Northeast and Kerala, it is below 0.1 signifying that less than one out of ten Muslims speaks Urdu.

These maps based on the ratio of diffusion of the main twin languages show that the Muslim communities are the strongest agents of propagation of Hindustani outside the Hindi Belt particularly as a mother tongue. However, Hindi as an additional language is flourishing in the Northeast, Orissa and Deccan, comparable to (or even higher than) the standard it has already reached within the Hindi Belt.

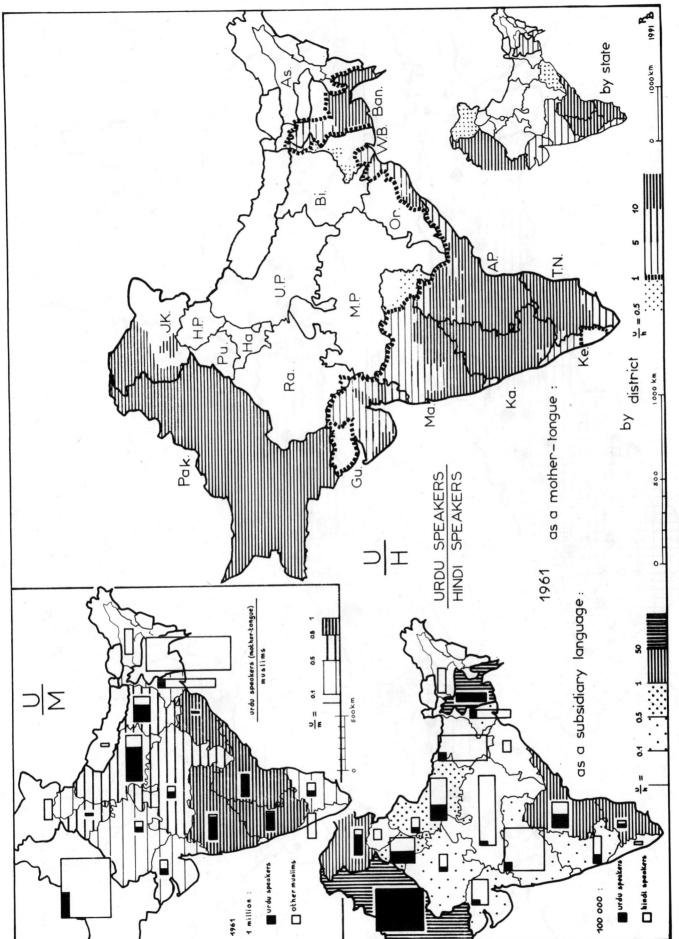

URDU SPEAKERS / HINDI SPEAKERS

U/H

1961   as a mother-tongue :

U/M

as a subsidiary language :

by district

by state

Plate 14: Urdu-Hindi

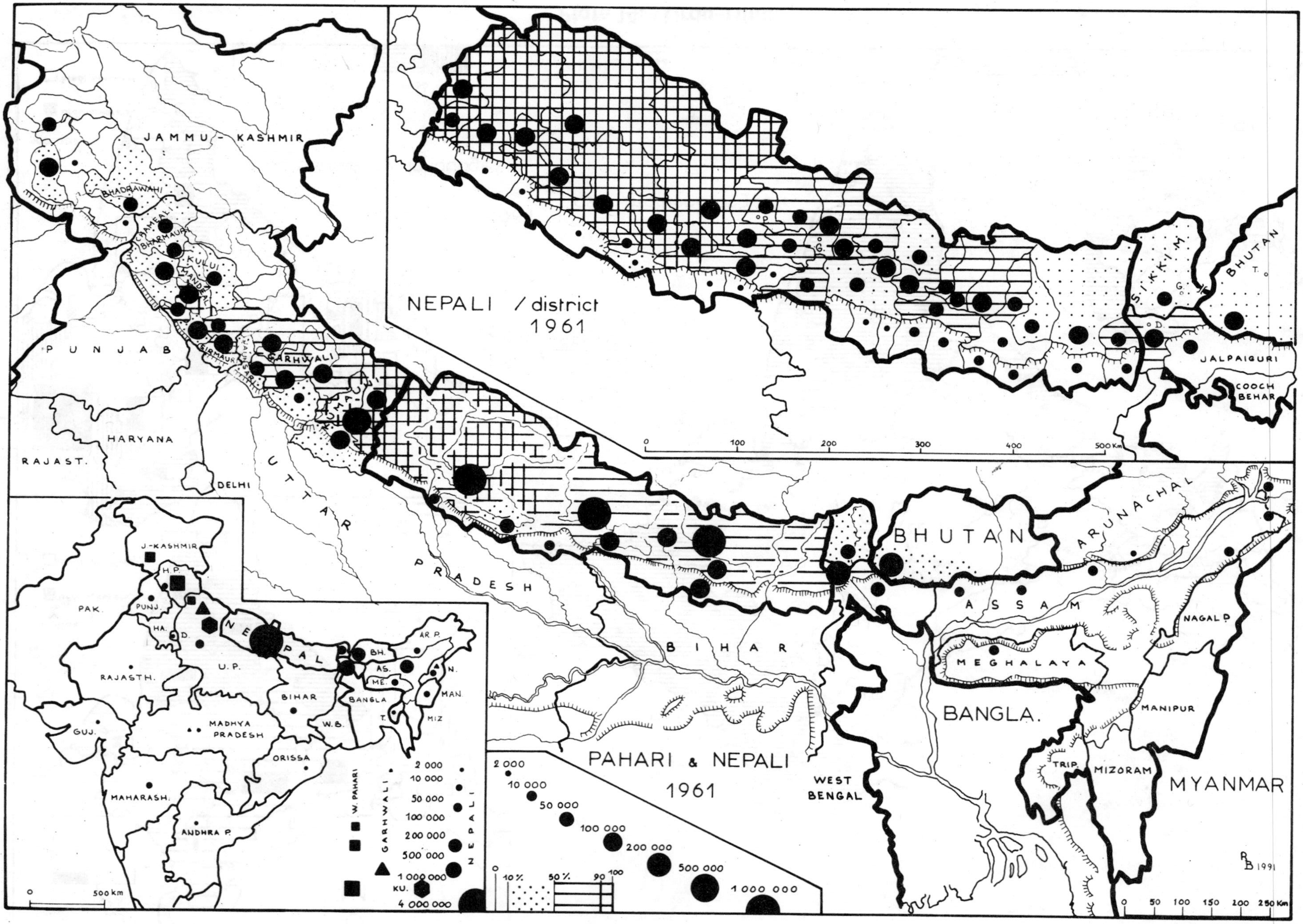

Plate 15: Pahari and Nepali

CHAPTER 8

THE HIMALAYAS AND THE NORTHEAST

PLATE 15: PAHARI AND NEPALI

Plate 15 deals with the geographical distribution of all Pahari speeches including the Nepali language in India, Nepal and Bhutan in 1961. Three dotted maps illustrate this distribution: the first map on the top right shows the distribution in the core area, mainly Nepal, the second map in the centre of the plate shows the distribution all along the Himalayan range, and the third map on the bottom left, shows the spread throughout the subcontinent. A scale of shading and dots is provided below.

- The first map shows both proportion and absolute volume of Nepali mother tongue speakers in Nepal, Sikkim, northwestern Bengal and Bhutan at the district level. It depicts the diffusion of the Nepali language all over the middle mountain zone from one end of Nepal to the other, and eastwards in the Darjeeling District of West Bengal, Sikkim and southern Bhutan. There is some minor penetration in the Terai lowlands of Nepal and in the Duars of Jalpaiguri District in West Bengal. A high proportion (more than 90 per cent) is found in western Nepal where no significant local tribe lives, followed by a sizeable concentration (from 50 per cent to 90 per cent) in central Nepal, the home of the biggest Gurkha tribes, and less than 50 per cent in eastern Nepal. However, an increasing proportion is being located in Darjeeling, the melting pot of all Nepalese immigrants who prefer Nepali to other ethnic languages.
- The map in the middle of the plate packs previous data from districts of Nepal at the regional level and adds western Pahari dialects from India extending from northern Uttar Pradesh (Kumauni, Garhwali and Jaunsari) and Himachal Pradesh (Sirmauri,

Mandeali, Kului, Bharmauri and Chameali) to Jammu & Kashmir (Bhadrawahi). In the east, the diffusion of Nepali (Gorkhali) is seen in Assam and other northeastern states such as Arunachal Pradesh and Meghalaya.
- The map on the left mentions the state- or province-wise stand of the main Pahari mother tongues: Nepali is represented by circles, Kumauni by hexagons, Garhwali by triangles and western Pahari by squares based on a common scale.

Based on the 1961 Census, Pahari/Nepali mother tongue speakers were 9,458 million all over the subcontinent, with the exception of the Bhutanese population where they could be more than 200,000. Of the 9,458 million, 3,541 million were eastern Pahari speakers (4,797 Nepali speakers in Nepal and 1,021 Gorkhali speakers in India). Other Pahari speakers numbered 3,541 million. There are two central Pahari dialects, Kumauni (1,030 million) and Garhwali (0.81 million), and many western Pahari languages: Jaunsari (54,000), Sirmauri (111,000), Mandeali (227,000), Kului (50,000), Bharmauri–Gaddi (56,000), Chameali (46,000) and Bhadrawahi (34,000). Further, there are 1,015 million unspecified Pahari speakers and 26,000 Mahasu Pahari ones, which should be geographically included in western Pahari.

It is important to further analyze how the census classification recognizes Gorkhali/Nepali as a separate language in India, added to the list of scheduled constitutional languages since 1991, and at the same time how it considers other central or western Pahari dialects as mother tongue *variants* to be grouped under the Hindi language along with other central Hindustani dialects.

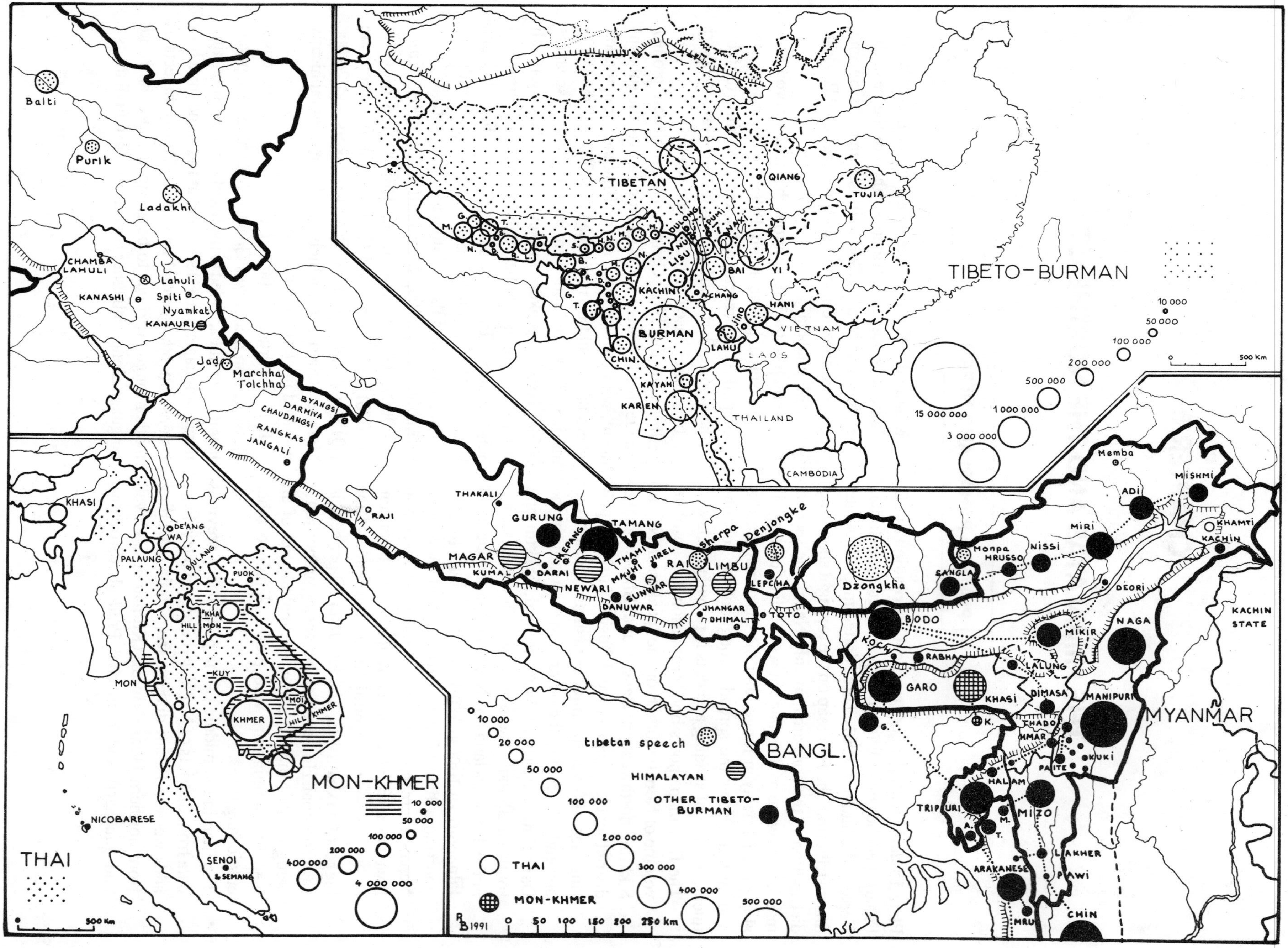

Plate 16: Tibeto-Burman, Mon-Khmer and Thai

PLATE 16: TIBETO-BURMAN, MON-KHMER AND THAI

Plate 16 illustrates the geographical distribution of languages belonging to the three families from the northeastern margins of the subcontinent, Tibeto-Burman, Mon-Khmer and Thai. Their settlement within the subcontinent (from the Himalayas to the Burma range) is detailed in the main map in the middle of the plate. The distribution of languages belonging to each of the language families is shown in two other maps: extending up to China for Tibeto-Burman (top right), and till Southeast Asia for Mon-Khmer and Thai (bottom left).

- The main map shows each of these languages, identified through proportional circles with various shadings: circles with a stippled effect for Tibetan, striped circles for 'pronominalized' Himalayish or Himalayan, black circles for other Tibeto-Burman languages, crisscrossed circles for Mon-Khmer, and outline circles for Thai. Languages spoken in various states are shown with differing radii, and languages belonging to the same group are linked by dotted lines.

Proper Tibetan languages/dialects extend from Jammu & Kashmir (Balti, Purik, Ladakhi) to Himachal Pradesh (Lahuli, Spiti), Uttar Pradesh (Jad, Marchha, Tolchha), Nepal (Sherpa and Jirel), Sikkim (Denjongke or Sikkim Bhotia), Bhutan (Dzongkha or Bhutanese) and Arunachal Pradesh (Monpa and Memba), although the latter two may be classified under the eastern Himalayan branch. Thakali, Gurung and Tamang, close to the Tibetan language from central Nepal and which were previously considered Himalayan languages, are now shown distinctly.

Himalayish (i.e., western Himalayish within the Bodish set) includes Chamba Lahuli, Kanashi and Kanauri in Himachal Pradesh; Byangsi, Darmiya, Chaudangsi, Rangkas and Jangali at the border of the Himalayan Uttar Pradesh and Nepal; and Thami in central Nepal. Eastern Himalayan (i.e., outside the Bodish set, halfway towards eastern Tibeto-Burman), on the other hand, may now include Raji, Magar, Chepang, Newari and Sunwar in central Nepal; Rai and Limbu in eastern Nepal; and maybe Dhimal as Toto and Kami in India. However, some of these languages, such as Magar and Newari, have long been differently classified. Lepcha from Sikkim, previously considered

similar to eastern Himalayan, now seems to be more akin to the Assam group.

Arunachal language group, or the Mirish group, integrates Hrusso (Aka), Nissi (Dafla), Miri, Adi (Abor) and Mishmi as also Sangla from Bhutan, though it appears to be closer to Tibetan.

Baric includes Deori, Lalung and Dimasa centred around Bodo; Koch and Rabha centred around Garo; and further south, Tripuri, better known as Kokborok. Mikir or Karbi seems to make up a proper group with Meithei or Manipuri.

About 24 Naga languages now seem to be divided into two sets: the first set in the northeast, around Konyak, is more akin to Bodo, and the second set in the southwest, around Sema and Angami, is significantly named Naga-Kuki because of its southern connections.

The Kuki-Chin set is increasingly considered to comprise three clusters: Kuki proper or 'Old Kuki' along with Vaiphei and Halam in the west, Kuki-Chin or 'New Kuki' around Thado, with Paite and many small units in the north, and Chin, with Hmar, Mizo (ex-Lushai), Lakher and Pawi in the south, linked to the numerous Chin units of the Chin state in western Myanmar.

The Burmese language branch is mainly represented by Arakanese, or Mogh or Marma, a dialect from the Chittagong Hill Tracts in Bangladesh, and by some minor related groups such as Mru, while Burmese-Yi is represented by Singpho, or Kachin, a minor offshoot of the main language from northern Myanmar (Kachin state) in southern Arunachal.

All these languages and ethnic groups make up the extreme southwestern advance or vanguard of the Tibeto-Burman family within the subcontinent through the western margins of Tibet, the southern sunny slopes of the Himalayas and the western Myanmar–India Hills.

A similar process of language spread, though in the opposite direction, is visible in the Southeast Asian peninsula among the sparsely populated Mon-Khmer and Thai groups. The Mon-Khmer subfamily from the Austro-Asiatic family (akin to the Munda subfamily as a result of this relation) is represented by Khasis in continental India and by Nicobarese in the islands. The Thai subfamily from the Daic or Zhuang–Dong family is typified by small Khampti groups in the Brahmaputra upper plains, as the former Ahom language of the founders of the Assam kingdom has become extinct.

- The map on the right situates most of the Tibeto-Burman languages in the subcontinent covering large areas in southwestern China and in the north-western Indo-Chinese peninsula. It shows that the Indian mountain areas are the actual confines of this huge area including the whole of Xizang (Tibet proper) and Qinghai provinces in China, the western parts of Sichuan and Yunnan, most of Myanmar and fringes of Thailand, plus some isolated outposts, or rearguards, such as Tujia in central China.

- The lower dotted map locates most of the languages belonging to the other two foreign language sub-families. Mon-Khmer subfamily is now restricted to Cambodia, the hilly areas of Vietnam, interiors of Laos and southeastern Myanmar (Mon state). Formerly, it covered most of Southeast Asia, before the advent of Tibeto-Burman and Thai peoples, in a settling continuum of which Khasi might have occupied the westernmost outpost. The Thai subfamily now spreads over most of Thailand, parts of north Vietnam (the former Thai region), eastern Myanmar (Shan state) and fringes in Yunnan (Xishuangbanna and Dehong autonomous prefectures).

The Southeast Asian peninsula, between the Indian subcontinent and China, has experienced many historical flows of population which have disrupted the original panorama of language about which linguists disagree and cannot give a very clear picture. But south of the large Sino-Tibetan set of languages including Chinese and Tibeto-Burman, there could be another set constituting the *Austric* super-family. This set may include all Austro-Asiatic, Austronesian, Miao-Yao and Zhuang-Dong (with Thai) languages; e.g., the formerly identified Austro-Asiatic branches like Munda and Mon-Khmer; plus more uncertain ones such as Vietnamese and Indonesian languages still spoken in Taiwan, the Vietnam Hills and from Malaya to Madagascar, as also the Micronesian and Polynesian languages. These units, among which linguists include Khasi from India with Vietnamese, have undergone as many splits due to the Tibeto-Burman or Thai invasions from (present) southern China as have the Dravidian and Munda groups in India, under pressure from the Indo-European invasions from central and western Asia.

PLATE 17: ARUNACHAL LANGUAGES

Plate 17 attempts to locate the various and less known languages in the Indian state of Arunachal Pradesh formed in 1972, formerly known as NEFA (North Eastern Frontier Agency). It comprises two maps: the main one displays each group and subgroup of population and language, and the inset map shows the physical location of the region.

- The inset map is mainly orographic, i.e., it mentions the altitude divide for this area within the Indian boundaries. It delineates the Brahmaputra plains in Assam, below 200 metres over sea level (shaded with a stippled effect), and the rapid increase in altitude in the eastern reaches of the Himalayan range, from 2,000 to over 4,000 metres where most of the international border with China is located according to the MacMahon Line (delineated at the Simla Conference held in 1914). China, however, does not recognize this and keeps claiming a border that runs mainly along the foothills instead (shown by a dotted line in the main map). This map also shows the boundaries of Bhutan, surrounding provinces of India, and the five former frontier divisions of NEFA, replaced by present districts of Arunachal Pradesh which are marked in the main map.

- The main map aims at showing the complex ethnic division of the population, its settlement in the mountains and, above all, the relationship between new and old group designations in ethnic and linguistic contexts that is needed for any rational overview to understand their future classification.

Main language designations are written in bold type face along with formerly used names (given in brackets) which may now be erroneous (derogatory, etc.) or simply the proper ethnic (tribal) designation. Names of smaller units, ethnic or linguistic (dialectal), are mentioned in light type face. Various shadings show the linguistic connection between groups and subgroups. The basic location of tribes has been drawn mainly from notional maps of the 1961 Census of India (Vol. I, Part

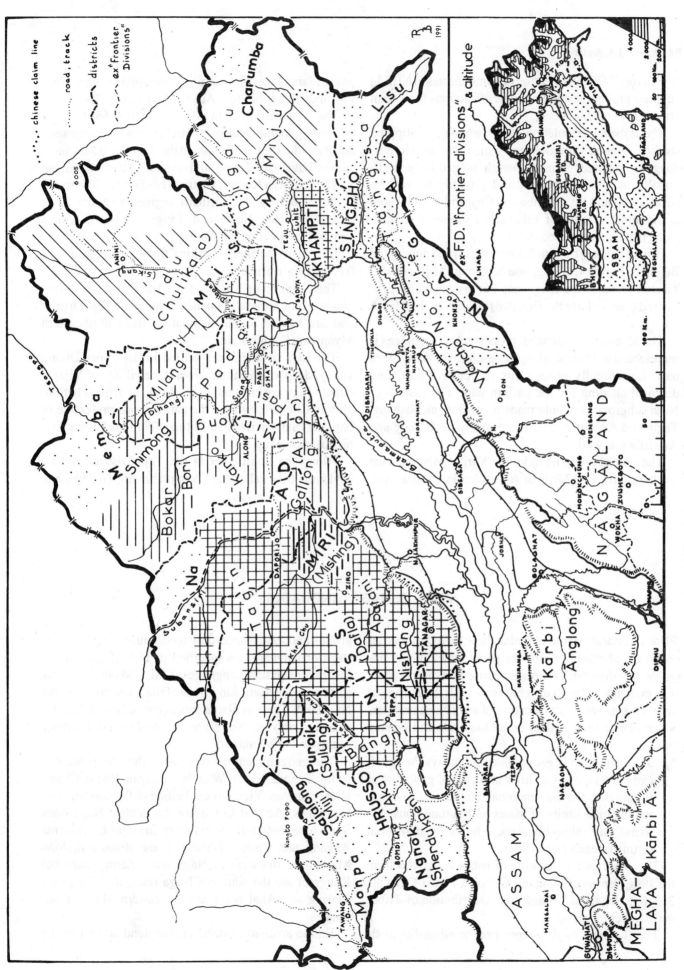

Plate 17: Arunachal Languages

II-C (ii) pp. 358–59: Location of communities in NEFA) but their groupings and linguistic affiliations have been drawn from other sources.

The Tibetan population is shown with a stippled shading: Ngnok (Sherdukpen) which may be close to Sangla in Bhutan; Monpa, though alleged to be traditionally akin to Tibetan, could possibly be eastern Himalayan; and Na, Memba and Charumba, all located in the upper reaches of valleys and supposed to have come from across the border.

Hrusso (spoken by both dominant Akas and dominated Buguns), Puroik (Sulung) and Sajalong (Miji) are still Tibetan unclassified languages but are generally considered (particularly the first two) as units of the Mirish set.

The Mirish (or Arunachal proper) set of languages is represented by three shadings: crisscross for the western part, horizontally striped for the central part, and diagonal shading for the eastern part. The eastern or Nissi subgroup is mainly made up of Bangni, Nishang, Tagin and Apatani tribes, and possibly the Sulung and Aka tribes as well.

The central group includes the Miri or Mishing tribe (including the Hill Miris of Arunachal Pradesh as well as the Plains Miris of Assam) and the Adi (ex-Abor) split into about ten tribes (the Adi-Gallongs, Adi-Pasis, etc.).

The eastern group, or Mishmi, is divided along a clear-cut geographical and dialectal tripartition between northern Idu (the Chulikatas and the dominated Mithuns), central Digaru, or Taaon, and southern Miju, or Kaman.

The southern Khonsa District (ex-Tirap F D) is mainly populated by the northern segments of the Naga tribes: Wancho, Nocte and Tangsa (denoted with a second type of stippled shading).

But, in its northern margins three small groups of foreign origin are settled:

The Singpho or Kachin, from the Burmese-Yi language group, are settled on the border of the Teju District and are related to the population from northeastern Myanmar (Kachin state).

The Lisu or Yobin are settled in the upper Diyum valley, deep in Myanmar, around the village of Vijayanagar. They are kinsmen of the Lisu, an official nationality in China, for whom the autonomous prefecture of Nujiang (Salwen river) in Yunnan (Nujiang Lisuzu Zizhizou) was set up.

Along the Luhit river in the Teju District, lives a Myanmar tribe called the Khampti having Thai kinship.

PLATE 18: NAGA LANGUAGES

Plate 18 endeavours to elucidate how the Naga mother tongues and ethnic groups are geographically and linguistically divided. Two maps are used for this purpose. The main map (drawn on a big scale with shaded areas) shows the geographical location of each Naga unit, and the inset map depicts their broad linguistic and kinship link.

• The main map is geographical (displays the relief, main rivers, railway lines and cities), geopolitical (highlights the international boundaries and administrative limits of states and autonomous districts) and ethno-linguistic (shows the territorial setting of each Naga tribe).

The geographical location of tribes is derived from the 1961 Census of India maps (Vol. I, Part II-C (ii) pp. 362–63: Nagaland Village-wise Distribution of Tribes and Mother tongues).

The shadings used to represent the ethno-linguistic groups are chosen according to the main linguistic kinships of languages as specified in 1991 at the Central Institute of Indian Languages (CIIL), Mysore: central, eastern and western subgroups of the Naga group within Nagaland. There is also a less accurate and delineated shading outside Nagaland in Arunachal Pradesh, Manipur and Myanmar.

The geographical distribution is thus from north to south: Tangsa, Nocte, Wancho, Konyak, Phom, Chang, Khiemnungan, Yimchungre belong to the eastern Naga languages; Ao and Lotha are the central Naga ones; Sema (one central area with four main outposts), Rengma, Angami and Chokri, Khezha, Pome (Paomata), Mao, Maram are the western Naga ones; Zemi, Liangmei, Rongmei are the southern Naga ones; and Tangkhul, Maring and Anal Naga are the eastern Manipur languages.

Ethnic areas mentioned in Nagaland show how the

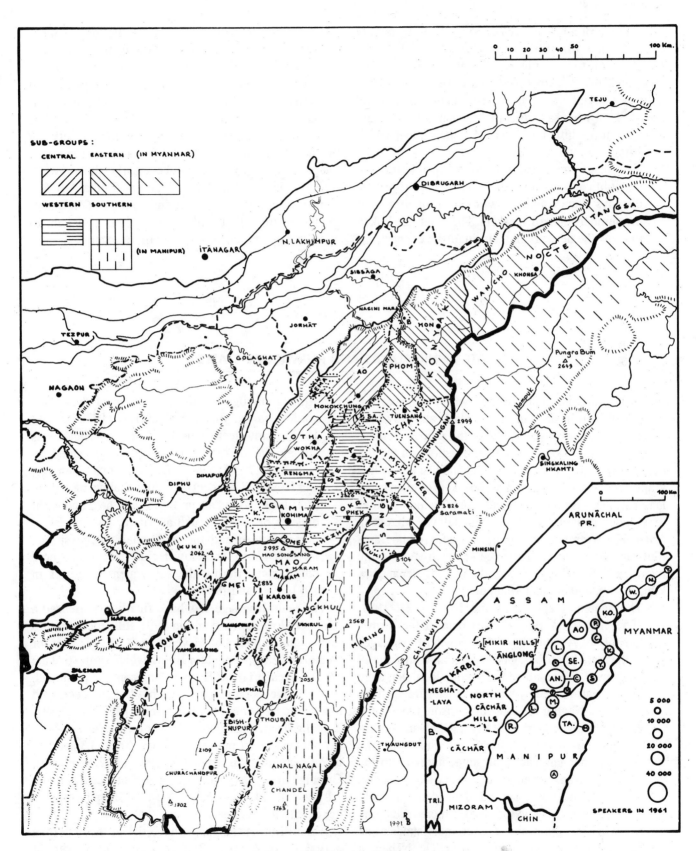

Plate 18: Naga Languages

delimitation of its new seven districts (there were only three districts till 1961) is an attempt to follow the puzzling ethnic divide of the province. Outside Nagaland, the Naga-peopled area covers most of the three new peripheral northern districts of Manipur and the whole of Khonsa district in Arunachal Pradesh, not to mention the hills bordering Myanmar about which scant information is available.

* The inset map, apart from recapitulating the geopolitical (basically ethnic) setting of the region, displays Naga languages with dots proportional to the numbers of their speakers. These dots are linked to show the network of their linguistic connections

according to CIIL data in 1991. Following more recent attempts to classify them, these linkages could be improved by adding Ao to the eastern (Konyak) languages' chain, while Tangkhul and Maring (from Manipur), and Lotha and Khiemnungan should be linked to the Sema (or western) group.

In this way the possible twofold distribution between the northeastern (Bara-Konyak?) and southwestern (Naga-Kuki?) groups could be clearly shown when splitting the previous central group (Lotha-Ao) and merging the western (Sema) and southern (Ze-Liang) groups. Further linguistic specifications will help to make this geographical mapping more accurate.

PLATE 19: HIMALAYAS AND PURVACHAL STATES

Plate 19 records the quantitative growth of language use, through the census data, in various states and provinces of the eastern Himalayan region of the subcontinent

A small-scale sketch map of the region, on the top right, shows the geopolitical setting and just below it, a graph denotes the change among speakers of main tribal languages in Assam in the broad sense (including states to secede from it later, i.e., Meghalaya, Mizoram, Nagaland) over half a century. Various ethnograms illustrate the changing language stand in each of the main territorial components of the region: Nepal, Sikkim, Assam, Tripura and Manipur.

* The general graph, using the 1911, 1921, 1931, 1951, 1961 and 1971 Census data of the former territory of Assam, shows the growth of languages of the main hill tribes. One exception, with actually no growth, is Santali which is not a local language but was introduced by workers of tea gardens from the Chota Nagpur area. In comparison, there is the example of Manipuri and Oriya, which are the immigrant but non-tribal languages shown on the graph. Other languages, all autochthonous to the region, with an uneven stagnation or a slow increase earlier, have known since Independence a rapid growth: an earlier one for Mizo, a more recent one for Miri and Mikir, and an even more sudden one for Khasi, Garo and Bodo, as well as Nepali, a non-tribal language but a shared lingua franca for many immigrant tribal groups coming from Nepal.

* Among ethnograms, the one on Nepal shows, according to the first two Censuses (1952–54 and 1961), a slow decrease in Tibeto-Burman languages among the more consistent sets represented by Nepali (48.7 to 51 per cent), the national language, and Hindi (28 per cent) provided that we include in this designation, as in India, all the Hindustani dialects or variants such as Tharu, Avadhi, Bhojpuri, Maithili and the colloquial village speech forms (*Dehati*). This slow decline has become more conspicuous during the subsequent Censuses in 1971, 1981 and 1991.

The main language sets have finally experienced a relatively low increase and in 1991 still stood close to their initial numbers of 41 years ago (50.3 per cent for Nepali and 28.4 per cent for Hindi) which shows that the erosion of each Tibeto-Burman language is widespread. The relative percentage of each of them decreased among the Nepalese population from 1952–54 to 1991: Tamang (from 6 per cent to 4.9 per cent), Newari (from 4.7 per cent to 3.7 per cent), Magari (from 3.3 per cent to 2.3 per cent), Rai (from 2.9 per cent to 2.4 per cent), Gurung (from 2 per cent to 1.2 per cent), Limbu (from 1.8 per cent to 1.4 per cent) and Bhote-Sherpa (from 0.9 per cent to 0.7 per cent).

Tibeto-Burman languages have, during the same time period, decreased from 21.8 per cent to 17 per cent of the whole population, in consonance with the constant centuries-old language shift from tribal ethnic mother

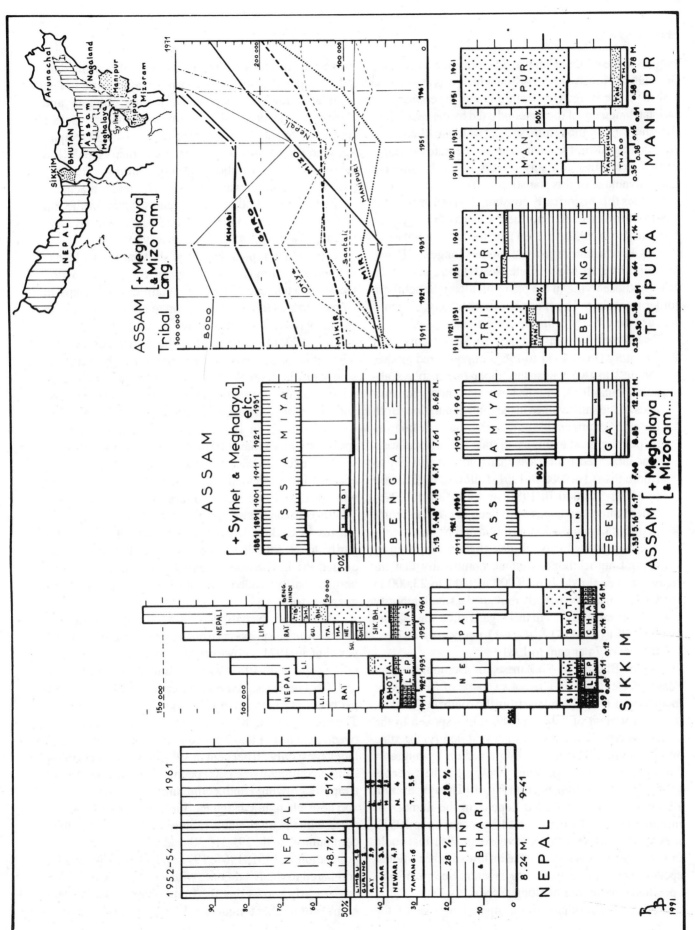

Plate 19: Himalayas and Purvachal States

tongues to the national language Gurkha. It is also called Gorkhali or Nepali or Khas-Kura which was at the same time the shared lingua franca throughout the country, the national language of the state and used by the educational system. Even though these relatively small changes in percentage do not result in disaster, the state language, already prevailing in many sectors of the population, takes advantage of this statistical shift.

Besides this historically constant but slow erosion of Tibeto- Burman local minorities, the steady position (28 per cent from 1952 to 1991) of the total number of various Hindustani registered mother tongues (Tharu, Avadhi, Bhojpuri, Maithili, etc.) leads us to consider the fact that those living in the plains all along the southern border may claim Hindi as their mother tongue even if they use the closely connected Nepali language.

• The two ethnograms dealing with Sikkim cover half a century (from 1911 to 1961) of registered mother tongues in two ways: the upper one displays absolute quantities, and the lower one shows percentages of the same values in the total population. Both the ethnograms enable us to notice the basic linguistic development in this small state with a population that increased from (less than) 90,000 in 1911 to (more than) 160,000 in 1961, followed by 210,000 in 1971, 316,000 in 1981, and 406,000 in 1991, where three languages have been in constant competition: Lepcha, Sikkim Bhotia and Nepali.

Lepcha, or Rong by its self-designation, is spoken by the central autochthonous ethnic community that increased rather slowly from 9,000 in 1911 to 23,000 in 1981, but which consistently remained a small minority in its homeland and was in this regard quite stable from 1911 to 1971 (11–11–12–10–9–11 per cent), however, it declined to 7 per cent in 1981.

Sikkim Bhotia, or Sikkimese, or Denjongke (language of Denjong, an alternative name of Sikkim), or incorrectly Lhoke (language from the south, in Tibetan), the local variant of Tibetan (Bhotia), is spoken in the upper reaches of valleys, by the royal family, the state and in monasteries, and easily picked up by migrants from other Tibetan-speaking areas, e.g., the Sherpas from Nepal or refugees from Tibet. Though Sikkim Bhotia scarcely superseded Lepcha in the number of mother tongue speakers (about 10 per cent up to 1951), it experienced a significant increase in 1961 that could only be partly explained by the inflow of other Bhotia-speaking people, registered as Tibetan, Sherpa or 'unspecified Bhotia' mother tongue speakers.

Nepali, or Gorkhali, is the main language of the numerous migrants who came from neighbouring densely populated valleys of eastern Nepal to settle in less populated regions such as Darjeeling, Bhutan and Assam. However, until 1951, most of these Nepalese migrants (i.e., 60,000 migrants as against 40,000 Nepali speakers) stated mother tongues other than Nepali: Rai (about 20,000), Limbu (15,000), Gurung, Tamang, Magar Newari, Sunwar, etc. In 1961, Nepali reached a total of about 75,000 mother tongue speakers while Rai and Limbu fell to 3,000 and 5,000 respectively, and Gurung, Tamang, etc., became nearly extinct.

This sudden typical language shift can easily be explained by willingly stated language transfers, showing the shared tendency of all mountain ethnic groups in Nepal towards their acculturation to Nepali, and which is accelerated abroad among migrants from mixed origins. Sikkim, in particular, illustrated this process when many legal steps were undertaken to grant citizenship to resident Nepalese and an official status to Nepali, which was already the lingua franca in the lower reaches and the second language for administrative purposes.

Interestingly, in 1951 all Nepalese languages were spoken by more than 110,000 people and in 1961 they scarcely exceeded 80,000. This loss could only be accounted in the sudden gain noticed in Sikkim Bhotia which showed that the acculturation of various small Tibeto-Burman-speaking groups to the dominant languages in Sikkim led them partly to Sikkimese and partly to Nepali. Both these official languages thus eroded the in- between migrant ethnic languages and perhaps partly eroded the autochthonous Lepcha language as well.

After 1961, Nepali, has increased its position in mother tongue speakers (from 46 per cent in 1961 to 64 per cent in 1971), however, it somehow decreased to 60.47 per cent in 1981, while Bhotia, including Sherpa and Tibetan, registered a significant decrease (from 36 per cent to 11 per cent in 1971 and 12 per cent in 1981). The remaining mother tongue speakers are divided between Lepcha (11 and 7 per cent) and other non-official languages: only 20 per cent in 1981 including a reviving Limbu community (20,000 people, i.e., 6 per cent) and a rapidly growing Hindi community (5 per cent).

These changing language kinships could be compared with the more stable religious ones. The Buddhist community, with 29, 31, 30 and 29 per cent of the population in 1951, 1961, 1971 and 1981 respectively, compared to the Hindu one, with 71, 67, 69 and 67 per cent, clearly shows that the first one exceeds the total number of mother tongue speakers of the two traditionally Buddhist peoples, Lepchas and Bhotias (23 per cent in 1971 and 19 per cent in 1981). This indicates that, between both alleged Bhotia-Lepcha and Nepali ethnolinguistic sets, there is still a fringe of people among whom mother tongue and religious affiliations are neither corresponding nor stable, but seem contradictory and moving.

• Both the Assam ethnograms are based on two different statistical series of the pre- and post-Partition territories of the province. The upper one (belonging to the pre-Partition period from 1881 to 1931 illustrates larger Assam including the densely populated Bengali-speaking Sylhet District, now in Pakistan. The lower one is that of the 1961 post-Partition smaller Assam province from which Meghalaya, Mizoram and Nagaland have later been withdrawn. All pre- and post-Partition (from 1911 to 1931, and from 1951 to 1961) figures are according to one of these two delineations.

Thus, the first ethnogram shows a large Assam province where Bengali was the language of almost half the population, and where both Assamiya or Assamese (from 28 to 23 per cent) and Bengali (from 50 to 46 per cent) decreased slightly when faced with an inflow of immigrants and consequently stronger numbers of the hill peoples. The second ethnogram shows a new Assam province without Sylhet, where the strong stand of Bengali has declined in the south in the Cachar District as well as in the north among the Brahmaputra valley immigrants.

A fact worth noting is that, between 1931 and 1951, there was a large and sudden increase in the Assamese mother tongue population which wins the absolute majority while Bengali speakers are significantly below their pre-Partition level (though they stand within the same administrative limits). Also observed was a reversal of the tendency of both languages to be constant: Assamese increased after having decreased while Bengali decreased after having increased. This change is due to the mass shift to Assamese by the Bengali migrants' children in the Brahmaputra valley.

• In Tripura (1911–61), another land for Bengali immigration, the process was different. Before Partition the balance was relatively even between the autochthonous Tripuri-speaking hill people (from the Tibeto-Burman family) and the Bengali population from the plains, though the former were decreasing slowly (from 41 to 39 per cent) while the latter were increasing (from 43 to 45 per cent). After Partition the Bengali population, as a result of mass inflows of refugees, increased from 61 to 65 per cent, while the Tripuris exhibited a marginal increase from 23 to 25 per cent. Since then, the Bengali net majority has increased to 68.8 and 69.1 per cent in 1971 and 1981 respectively, and the Tripuris have decreased to 23 per cent.

• In Manipur (1911–61), the Manipuris or Meitheis (of Tibeto-Burman linguistic kinships, settled in the central valley) are Hindus and the dominant people and played a predominant role as their numerical strength increased from 61 to 65 per cent. Thus various surrounding hill peoples could only keep, at best, a divided minority, whether they were of Naga or Kuki kinship, just as the Tangkhul in the north and the Thado in the south. In 1971 and 1981 the Manipuri mother tongue started to total 63 and 62 per cent respectively in favour of smaller groups, while Tangkhul and Thado became stable (10 per cent altogether).

All these diagrams illustrate complex language dynamics, matching various developments in the territorial spread, demographic increase and cultural shifts, which differently affect hill and plain peoples, including those who have been settled for long and those only recently. The status and development of each language, whether it is official, e.g., Assamese, Bengali, Nepali and Manipuri, or otherwise, are to be ranked among the most conclusive factors.

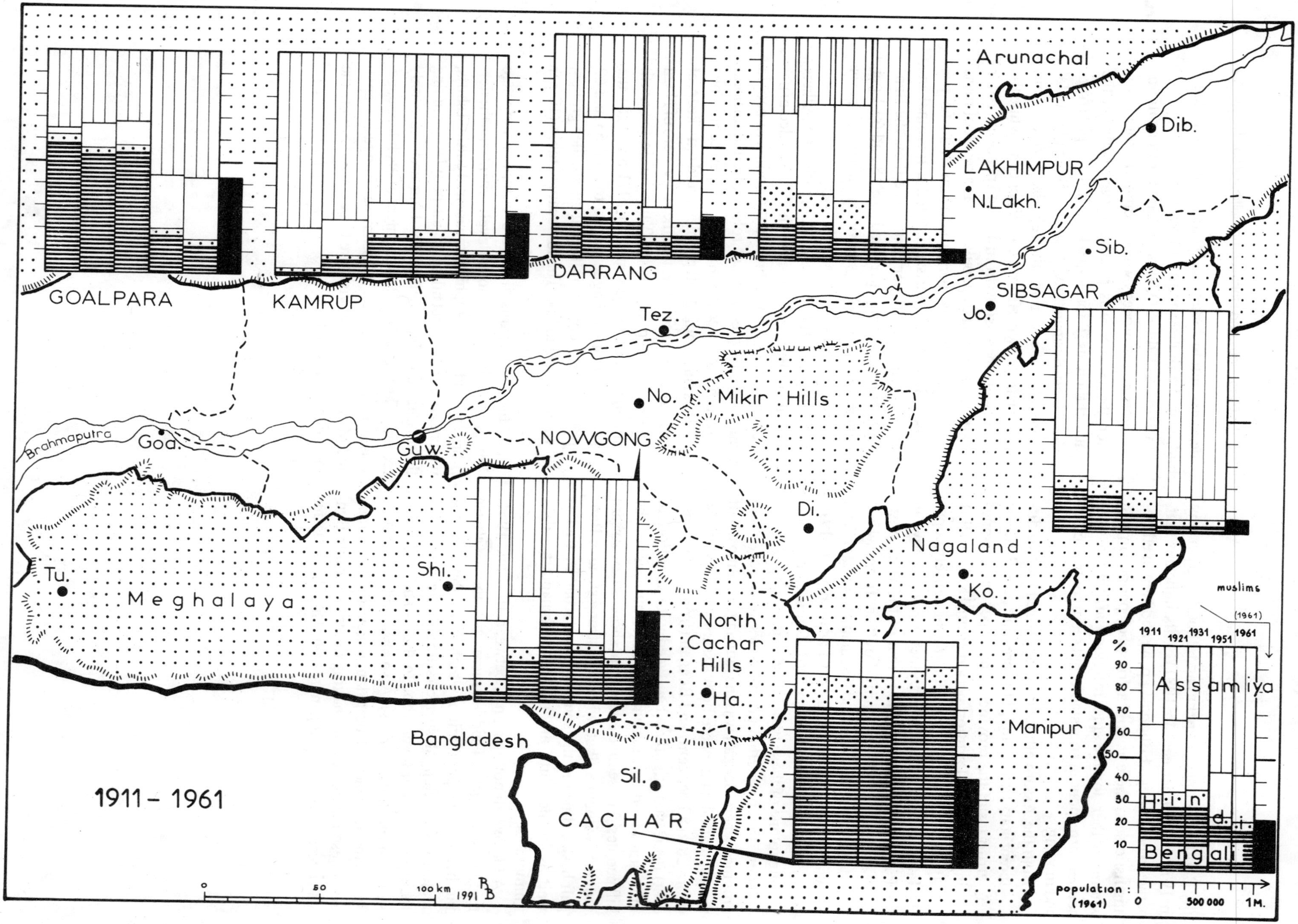

Plate 20: Assam Plains

1911 – 1961

PLATE 20: ASSAM PLAINS

Plate 20 deals with the central region of Assam state, i.e., the Brahmaputra and Cachar plains where most of the state's population resides, out of the Hill Districts (the Mikir Hills, now Karbi Anglong, and the North Cachar Hills). On a simplified map of this area, each of the former seven plains districts (the Brahmaputra plain now has 14 districts, and the Cachar plain, two) is shown through an ethnogram which illustrates the development of the percentage of mother tongue speakers during five successive Censuses (1911, 1921, 1931, 1951, 1961), as also the percentage of Muslims in 1961. At the bottom right another ethnogram displays the same data for the whole province of Assam.

* The ethnogram of the Assam province is basically similar to the one on Plate 19 called 'Assam [+ Meghalaya and Mizoram...]'. It is based on the population of Assam within its 1947–62 boundaries before the states of Nagaland, Meghalaya and Mizoram were defined. Each column is divided according to the percentage of mother tongue speakers: Assamese (Assamiya) at the top, the two other main languages, Bengali and Hindi at the bottom, while the blank portion in the middle represents Urdu and various languages of the hill peoples, either spoken in their homeland or brought into the plains by immigrants.

Plate 19 also indicates the sudden increase after Partition in Assamese speakers and the reversal of growth patterns, before and after this event: Assamese experienced a relative decrease followed by an increase and Bengali, an initial increase followed by a decrease. Both these facts reflect the significant acculturation of foreign settlers to Assamese, the predominant language in the state. The 1961 comparison with Muslims shows that they outnumbered Bengali speakers. What this does confirm is the universal rule of acculturation according to which immigrants and their descendants may give up their linguistic identity relatively more easily than their religious one. District ethnograms in this plate detail these facts. The descendants of former migrants from present Bangladesh who have adopted Assamese as their mother tongue but remained Muslims is a clear example.

* Each district ethnogram is based on the same rules as those followed for the Assam state and the width of columns is proportionate to the population of the district in 1961.

Goalpara (now divided into four districts) is that part of Assam which is closest to Bengal and is also the main entry point of incoming Bengali settlers. The majority of population prior to Partition spoke Bengali. Subsequently there was a shift to Assamese—a fact that cannot be explained only due to the migration of Bengali Muslims to Eastern Pakistan (i.e., Bangladesh) but which must also take into account the acculturation of a significant proportion of incoming migrants to Assamese. The 1961 comparison between percentage of Bengali speakers (12 per cent) and Muslims (43 per cent) shows that most of the Bengali-speaking population had shifted to the provincial language, which as a matter of fact, was close to their own native dialects (e.g. Mymensingha).

The same phenomenon can be noticed to a lesser extent in other districts in the middle Brahmaputra valley such as Kamrup, Nowgong, Darrang and Sibsagar, where Bengali speakers decreased in percentage and were barely half the Muslim population. Prior to Partition, in the remote eastern Lakhimpur District, Bengali migrants were outnumbered by Hindi speakers from Bihar and their current declining number is even below that of Muslims. This most probably is because of the conversion to Hinduism among Bengali city elite more than that among rural Bengali settlers.

Cachar District (now divided into two districts), situated south of the North Cachar Hills, geographically belongs to the Bengal plains and has always been part of the Bengali-speaking area. The Assamese language is of minor significance in this area and was spoken as a mother tongue by only 0.2 to 0.3 per cent from 1911 to 1961 while Bengali was increasingly spoken since Partition at the expense of Hindi and the languages of the hill tribes. Since 1961 (Amendment to Assam Official Language Act), Bengali is the administrative language of this area. And the fact that more than half the Bengali speakers are Hindus is not only explained by the inflow of Bengali Hindus since Partition but also by the later historical Islamization of this far eastern part of remote Bengali lands.

Assam has over half a century definitely included more Assamese speakers except for the southern plain which is Bengali-speaking. This is a result of a significant decline of Bengali in the Brahmaputra plains accompanied by a steady persistence of Hindi, Urdu and languages of the hill peoples.

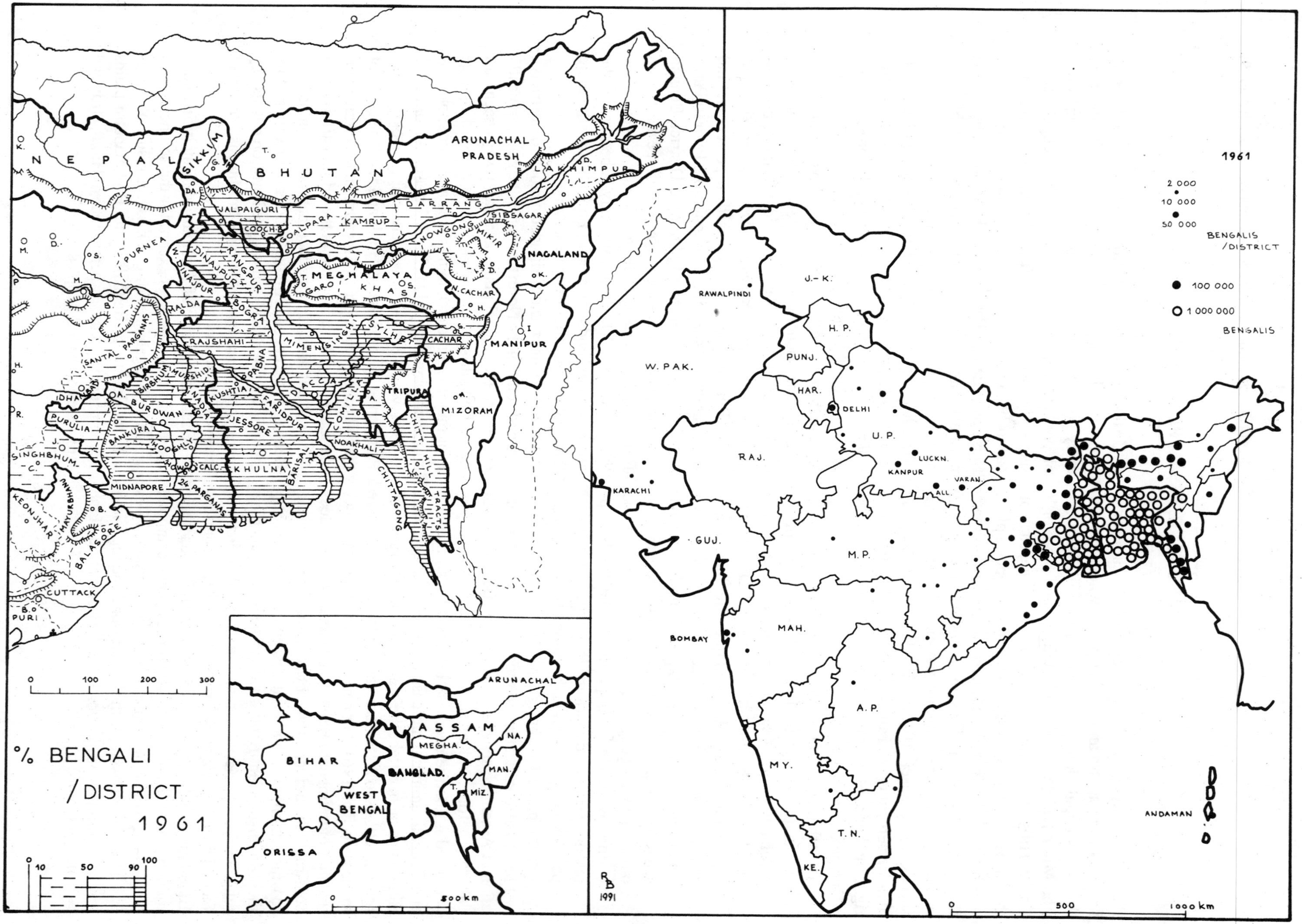

Plate 21: Bengali

1961

BENGALIS
/DISTRICT

BENGALIS

2 000
10 000
50 000

● 100 000
○ 1 000 000

% BENGALI
/DISTRICT
1961

10   50   90   100

0   100   200   300

ANDAMAN

1000 km

500

0

RAWALPINDI

W. PAK.

KARACHI

J.-K.

H.P.

PUNJ.

HAR.   DELHI

RAJ.

U.P.

LUCKN.

KANPUR

VARAN.

ALL.

GUJ.

M.P.

MAH.

BOMBAY

A.P.

M.Y.

T.N.

KE.

R
B
1991

NEPAL

SIKKIM

BHUTAN

ARUNACHAL
PRADESH

DARRANG

LAKIMPUR

SIBSAGAR

NOWGONG

KAMRUP

GOALPARA

MIKIR

KHAS.

N. CACHAR

NAGALAND

CACHAR

MANIPUR

MIZORAM

TRIPURA

MEGHALAYA

GARO   KHAS.

JALPAIGURI

COOCHBEHAR

PURNEA

W. DINAJPUR

RANGPUR

DINAJPUR

BOGRA

RAJSHAHI

PABNA

MYMENSINGH

KUSHTIA   FARIDPUR

JESSORE

NADIA

KHULNA

BARISAL

NOAKHALI

COMILLA

CHITTAGONG

CHITT. HILL TRACTS

MURSHIDABAD

BIRBHUM

BURDWAN

HOOGLY

CALC.

24 PARGANAS

BANKURA

MIDNAPORE

PURULIA

SANTAL PARGANAS

SINGHBHUM

KEONJHAR

MAYURBHANJ

BALASORE

CUTTACK

PURI

NEPAL

ARUNACHAL

A S S A M   NA.

MEGHA.   MAN.

T   MIZ.

BANGLAD.

BIHAR

WEST
BENGAL

ORISSA

500 km

100
90
50
10

CHAPTER 9

THE PERIPHERAL INDO-ARYAN AND THE CENTRAL ADIVASI BELTS

PLATE 21: BENGALI

Plate 21 deals with Bengali with the help of three maps: a regional shaded one on the top left, a subcontinental dotted one on the right and a small geopolitical sketch map in the centre.

- The sketch map draws the political setting of the historical Bengal region which, until the beginning of the century, included Assam and surrounding hilly areas, Bihar and Orissa. Through various Partitions (1905, 1912, 1947, 1971), this region was shaped into West Bengal, Bangladesh, Tripura, and the Cachar region in Assam.

- The regional map, with political boundaries and main orohydrographic traits, clearly shows (through shadings of 10, 50 and 90 per cent) that the proportion of Bengali speakers at the district level closely fits within the borders of West Bengal and Bangladesh which are mostly delineated by various foothills: Chota Nagpur in the west, Himalayas in the north, and Meghalaya and Purvachal in the east. Bengal lies in the delta region shared by the Ganges and the Brahmaputra. Throughout Bangladesh and in most of West Bengal, Bengali speakers comprise more than 90 per cent of the population—with the exception of the Duar-Terai region (Jalpaiguri 56 per cent), Ganga Barhind terraces (West Dinapur and Malda), Damodar basin (Burdwan 82 per cent, Hooghly 88 per cent, Howrah 85 per cent), Calcutta (64 per cent) and Purulia plateau (83 per cent), where various groups of people coming from the west have settled in either rural or industrial areas.

As seen previously, the Bengali settlement is predominant in Cachar District of Assam state (see Plate 20) and in the Tripura state (see Plate 19), and is now a declining minority in the Assam Brahmaputra valley (Plate 20). It has also extended up to Chota Nagpur's hilly areas (Santal Parganas, 13 per cent, Dhanbad, 12 per cent and Singhbhum, 21 per cent) primarily because there was need for industrial skilled labour in this region: Jamshedpur had 25 per cent Bengali speakers and 39 per cent Hindi speakers in 1951.

- The dotted map of the subcontinent displays Bengali speakers with two types of symbols: white circles (denoting 1 million people) and black dots (the bigger ones representing 100,000, the middle-sized ones denoting 10,000 to 50,000 and the small ones denoting 2,000 to 10,000). This representation enables us to appreciate the high concentration of population within the delta and a diffused one just around it, i.e., in Assam, Bihar and Orissa. A sprinkling is also visible all over the subcontinent: in the big cities along the Ganga plains and in many other urban centres within and outside India. This Bengali *diaspora* illustrates the propagation of the language in most parts of eastern India, among clerks, officers, managers and executives, by those in the civil service as also by business companies, and in areas where education was previously less widespread.

Plate 22: Oriya and Assamiya

Legend:
- ASSAMIYA (ASSAMESE)
- ORIYA
- Jungle tracts

Scale: 0 100 200 300 400 500 km

Main map labels: SIANG, LUHIT, SUBANSIRI, KAMENG, T.A., N.T., NAGALAND, BHUTAN, MIKIR, N.CACHAR, MANIPUR, MEGHALAYA, SYLHET, CACHAR, MIZO, TRIPURA, NEPAL, SIKKIM, MYMENSINGH, DACCA, CH., MITHILA, M. OD., MAGADHA, CHOTA NAGPUR, WEST BENGAL, CALCUTTA, SINGHBHUM, BALASORE, CUTTACK, BHUBANESWAR, KONARAK, PURI, BERHAMPUR, SRIKAKULAM, VIZAG., CHHATTISGARH, RAIPUR, DURG, BHILAI, BASTAR, NAGPUR, HYDERABAD

Rivers/places: Brahmaputra, Ganga, M. Ganga, Mahanadi

Inset (upper left): ASSAMESE — speakers / district 1961
Circle sizes: 2 000; 10 000; 50 000; 100 000; 200 000; 500 000; 1 000 000; 2 000 000

Inset (lower left): ORIYA — speakers / district 1961
Labels: UTTAR PRADESH, BIHAR, MADHYA PRADESH, MAHARASHTRA, ANDHRA P., BANGLADESH, ASSAM, AR. PR., NA., MA., MI., ME.
Scale: 0 500 km

Inset (center right): oriya / assamese — % 1961
Scale: 0 10 50% 90 100

R.B. 1991

PLATE 22: ORIYA AND ASSAMIYA

Plate 22 presents two eastern Indo-Aryan languages closely related to Bengali: Oriya on its southwest, and Assamiya, or Assamese, on its northeast which have a far less audience and spread. The percentage of mother tongue speakers according to districts is shown through a common regional map, spread diagonally across the plate, displaying the local distribution of both languages; two inset maps of Oriya, given on the top left, and Assamese, given below on the right; and two sketch maps, given below in the centre.

- The central regional map traces the natural and human background of the distribution of these languages: foothills, jungle tracts, main rivers and politico-administrative boundaries (international boundaries, boundaries of Indian states and districts, within or adjoining Assam and Orissa) along with main cities and towns. Within this framework, native homelands of the languages are shaded, i.e., lowlands in Assam in the Brahmaputra valley, in the coastal plains, the valley and basin of the Mahanadi in Orissa. Both these relative geographical isolations may explain the genetic separation of the languages from the Bengali central trunk, in a predominant situation within the Ganga–Brahmaputra delta. The same is probably true of the Gangetic plains, northwest of the delta, and of Maithili, Magadhi and Bhojpuri, which are linguistically close to Bengali and came later under the Hindustani influence.
- The inset maps mention the 1961 district figures for mother tongue speakers of these two languages. Assamese, as previously mentioned (Plate 20), is restricted to the Brahmaputra valley where each

district had between 1 and 2 million Assamese speakers. Some local settlement is to be found in neighbouring districts of Garo and Khasi (Meghalaya) and the Karbi (Mikir) Hills with about 10,000 to 50,000 people in each district, together with an even smaller number in Nagaland, Cachar and Calcutta, having about 2,000 to 10,000 people. Assamese is not spoken by a widely spreading ethnic community. However, in north Assam, it has had enough room for adoption among the numerous immigrants who have been attracted to it.

The map of Oriya shows that it has a lower concentration than Assamese and is less widespread than Bengali: each district in Orissa has from 1 to 2 million Oriya speakers, though there exist significant Oriya-speaking groups outside Orissa. Districts of neighbouring Andhra Pradesh and Madhya Pradesh are partly populated with Oriyas, mainly settled in littoral reaches and the Chhattisgarh basin. They have also migrated further away having been attracted by industries in Calcutta and its suburbs and the Damodar valley, or by plantations in North Bengal Terai or in the Assam foothills, in the upper Brahmaputra valley as also in Cachar and Tripura.

- This opposition between the territorially self-sufficient Assamese and spreading Oriya is also depicted by the sketch maps where Oriya covers the whole state of Orissa: more than 90 per cent of the population along the coast and in the core areas of the Mahanadi valley but more than 50 per cent in all other hilly districts while Assamese only exceeds 50 per cent in the Brahmaputra valley. Hill people and plains minorities are still far more prominent in Assam than in Orissa.

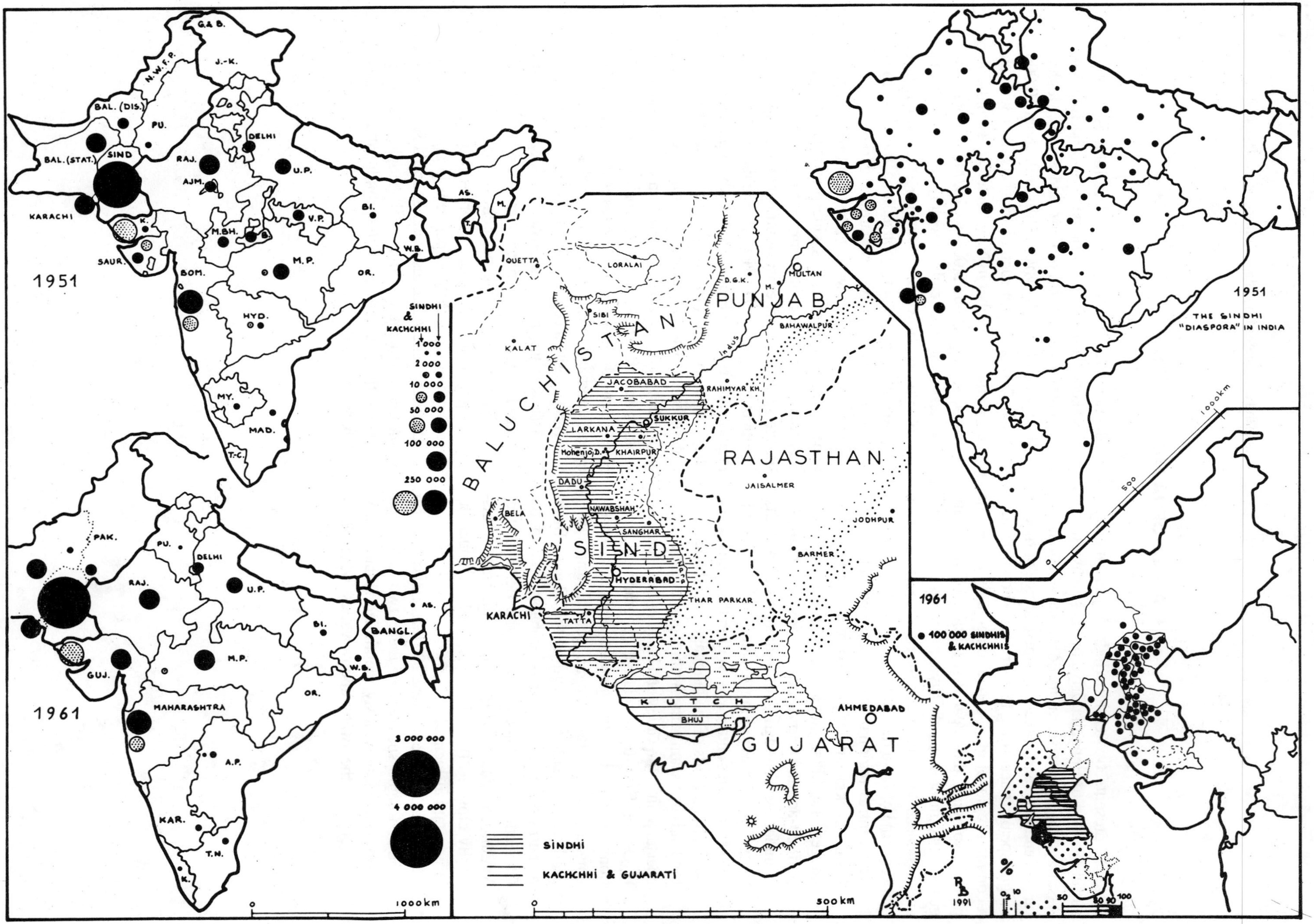

Plate 23: Sindhi

THE SINDHI "DIASPORA" IN INDIA

1951

1961

● 100 000 SINDHIS & KACHCHHIS

1000 km
500

%
100
90
80
50
10
1

1951

1961

PUNJAB
MULTAN
BAHAWALPUR
D.G.K.
RAHIMYAR KH.
JACOBABAD
SUKKUR
LARKANA
Mohenjo D.A
KHAIRPUR
SANGHAR
DADU
NAWABSHAH
SIND
HYDERABAD
TATTA
THAR PARKAR
KARACHI
BELA
LORALAI
SIBI
QUETTA
KALAT
BALUCHISTAN

RAJASTHAN
JAISALMER
JODHPUR
BARMER
AHMEDABAD
GUJARAT
KUTCH
BHUJ

R.B.
1991
500 km

SINDHI

KACHCHHI & GUJARATI

SINDHI & KACHCHHI
1 000
2 000
10 000
50 000
100 000
250 000
3 000 000
4 000 000

1000 km

1951
KARACHI
BAL. (STAT.)
SIND
G.A.B.
N.W.F.P.
J.-K.
PU.
RAJ.
AJM.
K.
SAUR.
BOM.
DELHI
U.P.
V.P.
M.P.
M.BH.
HYD.
MY.
MAD.
W.B.
OR.
BI.
AS.
M.
T-C.

1961
PAK.
DELHI
PU.
RAJ.
GUJ.
MAHARASHTRA
M.P.
U.P.
A.P.
KAR.
T.N.
K.
OR.
BI.
W.B.
AS.
BANGL.

Plate 23 deals with the diffusion of Sindhi across the subcontinent—both in its homeland, i.e., in the Sind province in Pakistan, and in its diaspora that is more widespread in India since Partition. A central regional map shows the natural and political setting of its homeland and, the four dotted maps around it depict the distribution of Sindhi speakers in their homeland as also in the diaspora.

- The regional maps show the topography of Sindhi lands: the plains of the lower Indus basin between the Baluchistan Hills in the west and in the north, the Great Indian Desert of Thar, or Marusthali, in the east, and swamps of the Rann of Kachchh in the south. Thus, Sindhi lands match most of the inhabited parts of the Sind province and Las Bela lowlands in southeastern Baluchistan. Following linguistic analyses, if we consider Kachchhi as a Sindhi and not a Gujarati dialect, we should include the Kachchh peninsula and islands, from where Kachchhi speakers originate but who have mingled with Gujarati-speaking immigrants.
- The smaller dotted map (bottom right) with a reduced shaded inset map depicts the distribution of most Sindhi speakers over their geographical core area. In the dotted map, each dot represents 100,000 Sindhi speakers by district in 1961. Of the total 5 million Sindhi speakers in Pakistan, 4.8 million lived in the Sind province and the rest in nearby districts of Las Bela and Kalat, and of the 1.4 million Sindhi speakers in India, 0.3 million lived in Kachchh and 1.1 million in the diaspora.

The shaded inset map shows the percentage of Sindhi (and Kachchhi) speakers in each district population. In the Sind province and Las Bela it is between 50 and 90 per cent, except in three districts where it is more and in Karachi where it is under 10 per cent (see Plate 40). Outside the core region, i.e., in Kachchh and Kalat, Sindhi speakers are in a minority of over 10 per cent. In the rest of Gujarat as in south Baluchistan and Punjab they are between 2 and 10 per cent in few districts. That demonstrates the rather low propagation of Sindhi, through proximity, around Sind and Kachchh.

- The three subcontinental dotted maps illustrate a

different phenomenon: a much wider extent of the smaller groups of the Sindhi diaspora which has spread after Partition, when 1 million Hindu Sindhis left Pakistan for India. Both maps use dots as symbols of representation (black ones for Sindhi and stippled ones for Kachchhi) but have two different scales of length: the top right map about India in 1951 is bigger in size as compared to the two subcontinental maps of 1951 and 1961 shown on the left.

The top right dotted map presents the district-wise distribution of Sindhi and Kachchhi within India in 1951 according to the then prevailing provincial boundaries. Outside Kachchh, Kachchhi was limited to the Kathiawar peninsula, Bombay and its suburbs. But Sindhis, originally from the Sind province, were already less numerous as compared to their population four years after Partition and had spread much further away: all over the northern Bombay province (Gujarat), Madhya Pradesh, Madhya Bharat, Bhopal, Vindhya (Vindhya Pradesh), Uttar Pradesh, Delhi, and above all in Rajasthan. Some more isolated and smaller groups could be located in south, east and northeast India.

Both the dotted maps on the left of the plate depict the provincial distribution of Sindhi and Kachchhi speakers all over the subcontinent in 1951 and 1961 according to the existing administrative boundaries. Both summarize the earlier mentioned district-wise distribution in India and specify the corresponding location of the inner smaller diaspora in Pakistan, already identified as remaining closer to the Sind borders.

All these maps mainly depict a demographic and linguistic consequence of the Partition: the movement of one part of a language community out of its homeland, transiting through neighbouring Gujarat, Bombay and its suburbs (e.g., Ulashnagar township) towards the whole of north central India. Registering Sindhi as the fifteenth 'scheduled' language in the Constitution of India in 1966 gave it recognition as a major language, in spite of its low number of speakers and its lack of territorial concentration within India. This also prevented Sindhi from being considered as a regional language in much the same way as Sanskrit and Urdu outside Kashmir.

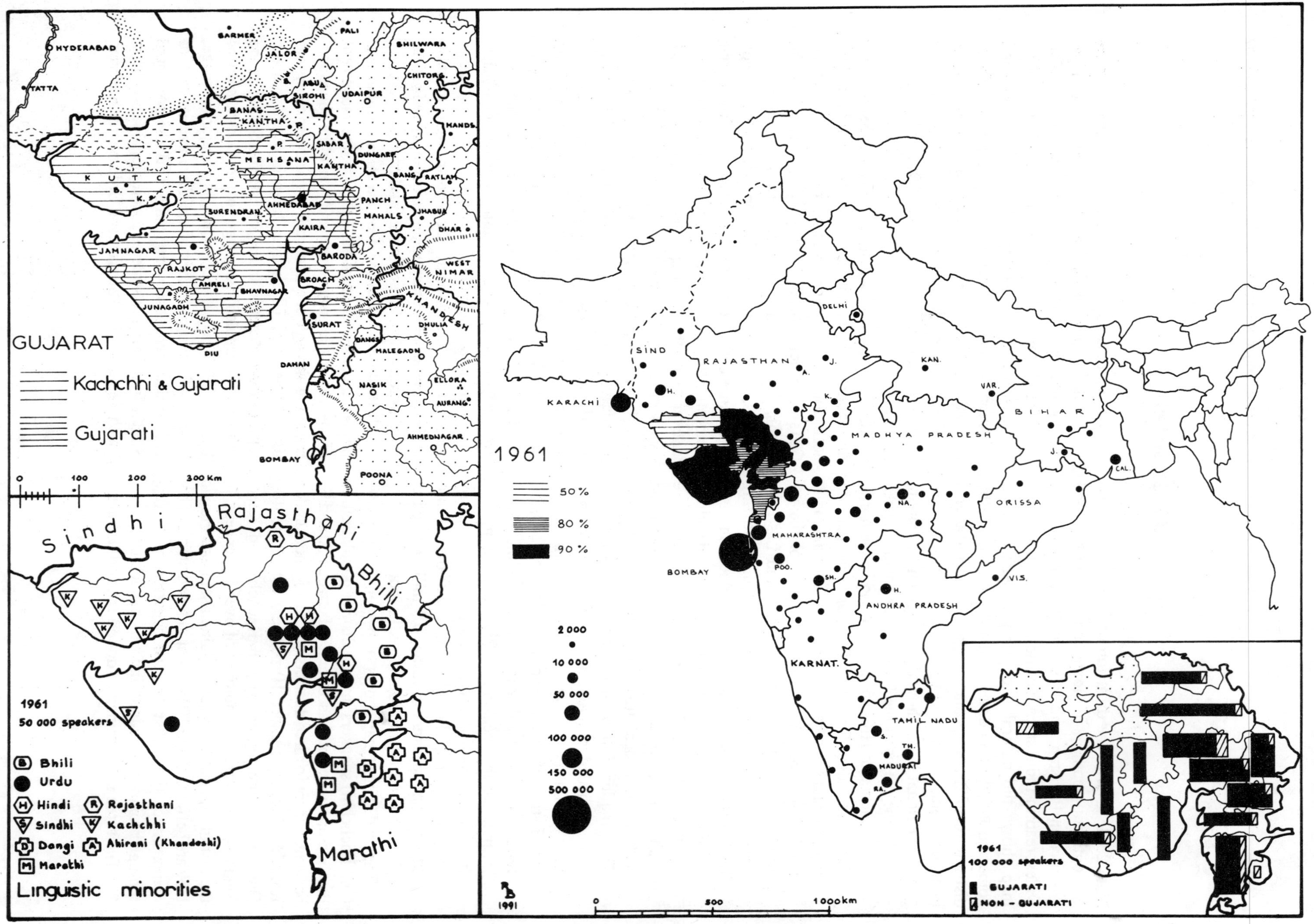

Plate 24: Gujarati

PLATE 24: GUJARATI

Plate 24 refers to Gujarati in 1961 with the help of four maps: a large subcontinental one and three smaller regional ones limited to Gujarat. Among the latter, the first regional map on the top left shows the physiographic framework of Gujarati lands, the second on the bottom left shows the inner and outer linguistic minorities, and the third on the bottom right sums up the resulting district majorities.

- The first regional map depicts Gujarati lands in their physiographic framework, between the Arabian Sea and the Deccan scarp line in the east, and the Indian desert in the north, with all national, state and district boundaries as in 1961. It shows Gujarat as a well-delineated set of lowlands with the Rann of Kachchh and the Bay of Cambay which divides it into three parts: Kachchh, Kathiawar Peninsula and eastern Gujarat lowlands. This natural unit is almost linguistic, except for Kachchh where the local speech is closer to Sindhi.

- In the second map minority languages are represented by symbols each depicting 50,000 speakers. Kachchhi, i.e., Sindhi (see Plate 23) is mainly localized in Kachchh, and the neighbouring languages such as Rajasthani, Bhili and Marathi are concentrated in the north, east and south respectively. Languages of diasporas are also presented: Urdu spoken by many Gujarat Muslims, Hindi used in bigger cities and, of course, Sindhi for the diaspora coming from Sind province. Added to these are local variants of Khandeshi (an in-between 'language' close to Gujarati, Marathi and Hindi), Dangi from the Dangs District, and Ahirani from across the border in Maharashtra.

- The small inset map (bottom right) summarizes the linguistic divide within each district using a rectangle proportionate to the district population and divided into two parts: the black portion denotes Gujarati while the hatched portion represents all the minority languages. The highest level of minority languages is in the Dangs District where Dangi is exclusively spoken, and in Kachchh where native Kachchhi was less spoken (45 per cent) than Gujarati (53 per cent). Other minorities can be found, though in a lesser proportion, in urban districts and almost nowhere in the rural districts of middle Kathiawar.

- The subcontinental map depicts the spread of Gujarati through two different ways. First, where Gujarati is spoken by most of the population of Gujarat,(except in the Dangs District), the shadings give the proportion of Gujarati speakers for each district population: between 50 per cent and 80 per cent in Kachchh, 80 per cent and 90 per cent in Ahmedabad, Baroda and Surat, and over 90 per cent in the rest of the state. Second, outside the Gujarati-speaking majority area, the dots are proportionate to Gujarati mother tongue speakers by district. Main Gujarati concentrations appear to be in Bombay and all around Gujarat, i.e., in Maharashtra, Madhya Pradesh, Rajasthan and Sind where Karachi is still the second Gujarati-speaking city outside Gujarat. In southern India, Tamil Nadu is the second centre of Gujarati language brought in by weavers, an occupational group which has maintained its Saurashtrian dialect in Madurai and in many other cities for centuries. Finally, Gujarati is also spoken in many other places in India such as in northern Deccan, Calcutta and Chota Nagpur—in areas wherever cities offered enough attractive working opportunities. The distribution of this language is quite different from that of Sindhi (Plate 23) which is heavily concentrated in the northern areas.

MARATHA POWER EXTENSION XVII-XVIII

GWALIOR (SINDHIA)
BARODA (GAIKWAR)
INDORE (HOLKAR)
NAGPUR (BHONSLA)
POONA (PESHWA)
TANJORE

1961

speakers by district outside Maharashtra.

2 000
10 000
50 000
100 000
200 000

% Marathi by district in Maharashtra.

70 80 90 100

Marathi

Plate 25: Marathi

PLATE 25: MARATHI

Plate 25 deals with Marathi by using four maps: a physiographic regional map (top left), a linguistic regional map (bottom left), an inset historical map (bottom right) and a main subcontinental map (centre right).

- The regional physiographic map on the top left shows the close connection between the boundaries (a thick unbroken line) of Maharashtra (the Marathi linguistic state) and the extent (a thick festoon-like broken line) of the *Trap* basalt lava extension over the old Deccan granitic block (an evenly spaced dotted shading). It also shows the limits (a dotted line) of the latter with rare alluvia (widely spaced dashes) lowlands in Gujarat, the Andhra littoral and the Tapti valley as also the forest cover (a thinner dotted shading). Thus, the only lands left blank are the *Trap* lava regions covered with permeable black fertile soils (*Regur*) and sprinkled with tree clumps. All these regions match with the Nimar and Malwa regions in Madhya Pradesh and with the small disputed fringe in northwestern Karnataka which has black soil but not the far eastern region of Maharashtra covered with Dandakaranya jungle tracts.

This indicates that the border between Marathi and Dravidian speakers approximates a geological divide: permeable fertile lavas against impermeable old platform, that need specific types of irrigation methods (either through wells or tanks) and thus promote specific patterns of settlement, cultivation and organization. This may be a clue aiding the explanation of the historical delineation and development of peoples in the Deccan region.

- The second regional map on the bottom left, drawn on a slightly bigger scale, shows the extent of Marathi-speaking areas by two shadings related to the population's density and seniority. A darker shading is used for the core of the Marathi country, also called the country par excellence, or the 'Desh'. A lighter one is used for the rest of the plateau where valleys stretching from the northwest to the southeast have been more recently, and less heavily, populated—except for the Tapti valley, running westwards, which offered a way to Berar and Vidarbha. Many of these border tracts, noted for rival sovereignties, archaeological remains and famous battlefields, are still disputed areas between linguistic states which do not agree with the present political delineation (see Plates 29, 31 and 47, for details on the Mahajan

Report). The major internal divisions of Maharashtra reflect its complex historical and geographical development: Konkan, Desh, Khandesh, Berar, Vidarbha and Marathwada, the latter being the former Marathi part of the Hyderabad Nizam's possessions.

- The historical map (bottom right) 'Maratha Power Extension XVII–XVIII' with the present delineation of the linguistic state captures the previous larger spread of the Maratha Empire, or Confederacy, consisting of the Peshwa, Bhonsla, Gaikwar, Holkar and Sindhia principalities and also including the smaller Maratha principalities in south India (Carnate, Arcote, Gingee, Tanjore, etc.). Together, they put up a united resistance against the Mughal as well as the British and French powers. All these historical political events may partly explain the present spread of Marathi.

- The data illustrated in the smaller more specific side maps is collectively represented in the main central map. It depicts the district-wise distribution of Marathi mother tongue speakers throughout the subcontinent in 1961 in two ways—by dot shadings showing the percentage of Marathi speakers in Maharashtra in the district population, and outside by dots proportionate to the total number of Marathi speakers in each district.

The decrease in the Marathi-speaking majority within Maharashtra is obvious from the west to the east: more than 90 per cent in Konkan, from 80 to 90 per cent in most of the central region, and between 70 and 80 per cent in the eastern reaches. Outside Maharashtra, Marathi speakers are mostly concentrated around the borders, (which, as in many other cases, do not match linguistic majorities) where there are a fair number of mixed areas, e.g., around Belgaum in Karnataka. But the spread of Marathi-speaking people goes far beyond the bordering areas into territories which were ruled by the Marathas more than two centuries ago, for instance in Baroda, Indore and Gwalior—strongholds of the Gaikwar, Holkar and Sindhia powers respectively. The spread is also visible in regions such as central and southern Karnataka, Tamil Nadu and Andhra Pradesh, which were originally close to territories directly ruled by the Marathas. Beyond this wide historical area, the spread of Marathi is less significant, with only a few thousand people in industrial centres like Calcutta or Jamshedpur.

PLATE 26: MUNDA, DRAVIDIAN AND INDO-ARYAN TRIBAL LANGUAGES

Plate 26 deals with languages of tribal ethnic communities in central India which belong to three different families: Munda, Dravidian and Indo-Aryan. These communities are scattered over northern Deccan, from the bend of the Ganga to the Ghats surrounding Gujarat, through a series of mountain ranges, hills and jungle tracts, extending from the Vindhyas to the Dandakaranya. This complex region involving eight states (Gujarat, Rajasthan, Madhya Pradesh, Maharashtra, Andhra Pradesh, Orissa, Bihar and West Bengal) is called the Tribal, or the Adivasi Belt, though members of Scheduled Tribes, i.e., Adivasis, seldom make up most of the population in any significant part of it now. In fact the overall population of India has since long moved through valleys and basins of this region, looking for vacant lands and mineral resources and bringing in a multiform development including all modern means of transport and urban networks.

This plate, consisting of only one map along with a small inset one that locates it within the subcontinent, combines physiographic, political, demographic and linguistic elements. Relief is denoted by scarp and foothill lines separating hills from lower places such as valleys, basins, littoral and delta lands. Main rivers give the overall direction of plateau slopes. Jungle tracts depicted with an evenly dotted shading cover most hilly regions and some minor parts of plateaus and plains.

Boundaries between states and provinces are represented by thick angular lines; the thickest line divides the Indo-Aryan Linguistic states, i.e., the northern and Dravidian states (Goa, Maharashtra, Madhya Pradesh and Orissa), and the southern ones (Karnataka and Andhra Pradesh). This delineation makes the ethno-linguistic divide more sensible, though the political delineation does not match all ethno-linguistic settlements, as for instance most Dravidian tribal languages are separated from the Dravidian set that comprises four states which are located south of this line.

Tribal languages are shown in the map with circles proportionate to the volume of their speakers along with their main geographical location. Major tribal languages, spoken in several states are represented by different circles which show the extent of these languages. Santali and Bhili in the eastern and western ends of the tribal area are represented respectively with a vertical and horizontal hatched shading. The Gondi extension is shown in the middle of the Adivasi Belt with black dots evenly spread over main inhabited hilly massifs.

With the help of these conventional designs, it is easy to point out three main territories for tribal languages: Chota Nagpur in the east, the Gondwana–Dandakaranya area in the centre, and the Bhil country, or Bhilwara, in the west.

Chota Nagpur, or Jharkhand (the 'Jungle Country') is mainly the southern half of Bihar state, covering the Deccan, while northern Bihar lies in the Ganga plain and is the home of Maithili, Magadhi and Bhojpuri; the latter extends to Chota Nagpur with its Sadri form, a kind of an intertribal lingua franca. But Chota Nagpur (or Jharkhand, claimed as a state) also extends to neighbouring margins of West Bengal (Purulia plateau), northern Orissa (Garjhat) and eastern Madhya Pradesh. This area is the centre of the Munda language family, a part of the big Austro-Asiatic set, which includes languages of the entire Southeast Asian peninsula along with Mon-Khmer and Vietnamese.

The northeastern Kherwari branch of Munda includes Santali and other related languages. The homeland of Santali—the major Kherwari language and the most-spoken tribal one in India—is traditionally located in the eastern fringe of Deccan (i.e., the Bihar–Orissa–West Bengal frontier area) but Santalis have also migrated to northern Bengal and Assam with other tribal plantation labourers. In 1961 out of 3.2 million Santali speakers in India, 1.5 million were in Bihar, 1.2 million in West Bengal, 0.4 million Orissa and 67,000 in Assam, plus about 66,000 in Bangladesh.

Among other Kherwari languages are Mundari (737,000), Ho (648,000), Bhumij (142,000), Koda/Kora or Khaira (32,000) and Korwa (17,000), mainly located in south Bihar, but also present in Orissa, Madhya Pradesh and West Bengal. Added to these are Asuri-Birjia-Agaria (7,000), Birhor (6,000) and Turi (1,600) belonging to tiny ethno-linguistic groups (see Part I, Chapter 2 for the special situation and status between Scheduled Tribe and Scheduled Caste, of some of these communities). Kharia (177,000) though not actually belonging to the Kherwari group is akin to the Munda languages of southern Orissa.

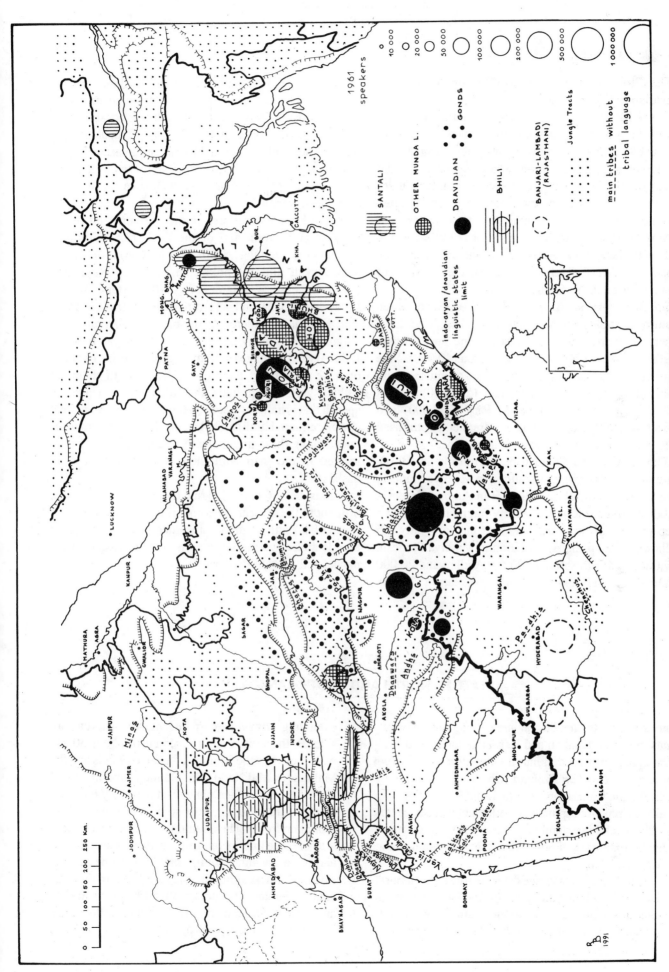

Plate 26: Munda, Dravidian and Indo-Aryan Tribal Languages

The Chota Nagpur area is also the homeland of two Dravidian tribal languages: Oraon, or Kurukh, (1.1 million) and Malto (89,000), the first located in the central part of the Ranchi plateau and the second at the tip of the Santal Parganas hills overhanging the Ganga bend.

The second main tribal set of languages has a wider spread but in a less clearly delineated region. It includes southern parts of Orissa and Madhya Pradesh (often referred to as the Dandakaranya), the central eastern part of Madhya Pradesh, the eastern reaches of Maharashtra and the northern tip of Andhra Pradesh, all of which are broadly speaking linked together due to the scattering of the Gond tribe in the Gondwana area.

Southern Orissa is the place of origin of three southern Munda tribes akin to Kharia. These tribes have spread from the north to the south and speak Juang (16,000), Savara (266,000) and Gadaba (40,000). Five Dravidian tribal languages have also originated here from the north to the south: Kui (512,000) Khond (168,000) and Konda (12,000), Parji (109,000) and Koya (141,000), the first three are frequently confused as they are spoken by the same Khond tribe.

Then comes the Gond tribe (4 million in 1961), scattered over four states (3 million in Madhya Pradesh, 446,000 in Maharashtra, 144,000 in Andhra Pradesh, 34,000 in Bihar, etc.), but heavily fragmented and in a deep process of acculturation. This has left only 1.5 million Gondi speakers: 1 million in Madhya Pradesh, 347,000 in Maharashtra, 78,000 in Andhra and 20,000 in Orissa. Closely akin to Gondi is Kolami (51,000),

spoken in eastern Maharashtra. In the northwestern end of the Gond area, in the western Mahadeo mountain range, across the Maharashtra–Madhya Pradesh border, we can find the Korku language (220,000 speakers), the westernmost outpost of the Munda, or Kolarian family, which maybe extended further west, for instance to the Koli community, whether or not its former linkage with Kolarian is verified.

A third main tribal area is the northern end of the Ghats region, homeland of the Bhils (3.8 million in 1961) whose language, Bhili, (2.4 million) is definitely Indo-Aryan and is spoken in southern Rajasthan (832,000), eastern Gujarat (276,000), western Madhya Pradesh (876,000) and northern Maharashtra (441,000).

If Bhili is considered as the only Indo-Aryan tribal language, then many Scheduled Tribes speak regional Indo-Aryan languages or some dialectal forms of them, or have elaborated their own speech from them. In Chhattisgarh, for instance, the Halbas speak Halabi, a speech that is halfway between the Chhattisgarhi dialect (from southern Hindi) and Marathi. The most numerous ones among these linguistically acculturated tribes are located in the map with their names underlined by dashes.

It must be borne in mind that the Rajasthani dialects, brought to the Deccan by wandering Scheduled Castes (not Tribes) called Banjari or Lambadi, are spoken over a wide area covering large parts of Maharashtra, Karnataka and Andhra Pradesh.

PLATE 27: NORTH AND SOUTH KANARA

Plate 27 depicts the littoral area along the Western Ghats, between Konkan and Kerala, belonging to Karnataka, and now divided into the two districts of *Uttar Kannad* and *Dakshin Kannad*, which were previously called North Kanara and South Kanara. A main map details the physiographic and settlement aspects of this region and its hinterland. The three inset dotted maps locate the extension of both native languages in Kanara: Konkani and Tulu.

- The main map shows the decisive role of the natural barrier in isolating the Kannad area. The Ghats scarp line runs from the north to the south of this area. It also depicts the biogeographical strip of vegetation

extending along this scarp line, mostly on its eastern side. Both make a natural screen of about 50 km wide, between the Kannad coastal lowlands and the Malnad (or Mal Nadu: Hill Country) and the upper part of the Karnataka plateau. It is mainly made up of rain forests along with some small patches of mountain forest. The natural landscape mostly consists of some lines of dry forest at the highest reaches and some savannah clumps including some dry tree savannah tracts along middle-sized tops in the Karnataka plateau. This geographical layout is among an overall landscape of cultivated and settled lands with a solid urban network (the size of cities is

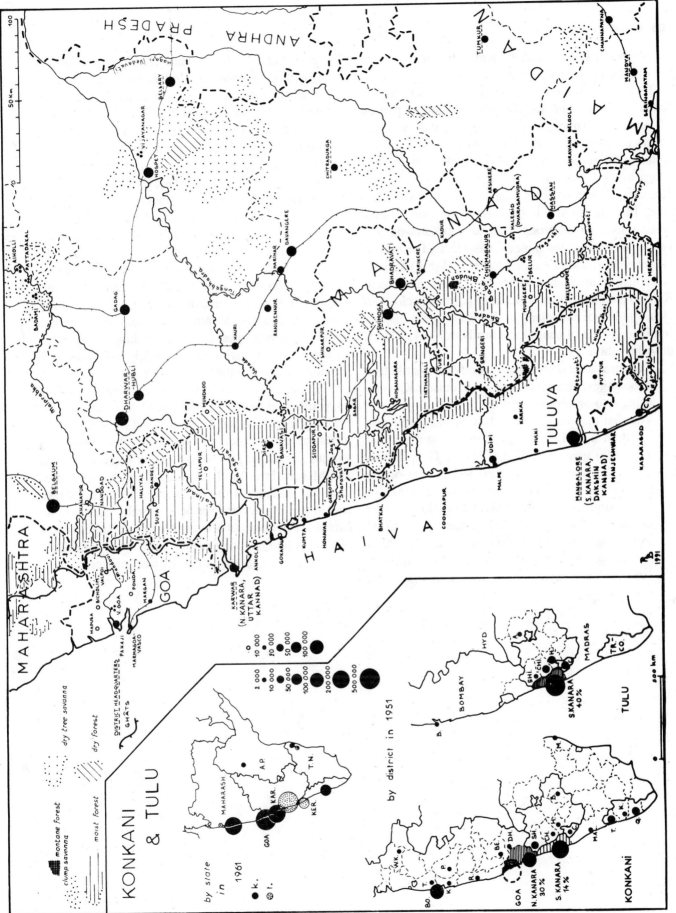

Plate 27: North and South Kanara

shown in the key) linked by railway lines (the map shows the most significant ones).

This orographic and biogeographical barrier, parallel to the coastline, explains Kannad's isolation, its pattern of human settlement, and linguistic peculiarity which shows the persistence of two speeches—Konkani and Tulu—different from the languages of the hinterland—Marathi and Kannada—though related to them. Konkani, spoken in Uttar Kannad and Goa, is distinct from Marathi though it belongs to the same southwestern Indo-Aryan group. Tulu, akin to Kannada, and having arisen from the same southern Dravidian branch is spoken in Dakshin Kannad. South (dakshin) Kannad is known as the Tulu country, or *Tuluva*, and North Kannad is called *Haiva*, which is linguistically closer to Goa, the actual homeland of Konkani, quite distinct from the speech of central and northern Konkan lands in Maharashtra.

- The three inset dotted maps specify the distribution of both these languages, within and outside Kannad, using a common scale of dots.

The first map on the top shows the state-wise distribution in 1961. With regards to Konkani, of a total 1,352,000 speakers, 557,000 were in Goa, Daman and Diu where they made up 89 per cent of the population; 492,000 in Karnataka; 215,000 in Maharashtra; 78,000 in Kerala and 11,000 in the rest of India. For Tulu, out of 935,000 speakers, 851,000 were in Karnataka; 68,000 in Kerala and 15,000 in the rest of India. The district-wise distribution in 1951 is shown separately for each language in the second and third inset maps. Konkani prevailed in Goa, not yet under the Indian government at that time, and made up 30 per cent of the North Kanara district, 14 per cent of South Kanara, and was widespread all along the eastern coast of India, from Bombay to Kerala (then Malabar, Trichur, Kottayam and Quilon districts), and in the nearby hinterland of Kanara and Goa (Belgaum, Dharwar, Shimoga, Chikmagalur, Hassan and Coorg districts). Tulu experienced a much smaller extension, limited to South Kanara (40 per cent of the population) and its four neighbouring districts.

This difference in distribution is linked to the historical expansion of many Konkani communities, either Hindus or Muslims, Brahmanical or trading groups, present in all active harbours and cities of the region, while the humbler peasant Tulu-speaking majority has a compact concentration which slightly overflows on to the ridges that close the horizon of *Tuluva*.

The linguistic consequences of both these kinds of geographical distribution are twofold. Konkanis, settled far away from Goa and North Kannad since some centuries, have kept their mother tongue but write it in various scripts: in Devanagari or Latin scripts in Goa and Maharashtra (partly according to their Hindu or Christian culture) in the Kannada script in Karnataka and in the Malayalam script in Kerala. Tulu has no current written use but is in fact the shared lingua franca of all populations living within Tuluva where the Tulu speakers enjoy a relative majority and anteriority.

CHAPTER 10

THE DRAVIDIAN SOUTH AND SRI LANKA

PLATE 28: THE FOUR MAIN DRAVIDIAN ETHNIES

Plate 28 depicts the numerical development over a century (1881–1981) of the four main Dravidian ethnies (ethnic groups, or ethno-linguistic communities, or big sociocultural aggregates). The development is reported for each language (Telugu, Tamil, Kannada and Malayalam) through each census. It is shown by:

* the total number of mother tongue speakers in India, i.e., the weight of the *ethnic group* (dots linked with a bold unbroken line);
* the total population in the present linguistic state—Andhra Pradesh, Tamil Nadu, Karnataka and Kerala (a broken line of dashes);
* the number of native speakers within the territory of the linguistic state (e.g., Telugu in Andhra Pradesh) is shown by a dotted line.

The space between lines referring to the same language has been, where possible, shaded by dots to make the difference more sensible. The comparison between number of speakers and provincial population enables us to underline the fact that the borders of linguistic states may have been rather approximately delineated for the language community, leaving various minorities of speakers outside the provincial borders and minorities of non-speakers inside. The *domestic* minority is that percentage of the state population which does not speak the regional language and the minority *abroad* is that percentage of the all-India ethnic group living outside (see Plate 43).

It is however essential to bear in mind that some figures may be missing due to non-availability in this trilogy: territory projections of linguistic states for 1881 and 1891, number of speakers within these states prior to 1911, and mother tongue data for the 1941 Census. As regards 1981, the loss of all mother tongue data in

Tamil Nadu due to a flood gives, for instance, the total number of Indian Tamil speakers only outside Tamil Nadu. The absence of Tamil Nadu data significantly reduces the number of Telugu speakers as well and, to a lesser extent, that of Kannada and Malayalam speakers. Thus, for 1981, the figures refer not to mother tongue but to 'the most spoken language in the household'. But each case must be examined separately.

In the case of Malayalam, the relatively lesser spoken of the four major Dravidian languages, the number of speakers had risen from barely 5 million in 1881 to 26 million in 1981—a more than fivefold (520 per cent) increase over a century. However, between 1911 and 1931, a small domestic non-Malayali minority within Kerala matched an equally small Malayali group outside the state: a balance showing the rather homogeneous linguistic composition of the state. But since 1961 Malayalis have been outnumbered by Kerala's total population and by 1981, there were nearly 26 million Malayalam speakers in the Indian 'household population' (according to 1981 Census definition of 'language mainly spoken in the households', but only in households of persons 'related by blood', not of 'institutional households', which are linguistically heterogeneous) compared with 24.2 million within Kerala, which amounted to 25.2 million household population (but 25.5 million inhabitants). Thus, if there were 1,000,000 non-Malayalis in Kerala (4 per cent of the state population), there were 1,800,000 Malayalis outside the state (7 per cent of the ethnic group). These small figures nevertheless showed that there was a growing spread of Malayalis outside their province whose population size remains quite close to its numerical ethnic weight.

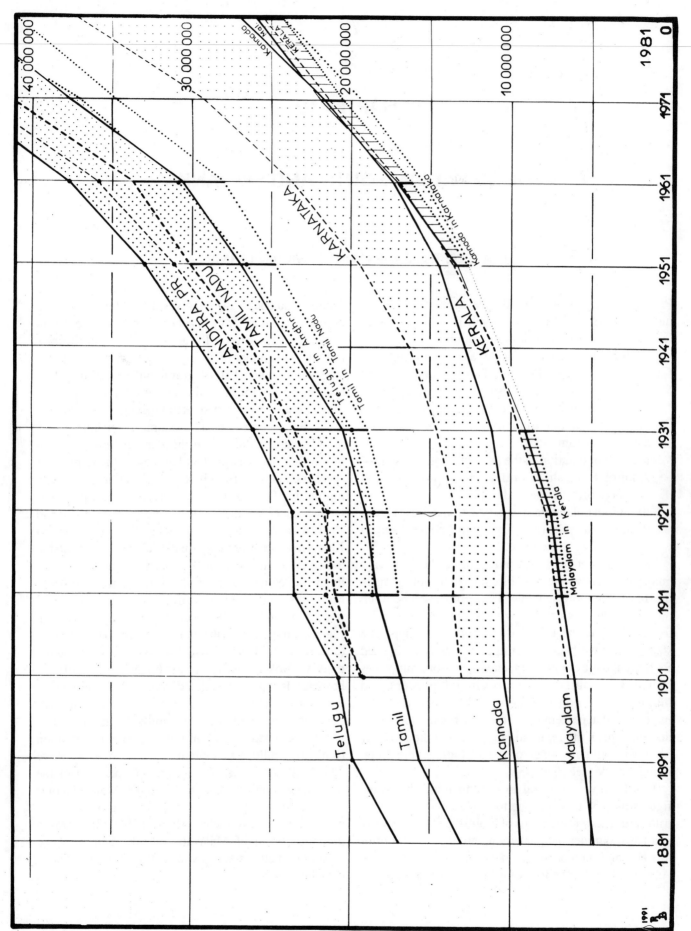

Plate 28: The Four Main Dravidian Ethnies

The case of Kannada is quite different. The number of speakers have increased from 9 to less than 27 million over a century, i.e., a threefold increase (300 per cent). Karnataka's population has always outnumbered the volume of Kannada speakers. There was a 36.8 million household population (out of 37.1 million inhabitants) in 1981 including 24.2 million Kannada speakers while the total Kannada household population in India had 26.9 million people. Thus, if the domestic linguistic minority had 12.6 million non-Kannada speakers (34 per cent of the state's population), there were only 2.7 million Kannada-speaking people outside Karnataka (10 per cent of the ethnic group)—an uneven balance showing Karnataka's heterogeneous linguistic design.

The number of Tamil speakers underwent more than a threefold increase (346 per cent) from 13 to 45 million people over the century. In 1981, among the overall Indian household Tamil-speaking population (44.7 million people), there was an almost similar division between the provincial Tamil-speaking total number (41 million people) and the overall provincial household population (53.2 million people out of 53.6 million inhabitants). Thus if in Tamil Nadu there was a non-Tamil population of 12.2 million people (15 per cent), Tamil speakers outside Tamil Nadu were 13.7 million people (8 per cent of the ethnic group): the figures were high but almost equal and slightly at the disadvantage of Tamil speakers.

Telugu speakers, the first Dravidian community in India, increased from 17 to more than 54 million people: thus a little more than a threefold increase (318 per cent). The number of speakers always outnumbered the provincial population but with a decreasing proportion. In 1981, the overall Indian household Telugu-speaking population had 54.2 million people including 45.3 million people within Andhra Pradesh, out of a provincial overall household population of 53.2 million people (out of 53.6 million inhabitants). Thus if non-Telugu speakers within Andhra Pradesh were 7.9 million (15 per cent), Telugu speakers outside the state were 8.9 million (17 per cent of the ethnic group). It is a significant but an almost even balance, slightly at the expense of the Telugu-speaking population.

Thus, the four major Dravidian ethnic groups have increased in varying degrees and have differently taken advantage of the set-up of linguistic states. In most of these states, the geographical design leaves nearly as many minority people inside than outside. Only in the case of Karnataka, the domestic minority greatly exceeds the one outside.

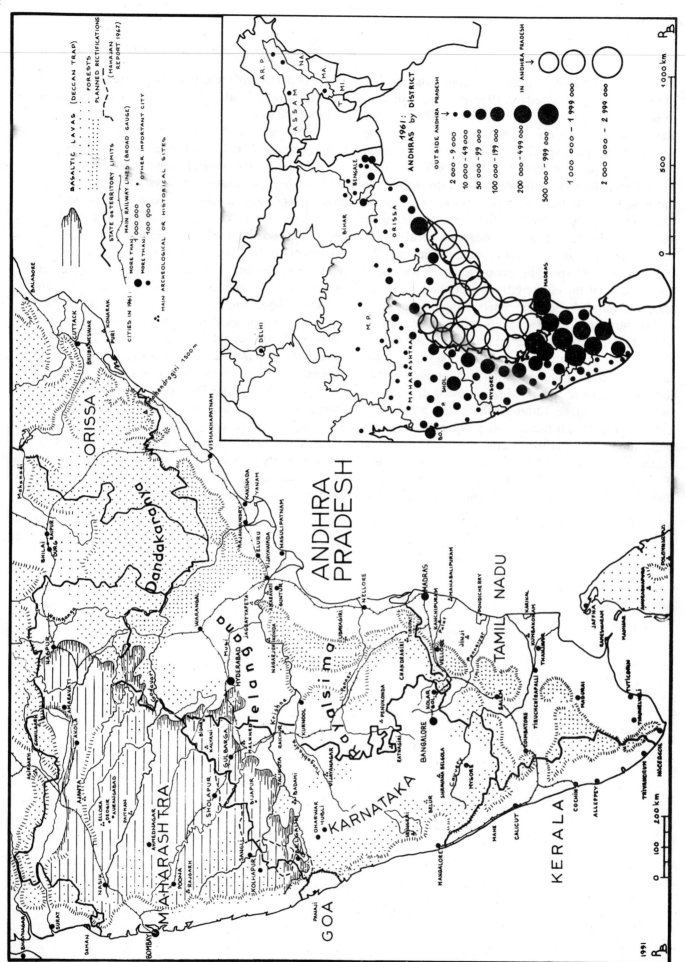

Plate 29: Andhra Pradesh, Telugu

PLATE 29: ANDHRA PRADESH, TELUGU

Plate 29 is based on Telugu. It shows a geographical map of the Dravidian Deccan on the left and a smaller dotted map of Telugu spoken in India on the right.

- The regional map shows the geographical division of (*a*) the whole southern Deccan into four major linguistic states and (*b*) their northern neighbours. State borders overlap physiographic data: main rivers, scarp lines of the Ghats and other foothills which delineate smaller massifs mostly covered by forests. The map also shows the extent of basalt lavas of the Deccan *Trap* which gives Maharashtra its specific landscape and extends over the northern border of Karnataka. In this border area, the changes with regard to state limits proposed by the Mahajan Report (1967) to stick to language areas are shown with dashes.

The Dravidian provinces thus seem to be delineated from the rest of India by the margin of the large basalt region in the northwest and by the wide forest lands of the Dandakaranya in the northeast. While the quadripartition in the Dravidian provinces brings to mind the close matching of these linguistic areas with various sets of natural regions, i.e., Karnataka from the western Deccan plateaus to the Kanara coastal lowlands, Kerala to the wider southern part of these lowlands, Tamil Nadu to larger plains isolating small massifs, and Andhra Pradesh from a flat littoral land to its hinterland including the non-basalt eastern Deccan plateau (Telangana) and its border basins and mountain ranges (Rayalsima).

Many archaeological sites remind one of significant historical influences that the Deccan area has undergone from the north to the south and vice versa, i.e., from Paithan, now in Maharashtra, the stronghold of the first Andhra empire (third century) extending to Nagarjunakonda and Amaravati, to Badami, Malkhed and Kalyani, strongholds of the Chalukya empire (from the sixth to the twelfth century). The Chalukya empire was situated around the basalt fringe from where the Bahmani sultanates of Gulbarga, Bidar, Bijapur and Golcunda (Hyderabad) invaded the Andhra–Kannada empire of Vijayanagar (from the fourteenth to the sixteenth century) which later withdrew to Penukonda and Chandragiri. The map also shows the railway network joining cities across the peninsula.

- The dotted map displays the district-wise distribution of Telugu mother tongue speakers in 1961 through the use of circles—white circles represent the distribution within Andhra Pradesh while black circles show the spread of the language outside the state. The map shows the demographic predominance of the Andhra littoral area (2 to 3 million people) over Telangana and Rayalsima. Outside Andhra Pradesh, the mass settlement of Telugu people is noticed in southeastern and eastern Karnataka and all over Tamil Nadu. This is due to historical reasons, dating back to the Vijayanagar empire having a large Telugu-speaking population. This spread has lasted for centuries. Beyond this contiguous and continuing presence, the more recent distribution of Andhra migrants is towards busy industrial centres all over Karnataka and Maharashtra, significantly in Sholapur, Pune and Bombay and further away in Bhilai in Madhya Pradesh, Jamshedpur in Bihar, Calcutta, and even in Assam.

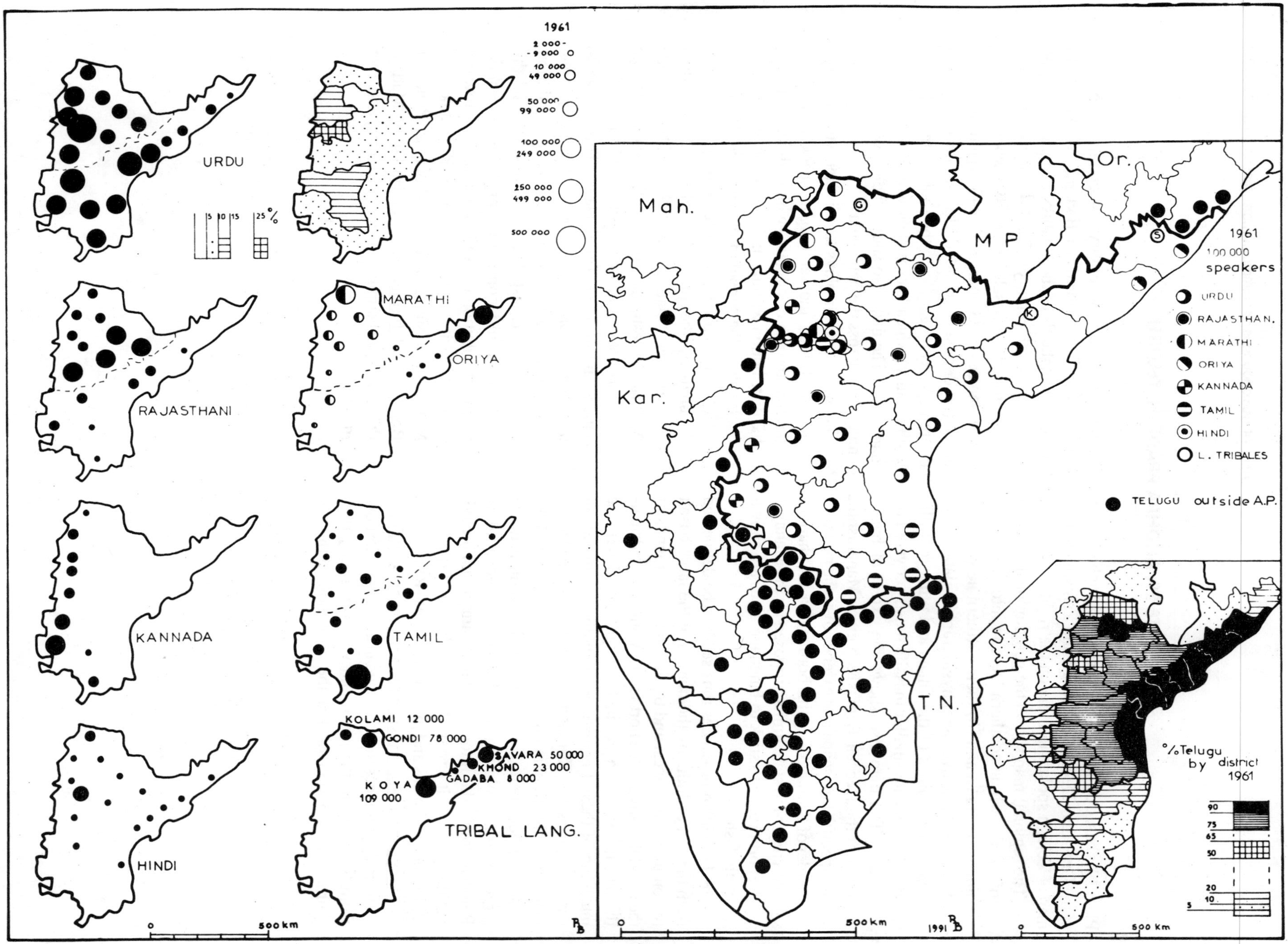

Plate 30: Andhra Pradesh, Linguistic Minorities

Legend and labels within the map:

1961 100 000 speakers

URDU
RAJASTHAN.
MARATHI
ORIYA
KANNADA
TAMIL
HINDI
L. TRIBALES

● TELUGU outside A.P.

%Telugu by district 1961
90 75 65 50 20 10 5

500 km

Or.

M P

Mah.

Kar.

T.N.

1991

1961 speakers
2 000 – 9 000
10 000 – 49 000
50 000 – 99 000
100 000 – 249 000
250 000 – 499 000
500 000

15 10 15 25 %

URDU

RAJASTHANI

KANNADA

HINDI

MARATHI
ORIYA

TAMIL

KOLAMI 12 000
GONDI 78 000
SAVARA 50 000
KHOND 23 000
GADABA 6 000
KOYA 109 000

TRIBAL LANG.

0   500 km

PLATE 30: ANDHRA PRADESH, LINGUISTIC MINORITIES

Plate 30 depicts linguistic minorities in Andhra Pradesh by district in 1961. They are first separately analyzed in eight small dotted maps on the left, then presented together in the big dotted map on the right which also shows Telugu-speaking areas outside Andhra Pradesh. The third map on the bottom right shows the percentage of Telugu-speaking people in Andhra Pradesh and its adjoining areas.

* The first set of dotted maps on the left use various circles drawn on the top right as symbols of representation. In 1961, 86 per cent of Andhra Pradesh's population were Telugu mother tongue speakers and half the population (7 per cent) among others (14 per cent) were Urdu speakers, matching the majority of the Muslim population (8 per cent). This Urdu minority is shown in two maps with dots for absolute numbers on the left and with shadings for the percentage of people on the right. Both show that Urdu extends from the Telangana area (former Nizam's possessions) to Rayalsima and to the southern littoral, and, in lesser numbers, to the northern Circars littoral. However, the Hyderabad District, (former stronghold of the Nizam's power) experiences the highest score (more than 25 per cent).

A second minority, also belonging to the Hindustani set of languages, is the nomadic Lambada Scheduled Caste (basically porters) which is reported to have come along with the Muslim armies. Their Rajasthani dialect is found all over Telangana mainly in its southeastern outer ring and, to a much lesser extent, further south and east.

Marathi and Oriya are closer to their native provinces but Marathi is more widespread due to the former Maratha power. Kannada is strictly confined to the bordering lands of Karnataka. Though Tamil has a mass settlement in the south, it is quite evenly distributed throughout the province. It was brought in by various communities which were traditionally intermingled with the Andhra society. Hindi, though numerically far less important than Urdu and Rajasthani, is distributed among numerous civil or army servants and other officers coming from the North in public and private concerns. Urdu, Rajasthani and Hindi make up 9 per cent of the population altogether.

Tribal languages were also mainly attached to tribes living in the hilly forested lands in the northern reaches of the province, the Dandakaranya area. Most belong to the Dravidian family (Koya, Gondi, Khond and Kolami) and the others to the Munda family (Savara and Gadaba). But all of them are mainly settled on the other side of the border, i.e., in Orissa, Madhya Pradesh or Maharashtra.

* The main dotted map sums up the importance of all minorities inside Andhra Pradesh and compares it with Telugu minorities outside. Each dot represents 100,000 speakers for one language other than Telugu in one district. The general impression given by the map is that of density and diversity of minorities in the capital (in Hyderabad District, Urdu is spoken by 500,000 people while Rajasthani, Hindi, Marathi and Tamil each have 100,000 speakers) followed by relatively bigger settlements close to the western and the southern border (Marathi, Kannada and Tamil) and, finally, the predominant scatter of Urdu all over the province.

Outside Andhra Pradesh, the black dots denoting 100,000 Telugu speakers, show the distribution of this significant outer minority on the other side of the border, i.e., in Orissa, Maharashtra, Karnataka and Tamil Nadu. The concentration is heavy in southeastern Karnataka (Kolar with 700,000 and Bangalore with 400,000) and spread over Tamil Nadu (Salem 600,000, Coimbatore 700,000 and Madurai 400,000). Apart from the difficulty of drawing a fair administrative boundary following mixed settlements, there was the impossibility of taking into account solid units which have been long cut off from their homeland.

* The final map on the bottom right displays the percentage of Telugu speakers in all districts of south Deccan. There are more than 90 per cent speakers in the core area spanning the whole of Andhra littoral followed by between 90 and 75 per cent in interior Andhra districts, between 65 and 50 per cent in Adilabad, Hyderabad and 53 per cent in Kolar in Karnataka. Finally, there is an outer ring where Telugu is spoken by about 20 to 10 per cent in most of eastern Karnataka, north and west Tamil Nadu and south Orissa.

PLATE 31: KARNATAKA, KANNADA

Plate 31 is made up of two maps. The bigger one on the left entitled 'Karnataka' uses dots to show various languages over a physiographic background and the smaller one on the right entitled 'Kannada' shows the spread of the language throughout India through circles with different radii.

- The 'Karnataka' map is primarily physiographic depicting the natural location of the region: foothill lines, forest areas and main rivers along with state borders and district limits. The names of each district are marked. The remaining part around the disputed Maharashtra–Karnataka border is also indicated: the border claimed by Maharashtra (shown with a double dotted line) and the arbitrary correction proposed by the 1967 Mahajan Report (shown with double dashes).

Against this basic background, various dots depict various mother tongue speakers. Each dot represents 100,000 people and most of the dots are of the same size except three at the bottom left which are divided into sectors representing the three main cities and their suburbs. Districts in the Karnataka state and the Nilgiri district in Tamil Nadu are filled with dots. Outiside Karnataka, only those Kannada- or Tulu-speaking groups are shown which number 100,000 in a district.

In this way we may compare the spread of Kannada in and around its province with various minority languages within it. Eleven languages are specifically symbolized:

Kannada, or Canarese, along with three related languages, i.e., Tulu from the Mangalore region, Coorgi or Kodagu from the Coorg District (a former princely state) and Badaga, an ethnic dialect from the Nilgiri Hills.

Three other major Dravidian languages, i.e., Telugu, Tamil and Malayalam.

Both the neighbouring Indo-Aryan languages, Marathi and Konkani, and those significantly spread all over the province, i.e., Urdu and Rajasthani (the Banjari-Lambadi dialect).

This display helps to visualize the main homelands of the Kannada language. Its densely populated settlements include the region along the Ghats called the Malnad (Mal Nadu) or the hilly country in the west and the Maidan (or meadows) in the Mysore plateau leading to a circle of southern mountain tops overhanging Kerala and Tamil Nadu in the south. Eastwards and northwards, in the northern and central lower Karnataka plateau, the density of the population decreases and there are more minorities. Westwards, down the Ghats scarp line, minorities make up most of the population: this is the Kanara, or Kannad, country (cf. Plate 27) where Konkani and Tulu are widely spoken languages.

A scrutiny of this province may reveal other internal or external language minorities. In the main town of Mangalore District as also in Coorg and the Nilgiri Hills, Malayalam is still being more spoken than Kannada in the main town, but far less than Tulu. Tulu is traditionally the language of northern Kasaragod District on the other side of the border. Once a taluk of Karnataka, it was granted to Kerala in 1956, however the 1967 Mahajan Report suggested that its northern part be granted to Karnataka. But the entire taluk is still claimed by Karnataka. In Coorg, Kodagu or Coorgi (29 per cent), fell to a minority as a result of the inflow of Malayalis and Kannadigas. Similarly, in the Nilgiri Hills, native Badaga peasants and Kurumba shepherds speaking Kannada dialects, and Toda cowherds and Kota craftsmen having their own Dravidian language have all been outnumbered by Malayalis and Tamils coming from surrounding plains.

In the Mysore plateau, Tamils mostly live in cities: according to 1961 Census, only half the population of Mysore city spoke Kannada, a quarter of the population of Bangalore spoke Kannada, the rest spoke Tamil (Kolar goldfields were predominantly inhabited by Tamil speakers). The minority of Tamils present further west, for instance, as plantation labourers, is numerically equivalent to Kannadiga people traditionally living outside the border in historical settlements within western Tamil Nadu.

A different phenomenon is observed along the eastern border of Karnataka, west of which there are four times as many Andhras as the member of Kannadigas along its eastern side, particularly, in the Kolar District where most of the population speaks Telugu. Within the Karnataka plateau, the main minorities are Urdu speakers mainly living in cities and towns. The other minorities are the Banjara porters who are closely affiliated to the Lambadas of Andhra Pradesh and are faithful to their Rajasthani dialect. The reorganization

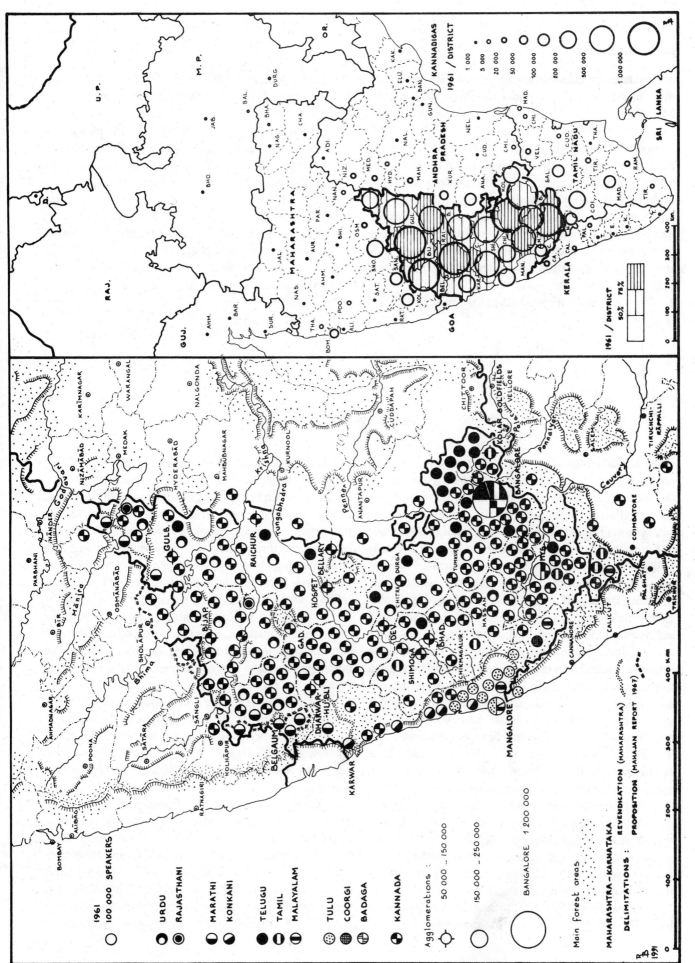

Plate 31: Karnataka, Kannada

of the states of Maharashtra and Karnataka created the most disputed border problem in 1961 with 1 million Marathi speakers on the Karnataka side and half a million Kannadigas on the Maharashtra side. The border claimed by Maharashtra, splitting Bidar, Belgaum and the northern Kanara Districts was meant to unite most of these Marathi populations to Maharashtra. The 1967 Mahajan Report recommended a compromise to transfer less territory to Maharashtra balanced by an opposite transfer of the Kannada-speaking territory to Karnataka. However, there has been no implementation, only several commemoration demonstrations are held every year.

* The 'Kannada' map uses dots to represent the Kannada- speaking people all over India. This language is localized within its linguistic state with a rather low density: seven districts with more than 75 per cent along with two settlements in the plateaus of Mysore and north Karnataka, nine other districts having between 75 and 50 per cent, the centre and on the periphery. The last three districts with a density below 50 per cent are Mangalore, Coorg and Kolar. Outside Karnataka, Kannada is mainly found along the disputed Maharashtra border, in the northern regions of Tamil Nadu, and to a lesser extent, in eastern Andhra Pradesh. Apart from Bombay, there no significant concentration further away.

PLATE 32: KERALA

Plate 32 deals with a single map that shows the natural position of Kerala. Its single linguistic trait is depicted by the border of the three linguistic states which encompass the population belonging to the three languages: Malayalam in Kerala, Tamil in Tamil Nadu, and Kannada in Karnataka. These state boundaries, which are primarily political limits, may now be taken as factual linguistic lines. This is validated by the fact that the boundaries are the actual framework within which each language is officially predominant in every field, and that they were supposed to coincide with the limits of the linguistic area.

If, in India, three language areas can become three linguistic states, it is because there were three natural areas allowing different modes of cultivation, settlement and feeling. Each of these states has a distinct form of speech, comprehension, expression and writing, i.e., its own culture. If people could be either Malayalis, or Tamils or Kannadigas, it is also because three landscapes and three calendars for seasons, have been split into three different countrysides.

The three languages are by and large akin but definitely different. The long process of separation of these three languages has been achieved: for each language, a common consensus has been reached by all involved people on a single way of speaking and writing it with its own grammatical rules.

This map, depicting the limits of three languages, is basically and predominantly biogeographical. It displays, with the most possible accuracy, the subtle reality and intermingled extent of the natural and physical elements which brought about changes in the landscape of the tip of India; and, in the same way, between the three major languages spoken there and consequently between the three states. The government along with administrators, had in 1956 shaped these new political boundaries after having taken into account the population's wishes and interest. Finally, these new boundaries happened to follow natural limits observed for centuries by social scientists (linguists and ethnologists) scrutinizing human communities, and by ecologists and botanists interested in ecosystems, biomasses, flora and fauna. These ecological barriers thus permitted the birth of three different language communities and eventually three states were set up. Here the ecology of both languages and societies may be joined—from the actual environmental ecology of the vegetative cover to the geopolitical set-up, through the spontaneous creation of language.

The vegetation consists of mountain forests and grasslands, evergreen rain forests, deciduous and semi-evergreen rain forests, and rain forest savannah or dry forest savannah. Both sides of the Ghats and other main scarps may or may not be populated. There are thick screens or wide buffer areas through which language uses from the plains are not transmitted; thus there are possibilities of new speeches being born. Geometrical

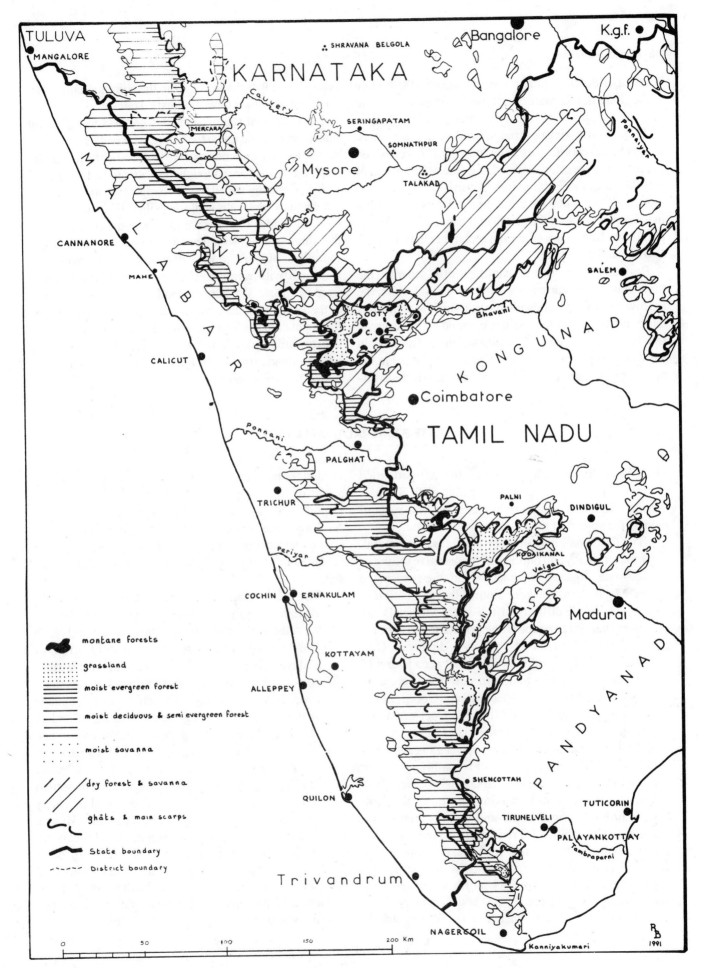

Plate 32: Kerala

boundaries do not rigidly follow the indented scarp line of the Ghats nor the watersheds, but they are not far from them (in fact just across various forest clumps).

They mostly zigzag through wild vegetation areas. Actual human borders are to be found only in cultivated plains which are often disputed, e.g., the northern end of Kerala (south of Mangalore) (north of the natural threshold) is a Tulu-speaking area but it is still within the Kerala state (see Plate 31) and has not been incorporated in Karnataka as per the recommendation of the 1967 Mahajan Report.

Basically, hilly forest massifs neatly separate the three states, and correspond to three natural units: the narrow windward Kerala plains receiving the monsoons and overhung by the Ghats ridge covered with evergreen rain forests in the south; the wider and dryer Tamil Nadu leeward plains; and the cooler Karnataka plateau in the north. These three natural regions, cradles of three different languages diverging from the common Dravidian basis, later formed three linguistic states.

Minor natural subdivisions did not lead to consistent human or political units: the Coorg state and its ethno-linguistic Kodagu community were included in the Karnataka state; the Wynad area, though the Cauvery laps its shores, was ecologically added to the Kerala state, and has been inhabited by Malayalis while the Nilgiri Hills were joined to Tamil Nadu. The hills are located at the crossroads of the three states, with specific ethno-linguistic communities, but are more open to the east, which is traversed with rivers and where most migrants come from (see Plate 31). Further, south, between the very end of the Ghats mountain ridge and Cape Kannyakumari, the population has linguistically leant more towards Tamil than towards Malayalam. Thus, Nagercoil District, a part of Nanjilnad, formerly of the Travancore state, was united to Tamil Nadu.

PLATE 33: KERALA, MALAYALAM

Plate 33 is divided into two parts: the left part titled 'Kerala' has four smaller maps dealing with Kerala's various languages and the right part titled 'Malayalam' depicts the spread of the language within India.

- The first small map on the right shows the natural, urban, railway and politico-administrative setting of the state. Against this background, the percentage of Malayalam speakers among the population is shown. In all districts of the state, Malayalis are more than 90 per cent of the population except for northern Kasaragod where Tulu is dominant. Outside Kerala, Malayalis numbered between 10 and 25 per cent of the population in only four bordering districts: Mangalore (10 per cent) and Coorg (21 per cent) in Karnataka, and Nilgiri (17 per cent) and Nagercoil in Tamil Nadu (see Plates 31 and 32).

Distribution of other language speakers is shown in the next three dotted maps. Tamil is mainly spoken in the bordering areas of the Palghat Gap where Malayali–Tamil interpenetration is maximum, i.e., in the Kottayam uplands among tea and rubber plantation labourers; and south of Trivandrum where there are many groups belonging to Tamil social communities. Konkani is found in the coastal parts among trading communities coming from the north since centuries though a part of them, e.g., in Goa and Kanara, prefer to state Marathi as their mother tongue. Tulu is strictly limited to the countryside north of Kasaragod, actually a part of traditional Tuluva, which the 1967 Mahajan Report recommended to transfer to Karnataka. This resolution was however strongly fought by all successive governments in Kerala. Telugu and Kannada are confined to smaller communities scattered all over the state.

- The 'Malayalam' map locates this language in its all-India geographical basis by two types of dots on the same scale: white ones within Kerala and black ones outside the state. The concentration of Malayalis is primarily in Kerala but their distribution outside the state is also significant. In Lakshadweep Territory, Malayalam is the native language of the whole archipelago but not of the island of Minicoy where the language is Mahl or Maldivian. Malayalam is also spoken by other language communities in Mangalore, Coorg, Nilgiris, Coimbatore and Nagercoil where Malayalis have for long settled and mingled. Malayalam is also found in many urban centres of Tamil Nadu and the former Mysore state where Malayali professionals are appreciated. For this same reason, they have moved to other industrial cities of the country and have been embraced along with other southerners with the overall appellation of 'Madrassis'. Their distribution is also seen in nodal places along main railway lines.

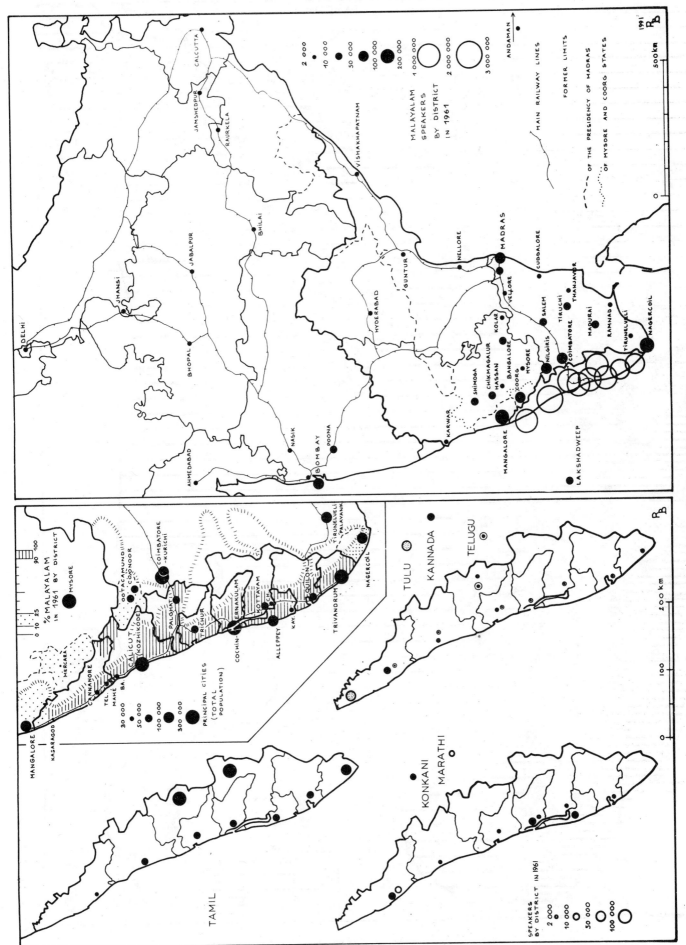

Plate 33: Kerala, Malayalam

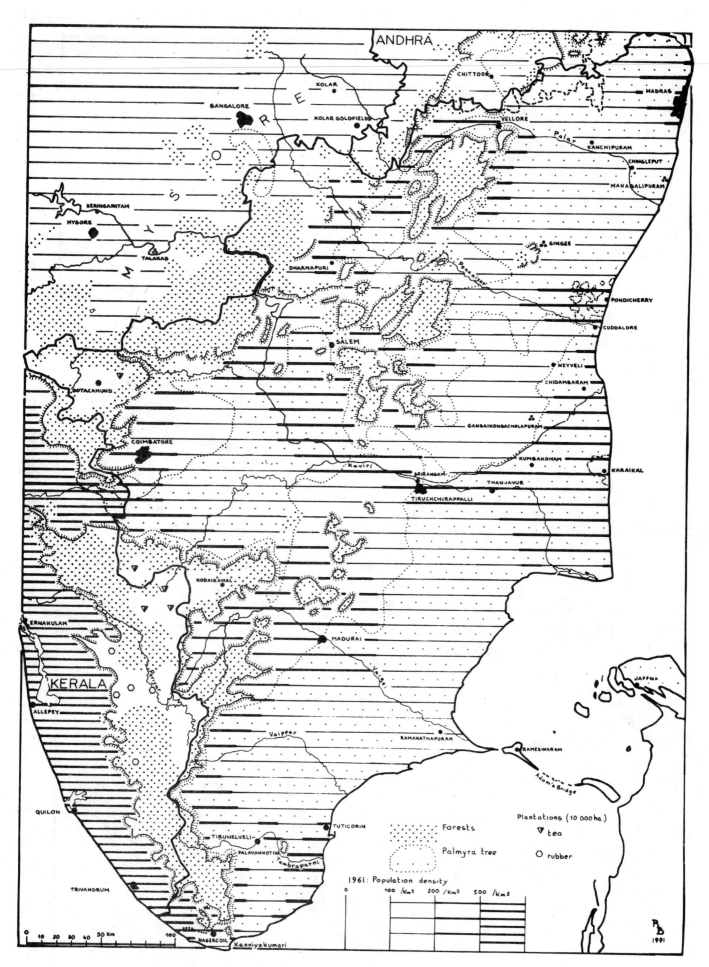

Plate 34: Tamil Nadu

PLATE 34: TAMIL NADU

Plate 34 shows on a single map the physiographic and demographic attributes of Tamil Nadu. This map only contains the linguistic state boundaries which is related to language. It is an evidence of what has been mentioned in Plate 32: a linguistic state is a language area and beyond that a natural area, rather consistent and well delineated from its neighbours.

This map is basically physiographic to the extent that it deals with relief: foothill lines of massifs plus rivers as well as directions of gentle or steep slopes. Two biogeographical traits have been illustrated: forests which are mainly located upon or near hills and the extent of the palmyra tree (*borassus*) which is typical of the Tamil landscape and economy. Also located in the map are plantations of tea and rubber which attracted migrant labourers to hilly regions. All these elements (including those in the map in Plate 32) have been taken from the series of the *International Map of the Vegetation and of the Environmental Conditions (1/1,000,000* signifying 1 centimetre for 1 million centimetres, i.e., for 10 kilometres) issued by the French Institute of Pondicherry.

Human settlement is represented by density of population at four levels: under 100, between 100 and 200, between 200 and 500, and over 500, by square kilometres in 1961. It is also represented by the location of main cities and their suburbs as also by former historical centres (Gangaikondacholapuram, Mahabalipuram, Gingee and Talakad).

These elements help create the landscape of Tamil Nadu which is different from that of Kerala and Karnataka. It is a moderately populated set of basins, plains and deltas, sprinkled with lines of hills as opposed to the densely populated coastal plains of Kerala and the sparsely populated Mysore uplands. It is neatly separated from Kerala by the Sahyadri mountain range and sur-

rounded by scarp lines of the plateaus of Karnataka and south Andhra Pradesh. All its boundaries wind through hilly and forest areas which are sparsely populated.

Some minor transfers occurred as a consequence of the reorganization of states in 1956 whose aim was to encompass language area within a territorial boundary, e.g., Nagercoil, east of Kannyakumari, was shifted from Trivandrum to Tamil Nadu, Kollegal Taluk from Coimbatore to Mysore, etc. In 1959, both Tamil Nadu and Andhra Pradesh agreed, under the Pastakar Award, to change their boundary: 317 Tamil-speaking villages in return for 148 Telugu-speaking ones were transferred which resulted in the effacement of the old boundary (a dotted line in the map, west of Madras) and significantly pushed the new one closer to the foothills.

Due to favourable weather conditions, the palmyra tree grows in abundance in most of the lowlands, basins, plains and deltas of Tamil Nadu. This tree is absent in Kerala and Karnataka. Coconut trees growing in abundance in Kerala are far less significant in Tamil Nadu. The extent of palmyra trees corresponds to Tamil-speaking areas.

The state has undergone, through three millennia, a linguistic transition from classical to modern Tamil. In areas close to Karnataka and Kerala, a matching development led the people to turn to Kannada and Malayalam. There is no direct link between the vegetation and linguistic phenomenon except for the fact that they ensue from the same environment and could extend within the same limits. Both the Tamil culture and Tamil cultivation pay a special tribute through the Tamil language to this tree which is as precious for Tamils as the coconut tree is for Malayalis. Links between nature and culture are numerous and often indirect, however, in few places like Tamil Nadu, this kind of relationship and similarity could be made obvious through a map.

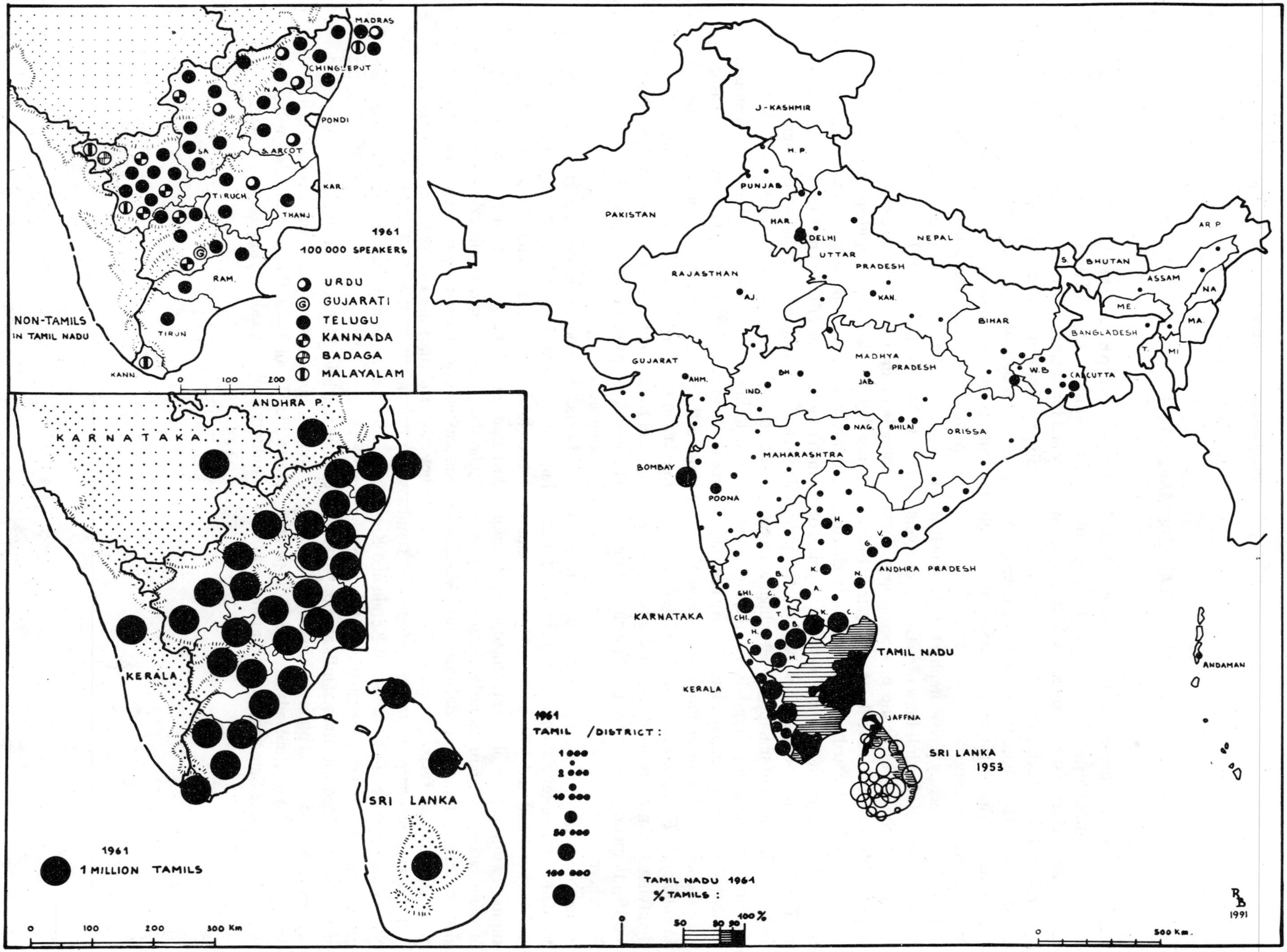

Plate 35: Tamil

PLATE 35: TAMIL

Plate 35 analyzes the distribution of Tamil in India (main map) and in Tamil Nadu (bottom left inset map), and looks at other languages spoken in Tamil Nadu (top left inset map).

- The bottom left inset map uses dots representing 1 million people to show the distribution of Tamil speakers in 1961 in Tamil Nadu, its neighbouring states and Sri Lanka. Out of 33.6 million Tamils, 28 million lived in Tamil Nadu and were almost evenly distributed all over the state. Further, 3 million lived in Sri Lanka, 0.5 million in Andhra Pradesh, 0.9 million in Karnataka, 0.5 million in Kerala and 0.3 million in the Pondicherry Territory plus 0.4 million in the rest of India.

- The top inset map shows with dots for 100,000 people, the district-wise distribution of non-Tamils in Tamil Nadu. Many Andhra communities such as the Reddi landowners or Komti traders have been living in the northern and western regions of Tamil Nadu since the Vijayanagar empire (from the fourteenth to the sixteenth century). Thus, Telugu speakers, in Tamil Nadu numbered more than 3 million (nearly 10 per cent of the population). The Kannadigas, less than 2 million (2.8 per cent), were confined to western uplands; the Badaga community, speaking a Kannada dialect, lived in the Nilgiri Hills; and Malayalis (0.4 million) were present on the border and in Madras city. Urdu speakers (0.6 million, 1.8 per cent) constituted only a small part of Tamil Muslims (1.6 million, 4.5 per cent) and were widespread in the northern part of this province since the settlement of Carnatic and Arcot Nawabs after the fall of Vijayanagar. On the other hand, most Tamil-speaking Muslims such as the Kerala Muslims and the Sri Lankan Moors (not shown in the map) are more numerous in southern Tamil Nadu. Then follows Gujarati (0.2 million),

the native language of the Saurashtra weavers living in Madurai since some centuries. Other languages had much smaller communities: Marathi (52,000) dates back to the Maratha confederacy in the eighteenth century, Hindi (39,000) was mainly brought by civil servants and employees of national companies and administrations.

- The overall map of Tamil speakers across the subcontinent shows their distribution with percentages of people in both their native areas: Tamil Nadu and northeastern Sri Lanka. This has been done using two kind of dots on the same scale: black ones in the rest of India barring Tamil Nadu and white ones in Sri Lanka.

Among Tamil Nadu's higher percentages of the population, 80 per cent are in coastal eastern districts and more than 90 per cent in the Kaveri (Cauvery) delta or Cholamandalam (Coromandel or Chola Nadu) and southern Pandyanad (Pandya Nadu). In the western half, numerous minorities have relatively outnumbered the Tamil majority (75, 68 and 79 per cent in Salem, Coimbatore and Madurai districts respectively) while in Nilgiri the Tamils being in the minority are rapidly increasing.

Outside Tamil Nadu, Tamils are spread beyond bordering areas mainly in all the other three Dravidian states, then in Bombay and Pune, and finally in all cities of north India particularly in Calcutta, Jamshedpur and of course Delhi, as also in the industrial belt of Chota Nagpur.

In Sri Lanka, the northern districts have the highest percentage (over 90 per cent). The eastern districts too, still have high percentages (over 80 per cent). But the dotted map shows that Tamils were on the whole more numerous in areas where they did not reach a majority, i.e., in Kandy or in Colombo (see Plate 36).

PLATE 36: SRI LANKA

Plate 36 consists of a general map on the right depicting Sri Lanka, five inset dotted maps for each *race* according to the 1953 Census, plus a Sinhalese-Tamil language map with percentages at the bottom right.

- The overall map is, as those in Plates 32 and 34, basically physiographic and aims to better illustrate the role of environmental factors in the ecology of human groups and their languages. The south central Kandy country, the highland heartland of the island, is indicated with its mountainous vegetation (over 900 m) and tea gardens, while slightly below are evergreen forests (up to 900 m) and rubber plantations. Coconut trees are predominant in the Low country along the western coast. Both these areas (Kandy highlands and coastal lowlands) receive heavy rainfall as they directly face the monsoon winds. Eastern lowlands are a leeward area where irrigation is done through tanks or canals. The northwestern and southeastern ends of the island are characterized by a typically dry vegetation.

This physiographic duality of southwestern windward low and high regions opposed to northern and eastern drier parts, had been for three millennia a major ethnic divide because Sinhalese settlement and power was centred in the southwest while Tamil settlement and power was in the north and northeast. There is a disputed in-between area of the former Sinhalese capitals: Polonnaruwa and Anuradhapura.

- The present distribution of people cannot be directly appreciated through language data because the Censuses of Sri Lanka (1953, 1963, 1971, 1981) do not collect and publish any information about mother tongues or languages but only about previously so-called 'races', now designated as 'ethnic groups'. Thus, due to the non-availability of information on the linguistic aspect of the country, the five inset dotted maps only show details about the ethnological aspect. But, as the five main ethnic components of Sri Lanka are traditionally and neatly distributed into two language sets, it is fairly easy to estimate the number of speakers present in each language community.

The Sinhala-speaking set of population was divided into two in 1963: Low Country and Kandy Sinhalese groups, this distinction got obliterated in 1981. The two dotted maps pertaining to these groups show a rather distinct geographical distribution. There is a marked absence of these groups in the northern and eastern parts of the island.

The other three inset maps relate to the three Tamil-speaking groups: Ceylon (or Sri Lanka) Tamils, Indian Tamils and Moors. Sri Lankan Tamils, settled in the island since some centuries, constitute the main native population in the northern tip of the island including the Jaffna peninsula and the eastern littoral. From there, the Sri Lankan Tamils (basically trading, clerical and professional communities) have spread all over the island, particularly, to Colombo and the Kandy country. The second group comprising the so-called Indian Tamils from Sri Lanka, on the other hand, are the descendants of Indian labourers who migrated to tea gardens since the nineteenth century and consequently settled from the Kandy highlands down to Colombo. Many of them, under the 1964 India-Sri Lanka agreement, were scheduled for a planned repatriation to India which was never achieved. The third group is that of the Moors who are Muslims belonging to the same kind of trading communities as those in Tamil Nadu and Kerala, and are spread all over the island with a higher density in the eastern coast, the Kandy area and Colombo. Very few of them (about 5 per cent) were considered as either Indian Muslims or Pakistanis.

From these five groups, totalling about 99 per cent of the entire population (98.8 per cent in 1963 and 99.2 per cent in 1981), it was easy to draw up percentages of Sinhalese or Tamil speakers within the population. These percentages have been displayed with shadings in the final inset map. In it, a clear-cut line is shown that divides the island into an almost entirely Tamil-speaking region in the north and in the east, and an area mostly Sinhala in the centre, in the west and in the south (though there are some mixed parts in the centre). In the eastern coast, the Tamil percentage was 93–98 in Jaffna and 85–86 in Manaar Districts. But, within predominantly Sinhalese lands, only 50–65 per cent of the population of the central Kandy country spoke Sinhalese except for the Nuwara Eliya District which is the tea area par excellence where 63 per cent spoke Tamil.

This ethno-linguistic division of the island, made worse by religious, social, historical and political factors, highlighted that the Tamil Elam claim for a Tamil-speaking autonomous area was not quite rational and

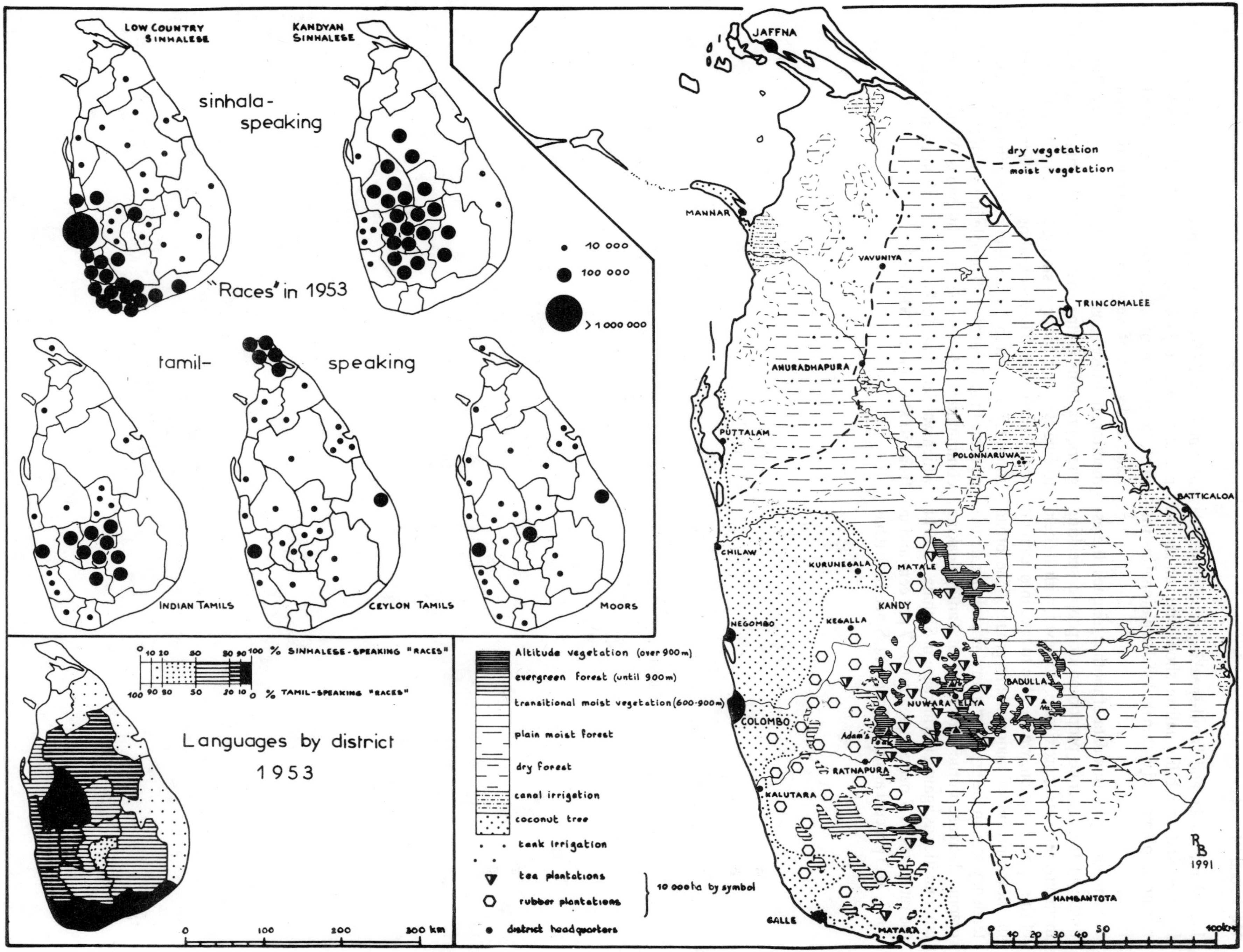

Plate 36: Sri Lanka

dry vegetation
moist vegetation

JAFFNA
MANNAR
TRINCOMALEE
BATTICALOA
VAVUNIYA
ANURADHAPURA
POLONNARUWA
PUTTALAM
CHILAW
KURUNEGALA
MATALE
KANDY
NUWARA ELIYA
BADULLA
KEGALLA
Adam's Peak
RATNAPURA
NEGOMBO
COLOMBO
KALUTARA
GALLE
MATARA
HAMBANTOTA

R B 1991

sinhala-speaking

LOW COUNTRY SINHALESE   KANDYAN SINHALESE

"Races" in 1953

10 000
100 000
1 000 000

tamil-speaking

CEYLON TAMILS   INDIAN TAMILS

MOORS

Languages by district 1953

% SINHALESE-SPEAKING "RACES"
% TAMIL-SPEAKING "RACES"

0 10 20 50 80 90 100
100 90 80 50 20 10 0

0   100   200   300 km

Altitude vegetation (over 900 m)
evergreen forest (until 900 m)
transitional moist vegetation (600–900 m)
plain moist forest
dry forest
canal irrigation
coconut tree
tank irrigation
tea plantations
rubber plantations
district headquarters

10 000 ha by symbol

logical as Sinhala- and Tamil-speaking people live side by side, and that bilingualism should be, or should remain, implemented within the local or national institutions.

Without any census data of mother tongues, the estimate of the accurate proportion of people speaking them only remains approximate. However, with the help of this approximation, we are able to take into account the development of major ethnic groups. The broad tendency seen in the present century, is a relative demographic decrease in the percentage of Tamil-speaking communities as against the increase in Sinhala. In 1911 the ratio was 31.7 per cent against 66.7 per cent and in 1943, 31.3 per cent against 67 per cent. Since 1946 it has declined from 28.9 per cent against 69.4 per cent, to 24.8 per cent against 74.4 per cent in 1981. Beside this twofold division of the population of the island, the relative decline of very small communities must be mentioned: Europeans, mainly English speakers; Burghers, gradually giving up their Indo-Portuguese dialect to English; and Malays, similarly losing their Creole Malay to English. They have altogether decreased from about 1.7 per cent to 0.7 per cent of the population with no more than about 50,000 people in each of these three communities. While the autochthonous Vedda tribe which was Sinhala-speaking since it is known, has fallen from 5000 to about 500 people.

CHAPTER 11

THE NON-REGIONAL LANGUAGES

PLATE 37: SANSKRIT

Plate 37 depicts the distribution of Sanskrit speakers in India according to the 1961 Census with the help of two dotted maps that show Sanskrit as an additional language on the right and as a stated *mother tongue* on the left.

- The map mentioning the state-wise distribution of Sanskrit as an additional 'subsidiary' language shows that in 1961 Sanskrit was stated by 194,433 people (173,036 men and 21,397 women). Thus, the figure was just slightly less than that required for a living language like Malayalam spoken by 17 million people. Another fact to be noted is the concentration of most Sanskrit speakers (137,000, about one for every 1,000) within the Hindi Belt. However, in the peripheral states the proportion is much lower except for Kerala (three for every 10,000).

- During every Indian census, many Indians amazingly use the option to state Sanskrit as their mother tongue as it is considered the most prestigious language in India and one of the initial 14 (now 18) constitutional languages in the country. This is illustrated by the map on the left. There were only 555 speakers in 1951 but 2,544 in 1961 (1,849 males and 695 females), 2,212 in 1971 and 6,106 in 1981. This rapid increase can be justly attributed to the recording of statements loaded with some individual motivation, deep attachment, cultural faithfulness, and spiritual allegiance, and is thus not an actual testification of a day-to-day, constant and collective working, spoken and thinking use of Sanskrit. It may rather reveal a behavioural and psychological bias more than the genuine legacy of an early childhood acquisition. 'Strange are the ways of ambition', wrote R.C. Nigam, a former Assistant Registrar General, in the 1961 Census

Volume about language (1964, ccxxiii). Whatever it may be, it should at least be taken into account as the expression of a significant intention and ambition and for this reason, the geographical analysis of its distribution is worth doing.

The map shows the district-wise number of all registered Sanskrit mother tongue speakers ranging from one person to more than 900 (926 in Allahabad) according to a gradual scale of dots. Each dot, representing more than five speakers, is divided where necessary into black and white sections to denote males and females (e.g., 674 males and 252 females in Allahabad).

This distribution is quite logistical because it indicates the presence, among various facts, of large groups of Brahmins, or other literate Hindus, all over India, and among them the predominance of men is not that surprising. However, some peculiar imbalances must be noticed, for instance, there were only two men and one woman in Banaras, 52 women in Kheri (Uttar Pradesh) and 89 in Ahmedabad with no male speaker. Notwithstanding these anomalies arising from people's statements or from the recording process, the resulting distribution in the map is relatively close to that shown in the map of Sanskrit as an additional language.

Two main pockets can be noticed: a large one in the Hindi Belt and a smaller one in southern Dravidian lands. The northern and historically central pocket is denser along the Ganga plain, though not exactly proportionate to the well-known traditional cultural centres. Some settlements are found in the Himalayas and in the forest reaches of Mahakantaka or Dandakaranya. The south Indian pocket, different from the previous map of Sanskrit as an additional language, is not centred around Kerala but around Karnataka and Tamil Nadu, and is spread in an equitable pattern with some concentration around Dharwar (probably a Lingayat

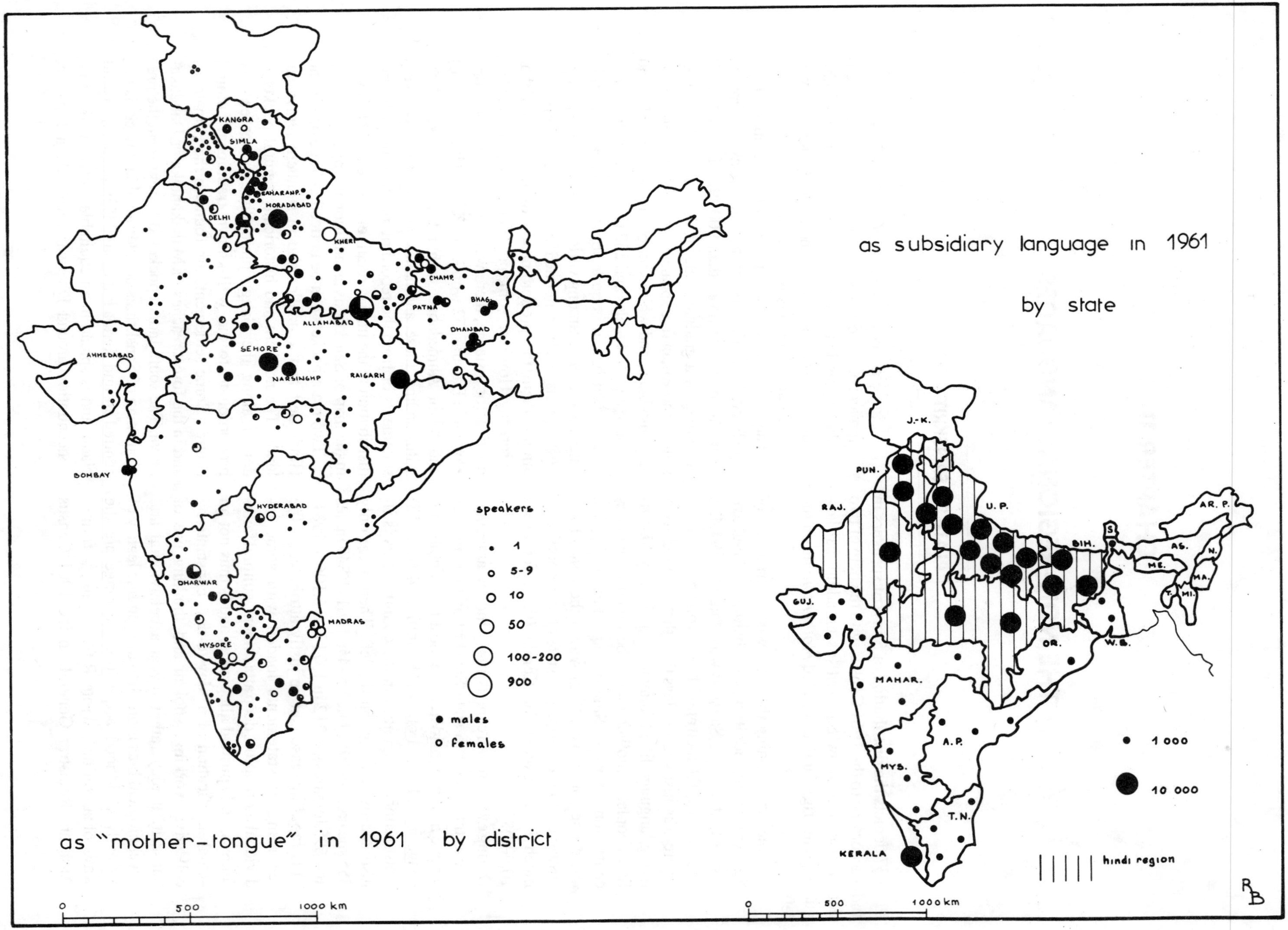

as subsidiary language in 1961

by state

1 000

10 000

hindi region

as "mother-tongue" in 1961 by district

speakers

1
5-9
10
50
100-200
900

males
females

Plate 37: Sanskrit

influence). As a matter of fact while we may find explanations for most concentrations, gaps are less easily justified. For instance, Kashmir, the land of the Pandits, had only three speakers (all women). The Dehra Dun District where Rishikesh is situated had only four speakers while Banaras had only three: Rishikesh and Banaras are famous centres of pilgrimage. Districts from the main Shaiva *maths* are not included as no Sanskrit speaker was registered in the upper Ganga valley (Uttarkashi and Chamoli) and neither in the whole of Orissa (not even Puri Jagadguru). There was only one speaker in Jamnagar District where Dwarka lies. But Chikmagalur District, the Sringeri centre of the Shankara order, had ten Sanskrit mother tongue speakers (three men and seven women).

This distribution, in spite of being discordant, confirms two facts. The first is that Sanskrit is alive and well, if the amount of publications including dailies was not enough to prove it, and that it reaches a persistent, scattered and conscious elite all over India—a situation which may have always been the same since some millennia when it split from the Prakrits. It kept a strong grip on the literate culture, besides and often in place of, Pali, Aramaic, Greek, Persian and English. It has never been a dead language nor a mass one. It has however been persistently, and even increasingly since its systematization by Panini, the cultural language of the small, influential and decisive minority which elaborated and transmitted over numerous centuries the religious, literary, philosophical, artistic and scientific treasures of India.

Second, in linguistic identity as in other fields, the Hindu world deliberately ignores standard situations and watchwords: individuals freely state their wants and preferences instead of following collective slogans and attitudes, and thus remain free to state any speech, mother tongue or heritage language, whichever they decide to honour most. All these statements are nonetheless facts and as such worth being assessed and included in a cartography.

1951

2 000 speakers

2 000 anglo-indians

BY STATE

1961

2 000 speakers

(S.LANKA : "BURGHERS, EURASIANS & EUROPEANS")

0   1000   2000 km

ASSAM   M   T   G   W.B.   BIHAR   ORISSA   U.P.   V.P.   BH.   M.P.   HYDERAB.   MYSORE   MADRAS   J.-KASHMIR   PU.   DE.   DELHI   H.P.   RAJASTH.   A.   BOMBAY   K   J   TRAVANCORE-C.

AS.   N.   M.   BANGL.   T.   BIH.   W.BENGAL   U.P.   OR.   M.P.   A.P.   MAHARASHTRA   MYS.   TAMIL NADU   KERALA   GOA   GUJ.   RAJ.   H.P.   J.-K.   PAKISTAN   SRI LANKA

by district
India 1951
Pakistan 1961

speakers
100
1 000
5 000
10 000

no data

KARACHI   MY.   BOMBAY   POONA   HYDER.   BAN.   MADRAS   IND.   NAG.   JAB.   DELHI   AG.   D.D.   LAH.   RAW.   LUCK.   KAN.   ALL.   PAT.   DHA.   JAM.   CAL.   DAC.   CH.   DARJEELING

R.B. 1991

0   500   1000 km

Plate 38: English as Mother Tongue

PLATE 38: ENGLISH AS MOTHER TONGUE

Plate 38 deals with the distribution of English as mother tongue in the whole subcontinent: the dotted map on the left shows the district-wise distribution in 1951 and 1961, and two small maps on the right show the distribution by provincial states in 1951 and 1961 using proportionate marks.

- The smaller 1951 map on the top right enables a basic presentation of this phenomenon. It compares the volume of English mother tongue speakers and Anglo-Indians who make up the only registered Indian community of English speakers besides other groups of English-speaking foreigners. In this way, we may assume that through a visual subtraction of the white mark (Anglo-Indians) from the black (total English speakers), it is possible to get the number of other English speakers (i.e., foreigners and other extremely few Indians).

This comparison shows that in most provinces, Anglo-Indians (111,637 in 1951) were actually close to the majority of English speakers (171,742). Among the other 60,000, English-speaking foreigners (30,000 British, 4,000 Americans, 2,000 Australians, etc.) were scarcely more than the natives of Portuguese and French territories in India (23,000 and 6,000 respectively) and were sociologically and linguistically amalgamated with Anglo-Indians. These other English-speaking populations neatly outnumbered Anglo-Indians in Bombay, Delhi and Assam, i.e., in places with numerous foreign residents. Rajasthan, with a number of English speakers lower than that of Anglo-Indians proves that this small community may linguistically merge in its human environment. In Sri Lanka, where language figures are not recorded in the census, the white rectangle shows the 'Burgher' community which is of partly Portuguese, Dutch or British descents.

- The second map depicts English speakers by states in 1961. It includes Pakistan and Bangladesh and shows that English-speaking communities have become widespread. The number of English language speakers which had been slowly increasing (224,000 in India in 1961) seemed to tend towards some stability (192,000 in 1971 and 202,000 in 1981).

- The dotted map is based on the Indian (in 1951) and Pakistani (including Bangladesh in 1961) censuses while areas (Nepal, Sri Lanka, Kashmir, Travancore) for which data is not available are indicated through striped areas. Delineations of former pre-reorganization provinces are shown with dotted lines along with present borders. The map details the distribution of both these main communities: Anglo-Indians and assimilated categories of Portuguese and French descents, and English-speaking foreigners. The focus of concentration is at the three main centres of economic activities—Bombay, Calcutta and Madras (four years of Independence, i.e., from 1947 to 1951, could not rank Delhi so high yet). Next in concentration were other economic centres of transportation and political life (Karachi, Delhi) with a special mention of hilly areas (Bangalore, Pune, Darjeeling, Dehra Dun, tea gardens of Assam, Coorg, Nilgiri Hills, Rawalpindi, etc.). The plate has thus illustrated English as the speech of two small communities and not as the additional language of most nations of the subcontinent.

PLATE 39: NON-INDIAN LANGUAGES

Plate 39 displays the distribution in India of the nine main groups of non-Indian mother tongues barring English from outside the subcontinent. Two subcontinental maps at the top deal with several Asian languages and four small Indian maps at the bottom each deal with a single European language.

- The map entitled 'Arabic and Persian' depicts the major Asian languages that had a paramount cultural influence on India. Persian was the official language of the Mughal Empire, the Maratha Confederacy and even that of the East India Company until the first half of the nineteenth century. In the twentieth century, Iqbal and Tagore continued to use it in many of their poems. Nowadays, it is the second most widely spoken foreign language in India after English and Arabic: 11,814 speakers in 1951, 8,885 in 1961, 10,509 in 1971. It enjoys the status of the main official language in Afghanistan (where it is known as Farsi or Dari), Tajikistan (where it is called Tajik) and Iran. It is traditionally used by trading groups in Pakistan in the region formed by Quetta, Karachi and Islamabad, and in India, i.e., in Bombay, Hyderabad, Bhopal, Aligarh and Chota Nagpur (Hazaribagh and its adjoining areas). The number of mother tongue speakers belonging to this community was 28,082 in 1961.

Arabic, the religious and classical language of Muslims, can be compared with Persian in India through the bulk of mother tongue speakers (7,914 in 1951, 17,840 in 1961, 23,318 in 1971 and 28,116 in 1981), while it is not possible to do so in Pakistan (3,334 in 1961) where it is mainly found in Sind (the first province won over to Islam) and Jacobabad (the outlet of business roads from Iran). In India, Arabs generally live in the same places as Afghans and Iranians do, i.e., along commercial roads coming from Irano-Afghan plateau and leading to the Gangetic valley, or to the western littoral. However, their traditional strongholds (7,000 in 1961) are in Karnataka's mountain areas or in Malnad. Here, they are known for having brought coffee growing in Mokka to India in the seventeenth century. This coffee cultivation was introduced by Babu Bhudan whose name has been given to the massif overhanging Chikmagalur (see Plate 27).

- Languages from eastern Asia are displayed on the dotted map on the right. Burmese, the national language of Myanmar (a former part of the Indian Empire) is mainly represented in the subcontinent by the Arakanese dialect, spoken in Arakan or the Rakhine state along the western coast of Myanmar. The Arakanese are traditionally settled in the Chittagong Hill Tracts district in Bangladesh where they are known as Moghs and make up one of the two main Buddhist communities. From there, they have spread to the northeastern hills in Bangladesh, Sylhet and India (in Tripura and Mizoram). However, since the local repression of 1978 in Myanmar, a number of Arakanese Muslim refugees called Rohingyas have fled across the border. They have been living in camps and are occasionally repatriated.

The 1951 Pakistan Census recorded 74,000 Arakanese and 40,000 Burmese speakers all over Bangladesh (among whom there were respectively 71,000 and 12,000 in the Chittagong Hill Tracts), but in 1961, there were only 2,000 Arakanese and 6,000 Burmese speakers and all of them lived in the Chittagong Hill Tracts. According to the 1961 Indian Census, there were 10,000 Arakanese and 3,000 Burmese speakers mainly in Tripura.

Chinese (9,214 speakers in 1951, 14,607 in 1961, 10,959 in 1971) was basically spoken by trading communities in Calcutta and Bombay. Japanese, with a much less numerous and a more recent settlement (985 speakers in 1961), was concentrated close to Japanese firms in Bombay, Calcutta, Baroda, Goa, Madras and Delhi.

- The four smaller maps at the bottom depict the four main European languages excluding English. Portuguese had 9,214 speakers in India in 1951 excluding Goa, 12,317 in 1961 including 9,161 speakers in Goa (14 per cent) and 6,029 in 1971. French similarly had 1,929 speakers in 1951 barring Pondicherry, and 2,593 in 1961 including 958 in Pondicherry where it is still alive. It was also extended to main business centres all over India, i.e., Madras, Bombay, Calcutta and Delhi, by Indians of French descent and foreign nationals (e.g., French-speaking people such as Belgians and Quebecers). German (1,665 in 1951 and 2,568 in 1961) is of recent settlement in India and is mainly found among foreign residents working with German firms such

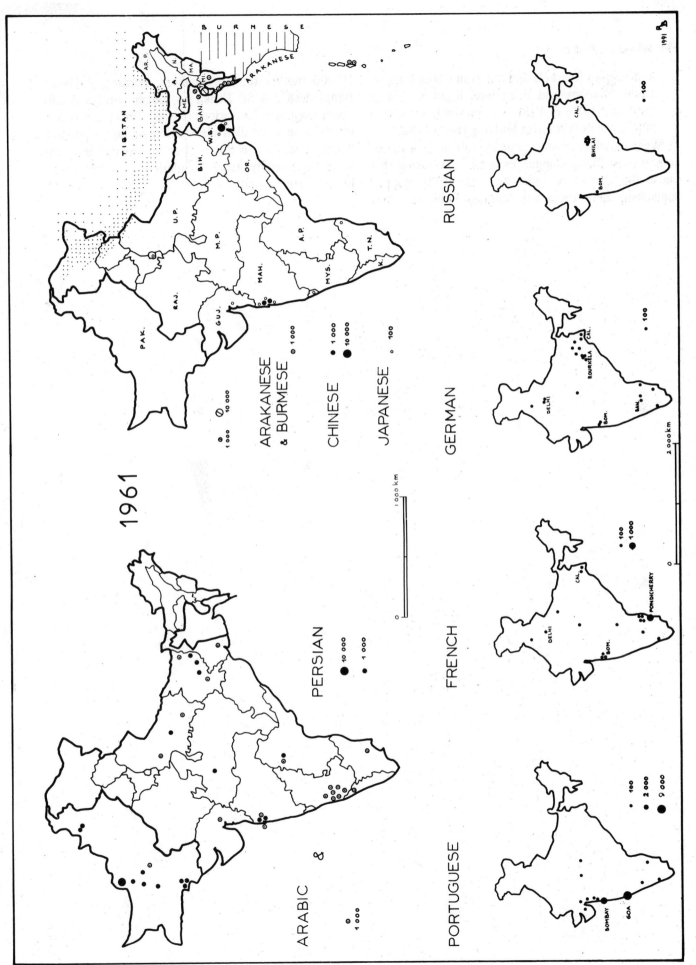

ARAKANESE
& BURMESE

CHINESE

JAPANESE

ARABIC &

PERSIAN

1961

FRENCH

GERMAN

PORTUGUESE

RUSSIAN

1991

Plate 39: Non-Indian Languages

as Krupp in Raurkela and others in Chota Nagpur, Delhi, Bombay and Bangalore. Russian (204 in 1951 and 1,036 in 1961) was presently located in Bhilai, the only Russian building site in India.

We cannot have any accurate idea about the distribution of most foreign languages in the subcontinent because the Census of India has since 1971 stopped registering data about any language with less than 10,000 mother tongue speakers. Further, Pakistan, Bangladesh and Sri Lanka no longer publish details about languages for various reasons. Enormous task is involved in a detailed registration of language data. There is also a fear that a clear representation of the linguistic diversity of their populations could be harmful to their national unity.

CHAPTER 12

THE LINGUISTIC STATES, THE MEDIA AND THE METROPOLITAN SITUATIONS

PLATE 40: LANGUAGES IN MAIN CITIES

Plate 40 shows the proportional development of mother tongue speakers in the five main cities of the subcontinent through five diachronic ethnograms. A central graph traces the development and tremendous increase in population of nine main cities of the subcontinent from 1891 to 1971.

- The graph begins with outlining the growth pattern of the five main cities.

    Calcutta and Bombay, two main ports as well as economic and administrative centres for long, are vying for numerical ascendancy. Of the two, Bombay has higher numerical strength mainly due to administrative reasons; Calcutta had a much lesser metropolitan population than Bombay: 10.9 and 12.6 million people respectively in 1991.

The modern capitals, Delhi and Karachi (8.4 and 7.7 million people in 1991), attained political and economic prominence. Karachi had a relatively stable economic and political position, notwithstanding the loss of its role of a national capital since 1959, and its restoration in 1970, though only as a provincial one. Delhi acquired a new leading economic position and role which is now decisive for the rest of India.

Though Madras (5.4 million people in 1991) is losing its place of third Presidency, the third largest city of India and a capital of a widely extended multilingual state, it remains the main city and business centre of all Dravidian lands.

The other four main regional metropolises include Lahore (4.5 million), Hyderabad–Deccan (4.3 million people), Bangalore (4.1 million) and Ahmedabad (3.3 million). Also, to be taken into account are political centres such as Dhaka (6.6 million in 1991; it became a capital since 1971), Colombo (1 million) and all the other cities reaching 1 million people—16 of which were in India, four in Pakistan and two in Bangladesh in 1991. The landscapes of these cities are less cosmopolitan and multilingual than those of the first major cities of the subcontinent.

- The Karachi ethnogram shows how significant the migrant population—coming from all over the subcontinent and mainly made up of Partition refugees (Muhajirs)—is in this city. The flow of Muslim migrants from the Hindustani Belt in northern India has since half a century given Karachi its particular physiognomy as being one of the biggest predominantly Urdu-speaking city of the subcontinent (since 82 per cent of Islamabad's population spoke Punjabi in 1981 while 11 per cent spoke Urdu and 4 per cent spoke Pushto). Between 1951 and 1961, Urdu speakers in Karachi increased from 50 to 54 per cent while native Sindhi fell from 14 to 9 per cent, ranking behind Punjabi (which also fell from 9 to 13 per cent). Other traditional minorities were similarly superseded: Gujarati, for instance, declined from 11 to 7 per cent because of the flow of Muhajirs from India and other migrants belonging to such ethno-linguistic groups of the country as Baluchi, Pushto, etc., from Pakistani provinces.

- The Delhi ethnogram is slightly different from the one in Plate 9. It shows how, in recent enumeration, changes in language terminology had a better impact on statistics or even on mass flows of population than any changes in linguistic use (language transfer). Prior to Independence, the population of this small Muslim regional market place in the process of becoming a capital and having a shared speech, could not decide between three designations:

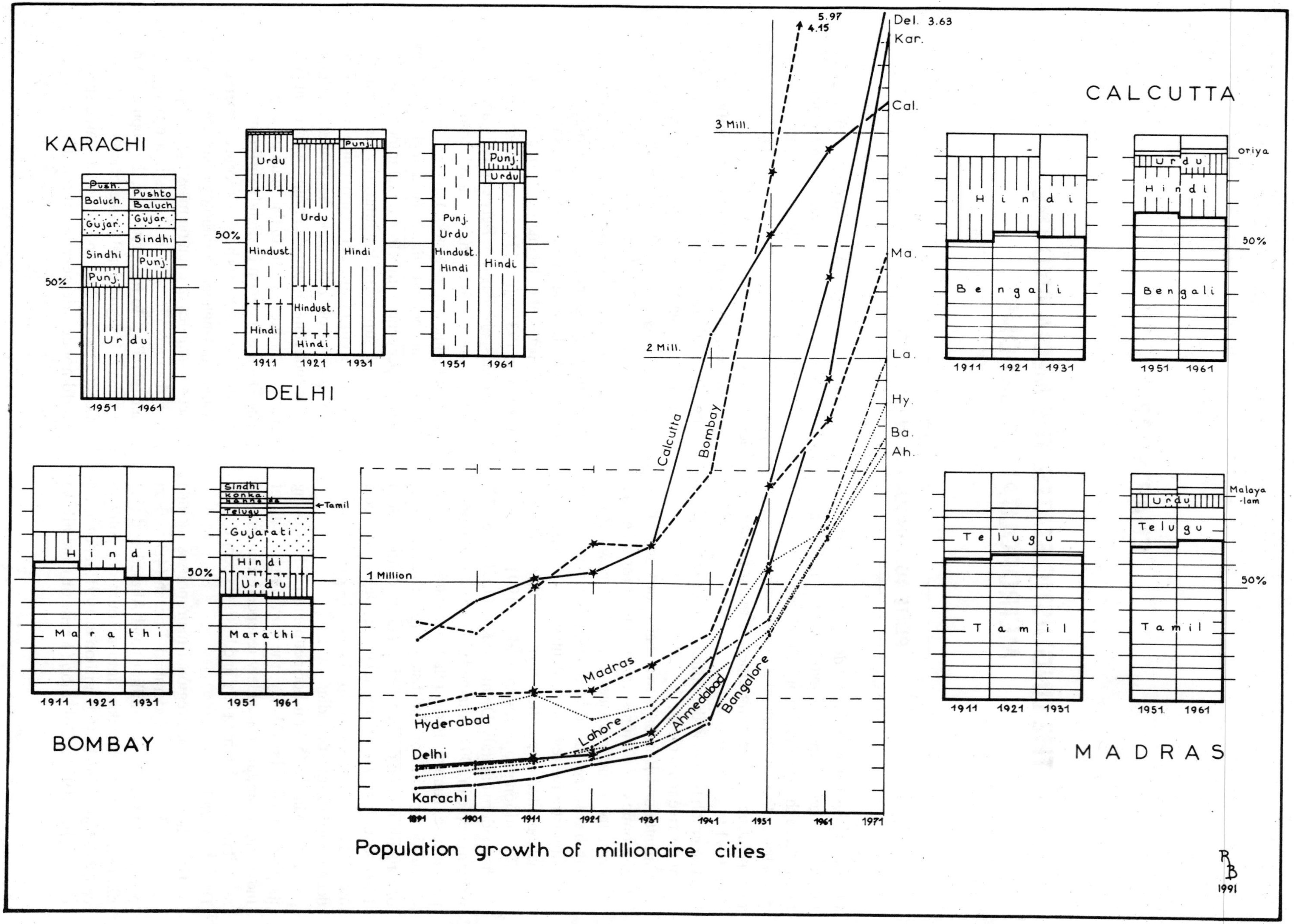

Plate 40: Languages in Main Cities

Hindi, Hindustani and Urdu. All these three languages were finally brought together in 1951 along with Punjabi as an additional language, due to the heavy inflow of refugees from the west.

Finally, in 1961, the break-up of the Hindustani language set showed that a large majority was inclined towards Hindi (77 per cent). Punjabi was spoken by more people (12 per cent) than Sikhs alone (8 per cent), and nearly as many spoke Urdu (6 per cent) than merely Muslims. These proportions have remained relatively stable. In 1971, Hindi was spoken as a mother tongue by 76 per cent, Urdu by 13 per cent (compared to 6.5 per cent Muslims), and Punjabi by 5.7 per cent (7.2 per cent Sikhs). In 1981, native languages of the population were Hindi spoken by 76 per cent, Urdu by 13 per cent (7.8 per cent Muslims) and Punjabi by 5.9 per cent(6.3 per cent Sikhs).

Roughly speaking, the three formal versions of commonly spoken Hindustani (Hindi, Urdu and Punjabi) comprised 95 per cent of the population in 1971. Earlier, it was 94 per cent in 1951, 96 per cent in 1931 and 1921, and 98 per cent in 1911. Through its complete transformation—from a sleepy and dying bazaar city with less than half a million people to a metropolis with more than 8 million people along with thousands of refugees and migrants—Delhi has almost retained the same linguistic ambience. The slight decrease in the predominant use of Hindustani is due to the new role of the city as a Union capital and world city, attracting residents from all over India (Bengali 1 per cent, Tamil, Malayalam and Sindhi a little less, etc.) and abroad.

- In Calcutta District, which comprises the core of the city and its suburbs, the inflow of migrants who do not come from Bengal is old and constant. Before Independence, Bengali was spoken by about 53 to 57 per cent of the population while the rest of the population, mainly coming from neighbouring Bihar, predominantly spoke Hindi. The Partition, bringing thousands of refugees from East Bengal, increased the percentage of Bengalis (66 per cent in 1951), though it later started to decline again (64 per cent in 1961). The number of Hindustani speakers increased from 25 to 28 per cent between 1951 and 1961 (20 and 19 per cent for Hindi, 5 and 9 per cent for Urdu) while, among the remaining 9 and 8 per cent, Oriya and other close neighbours had 1 per cent. The 1981 figures relating to native languages confirm this gradually increasing diversity of the core of the Bengal metropolis: Bengali 61 per cent,

Hindi 23 per cent, Urdu 12 per cent, Punjabi, Gujarati and Oriya with less than 1 per cent each.

- For the Greater Bombay District, the ethnogram shows a constant decrease (from 58 to 43 per cent between 1911 and 1961) in Marathi speakers among its inhabitants. (Although, at the same time, the total population of the district has undergone a fourfold general increase in Marathi speakers whereas it was less than threefold before.) The primary group of outsiders comes from neighbouring Gujarat and are either Parsis, Jains, Hindus or Muslim Bohras: Gujarati increased from 18 to 19 per cent between 1951 and 1961. The third linguistic group is Hindustani (from 17 to 18 per cent) with Urdu (10 per cent: less than Muslims 13 per cent) and Hindi (from 7 to 8 per cent). Among the Partition refugees, the most numerous were the Sindhis who peopled new townships such as Ulashnagar in Thane District. From the south, speakers of all Dravidian languages and of Konkani have been equally attracted by the diversity of opportunities that this economic capital seems to offer. Native language figures in 1981 nevertheless show some *re-Marathization* of the core of the city and its suburbs: Marathi 46 per cent, Gujarati 14 per cent, Hindi 12 per cent, Urdu 10 per cent, Punjabi 1 per cent, Sindhi, Konkani, Tamil, Telugu, Kannada and Malayalam about 2 per cent each. This cosmopolitan ambience in Bombay may partly explain the extremist reactions from some native Marathis about their allegedly being in the minority.

- As for Madras, the ethnogram shows an opposite tendency. From 1881 to 1961 the Tamil majority increased from 59 to 71 per cent. Conversely, the Telugu main minority decreased from 23 to 14 per cent while Urdu came to 6 per cent (compared with 7.5 per cent of Muslims), and Malayalam 3 per cent in 1961. Many differences separate the two former Presidencies: outsiders were in a less dominant leading economic position in Madras, and the growth of all Dravidian states focused on their own capitals maintaining many migration flows from within each state. Thus Madras now attracts fewer people from across the borders of Tamil Nadu and many more from within. At the same time, former migrants' children are being acculturated to Tamil. Native language figures in 1981 show this *Tamilization*: Tamil 75 per cent, Telugu 12 per cent, Urdu 5 per cent, Malayalam 3 per cent, Hindi 2 per cent, Gujarati and Kannada with less than 1 per cent each.

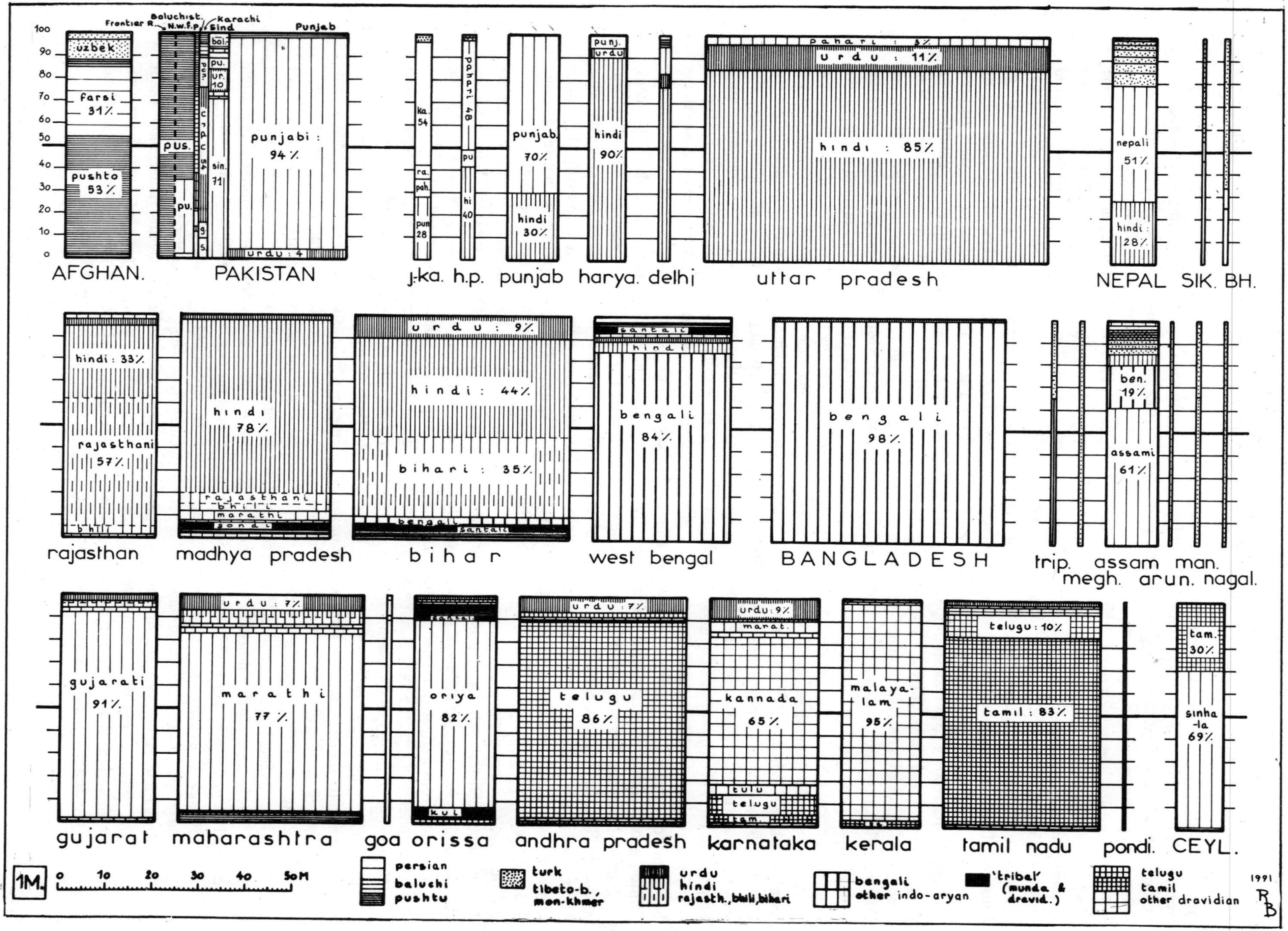

Plate 41: Languages by Region, 1961

Among other cities with 1 million people or more, few may offer such examples of tricky balances of majority against minorities. Like Hyderabad–Deccan in 1951, with 45 per cent of Urdu speakers within a Telugu environment, or Bangalore Municipal Corporation, where native Kannada had only 24 per cent in 1951 against Tamil (31 per cent), Telugu (18 per cent), Urdu (16 per cent) and others (11 per cent). The dynamics of formation and development of linguistic states entails various processes of language shifts and transfers leading to various stages of consistency or disparity.

PLATE 41: LANGUAGES BY REGION, 1961

Plate 41 displays the 1961 linguistic structure of each nation (mentioned in block letters) and region (mentioned in lower case letters) of the subcontinent through a single ethnogram that is proportional to its total population in width, and horizontally divided according to the percentage of its main spoken languages. The horizontal segmentation of the columns follow the geographical distribution of language minorities as much as possible from the north to the south. Each language or language family is indicated with the same shading pattern (provided below in the key) in all the ethnograms.

The study of each ethnogram presents a direct overview of the more or less complicated linguistic mosaic of each territorial unit. The comparison between them may lead to the appreciation of their common features when referring to their external linguistic identity and kinship as well as their level of internal consistency.

Some territorial units obviously look consistent, such as Bangladesh (Bengali 98 per cent), Kerala (Malayalam 95 per cent) and Pakistani Punjab (Punjabi 94 per cent). In many cases, this feature of consistency is concealed by a misleading opposition between formal versions of a common speech such as Hindustani with Hindi, Urdu and Punjabi. Thus, in Pakistani Punjab, the addition to colloquial Punjabi of Urdu which is the only taught and written language, would show a majority of 98 per cent. The same thing should occur in each province in the Hindi Belt when adding the figures of Pahari, Rajasthani, Bihari and even Bhili to all Hindustani variants. While doing that, many other united provinces may be considered in addition to the existing ones. The Hindi Belt provinces with predominant Hindustani variants are as follows: Himachal Pradesh (40 + 8 + 48 = 96 per cent), Indian Punjab (30 + 70 = 100 per cent), Haryana (92 + 5 + 3 = 100 per cent), Delhi (77 + 12 + 6 = 95 per cent), Uttar Pradesh (85 + 11 + 3 = 99 per cent) and Rajasthan (57 + 33 + 3 + 2 + 4 = 99 per cent).

When reducing or ignoring the inner rigid opposition between closely related languages, we may underline and emphasize, by way of contrast, that there are territorial units which are actually more deeply divided. Bihar is an example of provinces with more consistent but often disparate minorities: 88 per cent of its population speaks Hindi, Bihari, and Urdu while a 12 per cent minority speaks Bengali (3 per cent), Santali (4 per cent), Mundari, Oraon, Ho and Oriya (about 1 per cent each). Madhya Pradesh also reaches 88 per cent with Hindustani and Bhili, and a minority of 12 per cent divided into Marathi, Gondi, Oriya, Oraon, etc. Other states with a smaller majority but with many split minorities seem to have fairly solid bases, e.g., West Bengal (84 per cent), Orissa (82 per cent), Andhra Pradesh (86 per cent) and even Tamil Nadu (83 per cent) and Maharashtra (77 per cent).

When majorities get smaller, as in Sind (71 per cent) or Karnataka (65 per cent), this disparity may give rise to more difficulties. And when diversity takes the shape of duality, oppositions may lead to potential fragility and actual breakdowns as in Sri Lanka (69/30 per cent), Afghanistan (53/31 per cent), Nepal (51/28 per cent), Assam (61/19 per cent), Sikkim, Bhutan, Baluchistan, etc.

Linguistic states are seen as an empirical and never as a theoretical response to the challenge of a big diversity and irrational administrative limits. These states have enabled India to get out of many predicaments by presenting a united territory to major languages where most of its speakers could be ruled. Other less spoken languages were limited to the extent possible to a small population. But this distribution has been foreseen and achieved, only within the existing federal and democratic political framework of the national state. In such a background, if the territorial design of some linguistic states does not entirely satisfy everyone, the scope to develop it remains open.

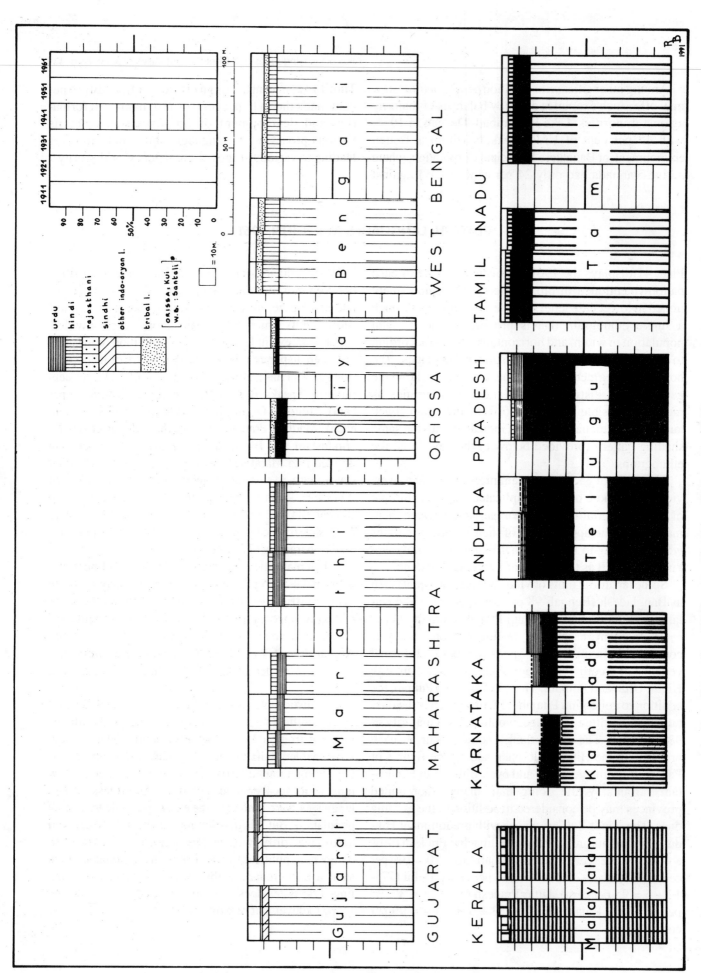

Plate 42: Linguistic States: The Three Major Languages, 1911-1961

PLATE 42: LINGUISTIC STATES: THE THREE MAJOR LANGUAGES, 1911–1961

Plate 42 depicts the development of the eight major Indian linguistic states outside the Hindi Belt from 1911 to 1961 through the respective distribution of their three main languages. It uses the diachronic ethnogram technique with a proportional width for each column, drawn to a common scale (shown in the key on the top right), pertaining to the population at that time. Each state language is shown with a particular shading that is used even when the language is spoken in other states. A shared shading is used in all ethnograms for main languages such as Hindi, Urdu, Rajasthani and Sindhi or for groups of languages such as Indo-Aryan, tribal languages, etc. The shared scale of population volume helps us to compare the linguistic minorities present in all these states of about the same size.

The scope and tendency of the language of the majority to increase relatively is significant in each state as seen in the cases of Tamil and Bengali since Independence. However, there has been a decrease in Telugu and Hindi minorities. A constant decline has also been noted in the proportion of Marathi speakers within Maharashtra; Kannada too has a weak position within its state; the tribal languages in Orissa and West Bengal have an insignificant position; and the distribution of Telugu outside Andhra Pradesh (in neighbouring Tamil Nadu, Karnataka and Orissa) is sparse. Finally, equally important is the ubiquity of Hindustani, through Hindi in Maharashtra, or through Rajasthani in Andhra Pradesh, and particularly its Urdu form in most of the south, from Gujarat and Maharashtra to Andhra Pradesh and Karnataka, strengthened by some linguistic consolidation of many Muslim communities. It is worth mentioning here that this phenomenon did not occur in Kerala in spite of a very consistent and old Muslim minority.

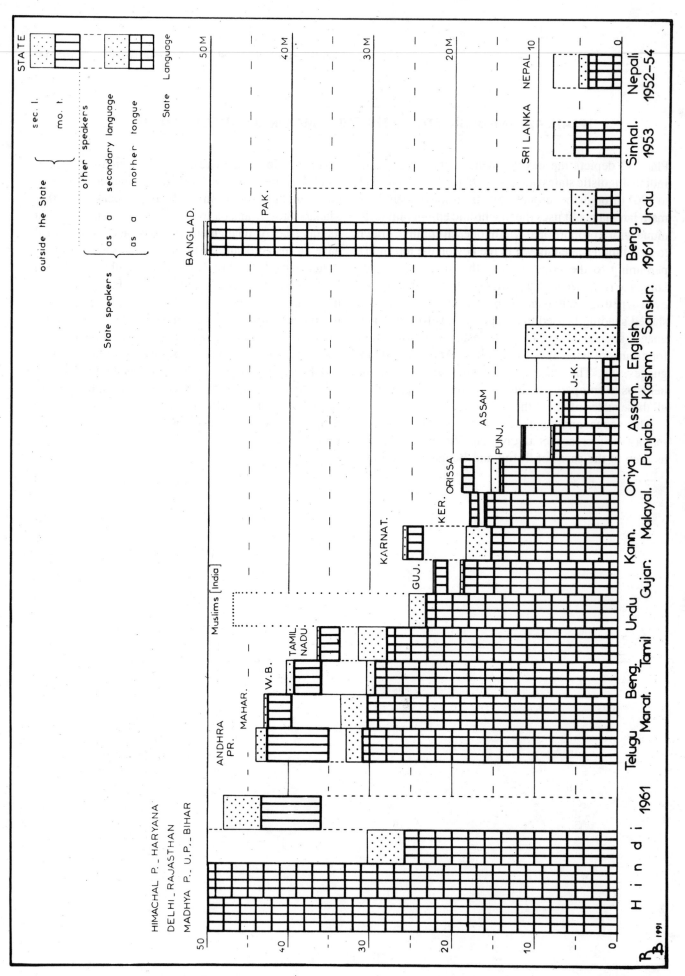

Plate 43: Official Languages and Population of States

PLATE 43: OFFICIAL LANGUAGES AND POPULATION OF STATES

Plate 43 tries to depict, for each of the 14 *constitutional* (and one *additional*) languages of India and for each *national* language of Bangladesh, Pakistan, Sri Lanka and Nepal, the respective volumes of people using them as mother tongues, as additional or as official languages. The census dates are close to each other: 1961 for India, Bangladesh and Pakistan, 1953 for Sri Lanka and from 1952 to 1954 for Nepal.

The histogram technique has been chosen, i.e., columns are divided into five parts according to a common scale and key (on the right). Each part represents:

- mother tongue speakers within the linguistic or national state (denoted by a grid);
- additional language speakers within the same state i.e., the *internal fringe of distribution* within the *inner minority* (evenly dotted areas);
- other language speakers within the state (blank areas), i.e., the part of the *inner minority* that does not speak the state language;
- mother tongue speakers outside the state, i.e., the *outer minority* (vertical lines);
- additional language speakers outside the state, i.e., the *external fringe of distribution* (evenly dotted areas).

This series of shadings show the influence of each language both inside and outside its territory. When looking at each language in its column, we can see three main sets of population, arranged according to their distance from their language:

- first, the *ethno-linguistic group* of native speakers together with the *bilingual fringe*;
- second, the *inner minority*, within the state, which does not speak the language but which is administrated through it (blank area);
- and, third, the *outer minority* of native speakers and the *external bilingual fringe* which are administrated through other regional languages.

The relative scope of these sets is significant to appreciate the extent of the distribution of each language within and outside its delineated territory. All the languages of India are displayed in descending order of their total native speakers within India and in other nations according to their size.

Hindi (125.8 million mother tongue speakers) spoken in the six provinces of the Hindi Belt (185.9 million inhabitants) has a large inner minority with a rather small bilingual fringe (4.4 million), and a consistent outer minority (7.5 million) and a bilingual fringe (4.5 million). These two bilingual fringes are the widest among all Indian languages (see Plate 44).

Other Indian languages present various situations, from being the most concentrated language in their states (like Malayalam and Gujarati with very small minorities, or like Punjabi, Assamese or Kashmiri with large minorities) to being the most split language community (like Telugu with a particularly significant outer minority). The balance between the volume of inner and outer minorities may throw light on the soundness of the considered linguistic state. A large outer minority may give way to dissatisfaction and to *irredentist* trends while a large inner minority may conversely raise claims of transfer to neighbouring states, or requests of autonomy from native consistent groups.

Outside India, the other national states of the subcontinent experience various linguistic situations, issues and fates, ranging from a high level of consistency, as in Bangladesh, to a low level, as in Pakistan, as also the dual split situations of Sri Lanka and Nepal.

The uneven importance of bilingual fringes shows the relative distribution of each language among the state's minorities. A higher distribution is found for instance in Tamil Nadu and Andhra Pradesh, and a lower one in Karnataka, Maharashtra and West Bengal. It also shows the relative distribution for Hindi, Telugu and Bengali outside the linguistic states.

PLATE 44: 'VEHICULAR' LANGUAGES AND MASS MEDIA

Plate 44 provides some tools for a comparative analysis between three aspects of the main languages of the subcontinent as speech vectors: their use as an additional language by people who have moved out of their native community and by the main mass media. A central graph compares the distribution of each of the most widespread languages as mother tongues and as additional languages (*Vehicular Languages* and/or LWC: *Languages of Wider Communication*). Two inset graphs depict the development of linguistic use as seen in the circulation of newspapers and output of films. Newspapers and films comprise the leading mass media in India.

- The central graph is a twofold horizontal histogram that shows, on the left x-axis, figures of mother tongue speakers and on the right x-axis, those of additional language speakers for each of the 27 main additional languages of the subcontinent (regional and national languages are written in block letters while other languages are written in lower case). The most widespread additional language of the subcontinent is shown at the bottom while the least one is shown at the top.

In order to visually notice the comparison between both these markedly different phenomena, two different scales, in million speakers, have been chosen for each series. The scale on the left for mother tongues is ten times smaller than the one on the right for additional languages. Thus, the same length on the left represents a tenfold increase in proportion than on the right: 10 million mother tongue speakers fill as much room as one million additional language speakers. This arbitrary selection is quite in perspective as there are ten times less additional bilingual speakers than native ones on an average for most languages. Through a rapid overview of the graph, it is easily verifiable that the length on both sides of the graph is approximately equal (i.e., ten times more people on the left than on the right). Anomalies noticed in the symmetry of the pyramid lead to significant exceptions.

This purports that the average ratio between both figures of mother tongue speakers (m) and secondary language speakers (s) can be mentioned as follows:

Additional language speakers/mother tongue speakers = 1/10 or 0.1 or 10 per cent.

This ratio [s/m] can be called the *ratio of language*

diffusion outside its mother tongue community (or *rate of vehicularity*, i.e., rate of use by other mother tongue speakers). When it amounts to 1/10, it represents the *average language diffusion level*.

Starting from this observation, we can mention that higher values of the ratio, i.e., s/m > 0.1 are *above the average*

(for instance, from 2/10 or 0.2 or 20 per cent, 10/10 or 1 or 100 per cent, to 100/10 or 10 or 1,000 per cent, etc.).

Lower values, i.e., s/m < 0.1, on the other hand are *below the average*

(for instance, from 0.5/10 or 0.05 or 0.05 per cent, to 0.1/10 or 0.001 or 0.001 per cent etc.).

Higher ratios, i.e., above one additional language speaker to ten natives (from two to ten or more), are the characteristics of a more or less significant diffusion: Languages of Wider Communication (LWC) such as national or regional languages, *lingue franche*, international languages, classical or liturgical languages, etc. Ratios lower than 1/10, i.e., where additional language speakers are less then 1/10 native ones, are related to languages with a lesser diffusion: those with relatively few speakers outside the native group.

Thus, in the graph, when the two striped bars on either side of the y-axis showing languages, have the same length we can say that it is around the average of one bilingual speaker out of ten natives. If the right striped bar is bigger than the one on the left, it indicates a fairly well-distributed language. But, if the right bar is smaller than the one on the left, it denotes a language with a lesser impact on non-native speakers' environment.

Fortunately each of the first censuses in the subcontinent recorded both these language uses. In India, beside mother tongues, there was one 'subsidiary' language in 1951, but two 'subsidiary' languages in 1961, two 'second' ones in 1971 and two 'additional' ones in 1981. In Pakistan, and nowadays in Bangladesh, 'additional' languages were recorded in 1961 with number of speakers; the same is true of Nepal from 1952 to 1954 with regard to 'secondary' language, but none in Sri Lanka where language statistics have never been recorded in the censuses.

Number of speakers for each language in the various nations of the subcontinent are added on the same bar though they are differently represented (shown in the

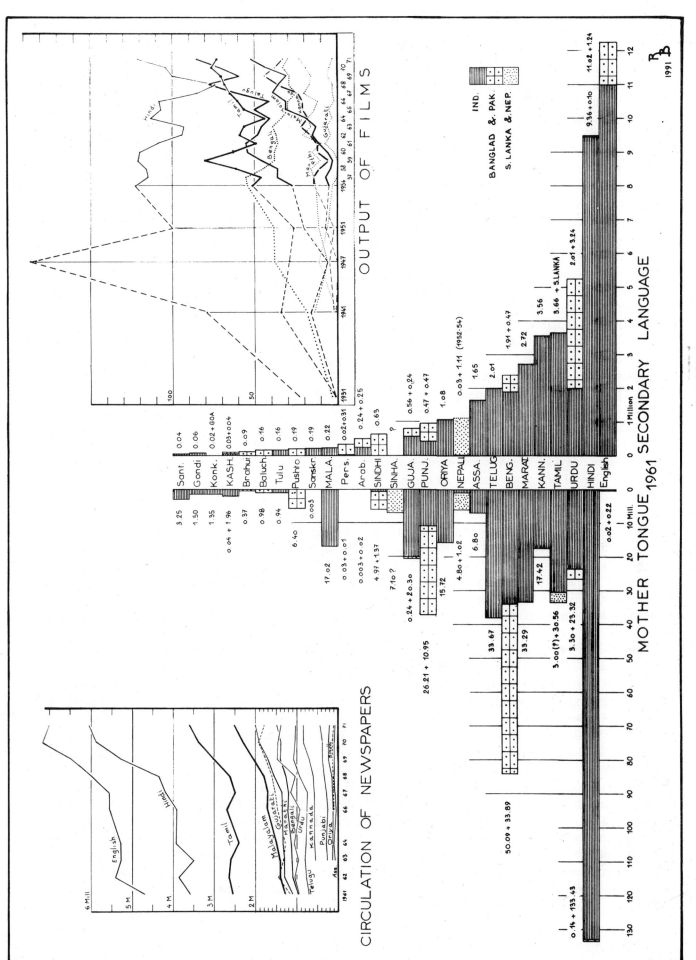

Plate 44: 'Vehicular' Languages and Mass Media

key) on the right. Going through the graph from the bottom to the top, we can notice a discrepancy with English which had 12.26 million second language speakers for only 0.24 million natives in India and Pakistan (11.02 + 1.24). Thus its s/m ratio (12.26/0.24 = 51) is typical of a major LWC.

English is followed by Hindi which is the widest native and second additional language all over the subcontinent. Its ratio of 9.37/133.57 = 0.07 (signifying that there was less than one bilingual person from outside out of 100 natives) is just below the theoretical average. This could be explained as a result of the concentration of the bulk of its native speakers mainly in the Hindi Belt and the fact that Hindi was the Union language till 1961, i.e., for less than 15 years.

For Urdu, the balance is just the opposite: s/m = 5.25/26.62 = 0.197 indicating two bilingual speakers for one native language speaker. This is because of its role of a national language in Pakistan. Both the Hindustani languages (Hindi and Urdu) were among the first second languages in the subcontinent.

The Tamil ratio s/m (quantified only in India) is 3.66 / 30.56 = 0.12. Being slightly above the average, this ratio shows an equitable distribution of the language among non-Tamils from Tamil Nadu besides its classical or literary prestige outside the state.

Kannada (s/m = 3.56/17.42 = 0.2) has a high ratio because of its role as a regional language within Karnataka which has a large number of linguistic minorities (35 per cent).

Ratios of Marathi (0.08), Bengali in India (0.06), Telugu (0.06), Oriya (0.07) are below the average because of the lower proportion of minorities within these states.

Higher ratios are obtained by Nepali in Nepal (0.275) and Assamese (0.24) which have a significant impact on minorities in their territory by virtue of being national or regional languages. Higher ratios are also obtained by Brahui (0.24), Tulu (0.17), Baluchi (0.16) and even Sindhi (0.125), all of which have a role as a regional language or as a local lingua franca.

This is the case, besides English, of classical languages such as Persian (1.25), Arabic (2.1) and Sanskrit (6.3, however controversial its figures as a mother tongue might be).

Though comparisons between both these quantities are highly enlightening, they must be carefully read and asserted, particularly when considering two languages very different in their development such as Malayalam

and Santali which have an extremely low ratio of diffusion (0.01).

The comparisons are carried out by way of a ranking of languages according to their usage as a second language and as a native language. The 1961 ranking comparison for the 14 constitutional languages in India was as follows (with mother tongue use given in brackets):

Hindi, 1 (1), Tamil, 2 (4), Kannada, 3 (8), Marathi, 4 (5), Telugu, 5 (2), Bengali, 6 (3), Urdu, 7 (6), Assamese, 8 (12), Oriya, 9 (10), Gujarati, 10 (7), Punjabi, 11 (11), Malayalam, 12 (9), Sanskrit, 13 (14), Kashmiri, 14 (13).

Progress in ranking for a second language use (compared with a mother tongue one) is linked to the scope of minorities of non-speakers within the administrated territory: Kannada holds 5 positions, Assamese 4, Tamil 2, Marathi and Oriya 1. The relative downgrading is due to a few minorities inside the linguistic state: Telugu, Bengali, Gujarati and Malayalam have lost three positions.

The wider diffusion of languages is more associated to the administrative power than to their cultural spread or development.

Data collected by Indian censuses on bilingualism may correct some of the above mentioned observations. The liability offered to anyone to state only one or two second languages besides their mother tongue has seemingly changed the ranking for at least the two main widespread additional languages, i.e., English and Hindi. Hindi, stated as a second language by 9.363 million people in 1961 (2.6 per cent of the population) reached nearly 17 million (3.1 per cent) in 1971 and 44 million (7.1 per cent) in 1981. According to the census data, figures for English as a stated second language were 11.02 million (3.1 per cent) in 1961, more than 24.9 million (4.6 per cent) in 1971 and about 3 million (0.5 per cent) in 1981.

The last figure is astonishingly incredible: more than 20 million speakers of English as a second language could not have vanished over ten years. It is also impossible that the number of delivered English courses could have had such a marginal impact on their (qualified or not) participants, among a population of 241 million literate people in 1981 and about 10 million students in the 9 to 12 standard and 3 million students in universities. However, on close examination this small figure could be accounted for as a direct consequence of the restriction to state only two second languages as also the gaps in recording data (e.g., language data for Assam and Tamil Nadu are missing).

After having stated a mother tongue, informants may have been in a dilemma to choose as a second language either English or other more frequently used languages, for instance, a home language, a lingua franca, a regional language, or the Union language. A second language is that which the informant has a fair 'working knowledge to converse with understanding' as required by the census. Thus any second language acquiring a third position (i.e., as the fourth one, including the mother tongue) had no place in published statistics. Trilingual Indians are so numerous (i.e., knowing two languages besides their mother tongue) that it is a pity not to take into account the additional contribution of quadrilingual ones.

In 1981, 13.34 per cent (13.04 per cent in 1971 and 9.7 per cent in 1961) of Indians were at least 'bilingual', i.e., more than 82 million including an unpublished number of trilingual and an unrecorded number of quadrilingual speakers. But the proportion varied greatly from one language community to another. It was much higher than the average in some small language groups (Coorgi: 83 per cent, English 74 per cent), or tribal groups (Gadaba 80 per cent), or scattered language groups (Konkani 68 per cent, Sindhi 57 per cent); and even in some compact groups mingled with significant minorities (Assamese 53 per cent, Tamil 50 per cent). The proportion was neatly below the average in other more concentrated language groups (Bengali 6 per cent, Hindi 5 per cent). Whatever be the actual number of people speaking English as a second language (if a fourth language was recorded), it is nevertheless significant to note that Hindi (the Union language) has gradually outnumbered English (the Union additional language) among the first three stated languages particularly among people living outside the Hindi Belt, i.e., Bengalis and Malayalis.

The graph on the top left dealing with 'Circulation of Newspapers' shows the development of the circulation of newspapers (dailies, weeklies, etc.) through million copies sold in each of the 15 main languages used in the press in India from 1961 to 1971. It shows some disparities with regard to increases in the ranking of the 15 Indian languages except for English which still ranked first:

1 Hindi, 2 Tamil, 3 Malayalam, 4 Marathi, 5 Gujarati, 6 Bengali, 7 Urdu, 8 Telugu, 9 Kannada, 10 Punjabi, 11 Oriya, 12 Sindhi, 13 Assamese and 14 Sanskrit, while Kashmiri did not figure in the press.

A decade later, in 1982, the circulation in Hindi had more than doubled, exceeding that of English, which had increased by only one-third, Malayalam exceeded Tamil, and Bengali exceeded Marathi. The resulting ranking (except for English now ranking second) for Indian constitutional languages was as follows:

1 Hindi, 2 Malayalam, 3 Tamil, 4 Bengali, 5 Marathi, 6 Gujarati, 7 Urdu, 8 Telugu, 9 Kannada, 10 Punjabi, 11 Oriya, 12 Sindhi, 13 Assamese, and 14 Sanskrit (two dailies), while there was still not a single daily in Kashmiri.

The overall ranking of dailies in 1990 showed that English held fourth position (with less than 200 titles) while national languages were as follows: 1 Hindi (more than 1,000), 2 Urdu (305), 3 Tamil (206), 4 Malayalam (187), Kannada (162), and so on till Sanskrit which still had two dailies.

Such a ranking is obviously more indicative of the number of literate people in each language than of the gross total number of its speakers.

- The graph on the 'Output of Films' shows the number of films produced over one-and-a-half decade (1956–71), plus milestones for 1931, 1941, 1947 and 1951. It highlights the seven major languages in which films are produced. Hindi ranked first with an annual production of approximately 100 films though there was no actual increase. It was followed sometimes closely by films made in Tamil and Telugu reaching around 80, those in Malayalam and Kannada showed a significant increase and were close to 50, and those in Bengali declined to about 30. Films produced in Marathi were more than 20 and those in Gujarati were less than ten.

Two decades later in 1992, the Indian film production—ranking first in the world, followed by the USA, Japan, Egypt, Russia, Hong Kong and France—had increased significantly though the order of the languages had altered.

Hindi still leads with about 200 films but is closely followed by Tamil and Telugu, each with nearly the same number of films. Malayalam is followed by Kannada with about 100 films. Bengali has maintained a stable figure of 50. Marathi reaches 30 while Gujarati, after having exceeded Marathi in the seventies and eighties with more than 30 films had fallen again to about ten. Thus, it was still behind less significant cinema languages such as Oriya, Punjabi, Assamese, Nepali and Manipuri, and recently even behind Urdu and Sanskrit.

The ranking of languages in which films are made, different from that of the press, draws attention to other factors. The first is obviously the interintelligibility among all Hindustani variants that explains the almost complete absence of Punjabi and Urdu films while most Hindi films, mainly directed in Bombay studios within the Marathi area, largely contain Urdu songs. There is also a close intelligibility of peripheral Indo-Aryan with Hindustani that explains the grave competition faced by Bengali, Marathi and Gujarati film production. Thus this factor of possible interintelligibility with Bengali as with Hindi may hamper the rise of Assamese or Oriya film production.

The second decisive factor is the geographical decentralization of south India's film industry. Film production has moved out of Madras studios towards the studios of Hyderabad–Deccan, Bangalore and Trivandrum. The decentralization is linked to the strong identity and linguistic differences of the four Dravidian languages, and the tremendous popularity of native films and actors among these populations.

The disparity in languages is due to the tendency within the production of mass media that favours some languages among the major ones, marginalizes the medium-sized ones and neglects all the minor ones. Television may increase this shared tendency. It has so far greatly promoted Hindi—a supremacy that will necessarily last and expand until regional studios would provide Doordarshan (India's television system) with enough competitive programs in regional languages.

The wider diffusion aspect is significantly based on the technical support of the media and on the extension of the state power than on the outer (i.e., from the local to the international) historical cultural prestige. Languages of Wider Communication thus refer to those which have film studios, a press, and a territorially established administration and are not those with several centuries of literature and learned knowledge or with a worldwide fame.

A brief attempt to compare the ranking of the present 18 constitutional languages (i.e., excluding any other Indian language, or English) according to their mother tongue speakers (in 1991) along with the number of second language speakers (in 1961), their press circulation (in 1982) and their film production (in 1992) would be as follows:

Hindi 1 1 1 1, Telugu 2 5 8 3, Bengali 3 6 4 6, Marathi 4 4 5 7, Tamil 5 2 3 2, Urdu 6 7 7 1 4, Gujarati 7 10 6 8, Kannada 8 3 9 5, Malayalam 9 12 2 4, Oriya 10 9 11 9, Punjabi 11 11 10 10, Assamese 12 8 13 11, Kashmiri 13 14 (?) (?), Sindhi 14 (?) 12 (?), Nepali 15 15 (?) 12, Konkani 16 16 (?) (?), Manipuri 17 (?) (?) 13, Sanskrit 18, 13, 14, 15[*].

The comparison of these rankings in each of the major languages, despite the unavoidable disparity to date the four indexes, may throw some light on its average position within the complex landscape of the cultural life of the Indian population.

[*] The question marks indicate that ranking data for these categories is not available.

CHAPTER 13

ETHNO-LINGUISTIC ISSUES THROUGHOUT THE SUBCONTINENT AND AROUND

PLATE 45: INDIAN POLITICAL MAP UNTIL INDEPENDENCE

Plate 45 aims at introducing the genesis of present national and regional units of the subcontinent through their territorial development in the first half of the twentieth century. The plate comprises two political maps of the former Indian Empire: the one on the left shows the first linguistic provinces in 1900 and after, and the second on the right shows the provinces on the day of the Partition, 15 August 1947.

- The map on the left shows the administrative set-up of the peninsula (excluding Burma which then belonged to the Empire of India and Sri Lanka) from 1900 to the Partition. Different shadings express the political distribution between provinces and presidencies of British India (blank areas) and Native India (dotted areas in three densities according to the size of princely states: from evenly dotted areas for the most important princely state to densely dotted areas for the smallest state).

Borders of political units are drawn in lines of varying thickness. Presidencies and bigger provinces are represented by thick lines while smaller ones are shown by lighter lines. Names, dates and border lines of political creations or suppressions from 1900 onwards are shown on the map (various dotted or broken lines for 1901, 1905, 1912 and 1936 in which new borders were created).

As a matter of fact, many of the geopolitical events from 1900 to 1947 already had an ethno-linguistic significance more than just a territorial background. In 1901, the secession of the North West Frontier Province from Punjab created a Pushto territory which was suited to the situation, physiognomy and settlement of the Pashtun people beyond the Durand Line. The union

of Agra and Oudh that resulted in the creation of United Provinces in 1902 and the union of Central Provinces and Berar in 1903 were developments that responded to local convenience without taking into account ethno-linguistic background.

But, in 1905, the decision of Lord Curzon to divide Bengal into two parts—eastern Bengal with Assam and western Bengal with Bihar and Orissa—was as much anti-Bengal as anti-nationalist. This is because Bengal and, in particular Calcutta, were considered as leading the Indian National Movement and as such liable to punishment by division and consequent downgrading. The creation of the new province of Delhi led to the relocation of the capital from Calcutta. The retreat of the Crown and the repeal of Lord Curzon's decision in 1911 that resulted in the formation of three provinces—a reunited Bengal, a recreated Assam and a newly built Bihar and Orissa—were obvious acknowledgements of the unquestionable reality of Bengali, Assamese and Bihari-Oriya specificities.

The British power had to face not only a strengthening all-India National Movement, struggling towards democracy and Independence but it had to also encounter, within the same movement, many growing local forces demanding the creation of *linguistic provinces*. These provinces would correspond to historical units of the Indian nation in place of the bizarre and artificial administrative set-up prevailing during the British regime. For instance, as early as 1913, the Telugu Districts Conference asked for the formation of an Andhra province severed from Madras. The Indian National Congress began to subdivide its own inner structure according to linguistic units: Orissa was separated

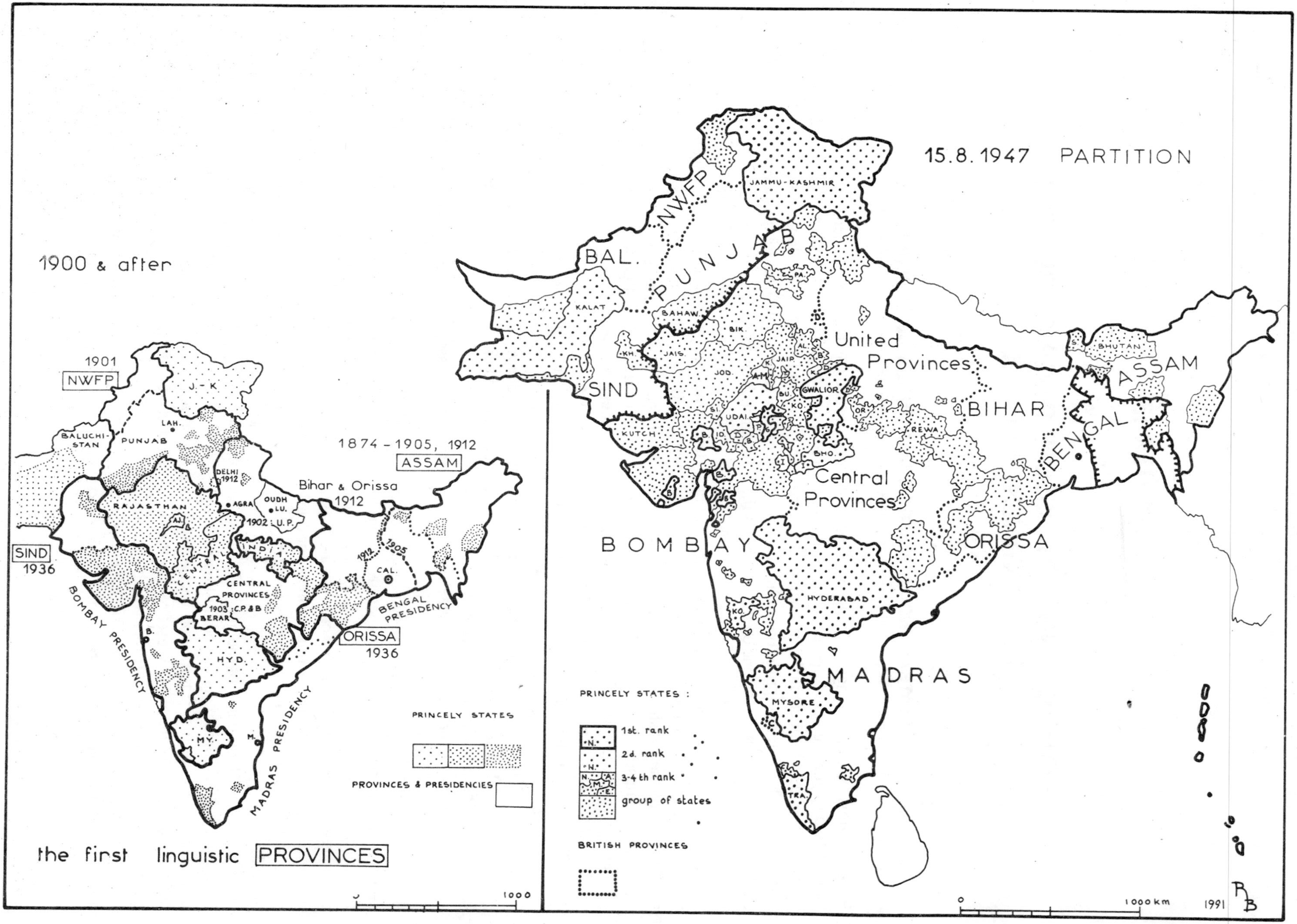

1900 & after
1901
NWFP
BALUCHI-STAN
PUNJAB
LAH.
J. - K
DELHI 1912
AGRA
OUDH
LU.
1902 U.P.
RAJASTHAN
CENTRAL PROVINCES
1903 C.P. & B
BERAR
HYD.
MY.
1874 - 1905, 1912
ASSAM
Bihar & Orissa
1912
CAL.
BENGAL PRESIDENCY
ORISSA
1936
SIND
1936
BOMBAY PRESIDENCY
MADRAS PRESIDENCY
PRINCELY STATES
PROVINCES & PRESIDENCIES
the first linguistic PROVINCES
1000
15.8.1947 PARTITION
JAMMU-KASHMIR
NWFP
BAL.
PUNJAB
KALAT
BAHAW.
BIK
JAIS
JOD
JAIP
UDAI
GWALIOR
BHO.
SIND
KUTCH
United Provinces
BIHAR
REWA
ASSAM
BHUTAN
BENGAL
Central Provinces
ORISSA
BOMBAY
HYDERABAD
MYSORE
MADRAS
TRA.
PRINCELY STATES :
1st. rank
2d. rank
3-4 th rank
group of states
BRITISH PROVINCES
0
1000 km
1991

Plate 45: Indian Political Map Until Independence

from Bihar in 1908, Sind and Andhra in 1917. In 1920, the Congress adopted the principle of general reorganization of administrative provinces on a linguistic basis, and in 1927 asked, as a first step, for the creation of new provinces of Andhra, Utkal (Orissa), Sind and Karnataka. However, among the constitutional reforms granted by London, only Orissa and Sind were created in 1936.

• The second map on the right presents the political situation on the eve of Independence and Partition, 15 August 1947. The 16 British provinces are shown as blank areas and demarcated by dotted lines (12 large provinces with their full name and four smaller provinces: Delhi, Ajmer–Merwara, Coorg and Andaman & Nicobar), and the princely states are shown by four dotted shades according to their official ranking (and the hierarchical honours of their head of state):

• five first class states (21 canon shots) with full name,

• six second class states (19 canon shots) with initial letters,

• 13 and 18 states of third and fourth class (17 and 15 canon shots) with delineated border and initials on the map,

• plus 17, 30, 23 states of fifth, sixth and seventh class (13, 11 and 9 shots), still belonging to the category of 'Salute States Rulers' (state rulers worth being saluted by a certain number of canon shots) and members of the House of Princes, graphically amalgamated on the map with 300 and more of the 'Non-salute States Rulers'.

The new international border of the two dominions, drawn under the Radcliffe Award, is shown by two barbed lines cutting the territory of the British provinces. Each princely state had to decide its accession to one of the two new states before the date of 'lapse of paramountcy' and 'transfer of power'. On 15 August, the decisions of the Khasi states, three feudal lords in Kathiawar, the Nizam of Hyderabad and the Maharaja of Jammu & Kashmir were yet to be made.

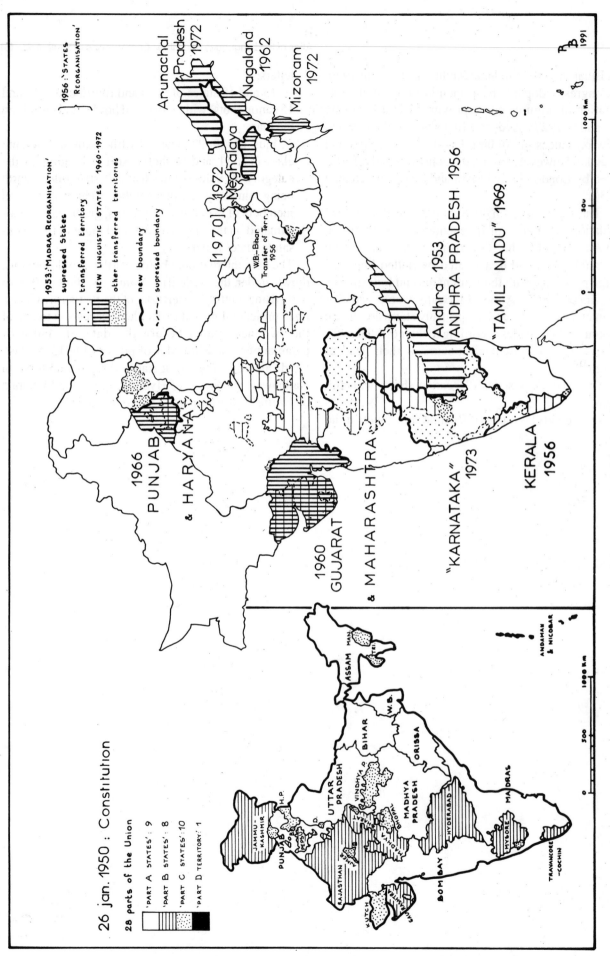

26 jan. 1950 : Constitution

28 parts of the Union

'PART A STATES' : 9
'PART B STATES' : 8
'PART C STATES' : 10
'PART D TERRITORY' : 1

1953 : 'MADRAS REORGANISATION'
1956 : 'STATES REORGANISATION'

supressed States
transferred territory
NEW LINGUISTIC STATES 1960-1972
other transferred territories
new boundary
supressed boundary

JAMMU KASHMIR
PUNJAB
PEPSU
RAJASTHAN
H.P.
D.
UTTAR PRADESH
VINDHYA P.
BHOPAL
AJMER
MADHYA PRADESH
HYDERABAD
ASSAM
BIHAR
W.B.
ORISSA
BOMBAY
MYSORE
MADRAS
TRAVANCORE —COCHIN
KUTCH
ANDAMAN & NICOBAR
MAN TRI

1000 Km
0 500 1000 Km

Arunachal Pradesh 1972
Nagaland 1962
Meghalaya [1970] 1972
Mizoram 1972
W.B.–Bihar Transfer of Terr. 1956
1966 PUNJAB & HARYANA
1960 GUJARAT & MAHARASHTRA
"KARNATAKA" 1973
Andhra 1953 ANDHRA PRADESH 1956
"TAMIL NADU" 1969.
KERALA 1956
1000 Km
0 500 1000 Km
R B 1991

Plate 46: Reorganizations

PLATE 46: REORGANIZATIONS

Plate 46 deals with the process of territorial reorganizations which, since Independence, brought the map of Indian federal political units to coincide with the language area map through the creation of the linguistic states. Two maps are presented: the first map on the left displays the parts of the Union of India as drawn under the Constitution of India, 26 January 1950. The second map on the right shows all the changes realized through various reorganizations from 1953 to 1972.

- Article 1 of the Constitution states that 'India that is Bharat shall be a Union of States', and is divided into 27 states and one Union Territory. The list of these divisions found in Schedule I had four parts from A to D. On the first map, the nine Part A states (big ex-British provinces) are shown as blank areas. The eight Part B states (former bigger princely states or union of states) are depicted with horizontal lines. The ten Part C states (former smaller provinces or states or union of states) are stippled. The only Union Territory (Andaman & Nicobar ex-province) is marked black. The making of this map, though representing much simplification and sound rationalization of the previous imperial map, has avoided any concession to the principle of linguistic states formerly supported by the Congress. Thus, in the years that followed immediately, the agitation for linguistic reorganization started and was especially strong among Andhra people.

- The second map gives the details of the changes operated on the political map of India by successive reorganizations.

In 1953, the 'Madras Reorganization' resulted in the creation of the state of Andhra, carved out of the multilingual Madras state.

The 'General States' Reorganization' of 1956 brought about the creation of the four unified Dravidian states—Andhra Pradesh, Mysore (*Karnataka* in 1973), Madras (*Tamil Nadu* in 1969) and Kerala—and the disappearance of most of the former princely state territories. The 'West Bengal–Bihar Transfer of Territories' put an end to a long-standing conflict.

In 1960, the 'Bombay Reorganization' separated Maharashtra and Gujarat, while 1962 saw the creation of the state of Nagaland.

The 1966 'Punjab Reorganization' led to the bifurcation of Punjab and Haryana, the creation of Chandigarh Territory and a unified Himachal Pradesh that incorporated former Himalayan Punjab districts.

The 'Northeast Reorganization' of 1972 effected in the appearance of the states of Meghalaya (autonomous since 1970), Mizoram and Arunachal Pradesh (ex-NEFA).

All these numerous changes in the shape and limits of the territorial units of the Union were meant to closely relate the federal map of India to its language map—at least to the map of its major languages, or of the most active ethno-linguistic minorities. Thus, each new border was intended to coincide, to the extent possible, with the limits of major language areas.

Beyond all controversies about linguism and its possible excess, it is not contestable that the present political map of India is more functional than that of 1950. The general life of Indian lands and its people focused on linguistic states in politics, economics as well as in any cultural or mediatic form of expression, is in agreement with Indian historical traditions.

Plate 47: Ethno-Linguistic Issues

NATIONAL & INTERNATIONAL QUESTIONS

REGIONAL QUESTIONS

LINGUISTIC & NATIONAL STATES

minorities
hindi NEPAL
nepali NEPAL
bengali
tibeto-b.
tamil CEY.

inter-states disputes & transfers
advocated new states & borders
supressed provinces & states (PAKISTAN)

nagas: insurrection 1955-64
MIKIR AUT. DIST.
N. CACHAR AUT. DIST.
kukis: autonom?
CACHAR: bengali
mizos: insurrection 1966
CHITTAGONG HILL TRACTS: autonom?

TRIBAL TERRIT.: 'TRIBAL AREAS'
'SCHEDULED AREAS'

regional languages:
urdu
hindi
other indo-ar.
dravid.
tibeto-b. & english

garo 1964: exodus
santal
nepali: minor.
newari
hindi

AR.P.
BHUTAN
SIKKIM
DARJEELING
NEPAL
MITHILA
BIHAR
JHARKHAND
OR
W.B.
U.P.
M.P.
VIDARBHA
MAHAR.
TELANGANA
A.P.
KE.
T.N.
TULUVA MY.
CEY.

VISHAL HIMALAYA
VISHAL HARYANA
HA.
GILGIT
BALTISTAN
LADAKH
KASHMIR
JAMMU
H.P.
PU.
CHANDIGARH
FAZILKA
PUNJAB
PAKISTAN
PASHTUNISTAN?
BALUCHISTAN
SINDHU DESH?
KALAT
KHARAN
MEKRAN
BAHA. WALPUR
RAJ.
GUJ.
DAMAN
DIU
GOA
BELGAUM
N. KASARAGOD
16-6-69 MALAPPURAM
N. DISTRICTS
MALNAD

rajasthani 1968: Constitution?
sindhi 1966 Constitution 1961: hindi offic!
1967: urdu offic! 1981
1959 D.
RAWALPINDI
Fed! Cap!. Ar.
1955-1970: 'One Unit Act'
Federal Capital Terr. 1948-59
Muhajirstan?

MAHAJAN REPORT 1967
'OPINION POLL' 1967
PATASKAR AWARD 1960
1964: SHASTRI-BANDARANAIKE AGREEMENT
tamil: 14-1-1966 offic!

1000 Km
1991

XINJIANG [SIN KIANG]
WEIWUER ZIZHIQU
TURKMENISTAN 1991
UZBEKISTAN 1991
TAJIKISTAN 1991
AFGHANISTAN
PUSHTO NAT'L.
1956 FARSI OFF'L.
1964 FARSI OFF'L.
IRAN

12-3-1963 PAK.-CHIN. TR.
1959 CHIN. OCC.
XIZANG [TIBET]
1965: BOD ZIZHIQU
CHIN. CLAIM
CHIN.-IND. TR.
1950: SIKKIM-IND. TR.
1961: SIKKIM SUBJECTS REGULATION ACT
1975: SIKKIM ACCESSION
NEPAL
KACHIN STATE!
DEWANGIRI
1949: RETROCESSION BHUTAN-IND. TR.
CHIN SPECIAL DIVISION
1958: ARAKAN STATE!
UNION OF BURMA
4-1-1948: INDEP.CE
1989: "MYANMAR"

1957: ACCESSION
23-3-1947: INVASION

PAKISTAN 14-8-1947: INDEP.CE
1956 CONSTITUTION URDU & BENGALI OFF'L. LANGUAGES
1948: URDU NAT'L.
JUNAGADH & MANAVADAR REVENDICATION (PAK.)
BALUCHISTAN: ex-'SPECIAL PROVINCE'
GWADUR 8-9-1958 CESSION
19-2-1968: DEMARCATION
KUTCH

"BANGLA DESH" 1971: INDEP.CE

CHANDERNAGORE 1947: CESSION 1952: TR.
YANAM
PONDICHERRY
KARAIKAL
MAHE
DAMAN
DIU
GOA
DADRA & NAGAR HAVELI 7-1954: OCCUPATION
20-12-1961: INCORPORATION
1-11-1954: CESSION 16-8-1962: TR.

CEYLON 4-2-1948: INDEP.CE
1956: 'OFF'. LANGUAGE ACT'
1972: 'SRI LANKA'

MALDIVES 26-7-1965: INDEP.CE

15-8-1947: INDEP.CE
26-1-1950: CONSTITUTION
26-1-1965: 'OFF'L. LANGUAGES ACT'
1967: 'OFF'L. (AMENDMENT) ACT'

0   1000 Km

R.B. 1991

PLATE 47: ETHNO-LINGUISTIC ISSUES

Plate 47, comprising three maps, strives to present the cartography of the ethno-linguistic issues in the subcontinent, other than those that were solved through the 'reorganizations'. The first map on the left deals with national and international issues within each nation, the second map is devoted to regional issues within each nation, while the third map on the right shows a classification of linguistic and national states according to the families of their official language.

* The map on 'National and International Questions' recalls many events, or pending issues, linked to language or ethnic problems within and around the subcontinent, at the national or international level. The existence of strong language groups and lasting language questions such as those concerning Baluchi in Iran; Farsi *vs* Pushto in Afghanistan; Turkmen, Uzbek, Kirgiz and Tajik in former USSR; Uygur and Tibetan in China; Kachin, Chin and Arakanese in Myanmar, have never been quite foreign to the life of the subcontinent. Most of these languages and peoples are partly present within the subcontinent, or are directly akin to the ones present within the subcontinent. The solutions offered or rejected may be considered with special attention.

Also of direct interest are the border disputes and aggressions, invasions, occupations, or flows of refugees on the very margins of the subcontinent. As opposed to this, the more peaceful cessions, incorporations or accessions of territories towards one or other of its seven nations are also pointed out. Attention is also drawn towards independences that occurred since 1947, changes in the names of nations, as well as the various fundamental laws on language use at the national level.

Thus, geopolitics is interfacing with language problems in various fields, and the linguistic issue is drawing out new facts and subjects to geopolitics.

* The main map in the centre on 'Regional Questions' displays a lot of factual information together with proposed new territorial units including controversial changes in designations and border lines. It is a map of achieved as well as of current or evolving processes or events. It is a map on which the accumulation of facts and possibilities gives a general impression of a moving landscape, and where many local details about recurrent or pending problems

may be found. But here the text deals only with the map as comments are less necessary.

As a matter of fact, since the last (1972) reorganization, further territorial changes seem less likely to occur. Claims for new states like Telangana, Vidarbha, Vishal Haryana, Vishal Himalayas (or Uttarkhand), etc., on a simple regional basis meet with scant real reception. Also, as these claims are not based on linguistic delineations, they have few chances to be taken into consideration as against those based on ethnic support. However, the examples of Gorkhaland (Darjeeling), Bodoland (Udayachal), Jharkhand, etc., prove that the most workable solutions would, most probably, rest on the pattern of some sort of autonomy, or territorial councils, or special administration, as it has been done in the case of Autonomous Districts (Karbi Anglong and North Cachar Hills), Tribal Areas (in Manipur and Mizoram), Scheduled Areas (for other states' tribal tracts), Gorkha Hill Council (Darjeeling), Bodoland Autonomous Council, and Jharkhand Area Development Council (Bihar) which is maybe better than carving out new states.

* The small inset map entitled 'Linguistic and National States' shows the linguistic affiliation of each basic territorial unit of the subcontinent. Since each unit is now officially monolingual, the map provides a general overview of the distribution of the subcontinent into four broad language zones.

The seven states of the Hindi Belt together with the Urdu set (Pakistan and the Indian state of Jammu & Kashmir) surrounding the small Punjabi area (Indian Punjab) constitute a broad Hindustani zone covering the entire northwestern and central half of the subcontinent.

The nine other Indo-Aryan languages (Nepali, Bengali, Assamese, Oriya, Sinhala and Dhivehi or Maldivian, Konkani, Marathi and Gujarati) form a peripheral chain around the Hindi Belt. The south is the massive block of four main Dravidian languages: Telugu, Tamil, Kannada and Malayalam. Further east, an outer crescent is formed by Tibeto-Burman languages such as Denjongke (Sikkimese), Dzongkha (Bhutanese) and Meithei (Manipuri) plus the minor languages of Hill states (Arunachal Pradesh, Meghalaya, Nagaland, Mizoram), all officially superseded by English.

One *Union* language (Hindi), six *national* languages (Urdu, Nepali, Bhutanese, Bengali, Sinhalese and Maldivian), 12 *constitutional* or *regional* languages (Punjabi, Assamese, Oriya, Konkani, Marathi, Gujarati, Tamil, Telugu, Kannada, Malayalam, Sikkimese and Manipuri) and one *additional* language (English), al-together add up to no more than 20 official languages of varying usages in society. Through these languages most of the written, administrative, cultural and mediatic activities of the subcontinent are operationalized.

PLATE 48: MAIN LINGUISTIC MINORITIES

Plate 48 shows the geographical distribution of the main linguistic minorities of the subcontinent through two maps. The smaller one on the left indicates the areas where languages other than the regional language are spoken by more than 40 or 50 per cent of the population, and the bigger one on the right shows the size of minorities (through circles) and the regional languages (through different shadings).

- The smaller map displays the extent of the areas where various minor languages (at the regional level) make up the majority (50 per cent) of the population, or nearly reach the majority (40 per cent) at the district level. Two kinds of shades are used for illustrating the majority position: either dotted for all Hindustani (Bihari, Rajasthani) or close to Hindustani (Bhili, Khandeshi) variants, or hatched for tribal languages or for languages from another region. A shading with horizontal lines represents a proportion between 40 and 50 per cent for any language or group of languages. The name of the regional language in each province is marked by its initial letters, and when it crosses a border an arrow connects it to its other location.

Areas where minority languages locally reach a majority position are (*a*) Rajasthan–Bhili region, Khandesh and northern Bihar, all having different Hindustani variants; (*b*) Himalayan region with Pahari in Uttar Pradesh, Hindi in Himachal Pradesh, Hindi and Himalayish in Nepal, Nepali in Sikkim, Darjeeling and south-western Bhutan; (*c*) south Assam with Karbi and Dimasa in Autonomous Districts, and Bengali in Cachar; (*d*) north of Jammu & Kashmir with Tibetan (Ladakh and Baltistan), Shina and Burushaski (Gilgit); (*e*) northern NWFP or FATA with Khowar and Kohistani; (*f*) around Punjab with Dogri in Jammu and Hindko in eastern NWFP (*g*) also some western borderlands, i.e., Baluchistan with Pushto in the north, Brahui in the centre and Sindhi in the southwest; Sind with Baluchi in the north, Urdu in Karachi; and Kachchh with Sindhi.

In central India, majorities of minor languages and tribal languages appear in scattered districts from south Bihar to Orissa, Madhya Pradesh and Andhra Pradesh. In central and south Deccan, Konkani, Tulu, Kodagu or some trans-border regional languages constitute the minor languages having a majority position while in Sri Lanka, it is Tamil.

In principle, however, regional languages command a majority position in most provinces (blank areas), except in Jammu & Kashmir, Baluchistan and Rajasthan.

- The main map presents the realm of each regional language (of one or several provinces) represented by a common shade and delimited by a thick border line, while, inside each of them, the regional or national boundaries are drawn by dotted or broken lines. Further, each language minority in each province is indicated by a circle of a specific shade, according to the legend, and proportionate to its population. Circles may be linked to the border of the province from where the language originated, or to other circles of the same language minority in other provinces.

Urdu minorities are the most important and are scattered all over the subcontinent. The spread of Hindi is far less as compared to Urdu and is always close to the Hindi Belt. Punjabi (including Dogri, Hindko, etc.) is diffused all around Punjab, Pahari in Himalayas, Rajasthani down to central Deccan (Banjari-Lambadi), Nepali in the eastern part of Nepal and Bhili around the Gujarat Ghats.

Other Indo-Aryan minorities are mainly found around their linguistic states except Sindhi and Konkani which spread much further. The same is true of the four main Dravidian languages whose diffusion is close to their home state.

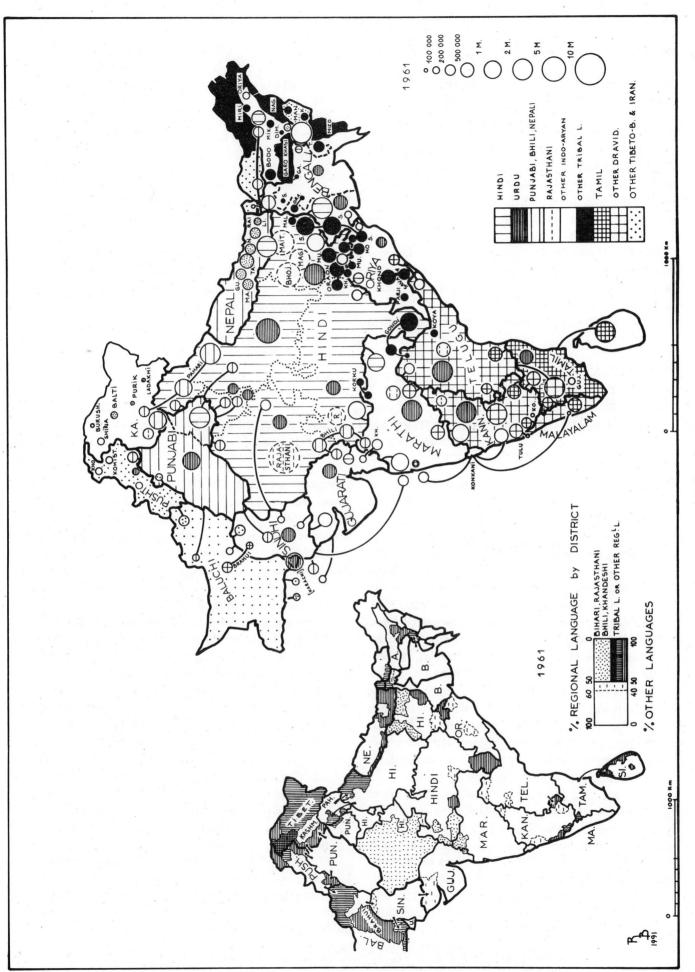

Plate 48: Main Linguistic Minorities

Most important tribal languages of eastern India are split into two main sets. The first, around Chota Nagpur, comprises most of the Munda group with Santali, Mundari, Ho, Kharia, plus Dravidian Oraon and Malto, with outposts extending to the Bangladesh plains. The second set, in Dandakaranya, is made up of tribal Dravidian languages with Gondi, Khondh (plus Kui and Konda), Parji and Koya. Also included are some Munda languages such as Savara, Gadaba and Korku which are territorially detached from the main group.

The Himalayas house many minor Tibeto-Burman languages, particularly in Nepal and to a lesser extent in Jammu & Kashmir with nearby Burushaski and Dardic minorities.

In conclusion it can be asserted that the geographical distribution of linguistic minorities follows four main patterns:
* border areas as far as regional languages are concerned once the creation of linguistic states was achieved;
* mainly hill regions for tribal languages where new autonomous institutions may be established;
* bigger metropolises like Karachi or Bombay where juxtaposition and intermingling are unavoidable;
* finally, a language like Urdu (or Rajasthani dialects to a lesser extent) is affected by quite a different type of distribution which results in an ubiquitous presence of minorities without a significant concentration in its linguistic state.

PLATE 49: ETHNO-LINGUISTIC PATTERN AND URBAN NETWORK AND ETHNO-LINGUISTIC FLOWS AND CULTURAL FOCUSES

Plate 49, consisting of two maps, is devoted to the ethno-linguistic composition of the subcontinent in both geographical and historical perspectives.
* The map entitled 'Ethno-linguistic Pattern and Urban Development' shows the division of the subcontinent into main linguistic regions on the basis of population. Zones of higher population density (over 100 inhabitants per square kilometre in 1961), or core areas, are represented by horizontal lines. All agglomerations over 100,000 are represented by squares (for capitals of states), or circles, proportionate to their population size. A network of principal railway lines connecting them emphasizes the chief urban and transport axis of each state or group of states. These three elements together determine the nature of the economic activity occurring within each region. The less important, more isolated, intermediary or marginal zones are left blank.

This hierarchy of economic and political centres based on the main and secondary axes gives shape to the linguistic areas, i.e., states. In fact, each ethno-linguistic set of population, born in its own environmental frame, has through centuries built its own network of cities and transportation, and has linked it to other ethno-linguistic sets till a common subcontinental system was formed.

The present territorial image is made by assimilating smaller units within larger national ones. Spatial organization, currently thought as based on purely economic criteria, is also deeply entrenched in the cultural background of people, e.g., technical and economic decisions of modern times often follow centuries-old well-known routes, such as the Grand Trunk Road or the Great Chord Line, running along ancient Uttarapatha.
* The map on 'Ethno-linguistic Flows and Cultural Focuses' delves deeper into the past. It shows the main physiographic elements that could have hampered human flows: main foothills or scarp lines, marshes or desert areas and those that facilitated them: valleys and rivers. Arrows indicate the historical directions of most known migrations. Some routes of migrations accompany names of languages or dialects (Malvi, Bundeli, Bagheli, Chhattisgarhi, Bhojpuri, Marathi, etc.) along their main axis of penetration. Tribal language areas, demarcated by dotted areas, coincide with the remote forested and hilly lands where Adivasis have for long been isolated. Locations of historic centres remind one of the place of origin and settlement of not only economic and political but also cultural and linguistic influences.

Migrations have changed the economy and the landscape. At the same time, these migrations have led to language waves which have modified the cultural atmosphere of regions to form the present linguistic and political pattern of the land.

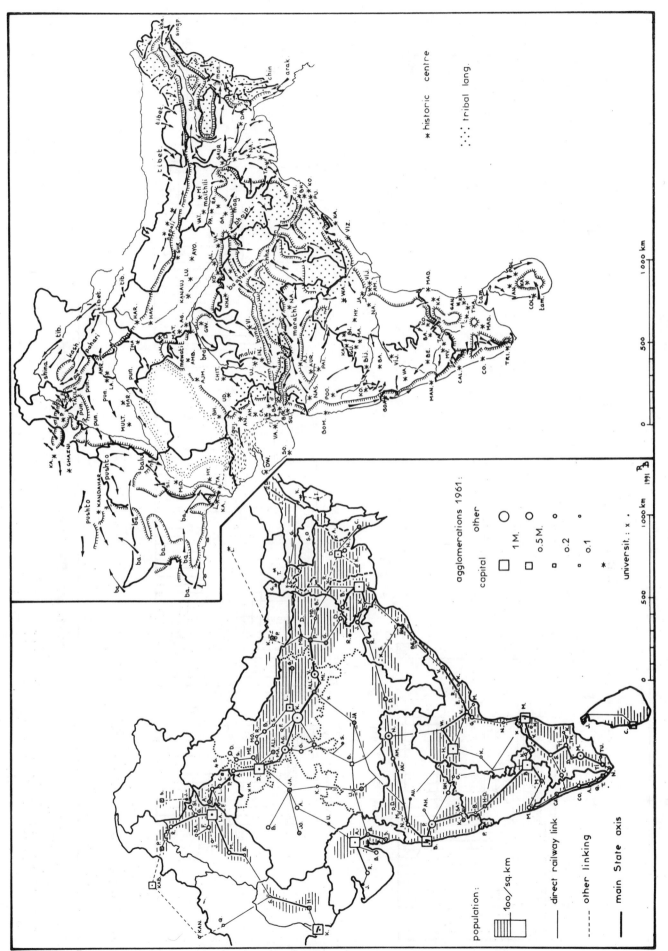

Plate 49: Ethno-Linguistic Pattern and Urban Network and Ethno-Linguistic Flows and Cultural Focuses

* historic centre

⋮ tribal lang.

population:
1oo/sq.km

—— direct railway link

- - - other linking

—— main State axis

agglomerations 1961:

capital | other
1 M.
0.5 M.
0.2
0.1

universit.: x .

1991
1000 km

500

0

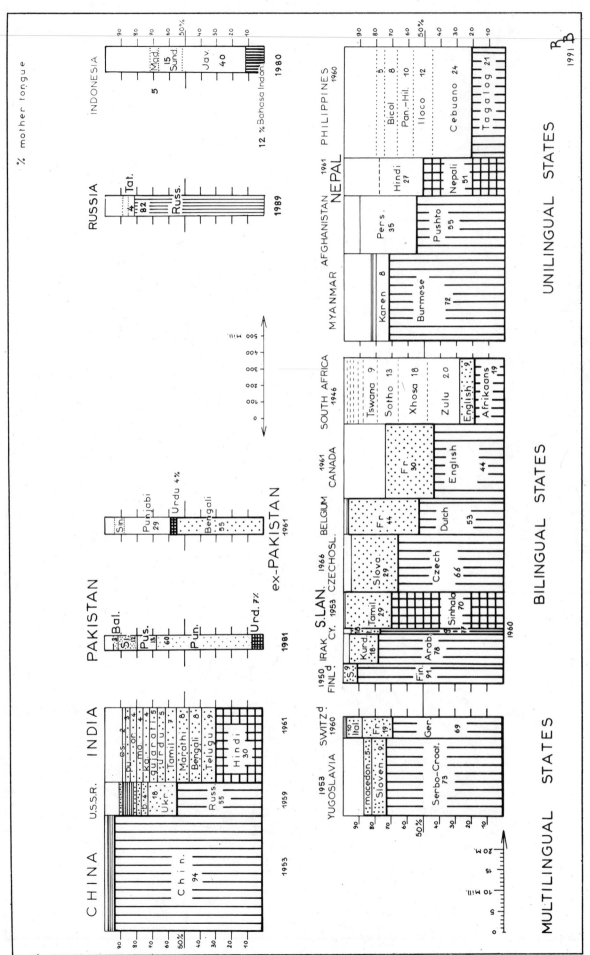

% mother tongue

Plate 50: Plurilingual States in the World

PLATE 50: PLURILINGUAL STATES IN THE WORLD

Concluding this series of plates on the language landscape of the subcontinent, Plate 50 gives an overview of these situations compared with that of other similar multilingual nations in the world. The main countries with complex ethno-linguistic composition are represented by ethnograms showing their mother tongues and the percentage of the population speaking them. The main language is identified by a dark shading, the other official one(s) by a dotted shading, and the non-official ones by blank areas.

There are two sets of ethnograms. The upper set is based on a scale of population that counts the inhabitants by hundred millions while the scale for the lower set is by millions only. The map deals with three categories of states—officially multilingual, bilingual and monolingual. Inside each category, states are ranked by order of decreasing percentage of the main language. The comparison has been done across varying dates, according to each state census that recorded mother tongue data. In the absence of formally published census data of mother tongues, the most recent official language figures have been used.

India is definitely the most multilingual country in the world on the basis of two counts. First, by virtue of the number of *constitutional* (and most of them de facto regional) languages to which all the other *national* languages may be added. Second, by the relative size of the languages among the population compared to the size of the main language Hindi which is only 30 per cent. If China has officially more than 50 ethnic nationalities which are theoretically liable to develop their languages, Chinese as mother tongue is spoken by more than 94 per cent of the population and very few other languages are actually used at the regional level. Even in former USSR, where, like in India, around 15 languages were official at the upper regional level, Russian was the mother tongue of 55 per cent of the population. The new Federation of Russia, though theoretically still multinational with 82 per cent Russian mother tongue speakers, is likely to leave regional languages with little power to be effective. Since the fall of multilingual and multiethnic Yugoslavia, the best existing working model of a multilingual state is Switzerland with only three official languages, German, French and Italian (plus Rumantsch, claimed as national though only used at the regional level) representing 69, 19 and 10 per cent of the population respectively.

Pakistan (also consisting of Bangladesh) was bilingual in 1961 having a far from even balance between Bengali (55 per cent) and Urdu (4 per cent), the latter used only in administration and education. In 1971, after the Independence of Bangladesh, Urdu (7 per cent) is still prevalent over the few regional languages (Sindhi and Pushto). Pakistan may be compared to Indonesia where the national language, Bahasa Indonesia, reaches as a mother tongue to only 12 per cent of the population. Despite its marginal figure, it is the only one used in administration and taught to every young citizen.

Sri Lanka which somehow reluctantly entered the category of bilingual states, with Sinhalese and Tamil (70 and 29 per cent respectively), might be compared to former Cyprus (Greek 77 per cent and Turkish 18 per cent), or to former Czechoslovakia (Czech 66 per cent and Slovakian 29 per cent) or theoretically to Iraq (Arabic 78 per cent and Kurdish 18 per cent). While the bilingual experiences of these countries is one of failure, one can look at Finland's harmonious existence in spite of its high numerical disequilibrium (Finish 91 per cent and Swedish 9 per cent). One can even look at Belgium (Dutch 53 and French 44 per cent) or Canada (English 44 per cent and French 30 per cent), two bilingual countries which have through different ways overcome their crisis. Not to speak of South Africa where past bilingualism (English 19 per cent and Afrikaans 9 per cent) is now giving place to something far from dual: 11 official languages in 1993.

Nepal falls in the category of monolingual states with one national language, Nepali, spoken as a mother tongue by 51 per cent of the population. It is similar to Philippines where the national language, Tagalog, also called Pilipino or Filipino, is the mother tongue of only 21 per cent of the population and also to Myanmar where Burmese is spoken by 72 per cent of the population. However, in Myanmar minority languages can theoretically benefit from regional autonomies (Kachin, Chin, Rakhine, Mon and Shan states). In the case of Afghanistan, the national language, Pushto (55 per cent), was in fact superseded by Persian (35 per cent), the official language since long. However, since 1990, Afghanistan was on the path to becoming a multinational country with at least eight nationalities: Pathans, Tadjiks, Nuristanis, Pashais, Baluchis, Uzbeks, Turkmens and Hazaras, each likely to receive its own administrative unit.

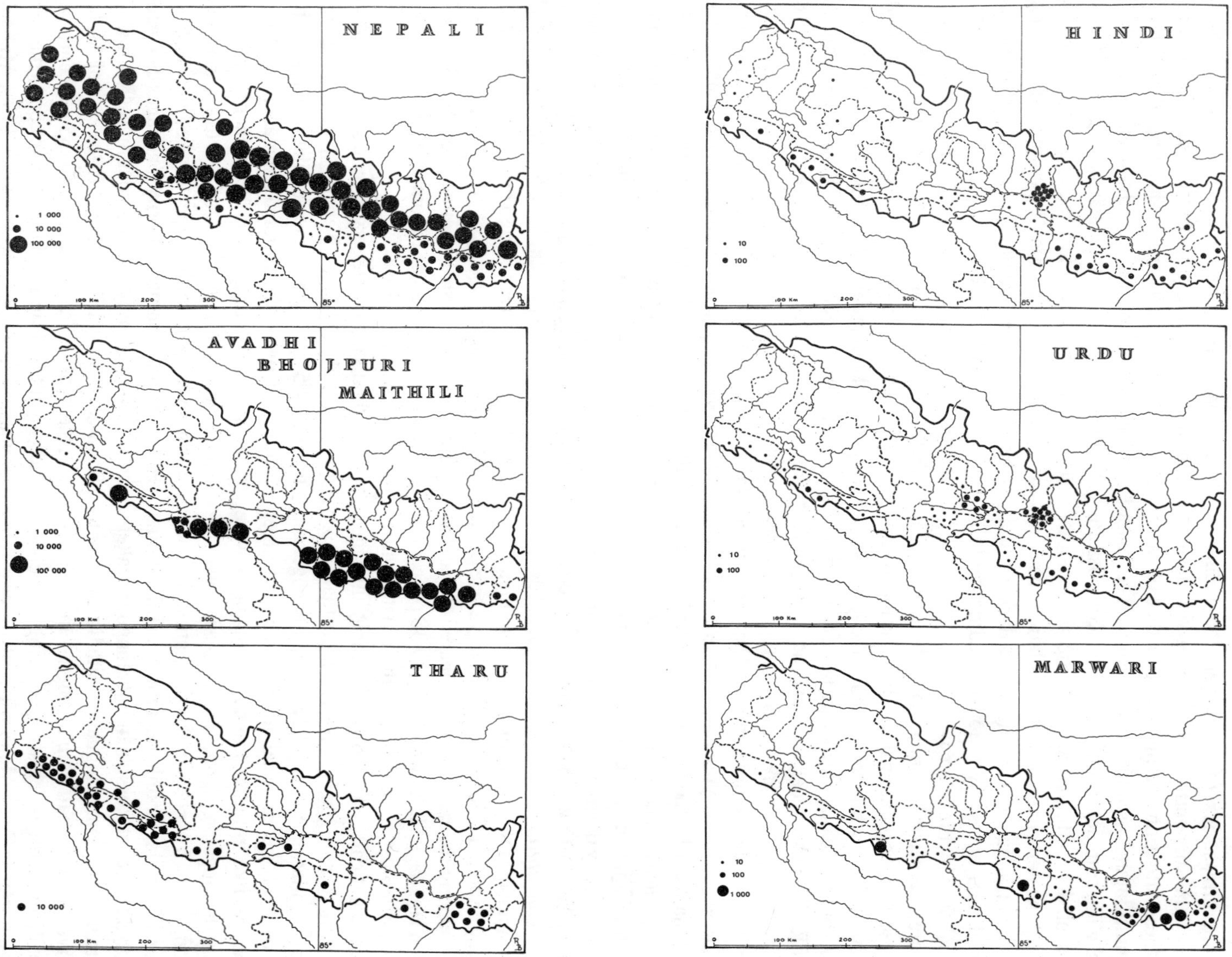

Plate 51: Nepal 1961: Main Indo-Aryan Languages

CHAPTER 14

THE LINGUISTIC SITUATION UP TO THE 1991 CENSUS

PLATE 51: NEPAL 1961: MAIN INDO-ARYAN LANGUAGES

Plate 51, the first in a series of three maps detailing the distribution of languages in Nepal in 1961, deals with the main Indo-Aryan languages of this country. Each language has two figures by thousand speakers: the first refers to the 1961 Census figures used in the map while the second refers to the 1991 Census. Six dot maps present mother tongue speakers by district:

Nepali (4,797, 9,303) extends quite evenly from the western to the eastern end of the middle mountain lands but has a low density in all Terai plains.

Avadhi (447, 375), Bhojpuri (577, 1,380) and Maithili (1,130, 2,192) are considered in India as Hindustani variants, though Maithili, and to a lesser extent Bhojpuri may be classified as eastern Indo-Aryan speeches which are more akin to Bengali than to Hindi. They are mainly concentrated in eastern and middle Terai with some moderate presence in western Terai.

Tharu (407, 993), the Hindustani dialect of the Terai, is mainly spread in its western part with some minor concentrations in central and eastern Terai.

Hindi (3,17) is displayed with a different scale of dots necessary for the small size of its figures like for the two foreign languages: Urdu and Marwari. It is mainly concentrated in the Kathmandu valley and scattered in the entire Terai. It has been brought in by the influx of Indian communities attracted by the capital city and its bordering areas.

Urdu (3,20) is again mainly present in the Kathmandu valley, Seti valley, Damauli, Pokhara and surrounding areas as also in Terai.

Marwari (7, 17) is mainly found in the eastern part of Terai in considerable proportions. It may also be linked to northern Bihar, Bengal or Calcutta as the language spoken by the business community. Thus, Hindi, Urdu and Marwari have been brought to Nepal by trading communities from India.

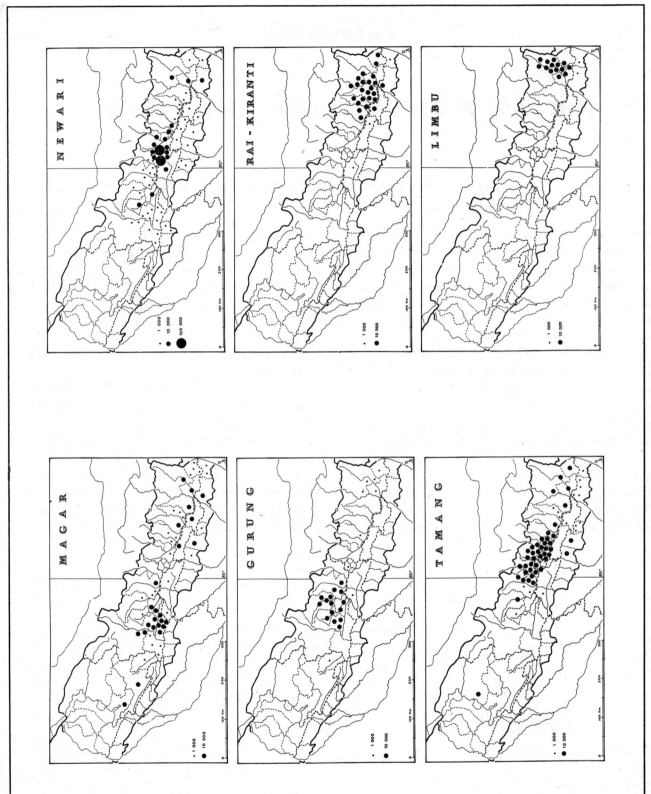

Plate 52: Nepal 1961: The Six Main Tibeto-Himalayan Languages

PLATE 52: NEPAL 1961: THE SIX MAIN TIBETO-HIMALAYAN LANGUAGES

Plate 52, the second in a series of three maps detailing the distribution of languages of Nepal in 1961, is devoted to the languages of the six main autochthonous hill peoples of the central and eastern mountains, historically included under the generic 'Gurkha' designation. All these languages belong to the Tibeto-Burman family. Each language has two figures by thousand speakers: the first refers to the 1961 Census figures used in the map and the second refers to the 1991 Census.

Magar, or Magari (255,430), now classified in a western Kiranti subgroup (eastern Himalayan branch), is mainly concentrated in the Kaligandaka lower valley which constitutes the Magar people's homeland. It is also found scattered in the middle mountain areas from the west to the east, especially along the Sun Koshi valley.

Gurung (158,228), closer to the Tibetan group, is the northern neighbour of Magari. It is more concentrated in its core area which is made up of the three valleys of Seti, Marsyangdi and Budhi Gandaki. A sprinkling of Gurung speakers is present in Kathmandu or in far eastern mountains.

Tamang (519,904) belongs to the Gurung group. It has a wider and more compact homeland situated north of Kathmandu in the central mountain valleys of Budhi Gandaki, Trishuli, Sun Koshi and Tama Koshi. It is also found in the Kathmandu valley eastwards up to the far eastern valleys.

Newari (378,700), an eastern Himalayan isolate, is heavily concentrated within the Kathmandu valley and its surrounding areas. From there, the Newar trading communities have taken it to central and eastern Nepal where it is mainly found in the Gurung country and in the far eastern valleys.

Rai-Kiranti (240,439) is the main component of the Kiranti group of the eastern Himalayan branch. Its country, western Kirant, is made up of the Dudh Koshi and Arun valleys in eastern Nepal. Divided into about a score of distinct dialects, it had a small expansion towards the far eastern Terai reaches.

Limbu (139,254) is the second component of the Kiranti group and is limited to its Tamar valley, or eastern Kirant, the easternmost part of Nepal mountains. Just like Rai-Kiranti, it is divided into about ten dialects and has marginally expanded to nearby Terai.

PLATE 53: NEPAL 1961: OTHER MINOR LANGUAGES

Plate 53, the third and last in a series of three maps detailing the distribution of languages of Nepal in 1961, is devoted to the 16 minor languages found in this country. Most of them are autochthonous but some are also present in adjoining Indian lands. Each language has two figures by thousand speakers: the first refers to the 1961 Census figures used in the map and the second refers to the 1991 Census.

Bhote-Sherpa (84,122) is the Nepalese designation of the Tibetan (Bhote) dialect spoken by the eastern populations (Sher-pa). It is mostly found in the upper reaches of eastern valleys of Bhote Koshi, Tama Koshi, Dudh Koshi, Arun and Tamar River; in the highest massifs of the Gaurishankar, Cho Oyu, Sagarmatha (Everest), and from Makalu to Kanchenjanga. However, the other Tibetan-speaking autochthonous mountain populations are more properly designated as Bhote-speaking because they are not Sherpa, i.e., from the east. All of them are traditionally found in other highlands of the border areas of Nepal, i.e., in Manasalu massif, north of Tamang and Gurung countries; in the Mustang valley; and in Dolpo area of western ranges.

The distribution of other minor languages may be better understood through their linguistic grouping (as shown in the upper chart on Plate 54) than through pure geographical display. Starting with the Tibeto-Burman family, the Plate proceeds by reviewing the languages closer to Tibetan and moves on to the more distant ones.

Jirel (2.7, 4.2), a Tibetan language akin to Sherpa, is found in the Tama Koshi valley.

Thakali (4.1, 7.1) in the Mustang valley belongs to the Gurung group.

Thami (9, 14), an eastern Himalayish language that is close to Tibetan and Gurung falling within the Bodish branch, is spoken in the same Tama valley as Jirel but in the upper reaches.

Raji (0.8, 3), belonging to the western Kiranti group (eastern Himalayan branch), is found in the western Terai and lower western mountains.

Chepang (9.2, 25) of the same group, linguistically and geographically close to Magar, is present in lower Budhi Gandaki and Trishuli valleys.

Sunwar (13 in 1961, 20 in 1971, 11 in 1981 and not reported in 1991) of the eastern Kiranti group is found in Kirant.

Dhimal (8.2, 15), an unclassified Tibeto-Burman language, is found in far eastern Terai. It may be akin to Bodo of Assam and would thus belong to Baric group; while Toto, found in some villages in India would be a dialect of Dhimal.

Jhangar (9.1, 15), is also spoken in far eastern Terai, but west of Dhimal. It has sometimes been related to Jangali, and thus classified under Himalayish like Thami. Currently, it is confused with Dhangar which constitutes the northernmost element of the Dravidian family and is found in a smaller community, 100 km westwards. According to recent field enquiries in eastern Terai, the Dhangar people are definitely Kurukh-speaking Oraons, settled for long in Nepal areas. Jhangar would thus only be a more recent offshoot of the Oraons, located here since Second World War and of course, having nothing in common with Jangali of western Terai.

Some still unclassified languages belonging to the Indo-Aryan family may be found in Nepal. Three of them, Darai, Kumal and Danuwar, may be grouped together and are possibly close to Dardic, i.e., to Kashmiri:

Darai (1.6, 6.5) is at the lower end of Magar and Gurung in the Narayan valley.

Kumal (1.7, 1.4), belonging to a community of potters, is present in the lower reaches of the Narayan valley. It also spread to Gurung and Tamang and to far eastern Terai.

Danuwar (12, 24) is spread with another community of peasants and fishermen to the east of Kathmandu and south of Tamang, all along the Sun Koshi valley.

Majhi (5.9, 11) spoken by a community of fishermen is widespread along the Sun Koshi and further east of Terai as also west of the Narayan valley. It seems to be closer to the languages of northern Bihar, possibly between Bhojpuri and Maithili.

Other easily identifiable minor languages of Nepal include Bengali (9.9, 28) spoken in far eastern Terai, close to the Indian border with Bihar and not far from West Bengal. Nepal's census traditionally distinguishes Bengali from its Rajbangsi dialect (56, 86) which has the same distribution and reflects a social division.

Santali (11, 8) of the Munda family is also found in the forests of this same far eastern part of Terai, as also Satar (19, 25) which is apparently a simple local variant

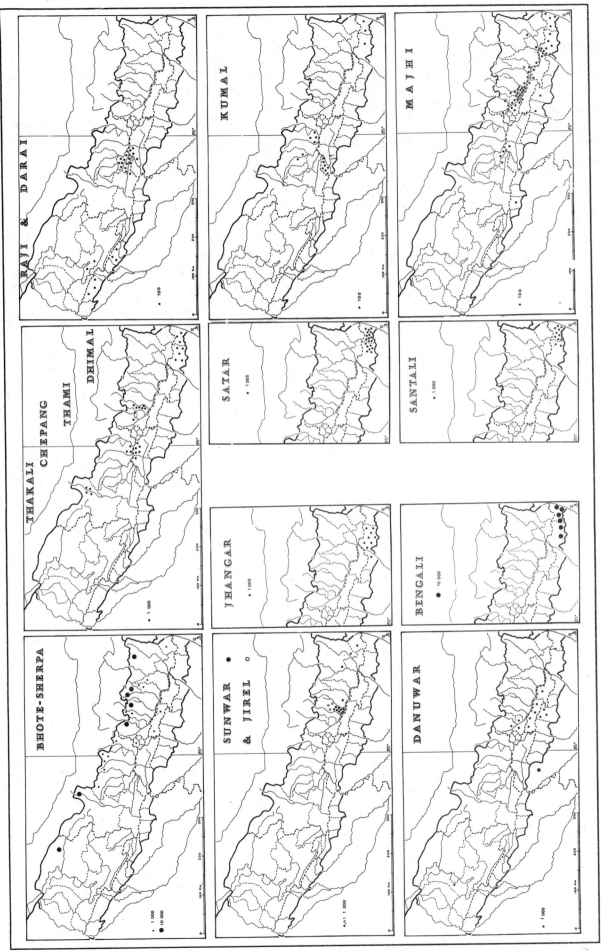

Plate 53: Nepal 1961: Other Minor Languages

of Santali, though some have considered it as Dravidian only because of the darker complexion of its speakers.

Other languages not represented in this series of maps are: Byangsi or Byangshi, omitted for whatever reason in 1961 Census but recorded in 1952–54 (1.8) and in 1991 (1.3), definitely belongs to the Himalayish group of the Bodish branch, and is spoken along the Indian border (Uttar Pradesh) at the far north western end of Nepal's territory.

Ksunda, or Kusunda, very recently extinct, was akin to Chepang (western Kiranti) and spoken in the same region.

PLATE 54: NEPAL 1991: LOCAL LANGUAGES

Plate 54 presents the 1991 distribution of Nepal's local languages, i.e., traditionally spoken by territorially settled communities, thus excluding foreign ones such as English, Hindi, Urdu, Marwari, regularly reported in the Census of Nepal. It consists of a distribution map entitled 'Layers of Language Communities' and a diachronic ethnogram showing the evolution of mother tongues of the three main language families, i.e., Tibeto-Burman, Indo-European and Austro-Asiatic.

*   The map gives an idea of the numerical volume of each language community by using spheres proportionate to the number of their mother tongue speakers (figures in thousands for 1991). Each sphere is located, as much as possible, at the original core area of the language community. And the extension of the whole language area of important languages has been indicated by shaded area delimited by dotted lines. Three regions based on the legend at the bottom demarcate the linguistic grouping: Himalayan, Bodish (i.e., Tibeto-Burman branch closer to Tibetan) or Indo-Aryan and Munda. The use of spheres instead of circles helps in visually comparing facts belonging to a much wider range of size: from 1,000 to about 10 million speakers.

The map shows the broad division of Nepal into two main language areas: Indo-Aryan in the western and southern parts, and Tibeto-Himalayan in the central and northeastern parts, with further distinction between Bodish, along the northern border, and Himalayan in three central blocks. The distribution of spherical symbols expresses the deep splitting up of Tibeto-Burman inside its own main present realm and its dispersal within the predominantly Indo-Aryan zone. This present intermingling reflects the gradual historical penetration of Indo-Aryans in the Himalayas, from the south in the Terai, and eastwards in the middle mountain zone, more than the expansion of Tibeto-Burman southwards. But, eventually, the later advance of the dominant axial west–east expansion of Nepali language in each valley was cartographically difficult to trace.

*   The upper chart is a graphic attempt to combine the representation of both the west–east and altitude-wise geographical distribution with the linguistic groupings of all Nepalese languages. This was possible through the well-known reality that Nepal's

ethnic groups traditionally inhabit different longitudinal zones, i.e., from Terai plain to central Himalayas through the middle mountain valleys. This natural ecology in altitudes more or less coincides with the main linguistic groupings. Thus, it facilitated the display of this upper–lower altitudinal distribution across the conventional west–east and left–right cardinal orientation. Furthermore, it was also easy to locate each mother tongue community linked with smaller subgroups corresponding to several language families, branches and groups according to their west–east situation along the quadripartition between far western and western, midwestern, central and eastern Nepal. Plus a broad distinction between the 13 major and 15 minor ethno-linguistic communities following the 100,000 members bar expressed by the two different sizes of dots.

Thus, the different zones of language communities, from upper to lower altitude, appear to correspond to a score of main groupings:

*   the mountain areas housing five groups/subgroups belonging to the Tibeto-Burman language family such as proper Tibetan, Gurung, Himalayish, Kiranti and Newari, together with Dhimal in the Terai, possibly the western end of the Baric group;
*   three Indo-Aryan groups: a possibly Dardic group of old settlement, the Pahari group of modern diffusion that constitutes the bulk of Nepal's population and the central (and eastern) group in Terai;
*   a small, but ascertained, Munda presence,
*   plus a smaller Dravidian group, subject to better delimitation and measurement, but yet to be officially recognized.

*   The ethnogram showing the general evolution of the proportion of speakers from 1952–54 to 1991, continues the representation carried out in Plate 19. The main factors were, first, the constant erosion of small ethnic Tibeto-Burman mountain languages due to the continuation of the historical progress of Nepali (48.7 to 50.3 per cent from 1952 to 1991) and, second, the stability of the Hindustani language block of the Terai (28 to 29.5 per cent) after a steady decline until 1981 (23.9 per cent).

As a matter of fact, the 1991 Census revealed a certain

Plate 54: Nepal 1991: Local Languages

Classification table

LANGUAGE FAMILY	BRANCH	GROUP (& Subgroup)	Far-Western & Western Nepal	Mid-Western Nepal	Central Nepal	Eastern Nepal
TIBETO-BURMAN	BODISH	TIBETAN (Southern)			JIREL	SHERPA
		GURUNG		THAKALI / GURUNG	TAMANG	
		HIMALAYISH (Almora & Eastern)	BYANSI		THAMI	JHANGAR
	EASTERN HIMALAYAN	KIRANTI (Western & Eastern)	RAJI	MAGAR	CHEPANG / SUNWAR	RAI / LIMBU
	unclassified	NEWARI			NEWARI	
		(Baric ?)				DHIMAL
INDO-EUROPEAN	INDO-ARYAN	unclassified (Dardic ?)		DARAI	KUMAL / DANUWAR	
		CENTRAL (Pahari)		NEPALI		
		CENTRAL & EASTERN	THARU	AVADHI / BHOJPURI	MAJHI / MAITHILI	BENGALI
AUSTRO-ASIATIC	MUNDA	KHERWARI				SANTALI / SATAR
DRAVIDIAN		NORTHERN				DHANGAR

LAYERS OF LANGUAGE COMMUNITIES
○ More than 100 000 persons
○ Less than 100 000 persons

NEPAL : % OF MOTHER TONGUE SPEAKERS

	1952-54	1961	1971	1981	1991
NEPALI	48.7	51	52.5	58.4	50.3
OTHER	23.3	21.5	22.01	17.7	20.2
		25.49	23.9		
HINDUSTANI & BIHARI	28	27.5			29.5

1991 NEPAL POPULATION CENSUS
(figures in thousands of mother tongue speakers)

Main language areas:
Indo-Aryan
Himalayan
Bodish

○ 1 000 000
○ 100 000
⊕ 10 000
● 1 000
mother tongue speakers

0   100   200 km

Map labels (figures in thousands of mother tongue speakers):

NEPALI 9 303
THARU 993
TAMANG 904
NEWARI 700
MAGAR 430
GURUNG 228
SHERPA 122
JIREL 4
THAMI 14
SUNWAR 11 ?
DANUWAR 24
MAJHI 11
KUMAL 1.4
THAKALI 7
DARAI 7
CHEPANG 25
AVADHI 375
BHOJPURI 1 380
MAITHILI 2 192
RAI 439
LIMBU 254
JHANGAR 15
DHIMAL 15
SANTALI 8
SATAR 25
BENGALI 114
BYANSI 1.3
RAJI 3

© Roland BRETON - 1994

rupture in this secular evolution. There was an expected decline in the erosion of minor languages. On the contrary, the rise of Nepali (48.7, 51, 52.5 and 58.4 per cent in 1952–54, 1961, 1971 and 1981 respectively) has been restrained with a loss of eight points in 1991 (50.3 per cent) while six among the seven main mountain ethnic groups, inversely controlled the decline of their mother tongue and it increased between 1981 and 1991: Tamang moved from 3.5 per cent to 4.9 per cent, Newari from 3 to 3.7 per cent, Rai from 1.5 to 2.4 per cent Magari from 1.4 to 2.3 per cent, Limbu from 0.9 to 1.4 per cent and even Bhote-Sherpa from 0.5 to 0.7 per cent, while Gurung alone remained stable at 1.2 per cent. This reversal did not allow these groups to regain their 1952–54 or 1961 positions in percentage of the total population. However, it generally brought them to catch up if not exceed their 1971 percentage.

While taking into account the language family distribution, we may notice that the Tibeto-Burman mother tongues numbering 17 per cent have gone beyond their 1981 score (12.1 per cent) and nearly regained the 1971 one (17.2 per cent) while all Indo-Aryan mother tongues statistically fell from 82.7 to 80 per cent. Munda approximated to 0.2 per cent and Dravidian, though not reported, was certainly lower. English (3,000) represented 0.015 per cent and other foreign languages (8,000), 0.045 per cent.

But, beyond the few 'not stated' census returns on mother tongue concerning each individual (9,000 i.e., 0.05 per cent), a linguistic uncertainty persisted with an 'other local language' category of nearly half-a-million returns (496,000), totalling 2.7 per cent in 1991 (5.1 per cent in 1981). This category certainly includes what was enumerated in earlier censuses under so-called 'local district dialects' or village speeches, *Dehati*, etc., that definitely belong to some form of Hindustani and Bihari variants. In scrutinizing their district break-up, it is clear that most of these 'other local language' returns were registered in the far western and far eastern Terai parts, i.e., in overwhelmingly Indo-Aryan speaking regions, while the remaining returns were scattered all over the country. One can therefore venture to presume that this mass (2.7 per cent) of residual returns belongs far more to Indo-Aryan (perhaps 2.5 per cent) than to Tibeto-Burman. The ratio between Indo-Aryan and Tibeto-Burman is roughly around 82.5 per cent to 17.5 per cent as against 80 per cent to 17 per cent, not including very small minorities between these groups: Munda (0.18 per cent), foreign languages (0.06 per cent) and Dravidian (not computed in the census but certainly lesser).

Plate 55 is devoted to Pakistan and its most recent data on languages. The 1951 Census of population provided statistics of individual mother tongue speakers; the 1961 Census added to it the number of people speaking other languages; the 1972 Census, after the secession of Bangladesh, omitted the language matter; and the 1981 Census gave province-wise data on percentage of household distribution by spoken language. The 1991 Census did not occur on account of political reasons.

Thus, to be able to compare Pakistan's language situation with that of other states of South Asia, it is necessary to rely on projections. Projections of 1981 household percentage data to provincial populations (between which household size varies) are used, also those of the 1981 figures to estimated demographic figures for 1991 estimates arrived at by international experts, based on different provincial growth rates. The figures of both the 1981 Census and 1991 projections are referred together.

This Plate consists of a map of all Pakistani languages. On the upper left, the Plate bears a pattern of language affiliations, and on the bottom right, there is a disc divided into sectors proportionate to languages. The language pattern makes the understanding of linguistic linkages of the communities displayed on the map coherent.

- The map shows the division of Pakistan into provinces and main language areas: the area speaking Iranian is represented by a lighter shading, Dravidian by darker shading and Indo-Aryan is left blank. Upon this background, symbols proportionate to the figures of the 1981 Census are superimposed: spheres as opposed to simple circles are used to allow the comparison of numbers ranging from 1,000 to 50 million speakers.

The Iranian area corresponds to most of North West Frontier Province (NWFP), Federally Administrated Tribal Area (FATA) and Baluchistan. The Dravidian area localizes to central Baluchistan and Indo-Aryan to the rest of the country, i.e., almost all of Punjab and Sind provinces, plus the northern and northeastern part of NWFP, or Dardic and Punjabi settlements, and some minor overlappings on the borders of Baluchistan and NWFP.

The numerical preponderance (93 per cent) of the two main provincial languages and one national language is as follows:

Punjabi was spoken in 48.17 per cent of Pakistani households in 1981 in a population of 84.3 million. In other words, the provincial figure is 39.5 million, not including its two local variants—Hindko (2.43 per cent or 2 million) in northeastern NWFP (former Hazara District) and Siraiki (9.84 per cent or 7.8 million), transitional to Sindhi. However, if Hindko and Siraiki are included, the figure is 60.44 per cent or 49.5 million. Thus the figure was 70 million in 1991 according to the estimate of Pakistan's population of 117.5 million (computed by Population Reference Bureau, Washington and preferred to the 115 million registered by UNO).

Pushto: 13.15 per cent, i.e., 11.5 million in 1981 and 15.5 million in 1991,

Sindhi: 11.77 per cent, i.e., 10.3 million in 1981 and 13.8 million in 1991,

Urdu: 7.6 per cent, i.e., 6.9 million in 1981 and 8.9 million in 1991.

After these follow the two languages of Baluchistan, raising the total to 97.19 per cent for the six main languages:

Baluchi: 3.02 per cent, i.e., 2.6 million in 1981 and 3.6 million in 1991,

Brahui: 1.21 per cent, i.e., 1.1 million in 1981 and 1.4 million in 1991.

The remaining 2.81 per cent, i.e., 2.3 million in 1981 and 3.3 million in 1991, is split into about a score of minor languages, whose number of speakers went unrecorded even in the 1951 and 1961 Censuses, perforce having to rely on SIL (*Ethnologue*) estimations.

They include Gojri, or Gujari, the Rajasthani dialect of the shepherds of lower Himalayan ranges (in former Hazara District of NWFP which had a large non-enumerated area in 1961) with 300,000 speakers in 1991.

Khowar is the most important of Dardic languages in Pakistan. It is the native language of the Kho people of Chitral state, now a district, with 98,000 speakers in 1961 and about 250,000 in 1991.

The locus of the Kohistani chain of languages is in the east of Khowar and had a total of 73,000 speakers in 1961. This group is divided into at least eight different languages: Diri, or Bashkarik, or Garwi in Dir District (12,000 (?) in 1961, 40,000 (?) in 1991) and Kalkoti

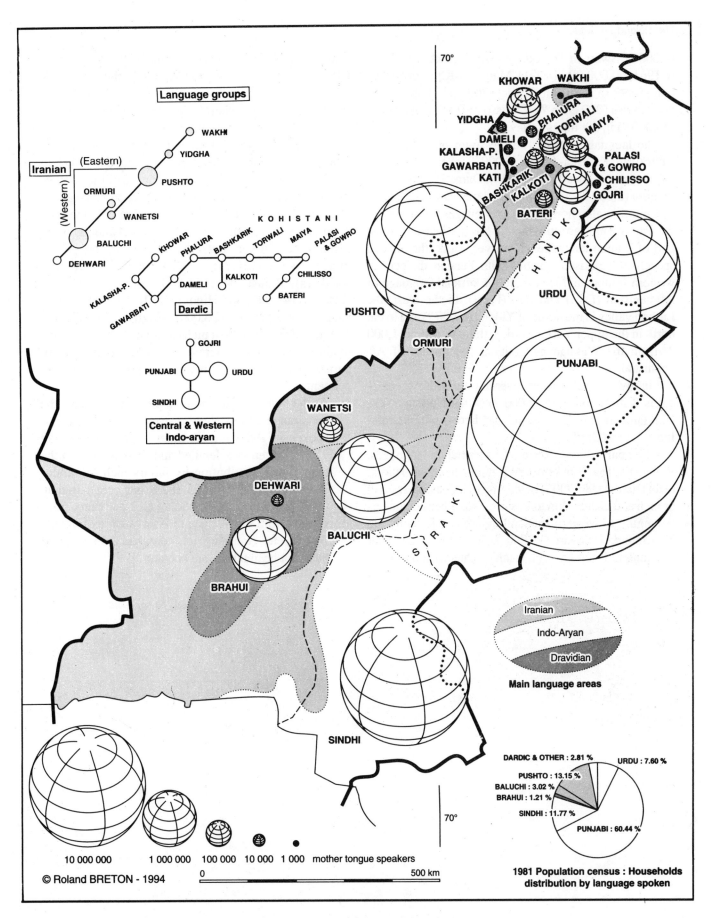

Language groups

Iranian

(Western) (Eastern)

WAKHI
YIDGHA
ORMURI
PUSHTO
WANETSI
BALUCHI
DEHWARI

KOHISTANI

KHOWAR PHALURA BASHKARIK TORWALI MAIYA PALASI & GOWRO
KALASHA-P. DAMELI KALKOTI CHILISSO
GAWARBATI BATERI

Dardic

GOJRI
PUNJABI URDU
SINDHI

Central & Western Indo-aryan

KHOWAR WAKHI
YIDGHA PHALURA TORWALI MAIYA
DAMELI PALASI & GOWRO
KALASHA-P. CHILISSO
GAWARBATI BASHKARIK GOJRI
KATI KALKOTI
BATERI

HINDKO

URDU

PUSHTO

ORMURI

PUNJABI

WANETSI

DEHWARI

BALUCHI

S I R A I K I

BRAHUI

Iranian
Indo-Aryan
Dravidian

Main language areas

SINDHI

10 000 000   1 000 000   100 000   10 000   1 000   mother tongue speakers

© Roland BRETON - 1994

0   500 km

DARDIC & OTHER : 2.81 %   URDU : 7.60 %
PUSHTO : 13.15 %
BALUCHI : 3.02 %
BRAHUI : 1.21 %
SINDHI : 11.77 %
PUNJABI : 60.44 %

1981 Population census : Households distribution by language spoken

70°

70°

Plate 55:   Pakistan 1981-1991

(4,000 ?); Swati, or Torwali, in Swat District (49,000 (?) in 1961, 60,000 (?) in 1991), Maiya, or Khili, or Kohistani proper in Kohistan District (200,000 ?) and Palasi and Gowro (200 each ?), Chilisso (3,000 ?) and Bateri (30,000 ?) in the Indus valley.

The languages located in the south of Khowar, in Chitral, are Kalasha–Pashai (5,000 ?), overlapping with Afghanistan, Gawarbati (2,000 ?), Dameli (4,000 ?) and Phalura (8,000 ?), all belonging to the Dardic branch.

Chitral is also home to two languages belonging to the Pamir Tajik group which is the northeastern-most part of Iranian languages. However, Tajik, the official speech in Tajikistan, blends with Persian dialects of western Iranian and is close to the official language of Afghanistan (Dari) and Iran (Farsi). In the west, the Lutkoh valley is the home of Yidgha (6,000 ?) and in the north in the upper Yarkun valley, there is Wakhi (1,000 ?) from the Wakhan geopolitical 'peninsula' of Afghanistan.

Finally in the southwest, overlapping with Afghanistan is Kati or Bashgali (5,000 ?) of the Nuristani (ex-*kafir* language family, intermediary between Iranian and Indo-Aryan (Dardic).

Other parts of Pakistan are far less rich in languages. Wanetsi is found in northern Baluchistan, near Harnai (Sibi District) (80,000 ?) belonging to the eastern Iranian branch and is thus akin to Pushto. Two other languages, belonging to western Iranian branch, i.e., Baluchi, are also found: Dehwari (10,000 ?) in Baluchistan (near Mastung in Kalat District, south of Quetta) and Ormuri

(3,000 ?) in NWFP near Kaniguram (south Waziristan). Other members of this latter residual ethno-linguistic community may be surviving (5,000 ?) in Afghanistan, south of Kabul while their kin are present north of Kabul (6,000 ?) and speak Parachi.

All the above mentioned minor languages, autochthonous in the Pakistan territory, amounted to only half a million people in 1991. Thus, nearly 2.8 million people may have, as their mother tongue, either some language of other parts of South Asia or a foreign one. Out of a population of 42.9 million in 1961 (it had undergone an increase of 274 per cent), the other main Indian languages were Gujarati (242,000 mother tongue speakers), Rajasthani (153,000), Bengali (46,000), Kashmiri (42,000) and Hindi (3,000). The foreign languages were Persian (26,000), English (18,000) and Arabic (3,000). It is difficult to estimate how much each of them could have increased or decreased in comparison with the average increase of population of 274 per cent.

- At the bottom of the plate, a pie-chart presents the percentage of household distribution by languages spoken in 1981: the six main languages reaching 97.19 per cent are detailed and shaded alike on the map. Their distribution by family includes: Indo-Aryan including Dardic (82.6 per cent), Iranian (16.2 per cent) and Dravidian (1.2 per cent). Languages from outside South Asia, such as English, Arabic, etc., (totalling not more than 0.05 per cent) have not been taken into account.

PLATE 56: BHUTAN AND BANGLADESH 1991

Plate 56 provides updated data on Bhutan and Bangladesh on a common map of the two countries. The geographical situation is specified by delineating borders, both national (continuous lines, thicker for Bangladesh and Bhutan, thinner for India and Nepal) and provincial in India and Myanmar (broken lines), as also limits of special autonomous districts in India (Darjeeling–Gorkha Hills, Karbi Anglong and North Cachar Hills). In this frame, the main mother tongues of Bangladesh and Bhutan are represented by spheres proportionate to the number of speakers.

- The language distribution of Bangladesh was detailed in the Censuses of 1951 and 1961, conducted by the administration of Pakistan. Soon after its Independence in 1971, the 1974 Census gathered scant language data, the 1981 Census, none, and the 1991 Census operations do not leave any hope of precision in this field.

The Bengali language has always enjoyed an ever-increasing preponderance within Bangladesh: 98.16 per cent in 1951, 98.43 per cent in 1961, 98.83 per cent in 1974. In a population of 109.9 million as reported in the 1991 Census (as against previously estimated figures of 116.6 million by the Population Reference Bureau, and 118.7 million by UNO), the 1974 percentage would bring the number of Bengali mother tongue speakers to at least 108.6 million. The total of other language speakers, on the other hand, would stand at around 1.3 million.

These other languages may be of two main types: (a) autochthonous, i.e., geographically entrenched on a territorial homogeneous basis, and (b) those which are brought in by migrants and spoken by their descendants mingled with autochthonous people.

In Bangladesh, the main language among those brought in from outside is Urdu: 268,000 speakers in 1951, 311,000 in 1961, 179,000 in 1974. This minority which had been mainly introduced at the time of Partition from Bihar, has after Independence (1971) been forced to leave the country on account of the alleged support of 'Biharis' to the Pakistan cause. Its decrease from 0.6 to 0.25 per cent of the total population seems to have ceased and official estimates maintained the latter percentage for 1981, bringing the figure to 218,000 persons. In these conditions the same percentage would have raised it to 275,000 in 1991.

Languages of other parts of the subcontinent were mainly brought by migrants working as agricultural labour force from neighbouring provinces of Bihar, Orissa and Meghalaya, and especially from tribal areas like Chota Nagpur. Thus, besides Hindi (123,000 in 1951 and 141,000 in 1961) spoken by Bihari labourers and settlers, and Oriya (17,000 and 13,000), the other languages are mostly tribal languages which were subsumed in the first two censuses under common designations: either 'Santali and Khasi' (111,000 in 1951 and 77,000 in 1961) or 'other Assamo-Burman' (112,000 in 1951, 136,000 in 1961), or, simply, 'other' (82,000 in 1961). Subsequently, in 1974, they were included under the general heading of 'Tribal Languages', together with all the autochthonous languages of Bangladesh's tribal areas. Thus, there was a total of 402,000 speakers (0.56 per cent of the population) of tribal languages which was officially projected as 558,000 for 1981 (0.65 per cent) by the census authorities.

The only way to get a statistical break-up is to infer it from the detailed district location of each category in 1961. And, to arrive at a tentative projection in 1991, it is necessary to presume an approximate doubling corresponding to the increase of the general population between the two dates. Thus, the figures in 1961 and 1991 would be: Santali 66,000 and 135,000; Oraon 55,000 and 110,000; Garo 84,000 and 170,000; and Meithei, which is not a tribal language, 19,000 and 40,000.

Apart from the tribal languages, the heading 'others', included in 1974 all mother tongues except Bengali, Urdu and tribal languages, i.e., languages of other parts of the subcontinent and of foreign countries. They were estimated as 244,000 (0.34 per cent) in 1974, and as 227,000 (0.26 per cent) in 1981. According to the 1961 Census, the other main South Asian languages, are attached to small urban communities: Punjabi 10,000, Sindhi 6,000, Gujarati 4,000, Pushto 4,000, Marathi 1,000 and Assamese 1,000. Languages from outside the subcontinent include English 3,000, Persian 2,000 and Burmese 7,000.

Autochthonous non-Bengali speaking populations of Bangladesh are concentrated in the south easternmost district of the Chittagong Hill Tracts, including the low ranges linking Tripura and Mizoram to Arakan in Myanmar. The main speech is Chakma, a Bengali dialect

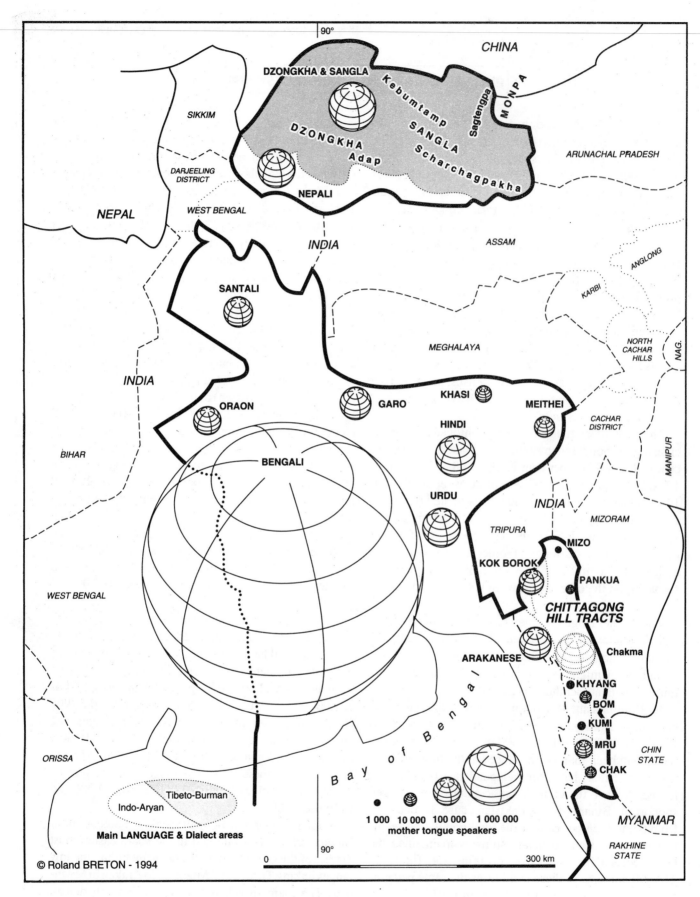

Plate 56: Bhutan and Bangladesh 1991

Map labels:

CHINA

DZONGKHA & SANGLA

Kebumtamp

Sagtengpa

MONPA

SIKKIM

DARJEELING DISTRICT

DZONGKHA
Adap

SANGLA

Scharchagpakha

ARUNACHAL PRADESH

NEPAL

WEST BENGAL

NEPALI

INDIA

ASSAM

ANGLONG

KARBI

SANTALI

NORTH CACHAR HILLS

NAG.

MEGHALAYA

INDIA

GARO

KHASI

MEITHEI

CACHAR DISTRICT

HINDI

ORAON

MANIPUR

BIHAR

BENGALI

URDU

INDIA

MIZORAM

TRIPURA

MIZO

WEST BENGAL

KOK BOROK

PANKUA

CHITTAGONG HILL TRACTS

Chakma

ARAKANESE

KHYANG

BOM

B a y   o f   B e n g a l

KUMI

MRU

CHIN STATE

ORISSA

CHAK

Tibeto-Burman

Indo-Aryan

Main LANGUAGE & Dialect areas

© Roland BRETON - 1994

1 000   10 000   100 000   1 000 000
mother tongue speakers

0   300 km

MYANMAR

RAKHINE STATE

belonging to those who have migrated from the coastal plains and have introduced wet rice cultivation along the inner valleys. A fact to be noted is that they are still Buddhists and wrote Bengali in Burmese script—a pointer to their being acculturated. Chakma speakers could be estimated to 100,000 in 1961 and 300,000 in 1991.

In the hills, around the Chakma peopled low valleys, various Tibeto-Burman languages are found. The main language is Arakanese (74,000 in 1951 and 150,000 in 1991 (?)) spoken in western Chittagong Hill Tracts along the coastal range from Tripura border to Arakan which is now the Rakhine state in Myanmar (locally Arakanese are also called Marma or Mogh). Here too, figures of tribal languages must be based on extra-census computations. The estimations for 1969 and 1991 would be as follows: various Tripuri dialects, now united under Kokborok (33,000, 75,000), Mru (12,000, 18,000), Bom (3,500, 7,000), Pankua or Pankhua (1,500, 3,000), Chak (3,000, 6,000), Khyang (1,000, 2,000), Kumi (1,000, 2,000), and Mizo (1,000).

Owing to the lack of 1991 data, it may therefore be stated from the report of the 1981 officially estimated percentages on 1991 population (109.9 million) that besides 108.6 Bengali mother tongue speakers (98.9 per cent), the remaining 1.3 million speakers (1.14 per cent) are split into: 275,000 (0.25 per cent) Urdu, 700,000 (0.64 per cent) tribal languages and 290,000 others (0.26 per cent). These estimated figures for tribal and non-tribal languages with an approximate doubling of some 1961 other language data, are roughly coherent with a further break-up of these categories.

The distribution by language family would thus be: Indo-Aryan (Bengali, Urdu, Hindi, Oriya, Punjabi, Sindhi, etc.) 109.5 million or 99.3 per cent, Tibeto-Burman (Arakanese, Garo, Kokborok, Meithei, Mru, etc.) 500,000 or 0.5 per cent, Munda (Santali) 0.1 per cent and Dravidian (Oraon) 0.1 per cent.

- Bhutan's language composition is not only the least known in the subcontinent but also the most controversial, due to the lack of any reliable census data. The recent language identification process is subject to heavy political interferences which manifest themselves in two forms.

First, the general figure of the only population Census (1969: 1,034,774 inhabitants), on which all later estimations were based, has been challenged by the present head of state, King Jigme Singye Wangchuk. He declared that it was a gross falsification resulting from his father's, King Jigme Dorji Wangchuk, fear that Bhutan would not get admission to the UNO in 1971, if the population of the kingdom was below 1 million. He added that, as a matter of fact, Bhutan's population more than 20 years later was only 600,000. Thus, instead of the UNO projection of 1,551,000 for 1991, the figure computed by the Population Reference Bureau of 700,000 appears more reliable.

The second factor is the well-known ethno-linguistic divide between native Bhutanese, called Drukpas, and the Hindu migrants from Nepal officially designated as Lhotshampas. The Drukpas, habitating the middle and upper reaches of the valleys, resemble the Tibetans by both their physical and cultural traits, including Lamaistic Buddhism and Tibetan dialects and language. The Lhotshampas have settled in the lower southwestern parts of the valleys. It is difficult to ascertain the numerical strength of this group. From official sources the proportion of Lhotshampas was only 25 per cent, from a population of not more than 600,000 in 1993. This defies previous estimations of 30–35 per cent or 40–45 per cent out of a 1.6 million population. Between these two extremes (150,000 ethnic Nepali to 450,000 ethnic Bhutanese, or 720,000 to 880,000) the unclear reality is now tempered by an important, temporary or definitive, exodus of Nepalese seeking repatriation to Nepal, presently living in refugee camps.

Nepali is actually the common lingua franca of the Nepalese, both nationally and abroad, whether they speak Gurung, Rai or any other mother tongue. Apart from Dzongkha, the national Bhutanese language belonging to the southeastern Tibetan group, distinct from classical and written Tibetan, many local speeches, also belonging to the Tibetan set, are still to be identified as dialects or languages. As far as it is known, Adap is spoken in the southern valleys, probably a dialect of Dzongkha. In the eastern valleys, Kebumtamp and Scharchagpakha would be dialects of a distinct Sangla language, which may belong to the same group as Monpa, spoken in the Indian Tawang district, but which also overlaps in the far eastern valley of Bhutan with Sagtengpa dialect.

Thus, it can be presumed that in 1991, out of a population of 700,000 inhabitants, a minimum of 30 per cent (200,000) spoke Nepali and 500,000 Tibetan, under various local forms.

MARATHI

MAHARASHTRA

GOA

KONKANI

TELUGU

ANDHRA PRADESH

KANNADA

TULU

KARNATAKA

TAMIL

TAMIL NADU

KERALA

MALAYALAM

LAKSHADWEEP

MALAYALAM

INDIA

80°

TAMIL

SINHALA

SRI LANKA

MAHL

MINICOY ISLAND

DHIVEHI

MALDIVES

Dravidian

Indo-aryan

Language areas

80°

0°

0°

10 000   100 000   1 000 000

mother tongue speakers

0   500 km

© Roland BRETON - 1994

80°

TAMIL

SINHALA

INDO-PORTUGUESE

CREOLE MALAY

80°

Sinhala

Tamil

Language majority areas by dictrict

0   200 km

10 000   100 000   1 000 000

mother tongue speakers
according to ethnic groups

Plate 57:   Sri Lanka and Maldives 1991

PLATE 57: SRI LANKA AND MALDIVES 1991

Plate 57 presents the language situation in the insular southern part of South Asia: the two states of Sri Lanka and the Maldives. It includes two maps: one is on Sri Lanka, and the other presents Sri Lanka and the Maldives, both in their geographical context and their linguistic relations with the southern part of the subcontinent.

• On the map of Sri Lanka, the two major language areas of the island are designed according to the distribution of the two sets of Sinhala- or Tamil-speaking ethnic groups within the former districts (see Plate 36 for details). The extension of the two shades delimits the northern and eastern Tamil majority region from the massive southwestern Sinhala block with its small central Tamil enclave. Two proportionate spheres drawn on the maps give an image of the volume of mother tongue speakers in the country. However, this method does not express the deep interpenetration of the two communities, especially in the central and western parts of the island. Two smaller autochthonous communities are gradually appearing and concentrating around the capital city, Colombo.

In the absence of the census figures it may be assumed that, in 1991, of the 17.4 million inhabitants (according to Population Reference Bureau), 74 per cent (12.8 million) spoke Sinhala, 25.3 per cent (4.4 million) spoke Tamil, and 0.7 per cent (120,000) spoke either Indo-Portuguese (60,000 ?), Creole Malay (40,000 ?) or English (20,000 ?).

• The general map shows the extension of the archipelago of the Maldives which had an estimated population of 223,000 inhabitants in 1991. The mother tongue Dhivehi is the national language and is also called Maldivian or Mahl, closely akin to Sinhala. The population also comprises a small community of Bohra traders of Gujarati mother tongue (0.15 per cent in 1946).

The main territorial affinities are brought into focus through the broad geopolitical divide between Sri Lanka, Maldives and India. These affinities are either between the four Dravidian linguistic states of India and the Tamil region of Sri Lanka. Another possible grouping could be between the south Indo-Aryan set of languages which unites the two national languages, Sinhala and Dhivehi, to the southernmost extremity of the Indo-Aryan continental realm occupied (about 1,000 kilometres north) by Konkani and Marathi. Malayalam (the language spoken in Kerala) is primarily spoken in the Indian Union Territory of Lakshadweep, however, the southernmost island, Minicoy speaks only Mahl or Dhivehi.

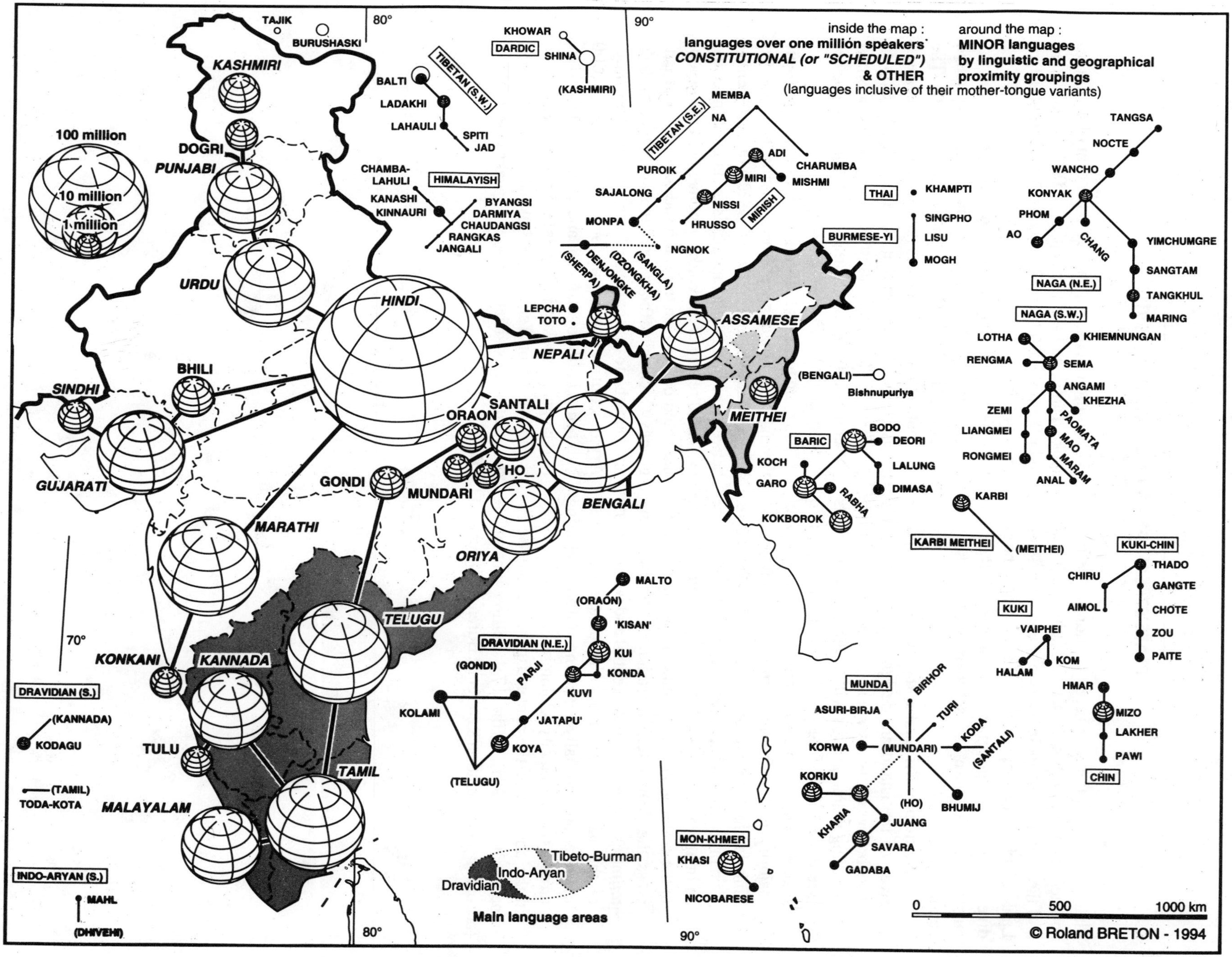

Plate 58: India 1991

inside the map :
languages over one million speakers :
CONSTITUTIONAL (or "SCHEDULED")
& OTHER
(languages inclusive of their mother-tongue variants)

around the map :
MINOR languages
by linguistic and geographical
proximity groupings

© Roland BRETON - 1994

Main language areas
Indo-Aryan
Dravidian
Tibeto-Burman

100 million
10 million
1 million

0   500   1000 km

PLATE 58: INDIA 1991

Plate 58 depicts the entire language distribution scenario of India with reference to 1991 data. Languages having over 1 million speakers are quantitatively represented within the boundaries of the country. All other languages are topologically displayed around the map.

- The map shows the political delimitation of the states, Union Territories and Autonomous Districts, which are shaded according to the legend at the bottom: darker dotted area for Dravidian, lighter for Tibeto-Burman and blank for Indo-Aryan. Upon this background are placed spheres, proportionate to the mother tongue speakers, numbers of the 25 languages which have at least 1 million speakers, whether they are constitutional (scheduled languages) or not. These spheres are linked by straight lines expressing the linguistic parenthood: Dardic, Indo-Aryan, Tibeto-Burman, Munda, Dravidian.

All autochthonous Indian languages with less than a million speakers (i.e., nearly 120) are clustered around the map according to their linguistic group. The cluster arrangement is topological: the attempt has been to situate each linguistic group along a direction radiating from the centre of the map towards the exterior. Languages constituting a linguistic group are displayed according to their geographical position with respect to cardinal orientation: north–south is upper–lower and west–east is left–right. Straight lines link the various languages according to currently acknowledged linguistic subgroups. The linkage with the closest language having 1 million speakers, shown in the map, is highlighted by mentioning the language in brackets. The name of the linguistic group appears in a rectangular box. Where numerical data are lacking—on account of being unpublished, as for Bishnupurya, or not enumerated, as for languages of Jammu & Kashmir on the other side of the Line of Actual Control (Shina, Khowar, Burushaski and Tajik are not enumerated at all while Balti is partly enumerated) estimated numbers are used and the spheres are replaced by empty circles of the same size.

About 20 schemes present the smaller language groupings.

Starting from north to south, there is Wakhi (Tajik) and Burushaski, which are isolated in India, followed by Dardic. Then, on the right, there are a dozen of Tibeto-Burman group schemes: southwest and southeast Tibetan, Himalayish, Mirish, Baric, northeast and southwest Naga, Karbi-Meithei, Kuki, Kuki-Chin and Chin, as also Lepcha and Toto, not yet clearly classified. Lepcha is between Himalayan and Naga while Toto, with nearby Dhimal, to Baric. Among them, is the grouping of the three Burmese-Yi language factions in India, the only Thai faction, and the easternmost Indo-Aryan speech, Bishnupurya (though it is only hypothetically full-fledged).

On the right are situated the Munda, Mon-Khmer and Northeast Dravidian schemes while on the left there are two smaller south Dravidian languages and the southernmost Indo-Aryan one.

The Andamanese language family with its three spoken languages is followed by their estimated number of speakers in 1981: Jarawa (250 ?) of Great Andaman, Sentinelese (50 ?) of Sentinel Island and Onge (100 ?) of Little Andaman.

(The data provided in this plate is prior to the publication of the 1991 Census data. Projected figures, based on 1981 distribution of mother tongues, and combined with regional rates of growth 1981–91 have been used. Figures and percentages derived from this estimation are found in the Annexures.)

PLATE 59: THE SOUTH ASIAN SUBCONTINENT 1991

Plate 59 presents the essential features of the language situation in the subcontinent in 1991, with a map bearing indications related to its 22 official languages and surrounded by seven pie-diagrams expressing the inner composition of each of the seven countries, by language family. Added to this are two other diagrams for the whole subcontinent, by language family and by main language.

• The map presents the political limits—international boundaries and regional state and province borders—arranged in a manner to emphasize the territorial distribution of the main language sets. For this reason, the regional limits between the six states of the Hindi Belt are drawn using dots instead of broken lines. The whole of the *Hindustani Belt*—including the Hindi Belt, plus Punjabi and Urdu states or provinces—is left blank so as to contrast with peripheral states and provinces which have other regional languages, and are shaded according to the affiliation of their regional language: darker grey for Dravidian, in the south, lighter grey for Tibeto-Burman in the northeast and peripheral Indo-Aryan and Indo-Iranian in the northwest.

This threefold zonal linguistic distribution is distinct from the Indian administrative delimitation of Regions A, B and C, as defined according to the 1976 Official Languages Rules. Because, if Region A (Hindi only) strictly coincides with the Hindi Belt (plus Andaman & Nicobar), Region B (Hindi with possibility of English) only includes Punjab, Chandigarh, Gujarat and Maharashtra, while Region C (English) comprises all other states of eastern and southern India, together with Jammu & Kashmir.

All 22 official languages are represented by circles, proportionate to the volume of their mother tongue speakers. In fact, indirectly proportionate, because these circles are only the outlines of proportionate spheres whose other traits have been effaced to make the map more clear and legible; while simultaneously allowing the division of the circle into sectors when one of these languages is official in different national territories.

The number of speakers (in millions) of the official language of each country is written in each circle. But, each language which is divided between two states shows the two figures inside each sector, beside the initials of each country. The total figure is given outside

the circle beside the language name. A small inset rectangle presents the total figures of Hindustani (Hindi–Urdu and Punjabi) speakers for each state and for the whole subcontinent.

Seven circles drawn around the subcontinent show the language family distribution of each of the seven countries of South Asia following figures used in Plates 54–58, thus excluding western and northern Jammu & Kashmir for which reliable data are lacking. An eighth subcontinental circle totals the data of the seven countries. These circles with thick circumferences are indirectly proportionate to the population and are drawn to the same scale. The Indo-Aryan and Iranian sector is left blank, Tibeto-Burman is represented by light dotted area, and Dravidian and Austro-Asiatic is indicated by darker dotted shading.

The pie-diagram on the right shows the distribution of the main languages and when a language has its speakers divided by country boundaries, a divide is designed by dotted lines inside each language sector. It specifies the central importance of the Hindustani set comprising three languages (Hindi–Urdu–Punjabi: 488 million or 44 per cent). Bengali, Telugu, Tamil and Marathi make up 33.2 per cent while the other 15 national or regional languages number 19 per cent, and all other 150 languages constitute only 38 per cent.

A note on Jammu & Kashmir data:

The western and northern areas of Jammu & Kashmir state under Pakistan occupation are (besides Bhutan) the only parts of the subcontinent where no census nor any language enumeration has taken place. This statistical gap tends to alter all regular population surveys, even those published by UNO. Here a purposive attempt has been made to measure this gap so as to enable an exhaustive and homogeneous evaluation of the language situation of the subcontinent.

But the task of language evaluation has proven even more difficult by the fact that the eastern and southern parts of Jammu & Kashmir under Indian administration constituted the only province of India where the census could not be conducted in 1991. Official estimation has, however, been published for this year: 7.719 million; and the projection from the 1991 total of the 1981 Census mother tongue figures could be considered as reliable as for the rest of India. The 1991 projected data for Jammu & Kashmir under Indian administration,

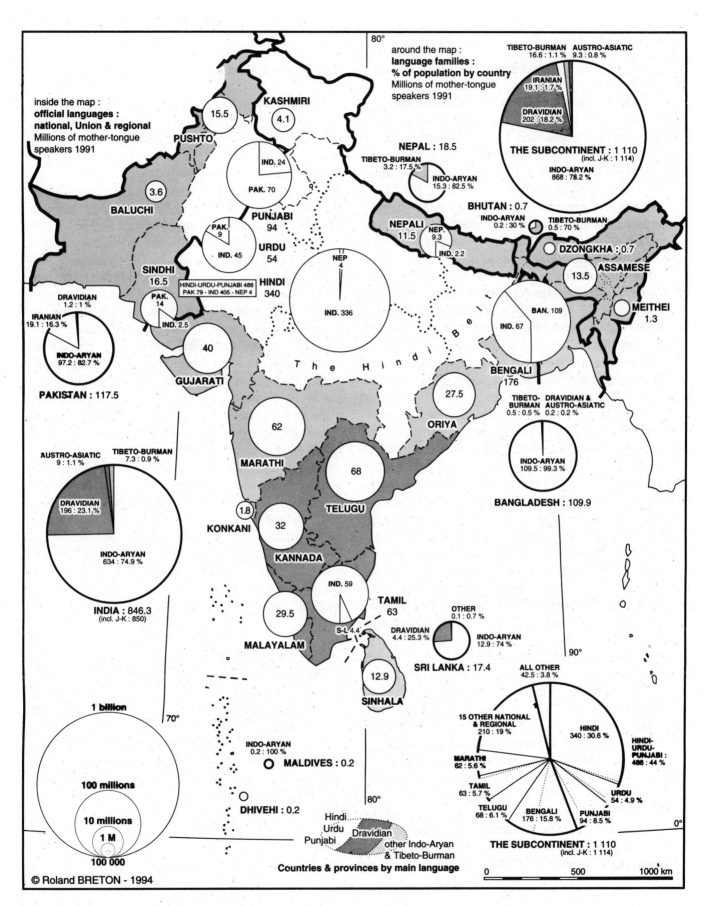

80°

inside the map :
**official languages :
national, Union & regional**
Millions of mother-tongue
speakers 1991

around the map :
**language families :
% of population by country**
Millions of mother-tongue
speakers 1991

TIBETO-BURMAN
16.6 : 1.1 %

AUSTRO-ASIATIC
9.3 : 0.8 %

IRANIAN
19.1 : 1.7 %

DRAVIDIAN
202 : 18.2 %

THE SUBCONTINENT : 1 110
(incl. J-K : 1 114)

INDO-ARYAN
868 : 78.2 %

KASHMIRI
15.5   4.1

PUSHTO

IND. 24
PAK. 70

NEPAL : 18.5

TIBETO-BURMAN
3.2 : 17.5 %

INDO-ARYAN
15.3 : 82.5 %

BHUTAN : 0.7

INDO-ARYAN
0.2 : 30 %

TIBETO-BURMAN
0.5 : 70 %

3.6

BALUCHI

PAK. 9
IND. 45

PUNJABI
94

URDU
54

NEPALI
11.5

NEP.
9.3

IND. 2.2

DZONGKHA : 0.7

ASSAMESE
13.5

SINDHI
16.5

PAK. 14

HINDI-URDU-PUNJABI 488
PAK 79 - IND 405 - NEP 4

HINDI
340

NEP.
4

IND. 336

BAN. 109

IND. 67

MEITHEI
1.3

PAK.
IND. 2.5

DRAVIDIAN
1.2 : 1 %

IRANIAN
19.1 : 16.3 %

INDO-ARYAN
97.2 : 82.7 %

PAKISTAN : 117.5

40

GUJARATI

The Hindi Belt

BENGALI
176

TIBETO-
BURMAN
0.5 : 0.5 %

DRAVIDIAN &
AUSTRO-ASIATIC
0.2 : 0.2 %

27.5

ORIYA

INDO-ARYAN
109.5 : 99.3 %

BANGLADESH : 109.9

AUSTRO-ASIATIC
9 : 1.1 %

TIBETO-BURMAN
7.3 : 0.9 %

DRAVIDIAN
196 : 23.1 %

INDO-ARYAN
634 : 74.9 %

INDIA : 846.3
(incl. J-K : 850)

62

MARATHI

1.8

KONKANI

68

TELUGU

32

KANNADA

IND. 59

S-L 4.4

29.5

MALAYALAM

TAMIL
63

OTHER
0.1 : 0.7 %

DRAVIDIAN
4.4 : 25.3 %

INDO-ARYAN
12.9 : 74 %

SRI LANKA : 17.4

12.9

SINHALA

1 billion

70°

100 millions

10 millions

1 M

100 000

INDO-ARYAN
0.2 : 100 %

MALDIVES : 0.2

DHIVEHI : 0.2

80°

90°

0°

ALL OTHER
42.5 : 3.8 %

15 OTHER NATIONAL
& REGIONAL
210 : 19 %

HINDI
340 : 30.6 %

HINDI-
URDU-
PUNJABI :
488 : 44 %

MARATHI
62 : 5.6 %

TAMIL
63 : 5.7 %

TELUGU
68 : 6.1 %

BENGALI
176 : 15.8 %

PUNJABI
94 : 8.5 %

URDU
54 : 4.9 %

THE SUBCONTINENT : 1 110
(incl. J-K : 1 114)

Hindi
Urdu
Punjabi

Dravidian

other Indo-Aryan
& Tibeto-Burman

Countries & provinces by main language

0   500   1000 km

Plate 59: The South Asian Subcontinent 1991

already used in the precedent plates and texts, are in round figures:

Kashmiri was spoken by 4.040 million in Jammu & Kashmir (52.3 per cent of Jammu & Kashmir under Indian administration) and 4.1 million for the whole of India, Dogri by 1.880 million (24.4 per cent) and 2 million in the rest of India; Hindi (including Pahari and Gojri) by 1.340 million (17.3 per cent), Punjabi by 220,000 (2.8 per cent) and Urdu by 8,000. Smaller languages would be as follows: Ladakhi 95,000 (1.2 per cent), Balti 65, 000 (0.8 per cent), Shina 20,000, Tibetan 6,000 and Nepali 5,000.

For the western and northern areas of Jammu & Kashmir under Pakistan occupation, projections are less easy to make. Taking the proportion of the last Census (1941) held in undivided Jammu & Kashmir (4.021 million), with 73 per cent of the population (2.947 million) later falling in the Indian administrated part and 27 per cent in the Pakistan occupied part, the latter may comprise 2.8 million inhabitants in 1991.

However, this does not coincide with Pakistan's published data of 1981 which tabulated 1.554 million (1.980 million for western Jammu & Kashmir and 574,000 for northern Jammu & Kashmir). If we use for these territories the average decadal growth rate given by the Population Reference Bureau for Pakistan (39 per cent), much higher than the general one observed in India (23.5 per cent), or estimated for Jammu & Kashmir in particular (28.9 per cent), the projected figure would be nearly 3.5 million for the whole territory under Pakistan occupation in 1991: 2.8 million for western Jammu & Kashmir and 700,000 for its northern territories. It is this total which has been added under each bigger outer circle of Plate 59, amending the population figure of India (850 million compared to 846.3) and of the subcontinent (1,114 million compared to 1,110.5).

The language distribution with reference to the 1941 Census is as follows:

Balti 250,000, Shina 300,000, Burushaski 100,000, Khowar 20,000 and Wakhi 10,000 in the north.

For the western part, the lacuna created by half a century of lacking language census has problematized the accurate conjecture of the divide between Punjabi, Pahari, Gojri and Kashmiri: 1 million, 1 million, 300,000 and 200,000(?) respectively. Or, according to the nomenclature rules of the Census of India: Dogri (instead of Punjabi) 1 million, Hindi (instead of Gojri and western Pahari) 1.3 million and Kashmiri 0.2 million.

Due to the lack of reliability, these figures have not been tabulated together with other 1991 figures, provided either by the census or by closer and safer projections.

A further note on the census data:

Due to the non-enumeration in western and northern Jammu & Kashmir, the uncertainty gap 3.5 million in the total population of South Asia (1,110.5 or 1,114?, i.e., 0.3 per cent) should not be exaggerated as it would affect the evaluation of mother tongue speakers.

Thus, due to a number of factors, one still has to rely on various projections for the non-enumerated countries. As a matter of fact, mother tongue distribution is still not available from every national census; many previous census enumerations can be contested in their methodology; and, last, the total population figures for 1991 have not been published for the South Asian countries. However, census population figures may themselves be contested. Even the Census of India, despite its more than a century of experience, can still be regarded as polemical.

Its final result for 1991—846.3 million—came as a surprise because it was notably below the UNO and Population Reference Bureau previsions—849.7 and 859.2 million respectively—as well as below those of the World Bank and UNO Population Division: 854 and 866 million respectively. It was also below the Census' own expectation: 850/855 million. The publication of the population figure could have been challenged by a specialist like Ashish Bose, who, starting from various possible underestimations concluded 'My estimate of the "correct" population of India would be between 870 to 880 million as of 1991' (1991: 49).

Following such an estimate, the margin of error could reach 4 per cent of excess over the quoted figure. It could consequently be the same for all language data used here besides other errors caused due to wrong declaration, registration, tabulation and interpretation. In this condition it is essential to use all language statistics cautiously. Further, as an absolute rule, they have to be used with reference to its precise date of collection and enumeration which situates it in its specific point in time. It may also be essential to use them with a critical assessment about the value of this source.

PLATE 60: DIFFUSION OF SOUTH ASIAN LANGUAGES AND SCRIPTS

Plate 60 gives an overview of the diffusion of South Asian languages and scripts outside the subcontinent. It includes two maps: the smaller one on the lower left is devoted to the main South Asian communities around the world while the main shows the Indian scripts in Asia.

- The main South Asian communities around the world are displayed on a world map, centred around the North Pole, with the continents diverging from it (through a triangular projection network placing around the northern hemisphere, a tri-partitioned southern hemisphere so as to respect the surface equivalence). They are symbolized by flower-like designs presenting a central image located in South Asia. The graphical representation is in three different sizes according to the importance of the various sets of population coming from South Asian countries.

The two biggest communities having around 1 million inhabitants are in Malaysia (760,000 in 1957, i.e., 11 per cent), Mauritius (672,000, i.e., 68.3 per cent in 1972) and South Africa (795,000, i.e., 2.9 per cent in 1980). The middle-sized communities with nearly half-a-million people are in Myanmar (roughly estimated as a maximum of 600,000 in 1976, i.e., 2 per cent of the population), Guyana (363,000, i.e., 52 per cent in 1970), Fiji (300,000 i.e., 51 per cent in 1976, but 335,000, i.e., 46 per cent in 1990), Trinidad (427,000, i.e., 40.3 per cent in 1980), Britain (400,000?), USA (331,000 Hindi–Urdu speakers in 1990), Canada (221,000 Asian Indian language speakers in 1986) and the Gulf Emirates (400,000?). The main smaller communities with around 100,000 inhabitants are in Singapore (155,000 in 1980, i.e., 4.5 per cent), Reunion Island (145,000, i.e., 25 per cent in 1993?), Surinam (70,000 i.e., 37 per cent in 1975), and Jamaica (28,000, i.e., 1.7 per cent in 1960). Altogether, there are more than 8 million people speaking Indian languages across the globe.

These communities mainly share a selection of some Indian languages. Hindustani in its different forms prevails here and there: Bhojpuri in Mauritius, Punjabi in Britain and Canada, Hindi, Urdu elsewhere. Tamil was leading in Myanmar, Malaysia, Singapore and South Africa. Gujarati, Sindhi and Konkani can be traced on the East African coast. Malayalam and Telugu were also sparsely present, but other Indian languages

were far less present overseas, for the evident reason that geographical proximity to seas and borders, and sociological ability to get abroad allowed the biggest mass emigration flows from the subcontinent. Over this original diversity, a certain trend towards an increasing diffusion of Hindi and Urdu is manifested at least among the main mass media, i.e., radio and the press.

Incidentally, to be truly exhaustive, the survey must take into account the gypsy populations, issued originally from the Dom communities of India that left the subcontinent and gradually got dispersed among the European peoples since the fifteenth century. Half a million of them were brought to deportation and extermination in Nazi Germany. Though they are not easily numbered, they are currently estimated to represent over 10 million people mainly in eastern Europe. They are also present in western Europe and even in the Americas. Among them a majority may still retain their vagrant or nomadic style of life, with an unknown proportion still speaking their ancestral language, Romani, or better known as Sinti-Rom because its two main dialects remind us of their origin (Sindhi and Dom) and which definitely belong to central Indo-Aryan more than to western Indo-Aryan (Sindhi) or Dardic, as it has been believed.

To have a global overview of south Indian languages, it is necessary to compare their relatively wide distribution over the world with a massive concentration in their home place: around 20 million speakers overseas against approximately 11 billion in their core area. This indicates a less than 2 per cent of outer diffusion; a low proportion compared to many other language communities. Besides that, none of these languages is yet considered international as they are overwhelmingly widespread in the same sector of the globe, and none is really used in international communications.

Nevertheless the twenty-first century world would at least consider the volume of South Asian languages, besides their well-known cultural and historical importance. In 1991 South Asian speaking population (around 1.135 billion within and outside the subcontinent) numbered about 21 per cent of the population of the world (5.384 billion) as against 18 per cent in 1900 and 26 per cent in 1850.

In projecting the known figures of the speakers to the last years of the twentieth century based on regional

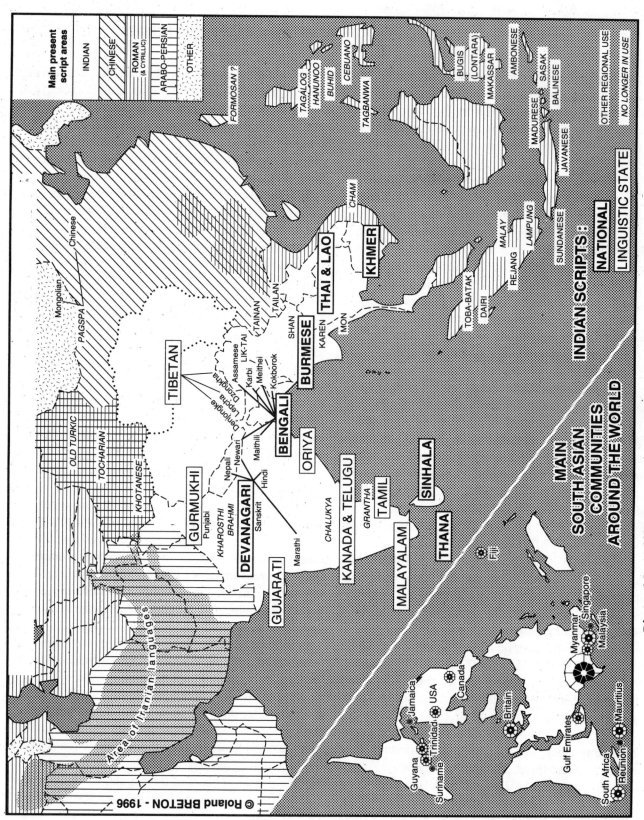

Plate 60: Diffusion of South Asian Languages and Scripts

© Roland BRETON - 1996

demographic previsions (Breton, 1994), the Indo-Aryan group ranks first (17 per cent of the world population) in the Indo-European family (43.5 per cent). But the Hindustani set of languages (10 per cent) is already the second in the world after Chinese (20 per cent). And, as a mother tongue, Hindi alone (6.8 per cent of the world population) is the second after Mandarin (14 per cent), Spanish and English (5.8 per cent each), and Arabic (5 per cent) while Bengali (3.7 per cent) occupies sixth position, followed by Urdu–Punjabi (3.2 per cent, an indivisible set, as the medium of instruction in most of the Punjabi areas is Urdu), Portuguese and Russian (2.7 per cent each), Japanese (2 per cent) German (1.7 per cent) and French (1.5 per cent). The Indian languages such as Telugu, Tamil and Marathi (1.3 per cent each of the world population) must be compared to Javanese (1.4 per cent), Korean (1.3 per cent), Vietnamese (1.1 per cent), Turkic, Italian or Thai (1 per cent). Gujarati is at the level of Persian while Kannada, Malayalam and Oriya are equivalent to Polish and Ukrainian in terms of percentage. Altogether, the ten first South Asian languages are at the level of 17 other first languages of the world.

The demographic weight is certainly not enough to qualify languages in the present world situation, as cultural and political positions are also heavily important. Nevertheless, the markets of communication as well as of general consumption, represented by the volume of speakers, is a first rank factor among others in the process of development and economic competition.

- The central map shows a certain cultural presence of Indian influence in many parts of Asia in the form of transmission of writing systems based on Indian scripts. This is the result of a millenary process reflecting the spread of Indian presence, lifestyle, religions and classical texts in two main directions. The first was in the north, towards Central Asia and along the Silk Route to China. The second was in the southeast, over the Indo-Chinese peninsula and the Indo-Malaysian archipelago, extending from Indian Ocean to China Sea. This created a continuous area where scripts of Indian origin have first been used and still prevail in certain parts.

Westwards, the realm of the Arabo-Persian alphabet, covering the whole Iranian language family area, is exihibited in the main languages of Pakistan (Urdu, Sindhi, Pushto, Baluchi, etc.) and of Jammu & Kashmir (Urdu, Kashmiri and Dogri). Eastwards, the area of the Chinese ideograms, or sinograms extends which

originally covered the whole Pacific fringe of Asia (China, Korea, Japan and Vietnam). This is presently recessing before different national writing systems (Korea and Japan) or the Roman alphabet (Vietnam and partly China for minor languages and to some extent in Chinese).

The South Asian subcontinent has also been the place where original scripts developed such as Kharosthi, Brahmi and Devanagari. These scripts travelled abroad with Hindu and Buddhist texts written in Sanskrit and Pali. Northwards, there exists some adaptation of Indian scripts which once reigned over the present Xinjiang basin, before the Turkization and Islamization of its populations. These populations have for long been Indo-European-speaking and were Hinduized. South of Taklamakan desert, there were Khotanese (seventh–tenth centuries) while north of this desert, there were Tocharian (fourth–seventh centuries) languages (Kuchean and Agnean), which have only been put in evidence since two centuries with archaelogical discoveries. Even Brahmi was first used to write Buddhist texts in early Turkic (ninth–tenth centuries).

Northwards, too, the Tibetan people inhabiting the high Central Asian massif have since the seventh century adopted, along with the Buddhist faith, the script in which its whole culture has been transcribed and registered. These Tibetan languages and script are prevalent not only in the so-called Tibet (Xizang) Autonomous Province (*Zizhiqu*) but also in the dozen Tibetan Autonomous Prefectures (*Zang Zizhizhou*) joined to neighbouring Qinghai, Gansu, Sichuan and Yunnan provinces. They are also present in Bhutan and Sikkim through their official Tibetan variants (Dzongkha and Denjongke) and even in the Lepcha ethnical language of Sikkim, including U-Chhen and U-Med variants of Tibetan script. At one time, an adaptatation of the Tibetan script, Pagspa, introduced by the Mongol or Yuan dynasty, was used in Chinese and Mongolian (both in the thirteenth to sixteenth centuries).

Within South Asia, Devanagari is used for Sanskrit, Hindi, Marathi, Newari and Nepali, and increasingly for Sindhi in India. Eight different scripts have evolved from Devanagari: Bengali (also used for Assamese, Meithei, Kokborok, Karbi, Maithili and initially for Newari), Oriya, Gujarati, Kannada and Telugu (these are similar to each other), Tamil, Malayalam, Sinhala and Gurumukhi (Punjabi). All these constitute modern scripts which have evolved from intermediate scripts such as the Gupta, Grantha, Chalukya, Cera-Pandya, Pallava-Chola scripts. They are now all attached to the official languages of 12 national or linguistic states. Also included is the Thana script of Maldives which borrowed letters from both Arabo-Persian and Kannada.

East of the subcontinent, various other scripts of Indian origin, mostly Brahmi, Pali, or early Tamil scripts, were adapted to several national or regional languages, each having different levels of success.

Four are definitely consecrated as the scripts of national languages: Burmese, Thai and Lao (both very similar), and Khmer. However, several minority languages of Myanmar made their own versions from these scripts: Mon (Austro-Asiatic, like Khmer), Karen (Tibeto-Burman), Shan and Khampti (both Thai languages), with Lik-Tai script. Similarly, in China, two other Thai speeches of two autonomous prefectures were constructed: Tainan script in Dehong and Thailan in Xishuangbanna.

The fate of Indian-originated scripts was less fortunate further east or southeast. On the mainland, the Cham script of the Cham language and Hindu kingdom (fifth–fifteenth centuries) which extended over present central and south Vietnam, was first superseded by Arabo-Persian and then quite disappeared with the dwindling Cham people. However, few Islamized survivors could be found in Cambodia.

In the archipelago, the Indian syllabic system was first used to write old Javanese, or Kawi, and old Malay. It has been superseded during the thirteenth–fifteenth centuries by the Arabo-Persian script used in middle Javanese or Pegon. Finally, modern Malay, or Malay-Indonesian (now officially called *Bahasa Malaysia* and *Bahasa Indonesia* in the two countries respectively) shifted in the nineteenth century to the Roman alphabet. Other regional Indonesian languages retained their original Indian-style scripts, e.g., Toba-Batak, Dairi Rejang and Lampung in Sumatra, or Sudanese, Javanese, Madurese in Java, Balinese and Sasak further east, and Makassar and Bugis in Celebes or Sulawesi, with their common Lontara script. Most of these languages have, however, mainly shifted to the Roman alphabet. All official administrative, educative and mediatic functions are conducted in Bahasa Indonesia, the one official language written in Roman alphabet.

North of the archipelago, Indian-style scripts were created for many local languages such as Tagbanwa in Palawan Island, Bisayan-Cebuano in central Philippine islands, Buhid and Hanunoo in Mindoro Island, and Tagalog, the present national language of the Philippines, now called Philipino or Filipino. All these languages have given up their Indian script in the

eighteenth century for the Roman alphabet. This is illustrated by Vietnamese which refrained from the use of Chinese ideograms while Malay-Indonesian relinquished the Arabo-Persian script. The existence of a Formosan Indian-style script in Taiwan, used in its Indonesian languages, before the massive Chinese settlement of the island, is highly controversial, for it may come from a scientific imposture dating from the beginning of the nineteenth century.

In any case, the present and past use of Indian scripts is far more than an isolated borrowing. It is the expression of the entire early Indianization (Sanskritization, Hinduization and Buddhization) of cultures and peoples through centuries of contact with India. The inner structure and the lexicon of each of these languages also reflect this deep influence of Indian civilization and languages. For instance, famous Khmer words like Cambodia (Kambudja), Mekong (Maha Ganga), Angkor (Nagar), Sihanouk (Singhanuka), etc., are of pure Sanskrit etymology, though the language is genetically far from Indo-Aryan. This type of borrowing is found in any of the Southeast Asian languages as Chinese loan words are found in great number in Korean and Japanese; Persian loan words in Arabic and Turkic; and Greek, Latin, French and English ones in any European language. The area covered by the diffusion of the Indian scripts is only an expression of the extension of one of the main great civilized areas of the world. If this could have also been manifested through vocabulary, myths and legends, scenic or graphic arts, or architecture, it would have been easier to represent it here through scripts.

For the moment, let it suffice to recall that the world communication landscape is distributed into writing system realms (as discussed in Plate 2). The Roman alphabet, used in all continents, includes parts of Southeast Asia (Malaysia, Indonesia, Philippines and Vietnam), southern China (Zhuang, Miao, and other ethnic minority languages) and central Asia since 1989. The Turkic peoples of central Asia officially reverted to the Roman script, following Turkey, and gradually gave up the Cyrillic or Russian script imposed under the Russian Soviet domination. Chinese ideograms were gradually restricted to China alone. Arabo-Persian script is now limited to the Middle East up to Tajikistan and to some Xinjiang languages in China. Cyrillic alphabet is consistently being restricted to some Slavic countries (Russia, Byelorussia, Ukraine, Bulgaria, Macedonia and Serbia-Montenegro). The Indian-style scripts cover most of continental South and Southeast Asia. This last realm is the most diversified in the world, with eight separate scripts for ten national languages: Devanagari (Hindi and Nepali), Tibetan (Bhutanese), Bengali, Sinhala, Maldivian, Burmese, Thai-Lao and Khmer. Added to this are six other scripts in Indian linguistic states or provinces: Oriya, Telugu–Kannada, Tamil, Malayalam, Gujarati and Gurumukhi. Thus, there are altogether 14 scripts plus at least a dozen of other regional ones, all in the Indo-Chinese peninsula or in the Indo-Malay archipelago.

ANNEXURES

A. PRESENTATION OF TABLES AND CHARTS

- The following tables present basic statistical data on languages in each country of South Asia, i.e., the national figures provided by various censuses of population. Each national census may differ from the other in terms of time and in the method of registering data. Many of them either omitted the language question or did not tabulate or publish the results. In the case of Sri Lanka, data only on ethnic groups (or, initially *race*) could be taken into account as information on languages is not collected. As a matter of course, in most countries, the *mother tongue* of every person is asked; but sometimes the enquiry is directed towards the language *mainly spoken* in households. This was the case observed in the 1981 Census of Pakistan and the 1981 Census of India at the first stage of publication (1987). Besides that, the tabulation of data on *mother tongue* needs a methodic classification under general *language* headings.

In the Census of India—regularly conducted every ten years and carrying detailed publications at all levels—the decision to classify certain speeches such as simple *variants* of main languages may be challenged by specialists. For instance, Maithili and western Pahari are put under Hindi while Khandeshi or Halabi are treated as full-fledged languages. It was thus necessary, at least at the national level, to take into account the gross provided figures. This is illustrated in the case of Hindi in India despite the changing official delimitation. The decision enforced by the 1971 Census of India withholding the publication of data on languages with less than 10,000 speakers, results in the non-entry/registering of all small figures since this date.

When for various reasons (such as non-enumeration of data due to civil wars or insecurity, partial destruction of documents, etc.), census data is lacking for one region leading to a notorious under-enumeration of the national total, the figures are preceded by the 'greater than' (>) sign.

Figures not available are replaced by '—'.

* Asterisks are put before figures of 'unspecified' generic language group designation which could not be clubbed with specific language returns.

All figures are rounded to the nearest 1,000 persons. The only exceptions being some very small Indian languages close to the 1,000 bar.

- The double purpose of the language classification chart is:

First, it recapitulates the general positions of all languages of the subcontinent within their distribution into families, branches, groups and subgroups. Most linguists may not agree to this or they may be differently revising their statements on many difficult points of classification.

Second, the chart attempts a totalization of the number of speakers of each language for the whole subcontinent through various national totals from the 1991 Census. This was possible by a harmonization between actual already published official data for 1991, and in its absence, with some safe projections based on previous census figures regarding languages and on other demographic sources. A larger provisional total for a few languages is added to the subcontinental total and to the country break-up. This provisional total takes into account the estimation of western and northern parts of Jammu & Kashmir where no language enumeration occurred since 1941 (see special note, Plate 58).

B. TABLES OF MOTHER TONGUES OF ETHNIC GROUPS OVER 1,000 PERSONS ACCORDING TO VARIOUS NATIONAL CENSUSES

BANGLADESH: 1961, 1974, 1981

BANGLADESH: Mother Tongues by 1,000 speakers, 1961–81

Bangladesh	1961	1974	1981
Total population	50,854	71,478	87,111
	mother tongues by 1,000 speakers		
Bengali	50,040	70,653	86,118
Urdu	311	178	218
Hindi	141		
Oriya	13		
Punjabi	10		
Sindhi	6		
Gujarati	4		
Persian	2		
Burmese	6		
Arakanese	2		
Other Tibeto-Burman	136		
Santali and Khasi	77		
Tribal languages		402	558
Others	82	244	227

INDIA: 1951, 1961, 1971, 1981

INDIA: Mother Tongues by 1,000 Speakers, 1951–81—(a)

India	1951	1961	1971	1981
Total population	356,879	439,235	548,160	616,880
18 Scheduled Languages				
Hindi	>108,759	133,435	209,514	264,514
Urdu	>13,572	23,324	28,621	34,941
Punjabi	>837	10,951	14,108	19,611
Hindi + Urdu + Punjabi	149,944			
Bengali	25,122	33,889	44,792	51,298
Oriya	13,296	15,719	19,863	23,022
Assamese	4,988	6,803	8,960	>80
Marathi	27,399	33,287	41,765	49,453
Gujarati	11,540	20,304	25,865	33,063
Kashmiri	—	1,956	2,495	3,177
Telugu	33,000	37,668	44,757	>50,625
Kannada	14,608	17,416	21,711	25,697
Malayalam	13,380	17,016	21,939	25,700
Tamil	26,593	30,563	37,690	>3,803
Sanskrit	1	3	2	6
Sindhi	745	1,373	1,777	2,044
Konkani	639	1,352	1,508	1,570
Nepali	436	1,021	1,420	1,361
Meithei	486	636	792	901

INDIA: Mother Tongues by 1,000 Speakers, 1951–81—(b)

India	1951	1961	1971	1981
		Other Indo-Aryan languages		
Shina	2	9	10	16
Dogri	—	880	1,299	1,531
Maldivian	—	5	—	—
		Other Tibeto-Burman languages		
		Tibetan		
Balti/Purik	—	34	40	49
Ladakhi	—	53	60	74
Lahauli	—	11	17	19
Denjongke/Sikk. Bh.	—	37	11	31
		Southeast Tibetan		
Sherdukpen/Ngnok	—	1	—	—
Monpa	—	15	26	33
Sulung/Puroik	—	2	—	—
Memba	—	2	—	—
		Himalayish		
Chamba–Lahuli	—	3	—	—
Kinnauri	0.224	29	45	53
		Arunachal/Mirish		
Hrusso/Aka	—	2	—	—
Nissi/Dafla	—	46	115	141
Miri/Mishing	58	137	181	—
Adi/Abor	2	95	99	125
Mishmi	—	15	22	24
		Baric		
Lepcha	27	24	33	28
Dhimal/Toto	0.3	0.3	—	—
Garo	240	307	412	>418
Bodo	215	362	557	>29
Deori	7	9	15	—
Lalung	8	11	11	—
Dimasa	6	33	40	—
Koch	5	8	14	17
Rabha	19	44	51	>22
Kokborok/Tripuri	171	300	373	502
		Karbi-Meithei		
Karbi/Mikir	131	154	199	>13

INDIA: Mother Tongues by 1,000 Speakers, 1951–81—(c)

India	1951	1961	1971	1981
(Other Tibeto-Burman languages: Naga)				
Naga unspecified	*12	*14	*23	*18
Northeast Naga				
Tangsa	—	>0.1	13	12
Nocte	—	>1.9	25	24
Wancho	—	>3.0	29	32
Konyak	9	57	72	76
Phom	1	13	18	24
Ao	49	58	75	52
Chang	1	11	16	22
Yimchumgre	—	13	20	27
Sangtam/Pochury	11	19	20	27
Tangkhul	35	44	58	80
Maring	5	8	9	12
Southwest Naga				
Lotha	22	27	37	58
Rengma	6	6	9	16
Sema	40	47	65	96
Khiemnungam	—	12	14	18
Angami/Chakru	29	53	69	41
Khezha	—	9	11	17
Zemi	10	10	6	11
Liangmei	2	10	13	17
Rongmei/Kabui	19	30	51	52
Paomata	8	8	9	—
Mao	14	21	35	59
Maram	3	5	—	—
Anal	3	6	7	11

INDIA: Mother Tongues by 1,000 Speakers, 1951–81—(d)

India	1951	1961	1971	1981
(Other Tibeto-Burman languages: end)				
Kuki				
Kuki unspecified	*36	*28	*32	*49
Vaiphei	4	9	12	16
Kom	3	5	6	10
Halam	12	17	19	19
Kuki-Chin				
Thado	10	32	51	58
Chiru	1	4	—	—
Aimol	0.3	0.1	—	—
Hrangkhol	1	8	—	—
Gangte	3	5	6	—
Chote	1	1	—	—
Zou/Simte	5	10	10	—
Paite	14	19	27	33
Chin				
Hmar	—	26	38	36
Mizo/Lushai	173	222	272	385
Lakher	6	10	12	16
Pawi	2	7	11	12
Burmese-Yi				
Singpho/Kachin	—	1	—	—
Arakanese/Mogh	—	10	12	17
Thai-Zhuang Languages				
Khampti	—	—	0.3	—
Mon-Khmer languages:				
Khasi	294	364	479	629
Nicobarese	12	14	18	22

INDIA: Mother Tongues by 1,000 Speakers, 1951–81—(e)

India	1951	1961	1971	1981
		Munda languages		
		Kherwari		
Santali	2,812	3,247	3,787	4,333
Mundari & 'Munda unspecified'	585	998	1,080	1,120
Ho	600	648	751	783
Bhumij	102	142	52	50
Koda/Kora	6	32	14	23
Turi	2	2	—	—
Birhor	—	1	—	—
Asuri	2	5	—	—
Birjia	2	2	—	—
Korwa	26	18	15	48
		West Munda		
Korku	189	220	307	348
		South Munda		
Kharia	11	177	191	213
Juang	13	16	12	19
Savara	256	266	222	209
Gadaba	54	40	20	28
		Other Dravidian languages		
		North Dravidian		
Malto	24	88	89	100
Kurukh/Oraon	644	1,142	1,236	1,334
		Central Dravidian		
Gondi	1,233	1,501	1,688	1,913
Kolami	43	51	67	84
Parji/Paraja	167	109	74	36
'Kisan'	66	50	74	159
Kui	207	512	351	522
Konda/Kubi	14	12	34	23
Kuvi/Khondi	281	168	196	196
'Jatapu'	33	19	36	23
Koya	137	141	212	240
		South Dravidian		
Tulu	788	935	1,158	1,417
Kodagu/Coorgi	69	79	72	93
Toda	1	1	—	—
Kota	—	1	—	—

NEPAL: 1952/54, 1961, 1971, 1981, 1991

NEPAL: Mother Tongues by 1,000 Speakers, 1952–91

Nepal	1952–54	1961	1971	1981	1991
Total population	8,236	9,413	11,556	15,023	18,491
Nepali	4,014	4,797	6,061	8,767	9,303
Hindi dialects	2,190	2,591	2,946	3,591	4,940
Hindi	80	3	—	—	171
Urdu	33	3	—	—	202
Tamang	495	519	555	522	904
Newari	383	378	455	449	690
Magar	274	255	288	213	430
Gurung	162	158	172	174	228
Rai	236	240	232	221	439
Limbu	146	139	171	129	254
Bhote-Sherpa	70	84	79	74	122
Jirel	3	3	—	—	4
Thakali	3	4	—	—	7
Byangsi	2	—	—	—	1
Thami	10	9	—	—	14
Jhangar	5	9	—	—	15
Raji	2	1	—	—	3
Chepang	14	9	—	—	25
Dhimal	6	8	—	—	15
Sunwar	17	13	20	11	—
Danuwar	9	12	10	14	24
Kumal	4	2	—	—	1
Darai	3	2	—	—	7
Majhi	6	6	—	—	11
Bengali	9	10	—	—	28
Rajbangsi	36	56	56	59	86
Santali	—	11	3	6	8
Satar	17	19	21	22	25
Others	70	114	487	765	507
Not stated	1	6	—	—	9

PAKISTAN: 1961, 1981

PAKISTAN: Mother Tongues (1961) and Households Language (1981)

Pakistan	1961	1981
Total population	42,880	84,254
	Mother tongues by 1,000 speakers	Languages spoken by % of households
Urdu	2,991	7.60
Punjabi (*)	26,200	60.44
Sindhi	4,964	11.77
Pushto	6,451	13.15
Baluchi	982	3.02
Brahui	366	1.21
Khowar	97	
Kohistani	209	
Kashmiri	42	
Gujarati	241	
Rajasthani	153	
Hindi	3	
Bengali	42	
Persian	28	
English	18	
Arabic	3	
Others	86	2.81

(*) including Hindko and Siraiki

SRI LANKA: 1946, 1953, 1963, 1971, 1981

SRI LANKA: Ethnic Groups by 1,000 Persons, 1946–81

Sri Lanka	1946	1953	1963	1971	1981
Total population	6,657	8,298	10,590	12,298	14,848
Ethnic groups					
Sinhalese	4,621	5,617	7,520	8,815	11,053
Tamils	1,515	1,859	2,351	2,333	3,652
Moors	409	710	689	666	1,026
Malays	23	25	24	19	43
Burghers and Eurasians	42	47	46	57	42
Europeans	5	7	7	7	—
Veddas	2	1	0	—	—
Others	41	32	20	7	32

C. THE LANGUAGE CLASSIFICATION CHART (WITH ESTIMATED MOTHER TONGUE SPEAKERS IN 1991 THROUGHOUT SOUTH ASIA)

L. Family

Branch

Group

(Subgroup)

Language	Total speakers:		(including west and north Jammu & Kashmir) (W & N JK)
	(by thousand)	(by country)	
Indo-European			
Iranian			
Western Iranian			
Baluchi	3,600	P	
Dehwari	10	P	
Ormuri	3	P	
Eastern Iranian			
Pushto	15,000	P	
Wanetsi	80	P	
Yidgha	6	P	
Wakhi	1	P	(+W & N JK 10 = 11?)
Nuristani			
Kati	5	P	
Indo-Aryan			
Dardic			
(Western Dardic)			
Pashaı	5	P	
Gawarbati	2	P	
Dameli	5	P	
Phalura	8	P	
Khowar	250	P	(+W & N JK 10 = 260?)
(Kohistani)			
Bashkarik	40	P	
Torwali	60	P	
Kalkoti	4	P	
Maiya	200	P	
Palasi	1	P	
Gowro	1	P	
Chilisso	3	P	
Bateri	30	P	
(Eastern Dardic)			
Shina	20	P	(+W & N JK 250=270?)
Kashmiri	4,100	I	(+W & N JK 200=4.3M?)
(possibly Dardic)			
Darai	7	N	
Kumal	1	N	
Danuwar	28	N	
Northwestern Indo-Aryan			
Sindhi	16,500	P (14 M) + I (2.5M)	
Central Indo-Aryan			
Dogri	2,000	I	(+W & N JK 1 M=3M?)

	Punjabi	94,000	P (70 M)+I(24 M)	
	Urdu	54,000	P (9 M)+I(45 M)	
	Hindi	341,000	I(336 M)+N(5M)+	
			(W & N JK 1.3 M=342 M?)	
	Gujarati	40,200	I	
Pahari				
	Nepali	11,700	N (9.3)+I(2.2)+BH (0.2)	
Eastern Indo-Aryan				
	Bengali	176,000	BD (109M)+I(67M)	
	Assamese	13,500	I	
	Oriya	27,500	I	
Southern Indo-Aryan				
	Marathi	62,000	I	
	Konkani	1,800	I	
	Sinhala	12,800	SL	
	Dhivehi	230	M (220)+I(10)	
Burushaski				
	Burushaski	?	I	(W & N JK 100 ?)
Tibeto-Burman				
Bodish				
Southwestern Tibetan				
	Balti (& Purik)	65	I	(+W & N JK 300=365?)
	Ladakhi	100	I	
	Lahauli	25	I	
	Spiti	?	I	
	Jad	?	I	
Southern Tibetan				
	Jirel	4	N	
	Sherpa	140	N (122)+I(18)	
	Denjongke	40	I	
	Dzongkha & Sangla	500	BH	
Southeastern Tibetan				
	Ngnok	3	I	
	Monpa	45	I	
	Sajalong	3	I	
	Puroik	5	I	
	Na	1	I	
	Memba	2	I	
	Charumba	1	I	
Gurung				
	Gurung	288	N	
	Thakali	7	N	
	Tamang	916	N (904)+I (12)	
Himalayish				
	Chamba–Lahul	?	I	
	Kanashi	?	I	
	Kinnauri	65	I	
	Byangsi	1	N	
	Darmiya	?	I	
	Chaudangsi	?	I	
	Rangkas	?	I	

	Jangali/Jhangar	15	N
	Thami	14	N
Eastern Himalayan			
	Magar	430	N
	Raji	3	N
	Chepang	25	N
	Newari	690	N
	Rai	439	N
	Limbu	279	N (254)+I(25)
	Sunwar	11	N
Baric			
Mirish			
	Hrusso	4	I
	Nissi	195	I
	Miri	300	I
	Adi	270	I
	Mishmi	35	I
Bodo-Garo			
	Lepcha	35	I
	Dhimal (& Toto)	16	N(15)+I(1)
	Garo	845	I(675)+BD(170)
	Koch	25	I
	Rabha	80	I
	Kokborok	745	I(670)+BD(75)
	Bodo	855	I
	Deori	20	I
	Lalung	15	I
	Dimasa	60	I
Karbi-Meithei			
	Karbi	310	I
	Meithei	1340	I(1 300)+BD(40)
Northeastern Naga			
	Ao	85	I
	Phom	40	I
	Konyak	120	I
	Wancho	45	I
	Nocte	35	I
	Tangsa	15	I
	Chang	35	I
	Yimchungre	45	I
	Sangtam	45	I
	Tangkhul	105	I
	Maring	15	I
Southwestern Naga			
	Lotha	90	I
	Rengma	25	I
	Sema	150	I
	Khiemnungan	30	I
	Angami	65	I
	Khezha	25	I
	Zemi	20	I

	Liangmei	25	I
	Rongmei	70	I
	Paomata	25	I
	Mao	80	I
	Maram	15	I
	Anal	15	I
Kuki			
	Vaiphei	20	I
	Halam	25	I
	Kom	15	I
Kuki-Chin			
	Thado	75	I
	Chiru	10	I
	Almol	2	I
	Hrangkhol	5	I
	Gangte	10	I
	Chote	2	I
	Zou/Simte	15	I
	Paite	45	I
Chin			
	Hmar	65	I
	Mizo	540	I
	Lakher	25	I
	Pawi	15	I
	Pankua	3	BD
	Khyang	2	BD
	Bom	7	BD
	Kumi	2	BD
	Mru	18	BD
Burmese-Yi			
	Singpho	3	I
	Lisu	?	I
	Arakanese	225	BD (200)+I(25)
	Chak	6	BD
Thai-Zhuang			
	Khampti	8	I
Austro-Asiatic			
Mon-Khmer			
	Khasi	875	I (855)+BD(20)
	Nicobarese	35	I
Munda			
Kherwari			
	Santali	5,655	I (5,485)+N(135)+BD(35)
	Mundari	1,385	I
	Ho	1,000	I
	Bhumij	65	I
	Koda/Kora	30	I
	Turi	3	I
	Birhor	3	I
	Asuri	10	I
	Birjia	5	I
	Korwa	60	I

Western Munda			
	Korku	440	I
Southern Munda			
	Kharia	265	I
	Juang	25	I
	Savara	250	I
	Gadaba	35	I
Dravidian			
Northwestern Dravidian			
	Brahui	1400	P
Northeastern Dravidian			
	Malto	125	I
	Dhangar	20	N
	Kurukh/Oraon	1,800	I (1,700)+BD (100)
Central Dravidian			
	Kolami	110	I
	Parji	50	I
	Ollari	20	I
	Kui	600	I
	Konda	15	I
	Kuvi	230	I
	Pengo	?	I
	Koya	300	I
	Gondi	2,400	I
	Telugu	68,000	I
Southern Dravidian			
	Tulu	1,700	I
	Kannada	32,000	I
	Kodagu	100	II
	Toda	1	I
	Kota	1	I
	Malayalam	29,500	I
	Tamil	63,000	I (59M)+SL (4.4M)

Abbreviations:

BD = Bangladesh, BH=Bhutan, I=India, M=Maldives, N=Nepal, P=Pakistan, SL=Sri Lanka

(Where 1991 Census data are lacking, figures have been estimated from previous censuses, with totals rounded off.)

Estimations for the part of Jammu & Kashmir occupied by Pakistan, where no language census occurred since 1941, have been deliberately added on to the right of the Chart.

SELECT BIBLIOGRAPHY

I. MAIN PUBLICATIONS OF VARIOUS CENSUSES OF POPULATION CONTAINING LANGUAGE DATA

CENSUS OF INDIA, 1881
Volume I–Report (Chapter VII: Language)
Volume II–Statistics (Chapter VII: Language)

CENSUS OF INDIA, 1891
General Report (Chapter V. A: Mother tongue).
Volume I General Tables (Chapter X: Parent tongues).

CENSUS OF INDIA, 1901
Volume I, India, Part I–Report (Chapter VII: Language).

CENSUS OF INDIA, 1911
Volume I, India, Part 1–Report (Chapter IX: Language).
Volume I, India, Part 2–Tables (Chapter X: Language).

CENSUS OF INDIA, 1921
Volume I, India Part 1–Report (Chapter IX: Language).
Volume I, India, Part 2–Tables (Chapter X: Language).

CENSUS OF INDIA, 1931
Volume I, India Part 1–Report (Chapter IX: Language).
Volume I, India, Part 2–Imperial Tables (Chapter XV: Language).
Volume I, India, Part 4–Social and Linguistic Maps.

CENSUS OF INDIA, 1941
Volume XXII, Jammu & Kashmir (Chapter XII: Language).

CENSUS OF INDIA, 1951
Census of India, Paper 1, 1954: Languages–1951 Census. Delhi 1954.

CENSUS OF INDIA, 1961
Volume, I, India, Part II-C (ii) Language Tables. Delhi 1964.

CENSUS OF INDIA, 1971
Census Centenary Monograph N. 10, R.C. Nigam: Language Handbook on Mother Tongues in Census. Delhi 1972.
India, Series 1, Part II-C (i) Social and Cultural Tables (including Tables C-V-A Languages and C-V-B Languages/Mother Tongues). Delhi 1977.
India, Series 1, Part II-C (iii) Volume I Social and Cultural Tables (including Tables C-VI Bilingualism). Delhi 1979.

CENSUS OF INDIA, 1981
Series 1, India, Paper 1 of 1987: Households and Household Population by Language Mainly Spoken in the Household. Delhi 1987.
Series 1, India, Part IV-B (i) Population by Languages/Mother Tongue (Table C-7). Delhi 1990.
Series 1, India, Part IV-B (ii) Population by Bilingualism (Table C-8). Delhi 1991.
Series 1, India, Part IX (ii) Special Tables for Scheduled Tribes on Mother Tongue and Bilingualism. Delhi 1991.

CENSUS OF NEPAL
Census of Population. Nepal, 1952/54 AD. Department of Statistics, Kathmandu 1958.
National Census of Population. Year 2018 (1961). Results. Second Part. Central Department of Statistics, Kathmandu 2024 (1967) (in Nepali).
Population Census, 1971: Social Characteristics Tables, Volume II, Part II. Central Bureau of Statistics, Kathmandu 1975.
Population Census, 1981: Social Characteristics Tables, Volume I, Part III, Nepal. Central Bureau of Statistics, Kathmandu 1984.
Intercensal Changes of Some Key Census Variables, Nepal 1952/54–81. Central Bureau of Statistics, Kathmandu, 4–5 March 1985.
Population Monograph of Nepal. Central Bureau of Statistics, Kathmandu. 1987.
The Analysis of the 1991 Population Census (Based

on Advance Tables). Central Bureau of Statistics, Kathmandu, March 1993.

Statistical Year Book of Nepal 1993. Central Bureau of Statistics, Kathmandu 1993. (Including: Population Distribution by Mother Tongue for Districts, 1991).

CENSUS OF PAKISTAN (and BANGLADESH up to 1961)

Census of Population, 1961. Volume 1: Pakistan (P.No. 158). Ministry of Home and Kashmir Affairs. Karachi n.d.

Census of Population, 1961. Volume 2: East Pakistan (P.No. 159). Ministry of Home and Kashmir Affairs. Karachi, June 1964.

Census of Population, 1961. Volume 3: Pakistan (P.No. 160). Ministry of Home and Kashmir Affairs. Karachi n.d.

Census Report of Pakistan 1981, (Census Report No. 69). Population Census Organisation. Islamabad, December 1984.

HandBook of Population Census Data. Population Census Organisation. Islamabad, December 1985.

CENSUS OF SRI LANKA

Census of Ceylon, 1953. General Report. Department of Census and Statistics. Colombo 1957.

ON CENSUS OPERATION

India 1991: Population Data Sheet. Delhi: Registrar General and Census Commissioner.

Bose, Ashish. 1991. *Population of India: 1991 Census Results and Methodology.* Delhi: B.R. Publishing Corporation.

—— 1991. *Demographic Diversity of India. 1991 Census State and District Level Data. A Reference Book.* Delhi: B.R. Publishing Corporation.

Premi, M.K. 1991. *India's Population: Heading Towards A Billion. An Analysis of 1991 Census Provisional Results.* Delhi: B.R. Publishing Corporation.

II. ON LANGUAGE DISTRIBUTION IN SOUTH ASIA

Breton, R. 1976. *Atlas Géographique des Langues et des Ethnies de l'Inde et du Subcontinent.* Quebec: Presses de l'Université Laval.

—— 1994. 'How Many Languages in India with How Many Speakers?' in Itagi, N.H., ed. *Spatial Aspects of Language, Mysore:* CIIL Silver Jubilee Publication Series, pp. 85–96, 2 tables.

Distribution of Languages in India in States and Union Territories (Inclusive of Mother tongue). 1973. Mysore: CIIL.

Emeneau, M.B. 1956. 'India as a Linguistic Area', *Language, Volume XXXII,* Part I, January–March. Linguistic Society of America.

Fussman, G. 1972. *Atlas linguistique des Parlers Dardes et Kafirs,* Volume LXXXVI. Paris: EFEO.

Grierson, G.A. 1902–27. *Linguistic Survey of India,* Volume I–XIX. Calcutta: Office of the Superintendant Government Printing. (Reprint: Motilal Banarsi Dass, Delhi 1957.)

Kloss, H. and G.D. McConnell. 1974. *Linguistic Composition of the Nations of the World. Volume I: South Asia, Central and Oriental Sectors.* Quebec: Les Presses de l'Université Laval.

Languages of India. Present Status of Christian Works in Every Indian Language. 1994. Madras: India Missions Association.

Mahapatra, B.P., G.D. McConnell, P.Padmanabha and V.S. Verma. 1989. *The Written Languages of the World: A Survey of the Degree and Modes of Use. Volume 2: India, Book 1 Constitutional Languages, Book 2 Non-Constitutional Languages.* Quebec: Les Presses de l'Université Laval (PUL).

Masica, C.P. 1976. *Defining a Linguistic Area: South Asia.* Chicago: University of California Press.

McConnell, G.D. 1992. *A Macro-sociolinguistic Analysis of Language Vitality, Geolinguistic Profiles and Scenarios of Language Contact in India.* Quebec: PUL/Centre International de Recherche en Aménagement Linguistique (ICIRAL).

Pandit, P.B. 1972. *India as a Socio-linguistic Area,* Pune: Deccan College.

Sarker, A. 1964. *Handbook of Languages and Dialects of India.* Calcutta: Mukhopadhyay.

Singh, K.S. and S. Manoharan. 1993. *Languages and Scripts.* People of India, National Series, Volume IX. Delhi: Anthropological Survey of India and Oxford University Press.

Tirtha, R. 1964. 'Linguistic Regions in India'. *Pacific Viewpoint* Vol. 5, no. 1, (May). Wellington Victoria University of Wellington.

Zvelebil, K.V. 1990. *Dravidian Linguistics: An Introduction.* Pondicherry: Pondicherry Institute of Linguistics and Culture.

III. ON WORLD LANGUAGE CLASSIFICATION

Breton, R. 1991. *Geolinguistics: Language Dynamics and Ethno-linguistic Geography*. Ottawa: University of Ottawa Press.

—— 1994. (third edition) *Géographie des Langues*. Que sais-je? collection. Paris: Press Université de France.

Grimes, B.F. 1996. (thirteenth edition). *Ethnologue: Languages of the World*. 3 Volumes. Dallas: SIL.

Klose, A. 1987. *Languages of the World: A World Index of the Language Families*. Paris and Munchen: K.G. Saur.

Matisoff. 1980. *The Languages and Dialects of Tibeto-Burman: An Alphabetic–Genetic Listing with Some Prefatory Remarks on Ethnonymic and Glossonymic Complications*. Berkeley: University of California.

Ruhlen, M. 1987. *A Guide to the World's Language. Volume I: Classification*. California: Stanford University Press.

Voegelin, C.F. and F.M. Voegelin. 1977. *Classification and Index of the World's Languages*. New York: Elsevier.

IV. ON SOUTH ASIAN ANTHROPOLOGY

Basu, Sajal. 1992. *Regional Movements. Politics of Language, Ethnicity—Identity*. New Delhi: Manohar Publications.

Biasutti, R. 1953. *Le Razze e i Popli Della Terra*. Turin: Unione tipografico torinese.

Bista, D.B. 1991. *Fatalism and Development: Nepal's Struggle for Modernization*. Calcutta: Orient Longman.

Brass, Paul R. 1991. *Ethnicity and Nationalism*, New Delhi: Sage Publications.

Danda, Ajit K. 1991. *Ethnicity in India*. Tribal Studies of India Series, T 144. Delhi: Inter-India Publications.

Das, N.K. 1989. *Ethnic Identity, Ethnicity and Social Stratification in North-east India*. Delhi: Inter India Publications.

Dumont, L. 1970. *Homo Hierarchicus: The Caste System and its Implication*. New Delhi: Vikas Publications.

Eickstedt, Egon von. 1934. *Rassenkunde und Rassengeschichte der Menschheit*, Stuttgart: Gustav Fischer Verlag.

Elwin, Verrier. 1961. *Nagaland*. Shillong: P. Dutta.

Guha, B.S. 1935. *The Racial Affinities of the People of India*: Census of India 1931, Volume 1, Part III-A

—— 1944. *Racial Elements in the Population*. Bombay: Oxford Pamphlet in Indian Affair.

Hutton, J.H. 1932. 'Races of Further India', *Man in India*, 3, Ranchi, India.

Majumdar, D.N. 1961. *Races and Cultures of India*. Bombay: Asia Publishing House.

Majumdar, D.N. and T.N. Madan. 1961. *An Introduction to Social Anthropology*. Bombay: Asia Publishing House.

Maloney, C. 1974. *Peoples of South Asia*. New York: Holt, Rinehart and Winston.

Olivier, Georges. 1961. *Anthropologies des Tamouls du Sud de l'Inde*, Paris: Ecole Française d'Extrême-Orient.

Sharma, K.L. 1990. *Indian Society*. Delhi: NCERT.

Singh, K.S. 1992. *People of India: An Introduction*. Calcutta: Anthropological Survey of India.

—— 1993. *The Scheduled Castes*. People of India, National Series, Volume II. Delhi: Anthropological Survey of India and Oxford University Press.

—— 1994. *The Scheduled Tribes*. People of India, National Series, Volume III. Delhi: Anthropological Survey of India and Oxford University Press.

Singh, K.S., V. Bhalla and V. Kaul. 1994. *The Biological Variation in Indian Populations*. People of India, National Series, Volume X. Delhi: Anthropological Survey of India and Oxford University Press.

Sopher, D. 1980. *An Exploration of India: Geographical Perspectives on Society and Culture*. Ithaca, New York: Cornell U.P.

V. ON LINGUISTIC STATES AND LANGUAGE ISSUES

Ambedkar, B.R. 1955. *Thoughts on Linguistic States*. Delhi. (Aligarh, Anand Sahitya Sadan, 1989).

Annamalai, E. 1979. ed. *Language Movements in India*, Mysore: CIIL.

Brass, Paul R. 1974. *Language, Religion and Politics in North India*. Cambridge: Cambridge University Press.

Constituent Assembly of India. 1948. Report of the Linguistic Provinces Commission. Delhi: Government of India Press.

Gandhi, M.K. 1954. *Linguistic Provinces.* Ahmedabad: Navajivan Publishing House.

Indian National Congress, n.d. *Resolutions on States Reorganisation 1920–1956.* Delhi: All India Congress Committee.

Rao, K. 1969. *The Language Issue in the Indian Constituent Assembly 1946–1950.* Bombay: International Book House.

Report of the States Reorganisation Commission 1955. Delhi: Government of India Press.

Singh, K.S. 1989. 'Ethnicity and Polity Formation in Tribal India'. *Human Science*: 38.

Srivastava, G. 1970. *The Language Controversy and the Minorities.* Delhi: Atma Ram.

Toba, S. 1992. *Language Issues in Nepal.* Kathmandu: Samdan Books and Stationers.

VI. MAPS AND ATLASES

An Atlas of India. 1990. Delhi: Oxford University Press.

Atlas of Pakistan. 1985 (1990). Rawalpindi: Survey of Pakistan.

Census Atlas, National Volume. 1988. Delhi: Census of India, 1981. Series 1, Part XII.

International Map of the Vegetation and of Environmental Conditions. 1/1,000,000. Pondicherry: French Institute of Pondicherry.

National Atlas of India, Selected maps (including 1978 Plate 232: Languages). Calcutta: National Atlas Organisation.

Schwartzberg, J.E. 1978. ed. *A Historical Atlas of South Asia.* Chicago and London: University of Chicago Press. (second edition, 1992 by OUP).

Singh, K.S. 1993. *An Anthropological Atlas. People of India National Series*, Volume XI. Delhi: Anthropological Survey of India and Oxford University Press.

Survey of India. *Topographical Maps, State Maps I: 1,000,000 scale, International Map of the World (IMW) 1/1,000,000.* Dehra Dun: Survey of India.

VII. FURTHER READINGS

Bertin, Jacques. 1981. *Graphics and Graphic Information–Processing.* New York: W. de Gruyter.

———. 1983. *Semiology of Graphics, Diagrams, Networks, Maps.* Madison: University of Wisconsin Press.

Chandrasekhar, S. 1950. *India's Population.* Madras: Annamalai University.

Chatterjee, S.P. 1968. 'La Géographie Régionale du Plateau de Meghalaya', in R.L. Singh, ed. *India, 21st International Geographical Congress. India: Regional Studies.*

Fuerer-Haimendorf. 1960. 'Unity and Diversity in the Chetri Case of Nepal' in Fuerer-Haimendorf, ed., *Caste and Kin in Nepal, India and Ceylon—Anthropological Studies in Hindu–Buddhist Contact Zones.* Bombay: Asia Publishing House.

Spate, O.H.K. 1957. *India and Pakistan.* London: Methuen. (third edition, 1967).

Srivastava, R.R. 1960. 'Tribe-caste Mobility in India: The Case of Kumaun Bhotias' in Fuerer-Haimendorf, ed. *Caste and Kin in Nepal, India and Ceylon—Anthropological Studies in Hindu–Buddhist Contact Zones.* Bombay: Asia Publishing House.

LANGUAGE CLASSIFICATION AND PLATE INDEX

Index of classification of the LANGUAGES, SPEECH FORMS and scripts, and of the related ethnic, **geographical**, and religious designations with their **main** occurrences on the plates.

LETTER TYPES USED

1. **BOLD CAPITALS** are reserved for main entries, i.e.: the most convenient designation of each of the full-fledged **LANGUAGE** unit spoken in, or around, the subcontinent. As far as possible it is the *auto-glossonym* (self-designation, or *autonym*, in the language itself). Exceptionally a different, already commonly used international (often English) term has been put on the same footing as the autonym, with a slash (/); ex.: **BENGALI/BANGLA** or **PUNJABI/PANJABI**.

2. Ordinary CAPITALS are used for all other LANGUAGE designations, as well as for other speech forms of an inferior level (DIALECT, DIALECT GROUP, etc.).

3. Lower case letters are used for language categories of a level superior to the language (Language group, family, etc.) and for all non-linguistic terms: names of scripts, ethnic groups (*ethnonyms*), social or religious communities, geographical places (*toponyms*), political units, etc.

4. Italics, whether in *CAPITALS* or in *Lower case letters*, are used for the least proper designations: erroneous, obsolete, derogative, etc., still found in some other publications, but presently becoming out of use or not recommended.

SYMBOLS USED:

⊂ is included in, belongs to, generally speaking
{ } includes what is under these braces
⇒ see (main entries)
≠ different from, not to be confused with

NUMBERS OF LANGUAGE SPEAKERS

Speaker numbers are given but only for each full-fledged **LANGUAGE**; and as a total within the territory of the seven countries of South Asia only (India, Pakistan, Bangladesh, Nepal, Bhutan, Sri Lanka and Maldives). Each round figure has been deliberately calculated as a projection from the previous census data till year 2001, according to regional rates of population increase, so as to reach a certain homogeneity with others. Therefore, these numbers are followed by an interrogation mark (?). When no recent data were available, they are followed by double interrogation marks (??).

REFERENCES TO THE PLATES

P. refers to Plate (Plate numbers are given for main occurrences only)

Note: This index has been created, after the completion of the plates and the fabrication of the text of this atlas, with the latest available information, such as those of the *People of India* series. As a result, some of the entries may not be found in the rest of the work. This is also the reason why the precise meaning given to some others may somehow differ from the sense used previously.

Abor ⇒ **ADI**

Achik, ethnic of **GARO**

ADAP ⊂ **DZONGKHA** P. 56

ADI, *Abor* ⊂ Mirish, Arunachal P. 1, 16, 17, 58, 230,000 ?
Adi-Bokar, Adi-Bori, Adi-Gallong, Adi-Karko, Adi-Milang, Adi-Padam, Adi-Pasi, Adi-Shimong, etc.: **ADI** subgroups P. 17

Adivasi, Adibasi, Adimjati, Tribe, Scheduled Tribe, Tribal People, P. 26

Adiyan or Erava Tribe, Wynad, Kerala ⊂ **KANNADA**

Afghan ⇒ Pathan

Afghanistan P. 4, 6, 47, 50

AGARIA ⊂ **ASURI** ⊂ Kherwari

AHIRANI ⊂ **KHANDESHI** P. 24

AHOM ⊂ Thai, Assam (extinct) P. 16

AIMOL ⊂ Kuki-Chin P. 58, 3,000 ??

AITON ⊂ Thai

AJMERI ⊂ **RAJASTHANI** P. 10

Aka ⇒ **HRUSSO** P. 16, 17, 58

Ambala District, Haryana P. 9

Amritsar District, Punjab P. 9

ANAL/PAKAN ⊂ Naga P. 18, 58, 20,000 ?

ANDAMAN, **AKA-ANDAMAN**, Great Andamanese ⊂ Andaman Language Family Branch 50 ??

Andaman, Andamanese Language Family Branch {**AKA-ANDAMAN, JARAWA, SENTINELESE, ONGE**}

Andaman & Nicobar Islands Union Territory P. 41

Andhra people ⊂ **TELUGU**

Andhra Pradesh P. 2, 28, 29, 30, 41, 42, 43, 46, 47

ANGA ⇒ ANGIKA

ANGAMI, TENIDYE, TJUNGUNI, MONR {TENGIMA, ZUNUO-KEYHONUO, CHAKHRU} ⊂ Naga P. 18, 58, 80,000 ?

ANGIKA, ANGIKAR ⊂ BIHARI

Anglo-Indian community, India ⊂ **ENGLISH** P. 38

AO, AOR {MONSEN, CHUNGLEI} ⊂ Naga P. 18, 58, 100,000?

APATANI, APA TANI, TANU ⊂ **NISSI** P. 16, 17

ARABIC P. 2, 3, 39, 44, 30,000?

Arabian, Arabo-Persian script P. 2, 60

ARAKANESE, MAGH, MOGH, MARMA ⊂ Burmese, Myanmar and Bangladesh P. 1, 16, 39, 56, 300,000??

Arakan or Rakhine state, Myanmar P. 47

ARLENG ⇒ **KARBI**

Arunachal Pradesh, ex-NEFA P. 17, 19, 46, 47

Arunachal Language Group ⇒ Mirish

ASHKUN ⊂ Nuristani, Afghanistan P. 6

Assam P. 2, 16, 19, 20, 22, 41, 42

ASSAMESE/ASSAMIYA ⊂ Eastern Indo-Aryan P. 1, 3, 19, 20, 22, 42, 58, 59, 25 million ??

Assamo-Burman, Baric, Bodo Group ⊂ Tibeto-Burman P. 16

Asur, ethnic of ASURI

ASURI ⊂ Kherwari P. 1, 26, 58, 10,000 ??

Austric set of Language families {Austro-Asiatic, Austronesian, etc.}

Austro-Asiatic Language Family P. 16

AVADHI, AWADHI ⊂ Eastern Hindi P. 1, 12, 51

AVESTAN ⊂ Old Iranian

AWE ⊂ PENGO

Badaga peasant community, Nilgiri District

BADAGA ⊂ **KANNADA**, Nilgiris

Badakhshan province, Afghanistan, P. 6

Upper Badakhshan, ex-Gorno-Badakhshan, Tadjikistan P. 6

BADKAT ⊂ NYAMKAT ⊂ Tibetan, Upper Kannawar P. 16

BAGHELI, BAGHELKHANDI ⊂ Eastern Hindi P. 1, 12, 49

BAGRI ⊂ HARYANI

Baiga or Parhaiya Tribe, Chota Nagpur, Madhya Pradesh

BAIGANI ⊂ CHHATTISGARHI

Baital, Nagari script, Rajasthan

BAITE ⇒ BETE

Balinese script, Indonesia P. 60

BALOCHI ⇒ **BALUCHI**

BALTI ⊂ Tibetan P. 5, 6, 7, 16, 500,000 ??

Baltistan P. 5, 6, 7, 41

BALUCHI, BALOCHI ⊂ Western Iranian P. 1, 4, 5, 47, 55, 59, 4.8 million ??

Baluchistan, Pakistan P. 4, 5, 41, 47

Baluchistan and Seistan, Iran P. 47

BANBHASHA ⇒ **JANGALI**

Bangalore Municipal Corporation P. 31

BANGALA/BANGLA/**BENGALI**

Bangladesh, ex-East-Pakistan P. 2, 21, 41, 47, 56

BANGNI ⊂ NISSI P. 47

BANJARI, BANJARI-LAMBADI ⊂ RAJASTHANI P. 11, 26, 30, 31

BANJOGI, BONZOGI ⊂ Chin P. 56

BANUM ⇒ BUNAN

BARA ⇒ BODO, PLAINS CACHARI

BAREL ⇒ BHILALI

Baric Group ⊂ Tibeto-Burman P. 16, 58

BATERI ⊂ Kohistani, Pakistan P. 55, 30,000??

Barman of Cachar Tribe, North Cachar Hills District

BASHGALI ⊂ **KATI** ⊂ Nuristani P. 6

BASHKARIK, GARWI, DIRI, KALAMI, ethnic Bashkar ⊂ Kohistani P. 6, 55, 40,000 ??

Bastar District, Madhya Pradesh P. 26

BAWN ⊂ **MIZO**

Bedia Tribe, Chota Nagpur ⊂ SADRI

Beldar vagrant caste, Maharashtra ⊂ Hindustani and Dravidian?

BENGALI/BANGLA/BANGALA ⊂ Eastern Indo-Aryan P. 1, 3, 19, 20, 21, 41, 42, 48, 53, 56, 58, 59, 220 million?

BETE, BIETE, BAITE ⊂ **HRANGKHOL**, ≠ BIATE ⊂ **MIZO**

BHADRAWAHI ⊂ Western PAHARI P. 15

BHARMAURI, GADDI ⊂ Western Pahari P. 15

BHATEALI ⊂ DOGRI

Bhatinda District, Punjab P. 9

BHATRI ⊂ **ORIYA**

Bhil Tribe P. 26

Bhilala Tribe

BHILALI, BAREL ⊂ **BHILI**

BHILI ⊂ Western Indo-Aryan P. 1, 10, 12, 24, 26, 6.5 million?

BHILODI ⊂ BHIL

BHODI, BODHI, BUDHI, **LADAKHI** P. 5, 6, 7

BHOJPURI ⊂ BIHARI P. 1, 11, 12, 49, 51

Bhot Tribe, Himachal Pradesh

Bhot Country, Upper Kumaon, Uttar Pradesh P. 3, 16

Bhote, **BHOTE-SHERPA**, Sherpa, Nepal P. 16, 19, 53, 54, 200,000 ?

BHOTIYA, BHUTIYA, TIBETAN P. 16, 19, 53, 54

BHRAMU ⊂ **KUMAL**

BHUMIJ ⊂ Kherwari P. 1, 26, 58

Bhutan, Druk-Yul P. 15, 16, 47, 48, 56, 59

BHUTANESE, DRUK-KE, LHO-KE, **DZONGKHA** P. 1, 15, 16, 56, 59, 300,000 ??

BIATE ⊂ MIZO, ≠ BETE

Bihar P. 2, 11, 41, 42, 47

BIHARI ⊂ Eastern Indo-Aryan

Binjhal, Binjhia, Binjhwar Tribe, Orissa and Madhya Pradesh ⊂ SADRI, **ORIYA** AND CHHATTISGARHI P. 26

Bir jungle Tribes {Asur, Birjia, Agaria} ⊂ **ASURI**

BIRHOR ⊂ Kherwari P. 1, 26, 58, 3,000 ??

BIRJIA, BRIJIA ⊂ **ASURI** ⊂ Kherwari P. 58

Bisayan ⇒ Cebuano script, P. 60

BISHNUPURIYA, BISHNUPRYA, ethnic *Mayang*, Dalu ⊂ **BENGALI** P. 58

Bodh Tribe, Jammu & Kashmir

BODHI, BHODI ⇒ **LADAKHI**

Bodhi, Tibetan script, P. 60

Bodic, Baric group ⊂ Tibeto-Burman P. 16

BODO, BARA {Mech, Plains Kachari, Borofsa, etc.} P. 1, 16, 19, 58, 1.5 million ??

Bodpa, ethnic of TIBETAN

BODSKAD ⇒ TIBETAN

Bod-Yul ⇒ Tibet

Bohra Muslim community, Sind, Gujarat, Mumbay

BOM ⊂ Chin, Bangladesh P. 56, 9000 ??

Bombay or Mumbay District, Maharashtra P. 40

BONDO, BONDO-PORAJA ⇒ REMO

BONZOGI ⇒ BANJOGI

BORO-KACHARI ⇒ BODO

Brahmi script of SANSKRIT P. 60

BRAHMAURI, GADDI ⊂ Western Pahari P. 16

BRAHUI ⊂ Dravidian, Pakistan P. 1, 4, 5, 41, 55, 59, 1.9 million ??

BRAJ, BRAJ BHASHA ⊂ Western HINDI P. 1, 12

BROKPA, BROQPA, BROKSKAD, BROKSAK ⊂ **SHINA**, Kargil District

BUDHI ⇒ BHODI

Bugis, Buginese script ⊂ Lontara script, Indonesia P. 60

BUGUN, ethnic Khowa ⇒ **PUROIC** P. 17

Buhid, Buoid script, Philippines P. 60

BUJUUR, MOYON ⊂ **ANAL**

BUNAN, BANAM, GARI ⊂ **CHAMBA LAHULI** P. 16

BUNDELI, BUNDELKHANDI ⊂ Western HINDI P. 1, 12, 49

Burgher community, Sri Lanka ⊂ **INDO PORTUGUESE** P. 36, 57

Burma ⇒ Myanmar

BURMESE ⊂ Tibeto-Burman P. 1, 3, 16, 39, 10,000 ??

Burmese script P. 2, 60

Burmic group ⊂ Tibeto-Burman

BURUSHASKI, ethnic Burusho P. 1, 5, 6, 7, 58, 59, 130,000??

Burusho {Hunza, Wershikwar} ethnic of **BURUSHASKI** P. 5, 6, 7

BYANGSI, BYANSHI ⊂ Himalayish P. 1, 16, 1,000 ??

Cachar District, Assam P. 20

CACHARI, HILLS CACHARI, **DIMASA** P. 16

CACHARI, PLAINS CACHARI, BARA, **BODO** P. 16, 19, 20

Calcutta District, West Bengal P. 40

CANARESE ⇒ **KANNADA**

Cebuano script, Philippines P. 60

Ceylon ⇒ Sri Lanka

CHAK, SAK, THET ⊂ Burmese-Yi, Bangladesh P. 56, 8,000 ??

Cha-Khe-Sang, CHAKRU–KHEZHA–SANGTAM ⊂ Naga P. 16

CHAKMA, CHAKAMA ⊂ **BENGALI** P. 16, 56

CHAKHRU, CHOKRI ⊂ **ANGAMI** AND 'Cha-Khe-Sang'

Chalukya script of **SANSKRIT**, South India P. 60

Cham script, Vietnam, Cambodia P. 60

CHAMBA LAHULI, LAHULI OF CHAMBA ⊂ Himalayish P. 1, 7, 16, 58, 3000 ??

CHAMEALI ⊂ Western Pahari P. 15

Chandigarh Union Territory, Punjab P. 47

CHANG, *MAZUNG* ⊂ Naga P. 18, 58, 45,000 ?

CHARUMBA {Meyor and Zakhring Tribes} ⊂ Tibetan, Eastern Arunachal P. 17, 58, 1,500 ??

CHAUDANGSI ⊂ Himalayish P. 16, 1,500 ??

Chenchu Tribe, Nalamalai Range, Andhra Pradesh ⊂ **TELUGU** P. 26

Chennai ⇒ Madras

CHEPANG ⊂ Himalayan P. 16, 53, 33,000 ?

Chero Tribe, Chota Nagpur ⊂ SADRI P. 26

Chetri, Khas community, Nepal

Chhattisgarh region, Madhya Pradesh

CHHATTISGARHI ⊂ Eastern Hindi P. 1, 12

Chibali ⊂ PUNJABI

Chik-Baraik Tribe, Chota Nagpur ⊂ SADRI

CHILIS, **CHILISSO** ⊂ Kohistani P. 55, 3,000 ??

Chin ⊂ Kuki-Chin ⊂ Tibeto-Burman P. 1, 16, 58

Chin state, ex-Chin Special Division, Chin-Hills, Myanmar P. 47

CHINESE P. 3, 39, 50, 15,000 ?

CHIRU ⊂ Kuki-Chin P. 58, 12,000 ??

Chirr Tribe ⊂ **YIMCHUNGRE**

Chittagong Hills Tracts District, Bangladesh P. 56

CHOKRI ⇒ CHAKHRU

Chota Nagpur, Chotanagpur, Jharkhand P. 22, 26, 47

CHOTE, CHOTHE, *PURUM* ⊂ Kuki-Chin P. 58, 3,000 ??

CHULIKATA ⇒ IDU P. 17

CHUNGLEI, CHUNGLI ⊂ **AO** (standard)

Chutiya, ethnic of **DEORI**

Coorg District, Karnataka ⊂ **KODAGU**, YERAVA, KURUMBA P. 32

COORG ⇒ **KODAGU** ⊂ Dravidian

CREOLE MALAY, Sri Lanka P. 57, 50,000 ??

Dadra and Nagar Haveli Union Territory

Dafla ⇒ NISSI

Dai, Daic, Thai Language Group ⊂ Zhuang-Dai Language Family P. 16

Dairi script, Indonesia P. 60

DAKHINI, DAKHSHINI ⊂ URDU P. 13

Dalu ⇒ Mayang
DAMELI ⊂ Dardic P. 55, 4,000 ??
Dandakaranya region, Madhya Pradesh and Orissa P. 26
Dang, Dhanka Tribe, Dangs District, Gujarat P. 24
DANGI, DHANKI ⊂ **KHANDESHI** P. 24
DANUWAR ⊂ Dardic ? Nepal P. 16, 53, 54, 35,000 ?
DARAI ⊂ Dardic ? Nepal P. 16, 53, 54, 10,000 ?
Dard, Dardic Language Family Branch P. 5, 6, 7, 55
DARI, FARSI ⊂ **PERSIAN**, Western Iranian P. 1, 3, 41, 47, 50
Darjeeling Gorkha Hills District, West Bengal P. 47, 56
DARMIYA ⊂ Himalayish, P. 16, 1,800 ??
Darrang District, Assam P. 20
Deccan, South India
DEHATI ⊂ Hindustani, Nepal
DEHWARI ⊂ Western Iranian, Pakistan P. 1, 55, 10,000 ??
Delhi District and Union Territory P. 9, 10, 40
DENDJONGKE, SIKKIMESE, SIKKIM BHOTIYA ⊂ Tibetan P. 1, 16, 19, 48, 50, 58, 55,000 ?
Deodhai, Ahom priestly caste, Assam
DEORI, ethnic Chutiya ⊂ Bara group P. 1, 16, 58, 25,000 ??
DESIA, Oriya Pidgin, Koraput
Devanagari or Nagari script P. 2, 60
DHANGAR ⊂ **KURUKH**, Nepal P. 55, 25,000 ?
Dhanka Tribe, Dangs District, Gujarat ⊂ BHILI P. 26
DHIMAL ⊂ Baric ? Nepal P. 16, 53, 54, 26,000 ?
DHIVEHI, DIVEHI, MAHL, MALDIVIAN ⊂ Southern Indo-Aryan, Maldives Islands and Minicoy P. 1, 33, 47, 50, 57, 300,000 ?
Dhodia Tribe, Gujarat ⊂ BHILI P. 26
DHUNDARI ⊂ RAJASTHANI P. 1, 11
DHURWA ⊂ **PARJI** P. 26
DIDAYI, DIDEY ⊂ **GADABA**
DIGARU, TAAON ⊂ **MISHMI** P. 17
DIMASA, HILLS CACHARI P. 1, 16, 58, 75,000 ??
DIRI ⇒ **BASHKARIK**
DIVEHI ⇒ **DHIVEHI**
DOGRI, ethnic Dogra ⊂ Northern Punjabi P. 5, 6, 7, 8, 54, 55, 4 million ??
Dokhpa, Drokshat Tibetan Tribe, Jammu & Kashmir ≠ Broq-pa
Donyi Polo Tribal Religion, Arunachal
DORLI ⊂ **GONDI**
DOWYAN ⇒ **LALUNG**
Dravidian Language Family P. 1, 26, 28, 54, 55, 57, 58, 59
Drukpa, ethnic Bhutanese
Dubla Tribe, Gujarat ⊂ BHILI P. 26
DUHLIAN, DUHLIAN TWANG, LUSHAI ⇒ **MIZO** standard

EMELA ⇒ **MAO**
EMPEO ⊂ **KACHA**
ENGLISH P. 3, 39, 44, 47, 300,000?

FATA ⇒ Frontier Region, Pakistan
Ferozepur District, Punjab P. 9
Formosan script, Taiwan P. 60
FRENCH P. 3, 39, 3,000 ??
Frontier Region, FATA, NWFP, Pakistan P. 4, 5, 6, 41, 47, 55

GADABA {DIDAYI, REMO, GUTOB} ⊂ Southern Munda P. 1, 26, 30, 58, 35,000 ?
Gadaba Tribe {**GADABA, OLLARI**}
GADDI ⊂ **BHARMAURI**
Gamit Tribe, Gujarat ⊂ **BHILI**
GANGTE, *RANGTE* ⊂ Kuki-Chin P. 58, 12,000??
Garhjat region, northern Orissa
GARHWAL BHOTIA {TOLCHHA, MARCHHA} P. 16
GARHWALI ⊂ Central Pahari P. 15
GARI ⇒ BUNAN
GARO, ethnic Achik, Kusik ⊂ Baric P. 1, 16, 19, 56, 58
GARWI ⇒ **BASHKARIK**
GATA ⇒ **GUTOB**
GAWARBATI ⊂ Dardic, Pakistan, Afghanistan P. 6, 55, 3,000 ??
GERMAN P. 3, 39, 50, 2,000 ??
Ghalcha, Ghalchah ⇒ Pamir Tajik
Ghats, Western Ghats or Sahyadri Range P. 24, 25, 26, 27, 32
Gilgit, Shinaki, Shinak country P. 6
Girijan Hill People, Andhra Pradesh
Goa state, former Goa, Daman & Diu Union Territory P. 27, 41, 47
Goalpara District, Assam P. 20
GOJALI ⊂ **WAKHI**, Hunza, Jammu & Kashmir P. 6, 7
GOJRI, GOJARI, GUJURI, GUJARI, GUJJARI ⊂ RAJAS-THANI, Jammu & Kashmir, Pakistan P. 6, 7, 11, 55
Golar, Golcar caste, Madhya Pradesh ⊂ **KANNADA**
GONDI, ethnic Gond (pl. Gondaru), Koi, Koitur ⊂ Dravidian P. 1, 26, 30, 58, 3 million ?
GONDLA ⊂ **LAHULI**
Gondwana region, Madhya Pradesh P. 26
GORKHALI, GURUKHA, KHAS KURA, NEPALI P. 15, 16, 19, 51, 54, 58, 59
GOWRO ⊂ Kohistani P. 55, 200 ??
Grantha script of SANSKRIT, South India P. 60
Gujarat P. 2, 24, 41, 42, 43, 47
GUJARATI ⊂ Central Indo-Aryan P. 1, 3, 23, 35, 43, 44, 48, 55, 58, 59, 45 million ?
Gurgaon District, Haryana P. 9
Gurkha, ethnic of GORKHALI
Gurumukhi, Gurmukhi, or Punjabi script P. 2, 8, 60
GURUNG ⊂ Bodish P. 1, 16, 19, 52, 54, 300,000?
GUTA, GUTOB, GATA ⊂ **GADABA**
Gyarung, Jiarong ⊂ Mirish, China

Haijong, Hajong, Hajang Tribe ⊂ **BENGALI**
Hairamba Tribe ⊂ **DIMASA**
Haiva country, North Kanara, Uttar Kannad P. 27
HALAM, HALLAM ⊂ Kuki-Chin P. 16, 58, 30,000?
Halba Tribe P. 26
HALBI, HALABI ⊂ Marathi–Hindi P. 1, 12, 25
Hanunoo script, Philippines P. 60
HARAUTI ⊂ RAJASTHANI P. 1
Haryana state P. 2, 8, 9, 41, 46, 47
HARYANI ⊂ Western HINDI P. 1
HAYU ⇒ VAYU
Himachal Pradesh P. 2, 9, 10, 12, 15, 41
Himalayas P. 6, 7, 15, 16, 17, 19

Himalayan, Eastern Himalayan Language Group ⊂ Tibeto-Burman P. 16, 19, 54

Himalayish, Pronominalized Western Bodish Language Subgroup ⊂ Tibeto-Burman P. 6, 7, 54, 58

HINDI ⊂ Hindustani P. 1, 2, 3, 9, 10, 11, 12, 14, 19, 24, 30, 43, 44, 47, 50, 51, 54, 56, 58, 59, 420 million?

Hindi Belt, Hindi Region, Linguistic Hindustan P. 11, 12, 14, 42, 58

Hindi Sansar ⇒ Hindi World

HINDKO ⊂ Northern **PUNJABI**, Pakistan P. 55

Hindustani ⊂ Central Indo-Aryan {**HINDI-URDU-PUNJABI**} P. 10, 12, 14, 51, 54, 58, 59, 60

Hingna script, Khamba, Arunachal

Hissar District, Haryana P. 9

HMAR ⊂ Kuki-Chin P. 16, 58, 80,000 ?

HO, ethnic Kol, Larka Kil ⊂ Kherwari P. 1, 26, 58, 1.2 million ?

HOJAI ⊂ **DIMASA**

Holija caste, Madhya Pradesh ⊂ **KANNADA**

Hoshiarpur District, Punjab P. 9

HRANGKHOL, HRANGKHAWL, HRANGKHWAL, RANGKHOL ⊂ **HALAM** ? ⊂ Kuki-Chin P. 58, 7,000 ??

HRUSSO, *AKA* ⊂ Mirish P. 1, 16, 17, 58, 5,000 ??

HUALNGO ⊂ **MIZO**

Hunza people P. 6, 7

Hyderabad (-Deccan) P. 13, 30, 40

Hyderabad (-Sind) P. 13, 23

IDU ⊂ **MISHMI** P. 17

Illaqas, Northern Frontier Tracts, NWFP, Pakistan P. 7

INDI ⊂ **PENGO**

Indo-Aryan Language Family Branch ⊂ Indo-European P. 1, 2, 54, 55, 56, 57, 58, 59

Indo-European Language Family P. 1

INDONESIAN, BAHASA INDONESIA, BAHASA MALAYSIA P. 3, 50

Indo-Iranian Language Subfamily {Iranian, Nuristani, Indo-Aryan Family Branches}

Indo-Pacific Language Family {Andamanese, Papu, Tasmanian, etc.}

INDO-PORTUGUESE, Sri Lanka, Burgher community P. 57, 50,000 ??

Iranian Language Family Branch P. 1, 2, 5, 6, 39, 47, 50, 55, 59, 60

IRULA ⊂ **TAMIL**

Irular Tribe, Kerala, Tamil Nadu

JAD, Jadh ⊂ Tibetan P. 16, 300 ??

JAINTIA ⊂ **KHASI**

JAMATIA ⊂ **KOKBOROK**

Jammu & Kashmir P. 2, 5, 6, 7, 41, 43, 47, 48, 58

Jammu & Kashmir under Pakistan occupation P. 5, 6, 7

JANGALI, BANBHASHA, RAWATI, RAJI, ethnic Ban-Raut ⊂ Himalayish P. 16, 20,000 ?

JAPANESE P. 2, 3, 39, 1,000 ??

Jatapu Tribe, Orissa, Andhra Pradesh P. 26

JATAPU ⊂ **KUVI-TELUGU-ORIYA** ? P. 26, 58

JARAWA ⊂ Andaman, 300 ??

JAUNSARI ⊂ Western Pahari P. 15

Javanese script, Indonesia P. 60

JEME, JEMI ⇒ **ZEMI** ⊂ Nage

JHANGAR ⊂ Himalayish or **KURUKH** P. 16, 53, 54, 20,000 ?

Jharkhand, Chota Nagpur Division, Bihar P. 26, 47

JHARKHANDHI ⇒ **SADRI**

JIMDAR ⊂ **RAI**

JINGPHO ⇒ **KACHIN**

JIREL ⊂ Southern Tibetan P. 16, 53, 54, 5,000 ?

JUANG ⊂ Southern Munda P. 1, 26, 58, 25,000 ?

Jullundur District, Punjab P. 9

KABUI, Nagaland ⊂ **RONGMEI**

KACHA, Manipur ⊂ **ZE-LIANG**

KACHARI ⇒ **CACHARI**

Kacchi Plain, Sewistan, Baluchistan

KACHCHHI, KUCHCHHI, KUTCHI ⊂ **SINDHI** P. 23, 24, 47

KACHIN, KAKHIEN, SINGPHO, JINGPHO ⊂ Burmese-Yi P. 1, 16, 58, 4,000 ??

Kachin state, Myanmar P. 16, 47

KAKHIEN ⇒ **KACHIN**

Ka-Dai, Kam-Thai Language Family P. 16

Kadar Tribe, Kerala ⊂ **TAMIL**

Kafir ⇒ Nuristani

KAHHA ⇒ **PHOM**

Kaikadi caste, Maharashtra ⊂ **TAMIL**

KAKBARAK ⇒ **KOKBOROK**

KALASHA ⇒ **PASHAI**

KALKOTI ⊂ Kohistani, Pakistan P. 55, 4,000??

KAMAN ⇒ **MIJU**

Kamarupa District, Assam P. 20

Kami Tribe ⊂ **DHIMAL** ?

Kanara or Kannad region, Karnataka P. 27

KANARESE ⇒ **KANNADA**

KANASHI, MALANI, MALANA, MALANESE ⊂ Himalayish, Himachal Pradesh P. 1, 7, 16, 58, 1,000 ??

KANAURI, KINNAWARI, MULTHANI ⊂ Himalayish P. 1, 7, 16, 58, 85,000

Kandyan Sinhalese P. 36

KANGRI ⊂ **DOGRI**

Kanikkar Tribe, Kerala ⊂ **MALAYALAM**

Kanjar vagrant caste ⊂ Hindustani and Dravidian ?

KANNADA, CANARESE, KANARESE ⊂ Dravidian P. 1, 3, 27, 28, 30, 31, 32, 33, 35, 41, 42, 43, 44, 48, 58, 59, 37 million ?

KANNAUJI ⊂ Western **HINDI** P. 1

Kapurthala District, Punjab P. 9

Karachi District P. 40

KARBI, AMRI KARBI, ARLENG, MIKIR ⊂ Tibeto-Burman P. 1, 16, 19, 47, 58, 580,000 ??

Karbi Anglong, ex-Mikir Hills District P. 17, 20, 56

Karmali blacksmith Tribe, Chota Nagpur

KARMALI ⊂ **SANTALI**

Karnal District, Haryana P. 9

KAREN ⊂ Burmese-Yi, Myanmar P. 1, 16

Karen script, Myanmar P. 60

Karnataka, ex-Mysore state P. 2, 27, 28, 31, 41, 42, 43, 44, 46, 47

KASHMIRI, KOSHUR, KASHIRU ⊂ Dardic P. 1, 5, 6, 7, 58, 59, 5 million ??

KATI, BASHGALI ⊂ Nuristani, Afghanistan P. 6, 55

Katkari Tribe Maharashtra ⊂ **MARATHI** P. 26

Kawar Tribe ⊂ CHHATTISGARHI

Kawi script, Indonesia P. 60

KEBUMTAMP ⊂ **SANGLA** P. 56

Kerala P. 2, 28, 32, 33, 41, 42, 43, 46, 47

KHAMBA, KHAM ZAYU ⊂ Tibetan, Arunachal Pradesh

Khampa Tribe ⊂ Tibetan, Himachal Pradesh

KHAIRA ⇒ **KODA** ≠ KHARIA ⊂ **KHARIA**

KHAMI ⇒ **KUMI**

KHAMIYANG, NARA ⊂ Thai

KHAMPTI, KHAMTI, KHAMTI ⊂ Thai, Myanmar, Arunachal P. 1, 16, 58, 10,000 ??

KHANDESHI ⊂ Western Indo-Aryan P. 24, 25, 26

KHARIA ⊂ Munda P. 1, 26, 58, 310,000 ≠ Khaira ⊂ **KODA**

KHARI BOLI, KHADI BOLI ⊂ Western HINDI P. 10, 11

Kharosthi script of SANSKRIT P. 60

Kharwar Tribe, Chota Nagpur ⊂ SADRI

Khas ⇒ Chetri community, Nepal

KHASI, RI LUM {BHOI KHASI, LYNGAM, JAINTIA, KHYNTRIUM, PNAR, WAR} ⊂ Mon-Khmer P. 1, 16, 19, 56, 58, 1.1 million

KHAS KURA ⇒ **NEPALI**

KHAWATHLANG ⊂ Kuki-Chin

Kherwari Language Group ⊂ Munda P. 26

KHETRANI ⊂ Western Punjabi

KHEZHA ⊂ Cha-Khe-Sang ⊂ Naga P. 16, 58, 30,000 ?

KHIAMNGAN ⇒ PNAR

KHIEMNUNGAM ⊂ Naga P. 16, 18, 58, 40,000 ? ≠ KHIAMNGAN ⊂ **KHASI**

Kho, ethnic of **KHOWAR**

KHOIRAO, KOIRAO ⊂ **MARAM**

Khond, Kondh, Kandh, Kandha Tribe ⊂ **KUI, KUVI, KUBI**

KHONGZAI ⇒ undifferentiated Naga, Assam

Khotanese script, Old Iranian, Central Asia, Xinjiang P. 60

KHOTTA, KORTHA ⊂ MAGAHI and SADRI

KHOUMI ⇒ **KUMI**

Khow, Khowa, ethnic of **BUGUN**

KHOWAR, CHITRALI, ethnic Kho ⊂ Dardic, Pakistan, India P. 1, 6, 7, 55, 330,000 ??

KHUN ⊂ Thai

KHIAMNGAN ⇒ PNAR ⊂ **KHASI**

KHYANG, SHO ⊂ Chin, Bangladesh P. 16, 56, 3,000 ??

Kinnawar District, Himachal Pradesh

Kinnawara, ethnic of KANAURI

Kirata, Kiranti Language group ⊂ Himalayan P. 16, 54

KIRGIZ, KIRGIZ, Kirghizstan, Tajikistan, Pakistan, China ⊂ Turkic P. 1, 6, 7, 500 ??

Kisan Tribe, Orissa, P. 26

KISAN ⊂ **ORAON–BHUMIJ–ORIYA** ? P. 26, 58

KOCH, PANI KÓCH ⊂ Baric P. 16, 58, 30,000 ??

KODA, KORA, KHAIRA ⊂ Kherwari P. 1, 26, 58, 35,000 ?

KODAGU, COORG, ethnic Kodava or Korava ⊂ Dravidian P. 1, 31, 58, 130,000

KODAKU ⊂ **KORWA**

Kodava or Korava community, Coorg District, Karnataka ⊂ **KODAGU** ≠ Korava Tribe, Orissa and Andhra Pradesh

Kohistani {**BASHKARIK, TORWALI, KALKOTI, MAIYA, PALASI, GOWRO, CHILISSO, BATERI**} ⊂ Dardic P. 1, 6, 7, 55

Kohl, Kohlarian ⇒ Munda

KOI ⇒ KOYA

KOIRAO, KHOIRAO, THANGAL ⊂ **MARAM**

KOIRENG ⇒ Gond

Koitor, Koitur ⇒ Gond

KOKBOROK, KOK BARAK, KAKBARAK, MRUNG {Tripura, Riang, Jamatia, Noatia, Uchai} ⊂ Baric P. 1, 16, 19, 56, 58, 1 million ?

KOKNA, KOKNI, KUKNA ⊂ **BHILI** P. 26

Kol, Kolha, Larka Kol, Lohar Kol Tribe ⊂ **HO**

KOL, Munda Pidgin, Orissa

Kolhan Country, Chota Nagpur

KOLAMI {NAIKI, NAIKRI} ethnic Kolam, Kolavar ⊂ Dravidian P. 1, 26, 30, 58, 120,000 ?

Koli Tribe (*Coolie*), Koli-Mahadev, Maharashtra P. 26

KOM, KOM REM ⊂ **MARING** P. 16

Komti caste, Tamil Nadu ⊂ **TELUGU**

KONDA, KUBI ⊂ Dravidian P. 26, 30, 58, 25,000 ?

Konda-Dora, Konda–Dhora, Konda–Kapu, Konda–Reddi Tribes ⊂ **KUBI**

Kondh, Kond, Kandha Tribes ⊂ **KUI** and **KUVI**

KONICHA ⇒ **SUNWAR**

Konkan region, Western Maharashtra P. 25

KONKANI ⊂ Southern Indo-Aryan P. 1, 25, 27, 33, 58, 59, 2 million ?

KONYAK ⊂ Naga P. 18, 58, 150,000 ?

KORA ⇒ **KODA**

Koraga Tribe ⊂ **TULU**

KORAKU ⊂ **KORWA**

Korava Tribe, Andhra Pradesh ⇒ Yerukula

KOREN, KOLREM, KOLRENG, KOIRENG ⊂ **THADO** ⊂ Kuki-Chin

KORWA ⊂ Kherwari P. 1, 26, 58, 70,000 ?

KOSHUR ⇒ **KASHMIRI**

Kota craftsmen Tribe, Nilgiris

KOTA ⊂ Toda-Kota ⊂ Dravidian P. 1, 31, 35, 58, 1,000??

KOYA, KOI ⊂ Dravidian P. 1, 26, 58, 340,000 ?

KUBI ⇒ **KONDA**

KUCHCHHI ⇒ KACHCHHI

KUI, KWI, KU, ethnic Kuisika ⊂ Dravidian P. 1, 26, 58, 700,000 ?

Kuki Language Subgroup ⊂ Kuki-Chin P. 1, 16

Kuki-Chin Language Group ⊂ Tibeto-Burman P. 16, 58

KULUI, KULVI ⊂ Western Pahari P. 9, 15

KUMAL, KUMKALE, BHRAMU ⊂ Dardic ? Nepal P. 16, 53, 54, 1,000 ?

KUMAUNI ⊂ Central Pahari P. 15

KUMI, KHUMI, KHAMI ⊂ Chin, Bangladesh P. 56, 3,000 ??

KURMALI, KURMI, KURUMALI, THAR, KUDMALI ⊂ SADRI

Kurmi, Mahato Tribe, Chota Nagpur

KURUKH, KURUX, ORAON ⊂ Dravidian P. 1, 26, 56, 58, 2.1 million

Kuruba forest Tribe, Mysore District

KURUBA ⊂ **KANNADA**

Kurumba shepherd Tribe, Coorg District, Karnataka and Nilgiri District, Tamil Nadu

KURUMBA ⊂ **KANNADA**

KUSUNDA ⊂ Himalayan, Nepal (extinct)

Kutch region, Gujarat P. 23, 24

KUVI, KHONDI, KONDHI ⊂ Dravidian P. 26, 58, 280,000 ?

KYON, KYONG ⇒ **LOTHA**

Labbai Muslim caste, Tamil Nadu ⊂ **URDU** ?

LADAKHI, BODHI, BHODI ⊂ Tibetan P. 6, 7, 16, 58, 125,000 ?

Lahaula community ⊂ **LAHULI**

LAHNDA, MULTANI ⇒ Western Punjabi

LAHULI, ethnic Lahula ⊂ Tibetan P. 15, 16, 58, 30,000 ?

LAHULI of CHAMBA ⇒ **CHAMBA LAHULI**

LAI, LAI HAWLH, ethnic Pawi ⊂ Kuki-Chin P. 16, 58, 20,000 ?

La

LAKHER, ethnic Mara ⊂ Kuki-Chin P. 16, 58, 30,000 ?

Lakhimpur, North-Lakhimpur District, Assam P. 20

LALUNG, DOWYAN, ethnic Tiwa ⊂ Baric P. 1, 16, 58, 20,000 ?

LAMBADI, LAMBANI, LAMANI ⇒ BANJARI

LAMGANG, LAMKANG ⊂ **ANAL** ⊂ Kuki-Chin

Lakshadweep Union Territory, Laccadive Islands ⊂ **MALAYALAM** P. 57

Lampung script, Indonesia P. 60

LARIA ⊂ CHHATTISGARHI

Latin or Roman script P. 2, 47, 60

LEPCHA RONG, RONG-KE, ethnic Rongkup ⊂ Baric ? P. 1, 16, 19, 58, 45,000 ?

LIANGMEI {KACHA, Manipur} ⊂ Ze-Liang-Rong ⊂ Naga P. 18, 58, 30,000 ?

LIMBU ⊂ Himalayan P. 1, 16, 19, 52, 54, 360,000 ?

Lik-tai script of **KHAMPTI**, Myanmar P. 60

LISH, LISHPA ⊂ MONPA

LISU, YOBIN, YAWYIN ⊂ Burmese-Yi, India, Myanmar, China P. 1, 16, 17, 58, 1,000 ??

Lingayat community, Northern Karnataka

Loba, Lhoba, Luoba, Loyoui ⊂ Mirish, China

Lodha Tribe, Chota Nagpur ⊂ **KHARIA**

Lohara, Lohra blacksmiths caste, Chota Nagpur ⊂ **SANTALI** and **MUNDARI**

LOI Tribe, Pyu ancient kingdom ⇒ **CHAK** ⊂ Burmese-Yi, Myanmar, Bangladesh

LOTHA, KYON, KYONG ⊂ Naga P. 18, 58, 115,000 ?

LUSHAI, LUSHEI, DUHLIAN TWANG ⇒ **MIZO**

Luso-Indian ⇒ **INDO-PORTUGUESE**, Sri Lanka

LYNG-NGAM ⊂ **KHASI**

Madhya Pradesh

Madhya Pradesh, ex-Central Provinces P. 11, 12, 41

Madras or Chennai District P. 35, 40

'Madrasi', South Indian

MAGADHI, MAGAHI ⊂ Bihari P. 1, 11, 49

MAGAR, MAGARI, MAGARKURA ⊂ Himalayan P. 1, 16, 19, 52, 54, 560,000 ?

MAGH ⇒ **ARAKANESE**

Mahar caste, Maharashtra ⊂ **MARATHI**

Maharashtra state P. 2, 25, 41, 42, 43, 47

MAHASU PAHARI ⊂ Western Pahari P. 15

Mahendragarh District, Haryana P. 9

MAHL, MAHAL, MALDIVIAN ⇒ **DHIVEHI**

Mahili, Mahli, Mahali, Maheli basket makers Tribe, Chota Nagpur ⊂ **SANTALI**

Maidan region, Southern Karnataka P. 27

MAITHILI ⊂ Bihari P. 1, 11, 49, 51, 40 million ?? ⊂ **HINDI**

MAIYA, MAIYAN ⊂ Kohistani P. 55, 200,000 ??

MAJHI, MANJHI ⊂ Central Indo-Aryan ? Nepal P. 16, 53, 54, 15,000 ?

Makassar, Macassarese script ⊂ Lòntara script, Indonesia P. 60

Makwara, Makware Tribe ⊂ **YIMCHUNGRE**

Malabar region, Northern Kerala P. 32

Malanad, Malnad country, Southern Kerala P. 47

Malay script, Indonesia P. 60

Malay, Creole Malay, Sri Lanka P. 60

MALANI ⇒ **KANASHI**

MALAYALAM ⊂ Dravidian P. 1, 28, 32, 35, 40, 41, 42, 43, 44, 48, 58, 59, 34 million ?

Malayali (1) people, Kerala ⊂ **MALAYALAM** P. 28, 32, 33

Malayali (2) Tribe, Tamil Nadu ⊂ **TAMIL**

Malayarayar Tribe, Kerala ⊂ **MALAYALAM**

MALDIVIAN ⇒ **DHIVEHI**

Maler ⇒ Sauria Paharia Tribe

Maldives Islands P. 47, 50, 57, 59

Malhar, Saora Malhar, Jora Savara Tribe, Orissa ⊂ **SAVARA**

Malnad, Mal Nadu region, Karnataka P. 27

Mal Paharia and Sauria Paharia Tribes ⊂ **MALTO**

MALPAHARYA ⊂ **BENGALI**

MALTO, MAL, MALE, ethnic Maler ⊂ Northern Dravidian, Rajmahal Hills P. 1, 26, 58, 150,000 ?

MALVI, MALWI ⊂ Rajasthani P. 1, 11

MANCHATI, PATNI ⊂ **CHAMBA LAHULI** P. 16

MANDA ⊂ PENGO

MANDEALI ⊂ Western Pahari P. 5

Mangalore, Karnataka P. 31

Manikfan ⊂ MALDIVIAN

Manipur state P. 19, 41, 47

MANIPURI ⇒ **MEITHEI**

Manic of Mia-Yao Language Family, China ⊂ Austric ?

MANJHI ⇒ **MAJHI**

MAO, EMELA, ethnic Pomai, Mao Mei, Memei, Imemei ⊂ Naga P. 18, 58, 100,000 ?

Mappilai or Moplah Muslim community, Kerala ⊂ **MALAYALAM**

Mara, ethnic of **LAKHER**

MARAM, ethnic Maramei ⊂ Naga P. 18, 58, 20,000 ?

MARATHI ⊂ Southern Indo-Aryan P. 1, 25, 40, 41, 42, 43, 44, 48, 58, 59, 78 million ?

MARCHHA ⊂ GARHWAL BHOTIYA

MARIA, MURIA ⊂ **GONDI**

MARING ⊂ Naga P. 18, 58, 20,000 ?
MARMA ⇒ **ARAKANESE**
MARWARI ⊂ Rajasthani P. 1, 11, 51, 13 million ?? ⊂ **HINDI**
Mayang, ethnic of BISHNUPURIYA
MAZUNG ⇒ **CHANG**
MECH ⊂ **BODO**
Meghalaya state P. 16, 19, 41, 46, 47
MEITHEI, MEITHEILON, MEITHI, MANIPURI ⊂ Tibeto-Bur-
man P. 1, 16, 19, 56, 58, 1.7 million ?
Meithei-Mayak script of **MEITHEI**
MEMBA ⊂ Tibetan, Arunachal P. 17, 58, 3,000 ?? ≠ **MONPA**
MEWARI ⊂ **RAJASTHANI** P. 1
MEYER, MEYOR ⊂ **CHARUMBA**
Miji {Don Mai, Non Mai} ethnic of **SAJALONG**
MIJU, KAMAN ⊂ **MISHMI** P. 17
MIKIR ⇒ **KARBI**
Mina Tribe ⊂ RAJASTHANI P. 26
Minicoy Island, Lakshadweep ⊂ **DHIVEHI** P. 57
Minyong ⊂ **ADI**
Mirdha Tribe, Orissa
MIRI {HILL MIRI or MISHING, PLAINS MIRI} ⊂ **ADI** ?
⊂ Mirish P. 1, 16, 17, 19, 58, 500,000 ??
Mirish or Arunachal Language Group ⊂ Tibeto-Burman P. 16, 58
MISHMI {IDU, DIGARU, MIJU} ⊂ Mirish, Arunachal P. 1, 16,
17, 58, 45,000 ?
MISHING ⇒ **MIRI**
Mithila country, Bihar P. 47
MITHUN ⊂ IDU
MIZO, DUHLIAN standard {LUSHAI, BIATE, RALTE, TLAU,
HUALNGO, BAWN, PANG} ⊂ Kuki-Chin P. 1, 16, 19, 46,
47, 48, 58, 725,000 ?
Mizoram state P. 46, 47, 48
Mohajir ⇒ Muhajir
MOINBA ⇒ **MONPA**
MOGH ⇒ **ARAKANESE**
MON ⊂ Mon-Khmer, Myanmar P. 16
Mon script, Myanmar P. 60
Mon-Khmer Language subfamily ⊂ Austro-Asiatic Language
Family P. 1, 16
MONPA, MONBA, MOINBA, ⊂ Tibetan P. 16, 17, 58, 60,000 ?
≠ **MEMBA**
MONSANG ⇒ SIRTI
MONSEN ⊂ AO
Mon-Yul ⇒ Monpa region
Moor Muslim community, Sri Lanka ⊂ **TAMIL** P. 36
Moplah or Mappilai Muslim community, Kerala
⊂ **MALAYALAM**
MORAN ⊂ Baric (extinct)
MOYON ⇒ BUJUUR
MRO, **MRU** ⊂ Chin, Bangladesh P. 16, 56
MRUNG ⇒ **KOKBOROK**
Muhajir, Mohajir, **URDU** mother tongue speaking refugees and
refugee descendants in Pakistan
MULTANI ⊂ LAHNDA
MULTHANI ⊂ **KANAURI**
Munda or Kolarian Language subfamily ⊂ Austro-Asiatic Lan-
guage Family P. 1, 26, 58, 59

Munda, ethnic of **MUNDARI**
MUNDARI ⊂ Khewari P. 1, 26, 58, 1,7 million ?
MURIA ⇒ MARIA
MURMI ⇒ **TAMANG**
Muslim community, India P. 13
Muthuvan Tribe, Kerala ⊂ **TAMIL**
MUWASI ⊂ **KORKU**
Myanmar, ex-Burma P. 47, 50
Mysore city, Karnataka P. 31

NA ⊂ Tibetan, Arunachal P. 17, 1,500 ??
Naga Language Group ⊂ Tibeto-Burman P. 1, 16, 17, 18, 19, 46,
47, 48, 58
Nagaland state P. 18, 46, 47, 48
NAGAMESE, Assamo-Naga Pidgin, Nagaland
Nagari ⇒ Devanagari script
NAHALI, NAHARI, East Madhya Pradesh ⊂ HALBI ?
≠ NIHALI?
NARA ⇒ **KHAMPTI**
Nasta'liq script ⊂ Arabo-Persian script
NEFA, NEFT ⇒ Arunachal Pradesh
NEFAMESE Assamo-Mirish Pidjin, Arunachal
Nepal P. 2, 15, 16, 19, 41, 43, 47, 48, 50, 51, 52, 53, 54, 59
NEPALI, GORKHALI, KHAS KURA ⊂ Eastern Pahari P. 1, 3,
15, 16, 19, 21, 41, 43, 44, 47, 48, 51, 54, 56, 58, 59, 15 million?
Newar, ethnic of **NEWARI**
NEWARI ⊂ Himalayan, Nepal P. 1, 16, 19, 51, 54, 900,000 ?
NGNOK, ethnic Sherdukpen ⊂ Mirish P. 17, 58, 4,000 ??
Nicobar Islands ⇒ Andaman & Nicobar Islands
NICOBARESE, NICOBARI ⊂ Mon-Khmer P. 1, 41, 58,
50,000 ?
Nilgiri mountains, Nilgiri District, Nilgiris, Tamil Nadu P. 31, 32,
34, 35
NIHALI, NAHALE, NAHUL ⊂ **KORKU** ? KHANDESHI ?
≠ NAHALI ?
NIMIADI, NIMARI ⊂ Rajasthani P. 1, 11
'Nishada' people, ancient Munda Language populations
NISHANG ⊂ **NISSI** P. 17
NISSI, NISI, NISU, NISHI, NISHING, *DAFLA* ⊂ Mirish P. 1, 16,
17, 58, 260,000 ?
NOATIA ⊂ **KOKBOROK**
NOCTE ⊂ Naga, Arunachal P. 17, 18, 58
NORA ⊂ Thai, Arunachal
North Cachar Hills District, Assam P. 19, 20, 21, 47, 48, 56
North Kanara District, Karnataka P. 27, 31
North Lakhimpur District, Assam P. 20
Nowgong District, Assam P. 20
NTENYE, Northern RENGMA ⊂ **RENGMA**
Nuristani Language Family Branch ⊂ Indo-European P. 1, 4, 5, 6,
41, 55
NWFP, North West Frontier Province or 'Pushtunistan', Pakistan
P. 4, 41, 47, 55
NYAMKAT, BADKAS, SANGYAS, Upper Kinnaur ⊂ Tibetan
P. 16
NZONG, NZONYU, Southern RENGMA ⊂ **RENGMA**

ODIA/ORIYA

Okkaliga dominant caste, South Karnataka

OI, OI Chiki script of **SANTALI**

OLLARI, OLARI {SALUR, POTTANGI} ⊂ Dravidian, Gadaba Tribe, 7,000 ??

ONGE ⊂ Andaman, 100 ??

ORAON/KURUKH, KURUX ⊂ Dravidian P. 1, 26, 58, 2.1 million ?

Orissa state, Utkal country P. 2, 22, 41, 42, 48

ORIYA/ODIA ⊂ Eastern Indo-Aryan P. 1, 19, 22, 30, 41, 43, 44, 58, 33 million ?

ORMURI ⊂ Western Iranian P. 1, 6, 55, 3,000 ??

Pagspa script, MONGOLIAN and CHINESE P. 60

Pahari ⊂ Central Indo-Aryan P. 1, 7, 9, 12, 15, 19, 48, 54

Pahariya Tribes {Mal Pahariya, Sauria Pahariya} ⊂ **MALTO** and MALPAHARYA

PAITE, PAIHTE, SIMTE, SAHTE ⊂ Kuki-Chin P. 16, 58, 55,000

PAKAN ⇒ **ANAL**

Pakistan P. 3, 4, 5, 6, 8, 13, 14, 23, 39, 40, 41, 43, 44, 45, 47, 48, 49, 50, 55, 59

PALASI ⊂ Kohistani, Pakistan P. 55, 200 ??

PALI ⊂ Middle Indian

Pamir Tajik or Pamirian, Ghalcha, Ghalchah Language Group ⊂ Eastern Iranian, Tajikistan, Afghanistan, Pakistan, India, China {WANCHI, YAZGULAMI, RUSHANI, BARTANGI, OROSHORI, SHUGNANI, ISHKASHIMI, SANGLICHI, MUNJANI, **YIDGHA WAKHI**, SARYKOLI} P. 6, 55 ≠ **TAJIK** ⊂ Western Iranian

Paniyan Tribe, Kerala ⊂ **MALAYALAM**

PANKUA, PANKHO, PANKHUA, PANG KHUA ⊂ **MIZO**, Mizoram, Bangladesh P. 56

Parangi or Parengi Paroja Tribe, Orissa ⊂ **SAVARA** ?

PAOMATA ⊂ **MAO**

PANJABI/PUNJABI

PARACHI ⊂ Western Iranian, Afghanistan P. 1, 6, 55

Paraja, Paroja Tribe ⊂ **PARJI**

Pardhan Tribe, Madhya Pradesh P. 26

Pardhi Tribe, Telangana, Andhra Pradesh ⊂ **TELUGU**

PARGANIA ⊂ SADRI

PARJI, ethnic Paroja & Dhurwa ⊂ Dravidian P. 1, 26, 58, 50,000?

PASHAI, KALASHA–PASHAI ⊂ Dardic, Afghanistan, Pakistan P. 1, 6, 55, 7,000??

PASHTO ⇒ **PUSHTO**

Pat desert ⇒ Sewistan

Pathan, Afghan, ethnic of **PUSHTO**

Patiala District, Punjab P. 9

PATNI ⇒ **BUNAN**

PAWI, PAWAI ⇒ **LAI**

PENGO, PENGU {INDI, AWE, MANDA} ⊂ **KONDA** ?

PERSIAN OR **FARSI**, Iran, **FARSI-KABULI** or **DARI**, Afghanistan, **TAJIK**, Tajikistan ⊂ Western Iranian P. 1, 3, 6, 39, 41, 44, 47, 50, 40,000 ?

PHALURA ⊂ Dardic, Pakistan P. 55, 8,000 ??

PHAKIAL ⊂ **KHAMPTI**

PHOM, KAHHA ⊂ Naga P. 18, 58, 50,000 ?

Plains Kachari ⇒ BODO

PNAR, SYNTENG, KHIAMNGAN ⊂ **KHASI**

POCHURY (SaPO-KeCHU-KhuRY), SOZOMI, SHOMLI ⊂ Naga 15,000 ?? ≠ SANGTAM

POMAI, POME, PAUMEI ⇒ **MAO** ≠ PUIMEI ⊂ **RONGMEI**

Pondicherry, Pondicherry Union Territory P. 34, 39, 41, 47

POONCHI, PUNCHI ⊂ Punjabi P. 6

PORTUGUESE P. 3, 39, 5,000 ??

POTTANGI ⊂ **OLLARI**

POTWARI ⊂ Western Punjabi

PRASUN ⊂ Nuristani, Afghanistan P. 6

PUIMEI ⊂ **RONGMEI**

Pulayan Tribe, Northern Kerala and Tamil Nadu **MALAYALAM** and **TAMIL** ≠ Pulayan caste, Southern Kerala

Punjab 1) Indian state P. 2, 8, 9, 10, 41, 43, 46, 47, 48, 49
2) Pakistan province P. 5, 8, 41, 47, 48, 49

PUNJABI/PANJABI ⊂ Hindustani P. 1, 3, 5, 6, 7, 8, 9, 10, 41, 43, 44, 48, 50, 55, 58, 59, 130 million ?

Purig-Yul, Purik region, Kargil District, Jammu & Kashmir P. 6

PURIK, ethnic Purig-pa ⊂ **SHINA** P. 16 ≠ **PUROIK**

PUROIK, ethnic *Sulung* ⊂ Tibetan P. 17, 7,000 ?? ≠ PURIK

PURUM ⊂ **CHOTE**

Purvachal, Eastern Mountains, Burma Range P. 19

PUSHTO, PASHTO, AFGHANI P. 1, 4, 5, 6, 7, 10, 41, 47, 48, 50, 55, 59, 20 million ?

'Pushtunistan' ⇒ NWFP P. 47

Pyu ⇒ **LOI** ⊂ Burmese-Yi P. 56

RABHA ⊂ Baric P. 1, 16, 58, 100,000 ??

RAI, RAI-KIRANTI, RAI-KURA ⊂ Himalayan P. 1, 16, 19, 52, 54, 570,000 ?

Rajasthan state P. 10, 11

RAJASTHANI ⊂ Hindustani P. 1, 10, 11, 12, 24, 26, 30, 57

Rajbangsi, Koch ⊂ **BENGALI** P. 54

RAJI, RAWAI, RAUT, MANUSH, JANGALI, BANBHASHA ⊂ Himalayan, Nepal, India P. 16, 53, 54, 4,000 ?

Rakhine ⇒ Arakan

RALTE ⊂ **MIZO**

RANGKAS, SHANKHYAKHUN ⊂ Himalayish P. 16, 600 ??

RANGKHOL ⇒ **HRANGKHOL**

RANGLOI, TINAN, GONDLA ⊂ **LAHULI OF CHAMBA**

RAUT, RAWATI ⇒ **JANGALI**

Rayalsima region, Andhra Pradesh P. 30

REANG ⊂ **KOKBOROK/TRIPURI**

Reddi, Reddy caste, Andhra Pradesh, Tamil Nadu ⊂ **TELUGU**

REDO, ethnic Bondo ⊂ **GADABA**

Rejang script, Indonesia P. 60

RENGMA {NTENYE, NZONYU} ⊂ Naga P. 18, 58, 30,000 ?

Riang Tribe, Tripura ⊂ **KOKBOROK**

Rohtak District, Punjab P. 9

ROMANI ⇒ **SINTI-ROMANI**

RONG, ethnic Rongpa ⇒ **LEPCHA**

RONGMEI PUIMEI, Manipur {KABUI, Nagaland} ⊂ **ZELIANGRONG** ⊂ Naga P. 18, 58, 90,000 ?

RUSSIAN P. 2, 3, 39, 1,000 ??

Russian or Cyrillic script P. 2, 60

SADRI, SADARI, SADANI, SHADRI, JHARKHANDI ⊂ Bhojpuri Pidgin, Chota Nagpur P. 11

SAGTENGPA ⊂ **MONPA**, Bhutan P. 56
SAJALONG, ethnic Miji ⊂ Tibetan, Arunachal P. 17, 58, 4,000??
SAK ⇒ **CHAK**
SALUR ⊂ **OLLARI**
SANGLA, TSANGLO ⊂ Tibetan, Bhutan P. 16, 56
SANGTAM, TUKOMI, SANTAMRR ⊂ Cha-Khe-Sang ⊂ Naga
    P. 18, 58, 45,000 ?? ≠ **POCHURY**
Sangrur District, Punjab P. 9
SANSKRIT ⊂ Old Indo-Aryan P. 37, 6,000 ?
SANTALI, HORKO ⊂ Kherwari P. 1, 19, 26, 53, 54, 56, 58, 7
    million ?
Saora, ethnic of **SAVARA**
Saoria Paharya, Sauria Paharia, Maler Tribe ⊂ **MALTO**
SARAIKI, SIRAIKI ⊂ Western Punjabi, Pakistan P. 55
Sart people ⊂ Middle Iranian, Central Asia, Xinjiang
SARYKOLI ⊂ Pamir Tajik, China P. 6
Sasak script, Indonesia P. 60
SATAR ⊂ **SANTALI**, Nepal P. 53, 54
SAURASHTRI, PATNULI, PATNU IKARAN, ethnic Saurashtra,
    ⊂ **GUJARATI**, Tamil Nadu
SAVARA, SORA, ethnic Saora ⊂ Southern Munda P. 1, 26, 30,
    58, 300,000 ?
SCHARCHAGPAKHA ⊂ **SANGLA** P. 56
Seistan region, Afghanistan, Iran, P. 47
SEMA, SEMI ⊂ Naga P. 18, 58
SENTINELESE ⊂ Andaman, 100 ??
Sewistan, Pat Desert, Sibi Plain, Kachi Plain, Baluchistan, Pakistan
    P. 23
SHA ⊂ **PHOM**
Shabara people, ancient Savara-speaking population
SHAN ⊂ Thai, Myanmar P. 1
Shan script, Myanmar P. 60
Sherdukpen, ethnic of **NGNOK**
SHERPA, **BHOTE-SHERPA** ⊂ Southern Tibetan, Eastern Nepal
    P. 16, 19, 52, 54, 200,000 ?
SHINA, ethnic Shin ⊂ Dardic P. 1, 6, 7, 58, 360,000 ??
Shompen Tribe ⊂ **NICOBARESE**
Sibsagar District, Assam, P. 20
Sikkim state P. 16, 19, 48, 50
SIKKIMESE, SIKKIM BHOTIA ⇒ **DENJONGKE**
Simla or Shimla District, Himachal Pradesh P. 9
SIMTE, SAHTE ⊂ **PAITE**
Sind province, Pakistan P. 5, 25, 41
SINDHI ⊂ Western Indo-Aryan, Pakistan, India P. 1, 5, 23, 40,
    44, 47, 55, 58, 59, 20 million ?
SINGPHO, JINGPO, KACHIN ⊂ Burmese-Yi, Arunachal P. 16,
    17, 58, 4,000 ??
SINHALA, SINHALESE ⊂ Southern Indo-Aryan P. 1, 3, 36, 47,
    50, 57, 59, 14 million ?
Sinhala or Sinhalese script P. 2, 60
Sinhalese people {Low Country Sinhalese, Kandyan Sinhalese}
    P. 36
SINTI, **SINTI-ROMANI** ⊂ Western Indo-Aryan, Central Asia,
    Europe, America
SIRAIKI, SARAIKI ⊂ Western Punjabi, Pakistan P. 55
SIRMAURI ⊂ Western Pahan P. 15
SIRTI ⊂ **ANAL**

SPITI ⊂ Tibetan, Himachal Pradesh P. 16, 3,000 ??
Sri Lanka, Ceylon P. 2, 36, 47, 48, 50, 57, 59
Sulung ethnic of **PUROIK**
Sundanese script, Indonesia P. 60
SUNWAR, SUNWARI ⊂ Himalayan P. 16, 19, 53, 54, 11,000 ?
Swangla, ethnic of MANCHAT
SWATI, **TORWALI** ⊂ Dardic P. 55
SYNTENG ⇒ PNAR ⊂ **KHASI**

TAAON ⇒ DIGARU ⊂ **MISHMI**
TABLENG ⊂ Naga ?
Tagalog script, Philippines P. 60
Tagbanwa script, Philippines P. 60
TAGIN ⊂ **NISSI** P. 17
TAI, TAI-PHAKE, TAI-RONG ⊂ Thai, Arunachal
Tailan script of DAI, China, Xishuangbanna
Tainan script of DAI, China, Dehong
Takri, Tankri script, Himachal Pradesh
Tana script ⇒ Thana script
TAJIK ⊂ **PERSIAN** ⊂ Western Iranian, Afghanistan, Tajikistan
    P. 1, 6, 7, 41, 50 ≠ Pamir Tajik ⊂ Eastern Iranian
Tajik ZZX or Tajik Autonomous District, China ⊂ Pamir Tajik
    P. 6
TAMANG, MURMI ⊂ Gurung group P. 1, 16, 19, 52, 54, 1.2
    million ?
TAMIL ⊂ Dravidian P. 1, 3, 28, 34, 30, 33, 35, 36, 40, 41, 42, 43,
    44, 47, 48, 50, 57, 58, 59, 70 million ?
Tamil Nadu, Tamilnad P. 2, 28, 34, 35, 41, 42, 43, 44
Tamil people, Sri Lanka {Sri Lanka Tamil, Indian Tamil} P. 36
Tamil script, P. 2, 60
TANGKHUL, THANGUL, THANGAL ⊂ Naga P. 18, 58,
    130,000 ?
TANGSA ⊂ Naga, Arunachal P. 16, 18, 58, 20,000 ?
Tanu, ethnic of APATANI
Tarao Tribe ⇒ **TATAOTRONG**
TATAOTRONG, ethnic Tarao ⊂ Kuki-Naga, Manipur, 1,000 ??
Telengana or Telangana region, Andhra Pradesh P. 29, 30, 46, 47
TELUGU ⊂ Dravidian P. 1, 3, 28, 29, 30, 35, 40, 41, 42, 43, 44,
    48, 58, 59, 80 million ?
TENGIMA ⊂ **ANGAMI**
Terai region, Southern Nepal, India
THADO, ethnic Thadu ⊂ Kuki-Chin P. 16, 58, 100,000 ?
Thai, Thai-Zhuang, Daic Language Family P. 16
Thailan script ⇒ Tailan script
THAKALI, THAKSYA ⊂ Gurung Language Group, Nepal P. 16,
    53, 54, 10,000 ?
Thakrufan ⊂ MALDIVIAN
THAMI ⊂ Himalayish P. 16, 53, 54, 20,000 ?
Thana script of **DHIVEHI** P. 60
THAR ⊂ SADRI
Thar Desert, Great Indian Desert, Marusthali, Western Rajasthan
THARU ⊂ Hindustani, Nepal Terai P. 19, 51, 54
THET ⇒ **CHAK**
Tibet, Bod, Xizang Zi Zhi Qu, P. 6, 47
TIBETAN, BHOTIA, BHUTIYA P. 1, 3, 5, 6, 16, 18, 19, 54,
    70,000 ?
Tibetan script P. 2, 60

SUBJECT AND AUTHOR INDEX

ABOUT THE AUTHOR

Roland J.-L. Breton is Professor Emeritus, University of Paris 8—Vincennes-Saint Denis. An eminent scholar, he is the recipient of two Fulbright scholarships and has held various assignments as a visiting professor at the universities of Washington and Hangzhou. Prior to this, he has been an active member of the French public service of national education where among other appointments he has been Cultural Counsellor, Warsaw, Assistant Professor at the universities of Aix-en-Provence, France, and Yaounde, Cameroon. He has also been Director of Research in Geolinguistics at the Human Sciences Institute, Yaounde.

As a member of the International Centre for Research in Language and Development in Africa, America and Asia at the University of Paris 10—Nanterre, he has been on various missions in South Africa, Ghana, Chile and Senegal, and is presently involved with the international project 'Logosphere' built on Anglo-French cooperation which aims to set up a global database-cum-atlas of world languages.

A distinguished geographer, he is known as a founder of geolinguistics, interested in the interlinking of ethno-linguistic and sociopolitical issues. He has specialized in the distribution of languages and ethnic communities with an emphasis on India, Black Africa, North America and eastern Europe. Professor Breton has contributed numerous articles to various journals and has previously authored several books including *Les Langues de l'Inde depuis l'Indépendance*; *Géographie des Langues*; *Géographie du Français et de la Francité en Louisiane*; *Les Ethnies*; *Géographie des Civilisations*; *Atlas Administratif des Langues Nationales du Cameroun*; and *L'Ethnopolitique*.